German Stoicisms

Also Available from Bloomsbury

French and Italian Stoicisms: From Sartre to Agamben, ed. Kurt Lampe and Janae Sholtz
The Art of Living Well, Paul van Tongeren, trans. by Thomas Heij
Hegel on Possibility: Dialectics, Contradiction, and Modality, Nahum Brown
Nietzsche and Epicurus, ed. Vinod Acharya and Ryan J. Johnson
Hans Jonas: Life, Technology and the Horizons of Responsibility, Lewis Coyne
Modernism Between Benjamin and Goethe, Matthew Charles

German Stoicisms

From Hegel to Sloterdijk

Edited by
Kurt Lampe and Andrew Benjamin

BLOOMSBURY ACADEMIC
LONDON • NEW YORK • OXFORD • NEW DELHI • SYDNEY

BLOOMSBURY ACADEMIC
Bloomsbury Publishing Plc
50 Bedford Square, London, WC1B 3DP, UK
1385 Broadway, New York, NY 10018, USA
29 Earlsfort Terrace, Dublin 2, Ireland

BLOOMSBURY, BLOOMSBURY ACADEMIC and the Diana logo are trademarks of
Bloomsbury Publishing Plc

First published in Great Britain 2021
This paperback edition published in 2022

Copyright © Kurt Lampe and Andrew Benjamin, 2021

Kurt Lampe and Andrew Benjamin have asserted their rights under the Copyright,
Designs and Patents Act, 1988, to be identified as Editors of this work.

For legal purposes the Acknowledgments on p. vi constitute an
extension of this copyright page.

Cover design by Charlotte Daniels
Cover images: Bust of Zeno © Jeanette Dietl / Shutterstock. Column illustration © iStock.
Column ruins by All Bong on Unsplash. Background by Mockaroon on Unsplash

All rights reserved. No part of this publication may be reproduced or transmitted
in any form or by any means, electronic or mechanical, including photocopying,
recording, or any information storage or retrieval system, without
prior permission in writing from the publishers.

Bloomsbury Publishing Plc does not have any control over, or responsibility for, any third-party websites referred to or in this book. All internet addresses given in this book were correct at the time of going to press. The author and publisher regret any inconvenience caused if addresses have changed or sites have ceased to exist, but can accept no responsibility for any such changes.

A catalogue record for this book is available from the British Library.

Library of Congress Cataloging-in-Publication Data
Names: Lampe, Kurt, 1977-editor. | Benjamin, Andrew E., editor.
Title: German stoicisms: from Hegel to Sloterdijk /
edited by Kurt Lampe and Andrew Benjamin.
Description: London; New York: Bloomsbury Academic, 2021. |
Includes bibliographical references and index.
Identifiers: LCCN 2020032485 (print) | LCCN 2020032486 (ebook) |
ISBN 9781350081864 (hb) | ISBN 9781350195462 (paperback) |
ISBN 9781350081871 (epdf) | ISBN 9781350081888 (epub)
Subjects: LCSH: Philosophers–Germany. | Stoics.
Classification: LCC B2521 .G47 2021 (print) | LCC B2521 (ebook) | DDC 193–dc23
LC record available at https://lccn.loc.gov/2020032485
LC ebook record available at https://lccn.loc.gov/2020032486

ISBN: HB: 978-1-3500-8186-4
PB: 978-1-3501-9546-2
ePDF: 978-1-3500-8187-1
eBook: 978-1-3500-8188-8

Typeset by Deanta Global Publishing Services, Chennai, India

To find out more about our authors and books visit www.bloomsbury.com
and sign up for our newsletters.

Contents

Acknowledgments		vi
List of Abbreviations		vii

1. Stoicism and Modern German Philosophy *Kurt Lampe and Andrew Benjamin* — 1
2. The Indifference of Reason: Hegel and Stoicism *Gene Flenady* — 23
3. Stoicism and the Development of the Human Sciences: Wilhelm Dilthey's Reception of Stoicism *Angus Nicholls* — 57
4. Nietzschean Stoicism: An Ascetic Strategy in Pursuit of Knowledge *Hedwig Gaasterland* — 85
5. Sovereign/Creature: Neostoicism in Benjamin's *Origin of the German Trauerspiel* and His Response to Carl Schmitt's *Political Theology* *Paula Schwebel* — 109
6. From *Oikeiōsis* to *Ereignis:* Heidegger and the Fate of Stoicism *Josh Hayes* — 137
7. Hans Jonas, Ancient Stoicism, and the Problem of Freedom *Emidio Spinelli* — 161
8. Dignity and Self-Making: Seneca, Pico della Mirandola, and Hannah Arendt *Andrew Benjamin* — 175
9. Hans Blumenberg and the Anthropology of Stoicism *Kurt Lampe* — 205
10. Planetary *Askēsis:* Peter Sloterdijk's Stoic Journey into Existential Spatiality *Sam Mickey* — 229

List of Contributors	257
Index	259

Acknowledgments

We gratefully acknowledge the support of the Arts and Humanities Research Council of the United Kingdom, which funded a research networking grant in 2016 under the title "Continental Stoicisms: Beyond Reason and Wellbeing." This volume began life as one half of that project.

Abbreviations

Note that with the exception of those named here, the titles of ancient Greek and Roman works are generally given in full.

Cicero, *ND*	*De Natura Deorum* (*On the Nature of the Gods*)
DK	Diels, Hermann and Walther Kranz (1951–2), *Die Fragmente der Vorsokratiker, Griechisch und Deutsch*, sixth ed., three vols., Berlin: Weidmann
DL	Diogenes Laertius, *Lives of the Illustrious Philosophers*
Epictetus	Epict.
Disc.	*Discourses*
Ench.	*Encheiridion* (*Handbook*)
LS	A. A. Long and D. N. Sedley (1986), *The Hellenistic Philosophers*, two vols., Cambridge: Cambridge University Press.
MA	Marcus Aurelius
Seneca	Sen.
Ep.	*Epistulae Morales* (*Moral Epistles*)
Ben.	*De Beneficiis* (*On Benefits*)
Helv.	*Ad Helviam* (*To Helvia*)
NQ	*Natural Questions*
Tranq.	*De Tranquillitate* (*On Tranquility*)
Vit. Beat.	*De Vita Beata* (*On the Happy Life*)
SVF	Hans von Arnim (1903–5), *Stoicorum Veterum Fragmenta*, four vols., Leipzig: Teubner.

1

Stoicism and Modern German Philosophy

Kurt Lampe and Andrew Benjamin[1]

1. Introduction

What is the historical and philosophical significance of Stoicism? The answer depends to a substantial extent on the place and time on which we choose to focus. Scholarship has made enormous progress in synthesizing and interpreting the difficult evidence for Greek and Roman Stoic doctrines and arguments in their original intellectual, practical, and cultural contexts. These ideas and exercises have recently taken on new life through the emergence and rapid expansion of Modern Stoicism.[2] Stoic reception has also become increasingly vigorous in the field of inquiry (e.g., Spanneut 1973; Colish 1990; Strange and Zupko 2004; Sellars 2016). Yet, even the 1,307 pages of *Stoizismus in der europäischen Philosophie, Literatur, Kunst und Politik: Eine Kulturgeschichte von der Antike bis zur Moderne* (Stoicism in European Philosophy, Literature, Art, and Politics: A Cultural History from Antiquity to Modernity, ed. Neymeyr, Schmidt, and Zimmerman 2008) pursue philosophical reception only as far as Friedrich Nietzsche. The presence of Stoic texts or ideas in German philosophy during the last 140 years is almost entirely uncharted.[3]

The present volume aims to begin mapping this territory. It has emerged from an international networking project devoted to the reception of ancient Stoic philosophy in modern continental philosophy.[4] One part of this project has brought together classicists, Germanists, and experts in modern European philosophy. Our aim has been not only to gather, elucidate, and critically evaluate existing responses to Greek, Roman, and neo-Stoic texts, but equally to create new conversations between these historically and conceptually distant systems of thinking and living. Given the novelty of this field of research, we cannot pretend to have achieved an exhaustive survey; indeed, we hope that other scholars will identify texts and topics for future research.[5] That being said, we hope to have opened up new vistas in intellectual history and revealed new philosophical significance in Stoic doctrines and practices.

The remainder of this introduction will not simply survey the chapters to come. Rather, our first aim is supplement their analyses with some additional contexts. Our second aim is to synthesize the coming chapters in order to hazard some general conclusions about German reception of Stoicism.

2. *Altertumswissenschaft* and Philosophy ca. 1850–1950

In Anglophone literature it is a commonplace that Hellenistic philosophy, including Stoicism, received relatively little attention until the mid-1970s. While it is true that Stoic doctrines are much better understood today than they were forty years ago, it is worth noting that they have been a major topic in German scholarship for well over 150 years. Some of the research produced around the turn of the century is still cited today. For instance, scholars still read Adolf Bonhöffer's studies of Epictetus (1890, 1894), and Hans von Arnim's compilation of the fragments of the Old Stoa—whose organization implies a comprehensive interpretation of their doctrinal system—remains the standard source for specialists (1903–5). Max Pohlenz completed his doctoral dissertation—in Latin—on Posidonius about the same time that Bonhöffer and von Arnim were writing (1898). Pohlenz's teaching and research on Stoicism would culminate fifty years later with *Die Stoa: Geschichte einer Geistigen Bewegung* (The Stoa: History of an Intellectual Movement, 1948), parts of which are still consulted today.

Of course, bare citations tell us little about the content or significance of this scholarship. In this regard two observations can be made. The first is that several important German philosophers conducted in-depth research on Stoicism early in their careers. It is well known that Friedrich Nietzsche's doctoral dissertation was on the sources of Diogenes Laertius's *Lives of the Illustrious Philosophers*, which contains one of our most important Stoic doxographies (DL 7.39–160, Nietzsche 1868). But there are far more striking examples. Few today remember Ludwig Stein, though he was internationally renowned as both a professor of philosophy and sociology and a journalist of international affairs ("Dr. Ludwig Stein," 1930; Haberman 1995). After completing rabbinical studies and a doctorate in philosophy, Stein become a protégé of the great historian of philosophy Eduard Zeller, with whom he cofounded the still-influential journal *Archiv für Geschichte der Philosophie*. Stein not only completed a *Habilitationschrift* on *Die Psychologie der Stoa* (The Psychology of the Stoa, 1886) but followed this with the much-longer *Die Erkenntnistheorie der Stoa* (The Epistemology of the Stoa, 1888). In the latter he makes significant progress toward rectifying Zeller's misunderstandings and dismissive judgments about Stoic logic, epistemology, and philosophy of language (Zeller 1865: 63–81). Stein's analysis is theoretically ambitious, since he tries to think through Stoic doctrines about concepts (*ennoēmata*), universals (*ideai, eidē, genē*), and "sayables" (*lekta*) in terms of a non-Stoic conception of linguistic and metaphysical "nominalism" (LS 30, 33; Stein 1888: 276–300). In this he develops a suggestion by Prantl (1855: 416), who was asking thought-provoking questions about this material as early as the 1850s (1855: 416–37; compare LS 28–29). It bears remarking that this attention to the metaphysical implications of Stoic theories about language foreshadows Émile Bréhier's much more well-known claims about Stoic sayables in *La théorie des incorporels dans l'ancien stoïcisme* (The Theory of the Incorporeals in Ancient Stoicism, 1908).

The second observation is that German scholarship has had surprisingly little impact on German philosophical reception of Stoicism. Bréhier's bold claims exerted considerable influence on Gilles Deleuze's *Logic of Sense* and several other thinkers (1969; see Lampe 2020). But the explorations of Prantl, Stein, and others have not inspired twentieth-century German philosophers in the same way. This point can be illustrated with another philosopher who began his career with a monograph on Stoicism. Günter Abel's *Stoizismus und Frühe Neuzeit* (Stoicism and the Early Modern Period, 1978) joins an ongoing debate about the role played by neo-Stoic cosmology in the emergence of what can loosely be called the "modern western worldview" (see Section 7). Yet German scholarship on Stoic philosophy of language does not appear to be among the inspirations for Abel's later work, central to which are theories of signification and interpretation.

The reasons for this missing dialogue between specialist scholarship on Stoicism and contemporary German philosophy undoubtedly vary from thinker to thinker. Here reference will be made to only one dimension of the explanatory background, which has to do with debates about the nature and purpose of *Altertumswissenschaft* (the "science of antiquity"). To simplify a great deal, models of *Altertumswissenschaft* were situated between two poles. For one, research aimed at inspiration and transformation of oneself and society, for which reason interpretation was in part intuitive, artistic, and oriented toward the interpreter's present-day concerns. For the other, research aimed at comprehensive reconstruction of a distant culture, for which reason interpretation was bound by technical methodologies and wholly focused on historicized frames of meaning. In the most famous episode in this debate, Friedrich Nietzsche fell closer to the former pole, while Ulrich von Wilamowitz-Moellendorf fell closer to the latter (Silk and Stern 2016: esp. 108–56; Landfester et al. 2006). The fact that Wilamowitz proved more influential might have something to do with the schism in the German reception of Stoicism. It would not then be coincidental that Pohlenz, the greatest German scholar of Stoicism in the first half of the twentieth century, was a devoted protégé of Wilamowitz (Dörrie 1962: 635).

This is clear in Pohlenz's polemic against Karl Reinhardt's study of the Stoic Posidonius. Reinhardt begins his monograph by decrying the sterility of both biographical and doxographical studies of ancient philosophers. He compares both to reconstructions of extinct animals based only on their bones (1921: 1). His methodology focuses instead on the "inner form" (*innere Form*) of the evidence:

> What we're calling the inner form does not depend on our discretion; in it we find instead a matter of impersonal and general necessity [*ein impersönliches und allgemeines Muß*]. Such a necessity, where it becomes known, leads to scientific knowledge [*Wissenschaft*]. . . . Through its comprehension we may hope, as they say, to reconcile scientific knowing and living [*Wissenschaft und Leben zu versöhnen*]. (1921: 1)

Reinhardt proclaims that good scholarship must grasp the principle that both animates the evidence itself and allows us to take part in that vitality; otherwise scholars can neither understand the evidence in its historical context nor find it meaningful for the present.[6] In his review, Pohlenz ironically welcomes Reinhardt's methodological challenge to the field:

> And we won't let our enjoyment [of Reinhard's innovative method] be ruined by the fact that R. also finds it necessary every couple of pages, with tedious monotony, to condemn the failure of understanding in all foregoing research; nor will we be annoyed when the author's inner form is unsympathetic to exact citations. (1965 [orig. 1926]: 173)

Pohlenz's criticism is clear. Not only is Reinhardt's referencing negligent and his treatment of prior scholarship dismissive, more importantly, given that none of Posidonius's works survives, Reinhardt eschews the usual methods of source criticism. Reinhardt supposedly uses his "feeling" (*Gefühl*) to identify which passages in surviving works represent Posidonius's influence (Pohlenz 1965: 175–6). For these reasons, Pohlenz thinks that Reinhardt's approach to scientific knowledge is fundamentally incorrect.

While it would be crude to posit a straightforward causal connection between Pohlenz's methodological conservatism and German philosophy's relative neglect of scholarship on Stoicism, there is no doubt that the great francophone scholarship of the period is more dynamically engaged with the philosophical concerns of its own time (e.g., Bréhier 1908; Goldschmidt 1953). It is also worth recalling that Pohlenz's work had its own methodological problem, namely its race-theoretical preoccupation with "Semitic" and "Hellenic" strands in the Stoic movement (Mates 1951; cf. Edelstein 1951: 427–8; cf. Foucault 1984: 585).[7] Whatever the full range of explanations may be, German philosophical reception of Stoicism has often been more indebted to Hegel's 200-year-old analysis than to more recent scholarship.

3. Techniques of Self-Cultivation: Paul Rabbow and Ilsetraut Hadot

Before moving on from German scholarship, it is important to acknowledge the influential work by Paul Rabbow and Ilsetraut Hadot. These scholars' research preceded by many decades the recent explosion of interest in philosophy as a way of life revolving around practices of self-cultivation.

In 1914, Rabbow published *Antike Schriften über Seelenheilung und Seelenführung auf ihre Quelle Untersucht, I: Die Therapie des Zorns* (Ancient Texts about Healing and Guiding the Soul Traced back to Their Sources, Volume I: The Therapy of Anger). Rabbow's goal of identifying the lost sources of surviving texts is not of direct concern; more relevant for subsequent philosophy is his focus on what he describes as "the techniques of methodically training yourself and shaping your volition [*die . . . Technik methodischer Selbsterziehung und Willensbeeinflüssung*] practiced in the first centuries of the Roman empire" (1914: 1). Rabbow's research in this area culminated forty years later with *Seelenführung: Methodik der Exerzitien in Antike* (Guiding the Soul: Methods of Exercise in Antiquity, 1954). While his arguments extend well beyond the Stoa, Seneca and Epictetus are among his most important points of reference.

Ilsetraut Hadot refined Rabbow's conclusions in *Seneca und die griechisch-römische Tradition der Seelenleitung* (Seneca and the Greco-Roman Tradition of Guiding the Soul, 1969). Her most significant innovation in this work is to emphasize the interpersonal dimension of Stoic ethics of cultivation, in which care for others occupies an important role alongside self-care (cf. Sharpe 2018).

Rabbow and Ilsetraut Hadot have unquestionably influenced subsequent European philosophy. Both Pierre Hadot and Michel Foucault acknowledge their debts to this scholarship (e.g., Hadot 2002: 66, 69, 106, 112–3; Foucault 1986: 50; 2005: 374, 392; 2018: 108). Matthew Dennis's and Sander Werkhoven's recent collection on *Ethics and Self-Cultivation*, which exemplifies the current importance of this theme, includes a chapter on Ilsetraut Hadot's updated and expanded French edition of her earlier German monograph (Sharpe 2018, discussing I. Hadot 2014). Finally, Peter Sloterdijk's *You Must Change Your Life!* again returns to Rabbow 1954 alongside the works of Pierre Hadot and Foucault (see Section 6).

4. Immanuel Kant

Turning to the philosophical reception of Stoicism, it is worth beginning with Immanuel Kant. Kant returned to Stoicism throughout his writings. His knowledge of the doctrines derives predominantly from his study of Cicero. He interpreted Stoicism as defined by a specific understanding of what it means to be a human being. Moreover, for Kant, Stoicism names a particular limitation within "ancient philosophy" conceived more broadly. Hence, he argues that the "ancients did not coordinate happiness and morality but subordinated them; because both amount to two different things whose means are distinct, they are often in conflict. The Stoic doctrine is the most genuine doctrine of true morals but the least suited to human nature" (Kant 2005: 422). The most sustained engagement with Stoicism as a named presence occurs in the *Critique of Practical Reason*, on which the following discussion will focus.

The question is, why would Kant think that Stoicism was the "least suited to human nature?" Note that what is at stake is "human nature" and thus Kant is addressing the question at the heart of a philosophical anthropology, namely, what is the being of being human? There are two elements that are inherent to any answer to this question. The first is what might be described as a capacity for error. The second is the recognition that human beings wish to derive pleasure from life. There is a drive toward "happiness." It is this drive and its complex relation to both reason and freedom that accounts as much for the errors that are made in its realization or actualization as it does for the human capacity to understand and thus rectify the errors that are made. (Rectification depends upon understanding.)

The point at which Kant is in agreement with Stoicism concerns the retention of a sense of the "highest good." The philosophical project that then arises concerns what for Kant is "the promotion of the highest good" (die Beförderung des höchsten Gut, Kant 1996: 231). It has to be willed. What has to be explained then is how the "highest good" is possible. Here the limit of Stoicism emerges. What Stoicism cannot account for is the possibility of the "highest good." Within both systems virtue can be equated with the highest good; and virtue and happiness have to be thought together. Thinking of them thus necessitates identifying the quality of each. The mistake made by Stoicism—though this is a position, for Kant, that they shared with Epicurus—was the failure to understand that virtue and happiness on the level of quality were "heterogenous concepts." As a result of this failure a "specious unity" is posited and thus their real difference unthought. Kant's argument is that the terms cannot be unified within any dialectic that attributes a similar quality to each. They are heterogenous in a precise sense, namely for Kant in regard to the highest good.

The reason Kant thinks that Stoicism cannot account for life is that intrinsic to Kant's philosophical anthropology is the claim that human beings are "compelled" to seek the highest good. There is a form of necessity. Compulsion here is the ineliminable work of reason. If this is the case, then for Kant virtue cannot be identified with the realm of the conditioned but must be the unconditioned element that accompanies all conditioned acts. Happiness is inevitably a conditioned state. What has to be thought therefore, for Kant, is the copresence of the conditioned and the unconditioned. The latter takes on the quality of the law. The "will" is operative within the domain of the conditioned acts in relation to the unconditioned quality of the law. Following the law—as a result of human freedom—is necessarily distant from the realm of inclinations in which happiness can be located. For Kant there is a different form of awareness involved, hence the claim that "an upright man cannot be happy if he is not conscious of his uprightness" (Kant 1996: 233). Stoicism's failure was its commitment to the position that happiness was already there in the consciousness of virtue. Not only is this false, but it firstly remains oblivious to the demands of reason and, secondly, cannot account for the necessity of virtue as inextricably bound up with the nonnecessity of happiness. The interplay of the two marks that which, for Kant, is intrinsic to human being.

5. Stoic Freedom: Critical Responses

One of the most important themes in the German philosophical reception of Stoicism has been the family of concepts encompassing freedom, agency, and responsibility. Recent anglophone scholarship has reconstructed the Stoics's attested positions in these issues (Bobzien 1998; Frede 2011: 27–36, 46–52), while francophone reception has explored how Stoic texts can help us to frame them differently (see Mitcheson 2017, Sholtz forthcoming). What sets German philosophical reception apart is the continuing influence of G. W. F. Hegel's compelling but simplified vision of Stoicism as a way of being in the world.

As Gene Flenady details, many scholars have discussed the importance for Hegel of Stoicism as the conceptually and chronologically first recognition of and attempt to actualize "the freedom of self-consciousness" (Chapter 2). In both the *Phenomenology* and *Lectures on the History of Philosophy*, Hegel argues that this attempt reveals its shortcomings through its partial failure: the Stoic practitioner rightly prizes the unity of thought as a space for self-cultivation, but by denying the value of personal and political relationships and institutions makes the actualization of that self in freedom impossible. Flenady adds that focusing on the Stoic concept of "indifference" allows for an expansion and refinement of this picture of Hegel's reception. Hegel approves of indifference to sensation, desire, and ungrounded opinion as a condition of reasoning, but condemns the Stoic for withdrawing her concern from externals, as if all material circumstances and relationships were indifferently supportive of self-actualization.

This Hegelian critique casts a long shadow, even though the advance of scholarship allows us today to see that it implies a partial misunderstanding: at least in middle and later Stoicism, the practitioner's virtue and happiness could not be conceived except through relationships and social roles. Thus the practitioner had good theoretical grounds for intervening in order to transform situations, and historical evidence shows that Stoics did so (Lampe 2020). That being said, it remains true that the success of these attempts at changing the world was deemed indifferent; it was the effort that mattered. Moreover, as Andrew Benjamin suggests, reception of "Stoicism" has often been directed at a "philosophical position with its own philosophical anthropology" rather than a complex and evolving historical system. Benjamin shows how Hannah Arendt, like Hegel, views Stoicism as an "illusion of freedom" that thrives when people are in fact "enslaved." Stoicism refuses to see that "enacted freedom" requires theorization and transformation of "the world" as the political space of action and dignity. In Arendt's terminology, human beings must aim at "virtuosity" as a quality of the world, not only at "virtue" as a predicate of individuals (Chapter 8, by Benjamin).

In this context, Hans Jonas's sustained analysis of Stoic freedom stands out for its erudite engagement with primary texts. For Jonas, as Emidio Spinelli explains, "the Stoa is the first philosophical school to devote explicit attention to freedom as a problem and goal for man." Jonas carefully reconstructs how the Stoics's position on freedom relates to their physics and theology. But this reconstruction only leads Jonas to reiterate Hegel's critique: not only do Stoics "confine our allegedly free action inside . . . the inner self" but even this inner self loses its autonomy through Stoic causal determinism. Jonas agrees that moral responsibility cannot be separated from necessity, but is not persuaded by the Stoic way of configuring their connection (Chapter 7, by Spinelli).

Although the reaction to Stoicism by Friedrich Nietzsche is not so obviously influenced by Hegel, it bears a family resemblance to the readings by Jonas and Arendt. As Hedwig Gaasterland explores, scholars have sometimes emphasized the continuity between Stoic and Nietzschean ethics through their shared concern with therapy of the passions. Gaasterland focuses instead on their shared commitment to the pursuit of truth. On this basis, she argues that Nietzsche's sympathy for Stoic equanimity in *Human, All Too Human* turns increasingly critical in *The Gay Science*, *Beyond Good and Evil*, and the *Genealogy of Morals*. This is because Nietzsche comes to believe that the pursuit of truth requires intensity and breadth of experience. Thus, Nietzsche's "love of fate" is strikingly different from that of the Stoics, to the extent that it could even be called "anti-Stoic": in addition to the Stoics's resolute, calm, and joyful acquiescence to whatever happens, Nietzsche's *amor fati* must embrace emotional suffering and the "dangerous game" of life (Chapter 4, by Gaasterland).

6. Stoic Freedom: Creative Appropriations

Another series of German philosophers have developed the creative more than the critical dimension of Hegel's reply to Stoicism. Some of the chapters in this volume both elucidate and extend this creative reception. It is well known, for instance, that Martin Heidegger's intense engagement with Greek philosophy more or less ends with Aristotle. But Josh Hayes argues that several moments in Heidegger's oeuvre can be read as parts of a submerged dialogue with the Stoic theory of *oikeiōsis*. *Oikos* means "household," and *oikeios* means "belonging to your household," "your own," "familiar," or "akin." *Oikeiōsis* is usually translated "appropriation"; for the Stoics, it is the lifelong process of intellectually and emotionally recognizing what naturally constitutes you by belonging to you (LS 57). Hayes connects it with an array of Heideggerian terms, from the "house of being" (*das Haus des Seins*) and the "uncanny" or "unhomely" (*unheimlich*) to "appropriation" (*Ereignis*) and "care" (*Sorge*). His argument culminates with

Heidegger's comments about Seneca in *Being and Time*. Through an innovative reading of this and related passages, Hayes suggests that the Heideggerian imperative to resolutely project ourselves toward our individual "fate" (*Schicksal*) and collective "destiny" (*Geschick*), which allows us to be "at home" in our thrown facticity, reconfigures the Stoics attempt to harmonize cosmic determinism with choice and moral responsibility (Chapter 6).

Finally, Sam Mickey elaborates the significance of Stoicism's recurrence in Peter Sloterdijk's recent publications. Sloterdijk explicitly discusses Stoic exercises of self-cultivation in *You Must Change Your Life!* (2014), where he not only cites Seneca, Epictetus, and Marcus Aurelius but also acknowledges his debt to Paul Rabbow, Pierre Hadot, and Michel Foucault. Mickey sets these citations in their broader philosophical context in Sloterdijk's oeuvre. Thus, we perceive that Sloterdijk "recovers" Stoicism as an ascetic "secession" from local cultural "domestication," rendering acculturated values "indifferent" in order to focus on individual and collective "vertical practice." One of Sloterdijk's key moves is to redefine the unit of ascetic practice with his image of nested "spheres"—the individual, the community, the world, and so on. This metaphor resonates with Hierocles's presentation of the Stoic practitioner surrounded by concentric circles of decreasing affinity, and Stoic *oikeiōsis* as the process of drawing these circles gradually closer to the center (LS 57G). In the Anthropocene, neo-Stoic care must be devoted to these nested spheres so that they do not become a "foam" of disorganized and diseased bubbles. Therefore, neo-Stoic self-cultivation will at the same time, for Sloterdijk, be care for the interconnected systems constituting our world (Chapter 10, by Mickey).

7. Physics and Philosophical Anthropology

As can be seen from the previous two sections, the individuals' relation to the sociopolitical and nonhuman world cannot be separated from questions about individual freedom. Already in the ancient texts, ethics is systematically grounded in physics, of which theology is one key component. Several of the German philosophers in this collection have focused on the explicit and implicit cosmology and anthropology of Stoic philosophy.

The contribution of Stoicism and neo-Stoicism to the so-called modern worldview has been repeatedly discussed in German philosophy, most notably by Wilhelm Dilthey, Hans Blumenberg, and Günter Abel (Chapter 3, by Nicholls). The Stoics posit an indwelling divine causal principle in all natural beings, which is the explanation for their qualities, dispositions, and the events involving them. Dilthey, Blumenberg, and Abel debate two general questions regarding the influence of this theory on early modern European thought. First, to what extent did it facilitate the rising emphasis on empirical investigation of natural laws? Second, to what extent did the Stoic ideal of aligning our thoughts with this immanent principle influence early modern ethics? These debates concern more than historical facts: on the one hand, they are ways of conceptualizing and critiquing "modernity"; on the other, they widen our understanding of the ways of life Stoic teachings can underpin.

Walter Benjamin's reading of neo-Stoic influence on German *Trauerspiele* offers a detailed case study for these debates about early modern ethics and Stoic cosmology. Paula Schwebel shows that for Benjamin the *Trauerspiel* dramatizes a neo-Stoic conception of "sovereignty" understood as emotional constancy in the face of creaturely mutability. This conception is not only psychological but cosmological, as can be perceived by appreciating Benjamin's implicit dialogue with Carl Schmitt. Schmitt's conception of sovereignty is deeply indebted to the work of Jean Bodin, who argued that just as God stands outside of the natural law created by his will, so the king grounds human law with his extralegal authority. By contrast, in the *Trauerspiel*, natural law is the necessary result of God's understanding of what is best. The core of human sovereignty is not law-giving authority, but acquiescence to the immutable natural law. Because human beings are mutable and limited, they are always "guilty" of misunderstanding this law and subject to passion. Although Benjamin's analysis is primarily historical rather than evaluative, he offers a subtle critique of neo-Stoicism: its anthropology and cosmology lead to the "mood of mourning" dramatized by the *Trauerspiel*. Similar arguments have been made about ancient Stoicism and Senecan tragedy (e.g., Rosenmeyer 1989).

Hans Blumenberg's engagement with Stoicism goes well beyond this particular controversy. As Kurt Lampe shows, throughout his career Blumenberg reflects on the precise Greek and Latin wording of Stoic texts. Blumenberg is interested in the nonconceptual "deep metaphors" of Stoic thought, which he claims provide the initial orientations for theoretical inquiries and practical deliberations. Though Blumenberg's discussions of Stoic epistemology prove insightful, it is his sustained attention to obscure areas of Stoic physics that most reward investigation. Lampe argues that many of Blumenberg's *conclusions* need revision: they rest on hasty arguments, and are unsustainable in the light of current scholarship. However, Blumenberg's *methods* give significance to texts that hitherto have appeared trivial, as Lampe demonstrates by applying them to several ancient passages (Chapter 9).

8. Karl Löwith

No discussion of recent German philosophical reception of Stoic cosmology would be complete without mention of Karl Löwith, whose ideas are often connected with Stoicism.[8] This is despite the fact that neither Stoic doctrines nor Stoic texts feature prominently in his publications. Certainly he emphasizes the values of pre-Christian Greece and Rome, but he most often speaks about "antiquity" as a whole. Individually, he cites a wide array of classical authors, including Homer, Hesiod, Heraclitus, Plato, Aristotle, and the pseudo-Aristotelian *On the Heavens*, Herodotus, Thucydides, Polybius, Celsus, Porphyry, Cicero, Pliny, and an Orphic hymn.[9] Although he also mentions Seneca several times, Stoicism is by no means his most conspicuous point of reference.

Indeed, it is Löwith's critics who have attached the label "Stoic" to him—most notably Jürgen Habermas in his short profile, "Karl Löwith: Stoic Retreat from Historical Consciousness" (1983 [orig. 1963]). It is worth insisting that this label is not only tendentious but also intended to be derogatory. This section will therefore begin by elucidating Habermas's explicit and implicit criticism. It will then be possible to dwell briefly on a few passages where Löwith genuinely engages with Stoic ideas.

A beginning can be made by explaining what Habermas means by "retreat from historical consciousness." Emphasis here will be on two essays in Löwith's *Gesammelte Abhandlungen*, namely "Mensch und Geschichte" (Man and History, 1960: 152–78) and "Natur und Humanität des Menschen" (Nature and Humanity of Man, 1960: 179–207). As Habermas rightly observes, one of Löwith's recurrent concerns is to challenge the belief that human existence is defined by historicity. "It is a contention of the most recent past," Löwith writes, "whose furthest origin is in the theologico-anthropological worldview of Christianity, that man exists historically" (1960: 154). Löwith is deeply critical of the position he associates especially with Hegel, Marx, Dilthey, and Heidegger, namely:

> The destinies of history [*Die Geschicke der Geschichte*], which we suffer and which fall to us inasmuch as we ourselves bring them about, appear so entirely to determine man in his existence that he can no longer even imagine anything other than being completely, utterly, inescapably bound to history. Modern man does not live in the *environment* of *nature*, he exists in the *horizon* of *history*. [*Der heutige Mensch lebt nicht im* Umkreis *der* Natur, *er existiert im* Horizont *der* Geschichte]. (1960: 158)

Löwith denies that the foundation of human being is historical rather than natural. Human beings have a nature, he insists, although this nature is a "determining orientation" (*Bestimmung*) rather than a "determined quality" (*Bestimmtheit*, 1960: 188). In other words, what is given to human beings by nature, in addition to their biological needs and capacities, is the thinking and speaking questioning of the given. Löwith is broadly in agreement with Hegel and Heidegger when he writes,

> In thinking and acting, man is related to and withdrawn from the natural world, because his thinking activity surpasses [*überschreitet*] everything given by nature. . . . In order to be able to live humanely, man must cultivate and thereby denature nature with work, that is with destructive appropriation [*man muß . . . die Natur durch Arbeit, d.h. durch destruktive Aneignung kultivieren und somit denaturieren*]. (1960: 196–7)

Note Löwith's acceptance that what is human only emerges through the thinking and active labor that "destroys" the given by "appropriating" it. However, Löwith argues that this questioning, surpassing, appropriating labor "reaches completion always still in the unsurpassable environment of nature" (1960: 205). The natural world is an intelligible organizing power independent of human beings, a "cosmos" in the ancient sense (1960: 186–7). It "is never 'ours' or the collective human perspective on it. . . . Rather we ourselves belong to it, even at that precise moment when we appropriate and surpass it" (1960: 205).

It should now be clear in what sense Löwith reasserts the natural foundation of being-human. Next it is essential to explain his assertion about "the theologico-anthropological worldview of Christianity." In *Meaning in History* (and frequently elsewhere), Löwith argues that Hegel and Marx exemplify the tendency to project the meaning of history into the future of its fulfillment or redemption (1949: 33–59). It is this pattern which Löwith traces back to Christian foundations. He diagnoses the same error in his fiercely critical essay on "The Political Implications of Heidegger's Existentialism," whose pathos of "resolution" and "destiny" he views as a post-Christian "faith" shared by National Socialism (1988 [orig. 1947–8]). Löwith attempts to recuperate classical cosmology as a remedy for these eschatological philosophies and ideologies:

> The ancients . . . did not presume to make sense of the world or to discover its ultimate meaning. They were impressed by the visible order and beauty of the cosmos, and the cosmic law of growth and decay was also the pattern for their understanding of history.. . . . This view was satisfactory to them because it is a rational and natural understanding of the universe, combining a recognition of

temporal changes with periodic regularity, constancy, and immutability.... As for the destiny of man in history, the Greeks believed that man has resourcefulness to meet every situation with magnanimity—they did not go further than that. (1949: 4)

As Richard Wolin, building on Habermas, concisely explains and thoughtfully critiques, Löwith's attempt to rehabilitate ancient Nature and Cosmos is in part an effort to come to terms with the disasters of recent German history (Wolin 2001: 70–100). Rather than seeing themselves as the heroic agents of world-historical destiny, people should instead recognize that there is no comprehensive and redemptive meaning to devote themselves to. They can then employ their "resourcefulness" and "magnanimity" in order to emotionally and practically handle whatever is currently happening.

It is now possible to appreciate both the tendentiousness and the insightfulness of Habermas's act of labeling. To begin with the former, it should be noted that there is nothing specifically Stoic about subordinating humankind to cosmic regularities or emphasizing our versatility and ability to rise above natural events. As Löwith's own citations attest, many other Greek texts articulate these ideas more memorably than Stoicism.[10] Next, it can be observed that by speaking of a "retreat from historical consciousness," Habermas unfairly transfers Hegel's critique of Stoicism to Löwith. As was seen in Section 5, Hegel accuses the Stoics of cherishing the unity of thought as the space in which *Geist* will be actualized, and therefore "retreating from" personal relationships and political institutions. But Löwith does not simply withdraw into the "freedom" of his own mind. To the contrary, among his central goals is to explain recent political events. Finally, while it is compatible with Stoicism to say human beings must "appropriate" nature (LS 57), it is profoundly un-Stoic to describe this as "destructive denaturing" of the given. This is not just a matter of terminology: whereas the Stoics believe that nature determines what each human being must appropriate, Löwith maintains that "the kind and manner and variety of needs and the kinds of satisfaction correlated with them surpass everything given or denied to him [i.e., to man]" (1960: 204). In other words, nature does *not* determine what each human being must appropriate.

The foregoing objections are important, since commentators sometimes accept without criticism the ascription of Stoic positions to Löwith. However, it is also true that there are allusions to Stoicism at some key moments in Löwith's works. Here we will limit ourselves to three examples.

Perhaps the most important example is in *Meaning in History*. In the Introduction to this volume, Löwith explains the ancient attitude to history by summarizing a passage from Polybius, whose *Histories* narrate the rise of republican Rome (1949: 8–9). This may already be covertly Stoic: scholars have frequently connected Polybius with Stoicism, as Löwith was probably aware.[11] Moreover, when Löwith says that "This mutability of fortune did not merely cause sadness to ancient man but was accepted with virile assent" (1949: 9), the idea of positively "assenting" to events recalls the Stoic injunction to "want" or even "love" whatever happens.[12]

Stoicism returns overtly in the book's Conclusion and Epilogue. In the former, Löwith argues that one should have the same attitude to historical events whether one believes in a humanistic cosmos or unfathomable divine providence, namely

> a definite resignation, the worldly brother of devotion, in the face of the incalculability and unpredictability of historical issues. In the reality of that agitated sea which we call "history," it makes little difference whether man feels himself in the hands of God's inscrutable will or in the hands of chance and fate. *Ducunt volentem fata, nolentem trahunt.* . . . (1949: 199)

Here the attitude of "assent" has been replaced with the less genuinely Stoic "definite resignation." But the Latin phrase comes from Seneca: "The fates lead the willing, but drag the recalcitrant" (Sen. *Ep.* 107.11). Seneca, in turn, is translating a lost Greek poem by Cleanthes, the Stoa's second scholarch. The attitude evinced by Cleanthes's poetry, like the effort to "assent" to whatever happens, rests upon the doctrine that god manages the entire universe intelligently and benevolently (LS 54, 63C3-4). Löwith by no means endorses this doctrine. However, he agrees with the Stoics that human beings belong to an organized natural world, and the rationale of this world is cyclical rather than eschatological. Therefore, human beings should use our naturally given abilities to address current problems, not to strive toward utopia. Stoicism appears one final time in the Epilogue, where Löwith mentions "the Stoic maxim, *nec spe nec metu* [neither in hope nor in fear]" (1949: 204).[13] Though human beings cannot live entirely without hope, Löwith believes it is "sober and wise" to repudiate the messianic hopes complicit in Germany's recent disasters and atrocities (1949: 205).

The second example of Löwith's Stoic reception comes from "Nature and Humanity of Man." Immediately after affirming that "with man a crack appears in nature, something questionable and equivocal, insufficient and invalid [*Unzulängliches und Nichtiges*]"—a position he explicitly connects with Hegel, Heidegger, and Sartre—Löwith refers once more to Seneca: "Man is sick with his own being-human. The human world, according to Seneca, is a giant hospital with a few wise doctors, who are philosophers" (1960: 198). The sentiment that folly is "sickness" is straightforwardly Senecan, but this pathology resists easy translation into existentialist idioms (Lampe 2008). Löwith's strategy is to connect both Senecan "sickness" and existentialist "invalidity" with "estrangement" from the given. Löwith describes this as "an originary *inadequacy* of man to himself and to the world," which makes humankind insatiable (1960: 200–4).

In order to describe the "remedy," Löwith turns to a different Senecan text, this time as quoted by Michel de Montaigne (1960: 206–7): "O quam contempta res est homo nisi supra humana surrexerit [How contemptible a thing is humankind, unless it raises itself above human things]!" According to Löwith, Montaigne is on good Stoic ground when he claims that humans cannot "surpass themselves" merely by reflecting on human virtues, but wrong to claim that "surpassing" must aim toward "supernatural transcendence." Montaigne fails to recall that this quotation comes from Seneca's *Natural Questions* (1.praef.5), in which there is no question of going beyond nature. Rather, *Natural Questions* elevates the questioner above "human things" through "participation in the divine, in other words cosmic natural reason" (1960: 206). Löwith's assertion here bears comparison with Pierre Hadot's claim that ancient physics is a "spiritual exercise" (Hadot 2002: 207–11; 2006: 182–9). But for his argument to work, Löwith must explain how this ancient exercise can be modernized. This is where the critiques by Habermas and Wolin are most incisive: it is not clear how Löwith's "nature" presents a viable alternative to "historical consciousness" as a basis for cultivating the "humanity" of individuals or societies.

This brings us to our final example. Habermas claims:

> When not long ago Löwith was asked to contribute to a radio series on the problem of the death penalty . . . without any sideways glance at the death penalty . . . he turned his attention exclusively to the Stoic philosophical *topos* of suicide as a sign of the freedom that is proper to philosophical mastery of life. One can only wonder if it is still wisdom when a thinker has to make assertions at the cost of so restricting his vision. (1983 [orig. 1963]: 88–9)

Here again Habermas both distorts Löwith's arguments and communicates a subtle insight. On the one hand, he is right that Löwith scarcely touches upon the death penalty in "Töten, Mord, und Selbstmord: Die Freiheit zum Tode" (Killing, Murder, and Suicide: Freedom toward Death, 1981 [orig. 1962]: 399–417), and spends almost the entire essay discussing philosophical arguments about suicide

(1981: 400–417). Moreover, though he alludes vaguely to several situations in which people committed suicide during the Second World War (1981: 403), Löwith shows not the slightest interest in relevant psychology or epidemiology. This certainly undercuts the "wisdom" of his analysis. It is also true that he implicitly links David Hume, the real hero of his essay, with Stoicism. First, he reports a comment Adam Smith made about Hume, that "there still existed genuine Stoics in the old sense" (1981: 413). Second, he quotes Hume quoting Seneca: "Agamus deo gratias, quod nemo in vita teneri potest (Thank god that no one can be detained in life)" (1981: 414).

On the other hand, Habermas makes it sound as though Löwith framed his entire discussion of suicide in Stoic terms. This is plainly false: Stoicism is only mentioned twice in passing, both times near the end of the article (1981: 413, 414). Stoicism is not mentioned at all in Löwith's other short essay on this topic, "Die Freiheit zum Tode" (Freedom toward Death, 1981 [orig. 1969]: 418–25). Löwith's primary points of reference are his familiar antagonists, namely Christianity, Hegel, and Heidegger. His principal argument is that commitment to totalizing meanings—the same eschatology that he attacks in *Meaning in History*—impedes intelligent evaluation of the ethics of suicide. His secondary argument is a critique of Heidegger's attitudes toward death, which is too subtle and complicated to summarize here. Overall, ancient Stoic texts and ideas play a very small role in Löwith's essays on this theme. The effort to connect them with a "Stoic philosophical *topos*" is best understood as part of Habermas's broader strategy to discredit Löwith.

9. Conclusion

The previous eight sections provide an initial idea of the variety and depth of responses to Stoicism in recent German philosophy. At the risk of some simplification, it might be said that most of this reception tradition revolves around two major themes. The first goes back to Kant and especially Hegel, and focuses on problematizing the relationship between the freedom of thought and the interpersonal, political, and ecological domains in which that thought must be actualized. The second focuses on the type of world projected by Stoic ways of life. Particularly important here is the doctrine of "appropriation," which designates the normative trajectory for Stoic exercises of cultivation—of ourselves, other human beings, and other aspects of the universe.

While these interpretations and critiques of Stoicism obviously have many similarities with those found elsewhere in Stoic reception, we believe they also offer something distinctive. Thus, it is hoped that, in combination with this book's companion volume (*French and Italian Stoicisms: From Sartre to Agamben*, Lampe and Sholtz 2020), they will expand and enrich philosophers' and scholars' appreciation for the significance of the Stoic tradition.

Notes

1. Kurt Lampe has written Sections 1–3 and 5–9, while Andrew Benjamin has written Section 4.
2. It is hazardous to generalize about this massive and diverse movement, but at the time of writing, the Modern Stoicism website is a good starting point: https://modernstoicism.com (accessed November 1, 2019).
3. A noteworthy exception is Majolino's forthcoming chapter on Husserl, which came to our attention only as this volume reached completion.
4. This project ran throughout 2016, and was supported by the Arts and Humanities Research Council of the United Kingdom.
5. For instance, we regret the absence of feminist philosophy from our coverage, although we are not aware of any German feminist philosophical engagements with Stoicism. (The phrase "German feminist philosophy" is itself slightly vexed: Nagl-Docekal 2005.)
6. This recalls Dilthey's theory of *Geisteswissenschaft*; in Chapter 3, Nicholls argues that this theory was inspired by (inter alia) Stoic sources.
7. Foucault is discussing Jürgen Habermas's surprise and disappointment to discover that one of his teachers had sympathized with Nazism. Foucault compares his own recent experience with Pohlenz, who "had for his entire life made himself the herald of Stoicism's universal values." Foucault has been reading Pohlenz's 1934 publication on *Antikes Führertum: Cicero de Officiis und das Lebensideal des Panaitios* (Ancient Leadership: Cicero's de Officiis and Panaetius's Ideal Life), about which he says, "Read the introductory page and book's closing remarks about the *Führersideal* and the true humanism constituted by a *Volk* animated by their leader's guidance . . . . [They show] with what gratitude Pohlenz would have greeted Hitler" (Foucault 1984: 585).
8. For example, consider the title of Richard Wolin's excellent chapter on Löwith in *Heidegger's Children*, to which this section is indebted: "Karl Löwith: The Stoic Response to Modern Nihilism" (2001: 70–100).
9. Representative passages include 1949: 6–9, 204–5; 1960: 153–7, 180–7, 230–2, 234–6; 1997: 116–21.

10   The breadth of Löwith's references to "antiquity" as a whole can be exemplified with just a couple of examples. In connection with natural and cosmic regularity—which are frequent themes in his work—Löwith mentions Herodotus, Thucydides, and Polybius, Homer, Goethe, a fragmentary Orphic hymn, the text *On the Heavens* ascribed to Aristotle, and Heraclitus (1949: 6–9; 1960: 155, 185–7, 231–5; 1997: 115–9). Resourcefulness and magnanimity are less common themes for Löwith, and it will be seen that Seneca is among the authors with whom he connects them. But one thinks also of Homer's Odysseus, the resourceful philosopher of Plato's *Symposium* (202c-4c), and the famous "Many are the wonders" ode of Sophocles's *Antigone* (334–83).

11   For references and an up-to-date appraisal, see Brouwer (2011).

12   See Seneca *NQ* 3.praef.12, *Ep.* 74.20; Epictetus *Ench.* 8; MA 5.8.5.

13   Though this string of words never actually appears in any classical Latin text, the thought is certainly Stoic: fear and hope are two of the four canonical "passions" to be avoided by any Stoic (LS 65).

Works Cited

Abel, Günter (1978), *Stoizismus und Frühe Neuzeit*, Berlin: de Gruyter.

Bobzien, Suzanne (1998), *Determinism and Freedom in Stoic Philosophy*, Oxford: Oxford University Press.

Bonhöffer, Adolf (1890), *Epictet und die Stoa: Untersuchungen zur Stoischen Philosophie*, Stuttgart: Ferdinand Enke.

Bonhöffer, Adolf (1894), *Die Ethik des Stoikers Epiktet*, Stuttgart: Ferdinand Enke. [(1996) *The Ethics of the Stoic Epictetus*, trans. William O. Stephens, New York: Peter Lang].

Bréhier, Émile (1908), *La théorie des incorporels dans l'ancien stoïcisme*, Paris: Librairie Alphonse Picard & Fils.

Brouwer, René (2011), "Polybius and Stoic *Tyche*," *Greek, Roman, and Byzantine Studies*, 41: 111–32.

Colish, M. (1990), *The Stoic Tradition from Antiquity to the Middle Ages*, 2 vols, Leiden: Brill.

Dörrie, Heinrich (1962), "Max Pohlenz," *Gnomon*, 34 (6): 634–6.

"Dr. Ludwig Stein, the Publicist, Is Dead" (1930), *The New York Times*, July 15: 23.

Edelstein, Ludwig (1951), "Review of *Die Stoa: Geschichte einer geistigen Bewegung* by Max Pohlenz," *The Classical Weekly*, 44 (7): 105.

Foucault, Michel (1984), *Dits et écrits 1954–1988, IV: 1980–1988*, eds. Daniel Defert and François Ewald, Paris: Gallimard.

Foucault, Michel (1986), *History of Sexuality 3: The Care of the Self*, trans. Robert Hurley, London: Penguin.

Foucault, Michel (2005), *The Hermeneutics of the Subject: Lectures at the Collège de France 1981–1982*, ed. Frédéric Gros, trans. Graham Burchell, New York: Picador.

Foucault, Michel (2018), *Histoire de la sexualité 4: Les aveux de la chair*, ed. Frédéric Gros, Paris: Gallimard.

Frede, Michael (2011), *Free Will: Origins of the Notion in Ancient Thought*, ed. A. A. Long, Berkeley: University of California.

Goldschmidt, Victor (1953), *Le système stoïcien et l'idée de temps*, Paris: Vrin.

Habermann, Jacob (1995), "Ludwig Stein: Rabbi, Professor, Publicist, and Philosopher of Evolutionary Optimism," *The Jewish Quarterly Review*, n.s. 85 (1/2): 91–125.

Habermas, Jürgen (1983), "Karl Löwith: Stoic Retreat from Historical Consciousness," in *Philosophical-Political Profiles*, trans. Frederick G. Lawrence, 79–97, London: Heinemann.

Hadot, Ilsetraut (1969), *Seneca und die griechisch-römische Tradition der Seelenleitung*, Berlin: de Gruyter.

Hadot, Ilsetraut (2014), *Sénèque: direction spirituelle et pratique de la philosophie*, Paris: Vrin.

Hadot, Pierre (2002), *What Is Ancient Philosophy?* trans. Michael Chase, Cambridge, MA: Belknap.

Hadot, Pierre (2006), *The Veil of Isis: An Essay on the History of the Idea of Nature*, trans. Michael Chase, Cambridge, MA: Belknap.

Kant, Immanuel (1996), *Practical Philosophy*, trans. Mary J. MacGregor, Cambridge: Cambridge University Press.

Lampe, Kurt (2008), "Seneca's Nausea: 'Existential' Experiences and Julio-Claudian Literature," *Helios*, 35 (1): 67–87.

Lampe, Kurt (forthcoming 2020), "Introduction: Stoicism, Language, and Freedom," in K. Lampe and J. Sholtz (eds.), *French and Italian Stoicisms: From Sartre to Agamben*, London: Bloomsbury.

Landfester, Manfred, Latacz, Joachim Latacz, Thomas Schmitz, Peter Lebrecht, and Jürgen Paul Schwindt (2006), "Philology," in Hubert Cancik, Helmuth Schneider, and Christine F. Salazar (eds.), *Brill's New Pauly*, http://dx.doi.org/10.1163/1574-9347_bnp_e15201850, consulted December 6, 2019.

Löwith, Karl (1949), *Meaning in History*, Chicago: University of Chicago Press.

Löwith, Karl (1960), *Gesammelte Abhandlungen: zur Kritik der Geschichtlichen Existenz*, 2nd ed., Stuttgart: W. Kohlhammer.

Löwith, Karl (1981), *Mensch und Menschenwelt: Beiträge zur Anthropologie*, Stuttgart: Meltzer.

Löwith, Karl (1988), "The Political Implications of Heidegger's Existentialism," trans. Richard Wolin and Melissa J. Cox, *New German Critique*, 45: 117–34.

Löwith, Karl (1997), *Nietzsche's Philosophy of the Eternal Recurrence of the Same*, trans. J. Harvey Lomax, Berkeley: University of California Press.

Majolino, C. (2020), "Back to the Meanings Themselves: Husserl, Phenomenology and the Stoic Doctrine of the *Lekton*," in *Phenomenological Interpretations of Ancient Philosophy*, eds. J. K. Larsen and P. R. Gilbert, Leiden: Brill.

Mates, Benson (1951), "Review of *Die Stoa: Geschichte einer geistigen Bewegung* by Max Pohlenz," *American Journal of Philology*, 72 (4): 426–32.

Mitcheson, Katrina (2017), "Foucault, Stoicism, and Self-Mastery," in Matthew Dennis and Sander Werkhoven (eds.), *Ethics and Self-Cultivation: Contemporary and Historical Perspectives*, 124–40, London: Routledge.

Nagl-Docekal, Herta (2005), "Feminist Philosophy in Germany: A Historical Perspective," *Hypatia*, 20 (2): 1–6.

Nietzsche, Friedrich (1868), "De Laertii Diogenis Fontibus," *Rheinisches Museum für Philologie*, 24: 81–228.

Pohlenz, Max (1898), *Quemadmodum Galenus Posidonius in Libris de Placitis Hippocratis et Platonis Secutus Sit*, Leipzig: Teubner.

Pohlenz, Max (1934), *Antikes Führertum: Cicero De Officiis und das Lebensideal des Panaitios*, Leipzig: Teubner.

Pohlenz, Max (1948), *Die Stoa: Geschichte einer geistigen Bewegung*, Göttingen: Vandenhoeckh & Ruprecht.

Pohlenz, Max (1965), *Kleine Schriften*, ed. Heinrich Dörrie, Hildesheim: Georg Olms.

Prantl, Carl (1855), *Geschichte der Logik im Abendland, erster Band*, Leipzig: S. Hirzel.

Rabbow, Paul (1914), *Antike Schriften über Seelenheilung und Seelenführung auf ihre Quelle Untersucht, I: Die Therapie des Zorns*, Leipzig: Teubner.

Rabbow, Paul (1954), *Seelenführung: Methodik der Exerzitien in Antike*, Munich: Kösel.

Reinhardt, Karl (1921), *Poseidonios*, Munich: Oskar Beck.

Rosenmeyer, Thomas (1989), *Senecan Drama and Stoic Cosmology*, Berkeley: University of California Press.

Sellars, J. (2016), *The Routledge Handbook of the Stoic Tradition*, London: Routledge.

Sholtz, Janae (forthcoming 2020), "Deleuzean Exercises and the Inversion of Stoicism," in K. Lampe and J. Sholtz (eds.), *French and Italian Stoicisms: From Sartre to Agamben*, London: Bloomsbury.

Silk, M. S. and J. P. Stern (2016), *Nietzsche on Tragedy*, Cambridge: Cambridge University Press.

Sloterdijk, Peter (2014), *You Must Change Your Life!* trans. Wieland Hoban, New York: Cambridge.

Spanneut, M. (1973), *Permanence du stoïcisme: de Zénon à Malraux*, Gembloux: Éditions J. Duculot.

Stein, Ludwig (1886), *Die Psychologie der Stoa, erster Band: metaphysisch-anthropologischer Theil*, Berlin: Calvary.

Stein, Ludwig (1888), *Die Erkenntnishtheorie der Stoa (zweiter Band der Psychologie)*, Berlin: Calvary.

Strange, S. K. and J. Zupko (2004), *Stoicism: Traditions and Transformations*, New York: Cambridge University Press.

Sharpe, M. (2018), "Ilsetraut Hadot's Seneca: Spiritual Direction and the Transformation of the Other," in M. Dennis and S. Werkhoven (eds.), *Ethics and Self-Cultivation: Ancient and Contemporary Perspectives*, 104–23, London

Wolin, Richard (2001), *Heidegger's Children: Hannah Arendt, Karl Löwith, Hans Jonas, and Herbert Marcuse*, Princeton; Princeton University Press.

Zeller, Eduard (1865), *Die Philosophie der Griechen: eine Untersuchung über Charakter, Gang, und Hauptmomente ihrer Entwicklung. Dritter Theil: Die nacharistotelische Philosophie, erste Hälfte*, 2nd ed., Leipzig: Fues's.

2

The Indifference of Reason

Hegel and Stoicism

Gene Flenady

Hegel's account of Stoicism in the *Phenomenology of Spirit* and in his *Lectures on the History of Philosophy* (*LHP*) is often—and understandably—cast in negative terms.[1] Hegel criticizes Stoicism as presenting an unrealizable conception of freedom, one that severs the necessary relation between individual freedom and its actualization in the world. In short, Stoicism is not for Hegel a "live option" for philosophy, in the sense that it disproves or undermines itself in the attempt to be lived out. Having no bearing on life outside of the subject who holds to it, Stoicism aims for freedom but grasps only emptiness and indeterminacy. In Judith Shklar's words, Hegel's Stoic "thinks himself unfettered in thinking and does not realize that his is the freedom of the void" (1976: 62). In spite of itself, Stoicism nonetheless provides an important Hegelian lesson, insofar as the necessary relationship between individual freedom and its actualization in determinate social relations is the most immediately graspable—and perhaps historically influential—moral of the Hegelian story *tout court*. Freedom cannot be coherently understood as the property of individuals, and Stoicism would be a particular version of that failed conception: taking the rational thought of the individual as necessary and sufficient for freedom.

It is not my goal in this chapter to determine how fair this criticism is to historical Stoicism.[2] My concern here is whether Hegel's criticism of Stoicism tells the whole story of its place in Hegel's philosophy. As such, I am primarily dealing with *Hegel's* stoicism. In my view, while Hegel in the *Phenomenology* and the *LHP* certainly is critical of stoicism in the way sketched earlier, its importance is nonetheless stressed in both texts, and, moreover, Hegel's philosophical engagement with stoicism is legible at other moments in his system.[3] I want to demonstrate the continuing presence of stoicism in Hegel by approaching his

Phenomenology and *LHP* treatments in terms of "indifference" (*Gleichgültigkeit*), the stoic *adiaphoron*.[4]

On one level, that Hegel would want to acknowledge the philosophical importance of stoicism is to be expected. If Hegel is to be true to what he takes be his own innovation, namely the dialectical logic in which error is a moment of the true (Hegel 2018: §2/4; 1986a: 12), stoicism must contribute in some way to what Hegel takes to be more self-consistent accounts of reason. In the *Phenomenology*, stoicism is first in the "history of Spirit" to explicitly link self-consciousness, the activity of thought, and freedom.[5] "As it consciously appeared [*bewusste Erscheinung*] in the history of Spirit [*Geschichte des Geistes*], this freedom of self-consciousness [*Freiheit der Selbstbewusstseins*] has, as is well known, been called *stoicism*" (2018: §198/118; 1986a: 157).[6] Hegel wants in the *Phenomenology* to develop these stoic resources, while at the same time arguing that stoicism's conception of self-conscious freedom as indifferent to sensible well-being *and* to sociopolitical actuality renders any further development *at their hands* impossible. Yet attendance to the concept of indifference in this critical account in turn brings into view the presence of stoicism elsewhere in the Hegelian system. Hegel, like the stoics, continues to think self-consciousness and freedom as constituted by indifference in some way. While stoicism is not explicitly mentioned in the Anthropology section of the *Philosophy of Mind*, Hegel's account there of the emergence of the individuated subject is, in my view, in tacit dialogue with his earlier account of stoicism in the *Phenomenology*.[7] Hegel offers an alternative account of the function of indifference in self-constitution that at once utilizes and refigures the stoic position. Similarly, Hegel's claim that we should be indifferent to mere opinion and attendant only to "scientific" or systematic reason (*Wissenschaft*) also marks a certain stoic inheritance, even if (again) Hegel is concerned to figure the relation of rationality to opinion in his own way.[8]

To put the argument as succinctly as possible, on Hegel's account, stoicism claims that to be free means to be indifferent to sensible well-being, and instead attuned only to freedom understood as the maintenance of thought's pure or "immediate" self-identity. But thought thus conceived is for Hegel necessarily indeterminate or empty, thus lacking the resources to provide determinate criteria by which particulars can be normatively distinguished, that is, as better or worse instances.[9] This picture broadly accords with Shklar's "freedom of the void" in the line mentioned above, as well as our commonsense understanding of indifference as a practical stance (as in the saying, "It's all the same to me"). But for the Hegel of the *Encyclopedia* system, to be free is nonetheless to be indifferent in the right way. First, in Hegel's Anthropology, self-identical subjectivity is constituted by *habitual* indifference to sensations and desires. Via the acquisition of habits (Hegel has certain fundamental habits in mind, for example the habit or walking, the habit of talking, doing such things without conscious attention to them), the subject is able to set aside the data of sensation and the arising and passing of natural desire, so as to regard itself as a self-same agent, and so one ultimately responsive to and responsible for reasons rather than merely to bodily affect. Indifference is in this sense a condition of entry into what Wilfrid Sellars has termed the "logical space of reasons" (1997: 76) though indifference to sensation and desire does not—as the stoics would claim—help us navigate that space itself. Secondly, rational agents on Hegel's account ought to be indifferent to arbitrary opinion, which, in providing no rational justification, is excluded from the space of reasons. Rational agents should instead be attentive or attuned to systematic thought (self-consistent reasoning),[10] and those social practices and institutions that actualize such thought. The stoics importantly indicate the constitutive role of indifference in agency, but conflate indifference to sensation and indifference to mere opinion, and wrongly claim that we ought as rational agents to be indifferent to social and political rationality.

As is always the case with Hegel—and perhaps equally with stoicism—the relation to Kant is salient. I want to begin the aforementioned trajectory by distinguishing Hegel's encounter with stoicism from Kant's. After pointing out, at a very general level, some similarities and differences between Kant and Hegel's respective engagements, I suggest that Hegel's account of stoicism as indifference—the indifference that accompanies reason itself—can be read as an involution of Kant's opening invective against "indifferentism" to metaphysics in the first edition Preface to the first *Critique*.

1. Kant, Hegel, Stoicism

Kant positions his practical philosophy with and against Stoicism. Indeed, that one of Kant's most celebrated lines—the "starry heavens above me and moral law within me" from the conclusion to the *Critique of Practical Reason* (CPrR 161)—shares its figures with Seneca's *De Consolatione ad Helviam* has been regularly noted.[11] Apart from shared literary allusions, the Kantian and stoic positions can been said to have two key conceptual similarities. First, Kant beginning the *Groundwork* with the unconditioned value of the good will is acknowledged by commentators as stoic in origin.[12] Second, it follows from this unconditioned value that Kant distinguishes between two forms of reasoning and their corresponding values, one moral and one nonmoral: between duty and inclination, and between categorical and hypothetical imperatives (Schneewind 1996: 290). As Julia Annas has shown, this sharp distinction between moral and nonmoral forms of reasoning has its analogue in the stoic distinction between virtue and "indifferents." "For the Stoics, nothing but virtue is good; other things have a different kind of value and are called indifferents. (This distinction can . . . be regarded as equivalent to the distinction between moral and value of a nonmoral kind.)" (Annas 1996: 240). Indeed, in the *Critique of Practical Reason* Kant explicitly mentions stoicism in working out the distinction between *Wohl* (mere well-being) and *Gut* (CPrR 59–60).

Kant's criticism is that stoicism in reducing well-being to a matter of indifference fails to formulate properly the relationship between virtue (*aretē*) and happiness or flourishing (*eudaimonia*), which follows from Kant's reconceptualization of human experience as conditioned by conceptual capacities *and* forms of sensibility. To say with stoicism that acting for the sake of the Good simply *is* happiness, regardless of (in indifference to) one's sensible well-being, fails to attend to finite, sensible conditions of human being. Hence Kant's claim to resolve the tension between stoicism and epicureanism (CPrR 110–14).[13] As Schneewind puts the Kantian position on the virtue-happiness relation: "Happiness, the satisfaction of desires, is indeed second in rank to worthiness to be happy, assured only by virtue; but it is nonetheless indispensable for needy dependent beings such as we" (1996: 292).[14] The reader sympathetic to stoicism can argue here that stoicism *does* provide a guideline for *relatively* justified motivation for and satisfaction in merely sensuous goods, namely in the distinction between preferred and "dispreferred" indifferents. Annas notes that the identification of happiness with virtue alone is "very unintuitive" and seems to "leave us with no rational basis for choice between health and disease, wealth and poverty," but that the stoics are not "forced into this absurd position," insofar as there are *nonmoral* reasons for why we should, in the domain of indifferents, and without any reference to virtue, prefer health to disease and wealth to poverty (Annas 1996: 240–1).[15] How closely this maps Kant's account of nonmoral practical reasoning cannot be tackled here. Suffice to say that Kant—like Hegel—nowhere directly engages with the preferred/dispreferred distinction (Schneewind 1996: 292), and that the Kantian would likely not be convinced by distinction *within* indifferent goods, given that *as indifferent* they would still occupy too peripheral a place in our account of the motivations and values of human agents. Hegel, as will be seen, takes the discussion elsewhere.

Perhaps partly due to a failure to engage with the above-mentioned distinction, both Kant and Hegel repeatedly claim that the stoic worldview is incomplete and requires supplementation. The difference for Hegel is that what supplements stoic rationality is not the sensible component of human nature, but an account of objectively rational social relations and institutions (what Hegel calls *Sittlichkeit* or "ethical life"). In other words, the *structure* of Hegel's critique of stoicism is the same as Kant's: stoicism lays the right groundwork but remains incomplete. Hegel however shifts the locus of that incompleteness from sensibility to sociopolitical reality. As Hegel puts it: "The internal freedom of self-consciousness is the foundation [*Grundlage*], but as yet it has no concrete shape [*hat aber noch nicht seine konkrete Gestalt*]; and everything legal or ethical the Stoics defined merely as something negative, indifferent [*Gleichgültiges*], or contingent that must be renounced" (2006: 278; 1986c: 295). In Hegel's view, it is not that stoicism is unworkable because it fails to acknowledge our sensibility as of justified interest to individual human beings, but rather because it takes social and political reality to be a matter of indifference, and, for Hegel, "in the concrete principle of spirit [*Im konkreten Prinzip des Vernünftigen*] it is by no means indifferent [*gleichgültig*] what circumstance I am in" (278; 295). What is missed in stoicism is the kind of social relations that would install or actualize rationality. This should accord with common (though of course contestable) framings of Hegel's idealism as introducing a constitutive moment of intersubjectivity ostensibly lacking—or at least not fully fleshed out—in Kant (Brandom 2002: 31).

The aforementioned draws some general lines around the shared lacuna and differing patterns of emphasis in Kant and Hegel's respective engagements with stoicism. It is of course not as simple as this. On the one hand, while Kant's engagement is in terms of rational and sensible components of individual moral agents, he includes the irreducibility of *obligation to others* in his critique of the stoic sage (Schneewind 1996: 292). On the other hand, Hegel suggests that the stoics were right to understand rational agency as requiring indifference to sensation and desire. Casting Hegel as defending indifference to sensibility, and Kant as arguing for the unworkability of such indifference (for sensibly conditioned beings), might strike one as prima facie odd. Isn't Hegel the thinker above all concerned to overcome any and all such Kantian dualisms? The answer is that Kant and Hegel are using stoicism to talk about different things. Hegel's treatment of stoicism is not *primarily* an account of the proper relation between the sensible and the rational motivations of embodied rational agents. Or, to return to the classical terms, it is not *primarily* about the proper relationship of virtue and happiness. The stoicism of the *Phenomenology* is part of an account of the structure of self-consciousness, and that preoccupation remains in the later *LHP*. There Hegel notes that the "ancient issue of the harmony of virtue (morality) with happiness [*der Harmonie von Tugend und Glückseligkeit*]," has "occupied us too, in the era of the Kantian philosophy," and Hegel marks, in basic agreement with Kant and the stoics on this point, that this harmony must be on the basis of a prioritization of "universal, rational definitions of duty [*Willensbestimmungen*], honor, and the like" rather than "external satisfactions [*äußerlichen Genüsse*] such as wealth, rank, and the like" (2006: 275; 1986c: 284). But Hegel then immediately moves to define the stoic identification of virtue and happiness in terms of self-consciousness: "So the Stoics said that happiness is the enjoyment or sensation [*Empfindung*] of this harmony itself, but it is to be posited only as inner freedom, independence, inner harmony with oneself [*Übereinstimmung mit sich selbst*]" (275; 285). Stoicism is for Hegel above all a theory of self-consciousness, but one that illegitimately abstracts self-conscious thought from its necessary corollaries, thus building from it a one-sided moral picture.

The remainder of this chapter is an attempt to explain the way in which Hegel makes use of the stoic distinction between rationality and that to which rationality is and ought to be indifferent, an appropriation that indexes his distinctive, post-Kantian philosophical approach more generally. Some brief account of this approach is required for what follows, insofar as Hegel's treatments of stoicism take place in the middle of Hegelian arguments, and the appropriation of indifference only makes sense within their contexts. I appreciate that any rapid characterization of Hegel's approach will be highly contestable; any account of the similarities and differences between Kant and Hegel's respective approaches will be even more so.[16]

Hegel is interested in providing a *developmental* account of philosophical content in a way Kant is not. Kant's transcendental arguments begin from certain experiences human beings indubitably have, and then seek to show that such experiences entail certain transcendental conditions.[17] In the practical sphere, for example, the fact of moral agency cannot be reduced to or understood with empirical resources alone, but is transcendentally dependent on the exercise of distinctly rational capacities. Hegel similarly wants to move from an indubitable experience (Hegel's word for this is "immediacy" [*Unmittelbarkeit*]) to an account of its conceptual conditions (the "mediation" [*Vermittlung*] of this immediacy).[18] His strategy is to begin with the logically simplest, most abstract (most "immediate") account of the exercise of a conceptual capacity, and show how that account of itself develops, through contradictions in its initial formulations, into a complete, self-consistent picture of the capacity in question. Importantly, the contradictions in prior accounts are moments of or contribute to the completed conceptual picture. This happens in different ways and in different registers in, say, the *Phenomenology*, the *Science of Logic*, the *Philosophy of Right*, and so on. In both Kant and Hegel, thought is able to produce through itself an account of the conditions of its own proper exercise; but Hegel's account is structured as a developmental narrative of successive negations and preservations of partial philosophical positions.[19]

Let me give an example of such a narrative directly relevant to what follows. In the *Phenomenology*, Hegel starts with the simplest, most immediate account of our power of empirical knowledge, a naïve realism which would take knowledge to be the nonconceptual, purely sensible consciousness of singular objects. This account, however, proves on closer inspection to be its opposite: the concrete and *singular* "this" we claim to know directly is in fact an utterly empty *universal* (a "this" indistinguishable from all other instances). The negation of this naïve realist position leads us to conceive of knowledge, more consistently, as the inherence of universal properties in singular objects (expressible in subject-predicate judgments). This is itself proven to be inconsistent, and so requiring further reformulation, and so on.[20] The first four chapters of Hegel's *Phenomenology* wants to demonstrate that the immediate intake of sensibility alone cannot account for determinate knowledge, but rather requires conceptual contributions—and that, ultimately, consciousness of empirical objects has to be understood in terms of *self-consciousness*, consciousness of the act of knowing such objects.[21] This is the point at which stoicism emerges in the *Phenomenology*, as the immediate philosophy of self-consciousness; the principle of self-consciousness explicitly taken up at *its* simplest and most abstract. Stoicism represents the immediacy not of knowing (with which the *Phenomenology* began) but of self-knowing.

A sense of this Hegelian explanatory mode—moving via negation from the immediate appearance of an explanandum to its explanans—can be provided by contrasting Kant's own usage of "indifference." Kant in the A edition Preface of the first *Critique* cites "indifferentism" as the enemy of metaphysics, understood as the science of reason in general, the self-clarification of reason by reason[22]:

> Now after all paths (as we persuade ourselves) have been tried in vain, what rules is tedium and complete *indifferentism [Indifferentism]*, the mother of chaos and night in the sciences, but at the same time also the origin, or at least the prelude, of their incipient transformation and enlightenment [*Aufklärung*], when through ill-applied effort they have become obscure, confused, and useless. (Ax)

Kant is diagnosing what he takes to be a specifically modern phenomenon: indifferentism to metaphysics results from the perceived fruitlessness of "dogmatic" rationalism, on the one hand, and modern, corrosive forms of skepticism emerging from empiricist "physiology" (Locke is mentioned by name), on the other. Metaphysics, in both its rationalist and empiricist forms, no longer merits attention, insofar as it has proved incapable of being put on the secure path of a science—or at least, compares unfavorably with the recent flourishing of natural science and its real-world application. Kant argues however that one must attend to reason, cannot be indifferent to it, insofar as it is human nature to think (Ax). Now, obviously, the stoics are not indifferentists in *this* sense: they take human being to be essentially rational[23]; indifference as we will see is rather intended to *secure* that rationality. As such, Hegel adds the following line of thought and makes stoicism its representative: stoicism is not the indifference to reason but *reason's own indifference*, the moment of indifference that constitutes the immediate self-presence of thought to itself. Stoicism makes explicit that indifferent withdrawal from the world installs rational agency. For Hegel, indifference by no means provides adequate guidance for such agency (as stoicism wrongly claims), but it is nonetheless a condition of its institution in the embodied individual. In other words, Hegel wants to say that reason, in its first appearance, in its immediacy as thinking self-consciousness, is *itself* bound up with indifference. It is the contradictions of this immediacy that Hegel is looking to follow in his treatment of stoicism.

2. Hegel's Critique of Stoicism

While the *LHP* account of stoicism is more detailed than the *Phenomenology*'s, that stoicism is treated in similar terms in distinct phenomenological and historical narratives raises here some well-known interpretive challenges of the *Phenomenology*, namely that it begins as an ahistorical treatment of the capacity of knowledge but then somewhat awkwardly modulates roughly halfway through to the real social conditions of rationality in European history since antiquity. While there is debate as to how well these two halves fit together, it appears that Hegel began by intending only the former, but found himself writing the latter (Forster 1998: 501–10).[24]

Hegel seemingly does not take himself to be treating a historical stoicism in the *Lectures* and a purely conceptual position (with passing resemblance to such history) in the *Phenomenology*. Stoicism is a historical philosophical position in both, and, interestingly, the *first* historical philosophical school to be mentioned by name in the phenomenological progress proper (i.e., excluding the Preface).[25] The history of philosophy had been tacitly present in the *Phenomenology* before the mention of stoicism.[26] But notably, the famous "Mastery and Servitude" section that immediately precedes Hegel's stoicism discussion takes place in no historically determinable place or time.[27] It can be taken as an allegory, the Hegelian equivalent of (and alternative to) the Hobbesian story of the transition from a state of nature to one of civilization, or perhaps even as an allegory for the human condition as such (Kojève 1980: 3–30). Hegel, however, is concerned to present the *historical* stoic as conceptually emerging from the *historically indeterminate* figure of the master and slave. The evidence here is provided by comparing the *Phenomenology* and *LHP* accounts. In the *LHP*, stoicism is treated briefly in its Greek origins, but the stoics of the Roman world for Hegel are the clearest expression of stoicism's own principles.[28] In the *Phenomenology*, the Roman world is referenced by all but name: "As a universal form of the world-spirit, it [stoicism] can only come on the scene during a time of universal fear and servitude [*Knechtschaft*] but which is also a time universal cultural formation [*allgemeinen Bildung*] that has raised culturally formative activity [*das Bilden*] all the way up to the heights of thinking" (2018: §199/118–19; 1986a: 157–8).[29] In both texts, the conditions of stoicism—at least the conditions of its flourishing into a "universal form"—are not purely conceptual, but historical and political. Thus stoicism represents the moment at which Hegel's conceptual story about knowledge and self-consciousness crosses over into real history.

The "Mastery and Servitude" section is importantly titled "Self-Sufficiency and Non-Self-Sufficiency of Self-Consciousness," and ends, as is well known, with the undoing of the master's claims to self-sufficiency and the slave coming to consciousness of their own self-sufficiency through work (*Arbeit*). On the one hand, the master proves to be paradoxically dependent on the slave, both materially (for sustenance, for satisfaction of their natural desires) and for recognition of their status as master (for recognition [*Anerkennung*], for satisfaction of their human desire to be acknowledged as a self-determining agent).[30] On the other hand, the slave, in laboring on objects, in giving objects a new form, recognizes in those objects their own agency: the form of the object, while it is "posited as external, becomes to [the slave] not something other than himself . . . therefore, through this retrieval, he comes to acquire through himself a *mind of his own* [*seiner durch sich selbst* eigener Sinn], and he does this precisely in the work in where there had seemed to be only some *outsider's mind* [*es nur* fremder Sinn *zu sein schien*]" (§196/116; 154)—that is, the intention and command of the master. The slave recognizes their own self-sufficient agency in their capacity to transform objects: as the work of art is a mirror for the artist, so the work object reflects the worker.

Crucial to the argument overall is the master and slave's respective *temporal* relationship to objectivity. The slave *works* on natural objects *for* the master; the master *consumes* them *for himself*. At first glance, the master acts *through* the slave, has his agency realized in the slave as a passive instrument. But the master's actions prove to be the empty, tedious repetition of reducing such objects to nothing (consuming them). The master satisfies their natural desire only for that desire to reemerge; their experience is not independence from nature (which they purport) but an endless cycle of dependence. On the other hand, the labor of the slave produces durable objects (dwellings, or, to stick with the example of food, durable skills), which enable a self-consciousness not pegged to the rising and passing of natural desires and their always temporary satisfaction. In mastery,

> desire [*Begierde*] has reserved to itself the pure negating of the object, and, as a result, it has reserved to itself that unmixed feeling for its own self [*unvermischte Selbstgefühl*]. However, for that reason, this satisfaction is only a vanishing, for it lacks the *objective aspect* [*gegenständliche* Seite], or *stable existence* [*das* Bestehen]. In contrast, work is desire *held in check* [*gehemmte* Begierde], it is vanishing *staved off* [*aufgehaltenes Verschwinden*], or: work *cultivates and educates* [*oder sie* bildet]. (§195/115; 153)

This distinction between mere repetition and vanishing, and a duration made possible by relationality, is central to Hegel's thought, but would take the analysis too far afield.[31] It is of interest here because Hegel in the Anthropology wants to show that our capacity to regard ourselves as a self-same I regardless of (in habitual *indifference* to) the arising and passing of sensations and natural desires marks the emergence of self-conscious agency from mere bodily capacity. The stoics are positioned at the corresponding moment within the *Phenomenology*: at the moment when vanishing is staved off in the slave's labor, the well-known stoic principle of *working on the self*—what amounts for Hegel to *maintaining* the self-identity of the I—immediately follows.

That stoicism can be meaningfully approached as work on the self is now well understood.[32] Hegel foreshadows this theme in modern scholarship, but with nuances resulting from its place within the phenomenological narrative. For Hegel, stoicism is the internalization of the slave's labor: the cultivation, the *Bildung*, of one's self in thought alone. Stoicism is the slave's labor *in thought*, and as such it is indifferent to really existing relations of mastery and servitude. That is, "whether on the throne or in fetters" (§199/118; 157)—whether as Emperor Marcus Aurelius or as former slave Epictetus—one can recognize oneself as oneself, without needing the intermediary of the object of labor. This makes the stoic in their indifference to mastery and servitude at the same time the unity of mastery and servitude: the stoic labors, like the slave, but without genuine relation to objectivity, like the master.[33] The dialectical neatness of this transition is satisfying: the stoic is neither master and slave and both master and slave; stoicism is thus the negation *and* preservation (the "sublation") of the master-slave relation within Hegel's phenomenological progression.

Now that we have stoicism positioned in the *Phenomenology*, we can unpack Hegel's account in closer detail. That account turns on the immediacy of the stoic conception of self-consciousness as entailing indifference. I will begin with "immediacy." This term is central to Hegel and so hard to economically summarize, but is linked (via its Kantian pedigree) to *direct* relationship to objectivity, the representation of an object that is "unmediated" by other or further representations (A19/B33). On Hegel's developmental reconceptualization of Kantian Idealism (briefly reconstructed in Section 1), the immediate is the as-yet-unelaborated, the conceptual conditions of which are implicit, not yet explicit.[34] Thus, the stoic account of rational freedom is "immediate," in the sense that it is first in the order of time to clearly formulate the concept of the "freedom of self-consciousness" (Hegel 2018: §198/118; 1986a: 157). What is material here is immediacy in a second but related sense: stoicism formulates the *concept* of self-conscious freedom *itself* in terms of immediacy. Whether Hegel can consistently argue for the necessity of this coincidence between historical and conceptual senses of immediacy—that temporally first positions are necessarily conceptually first—is itself a complex question, but the suggestion is nonetheless present in the *Phenomenology*'s account of stoicism and elsewhere.[35] Hegel summarizes freedom of self-consciousness in this way:

> Within thinking, I *am free* because I am not in an other, but rather I remain utterly at one with myself [*Im Denken bin Ich frei, weil ich nicht in einem Anderen bin, sondern schlechtin bei mir selbst bleibe*], and the object, which to me is the essence, is in undivided unity with my being-for-myself; and my moving about in concepts [*Bewegung in Begriffen*] is a movement within myself. However, in this determination of the shape of self-consciousness, it is essential to hold fast to this: that this determination is *thinking* consciousness *itself*, or its object is the *immediate* unity of *being-in-itself* and *being-for-itself* [*die* unmittelbare *Einheit des* Ansichseins *und des* Fürsichseins *ist*]. (§197/118; 156)

Thinking consciousness is understood as immediate in the sense of a direct or "simple" unity between observing and observed aspects of the self. In self-consciousness, the I as that which is to be known (the object, "being-in-itself") is unified with the I as that which knows (the subject, "being-for-itself"). It is a "difference that is no difference," a self-cancelling difference, or I = I.[36] This relation is qualitatively different from the relation between subject and object in empirical knowledge, treated in the prior "Consciousness" section of the *Phenomenology*. If the immediacy of self-consciousness (or *self*-knowing) were to be analyzed in terms of the relation of subject and object (merely *knowing*), self-coincidence would not be expressed, but rather an infinite regression in which self-coincidence is endlessly deferred. Such an account would take up only the *difference* between observer and observed, would render the observed term only an *object* and not *also* the subject of observation. It would fail, in Hegel's words quoted earlier, to "hold fast" to the immediate unity that characterizes self-consciousness—indeed such a false conceptualization is in its infinite regress indefinitely losing its grip. Now, the unity of self-consciousness had already emerged in the master-slave allegory: the initial combatants (those who are to become master and slave) take themselves as self-sufficient, self-identical beings, distinguished from and confronted by an other such being, purporting the same self-sufficiency. In stoicism, however, we have a consciousness that explicitly acknowledges unity as its principle, and so is *thinking*.[37] For Hegel, this making explicit *is* an achievement, and abiding in such unity, rather than in otherness, will remain the *structure* of freedom in Hegel's philosophy as a whole. But to take, with the stoics, the thought of the self-consciousness of the individual to exhaust the *content* of freedom is insufficient. Indifference here is the key to this achievement *and* its insufficiency.

The labor of self-consciousness so understood is to maintain its unity by indifference to what is other than it. The unity with oneself is won by indifference to otherness. Acting "according to reason" for the stoic thus means "a self-contained concentration [*die Konzentration des Menschen in sich*] such that one forswears, or is indifferent [*gleichgültig*] toward, everything pertaining merely to immediate sensation and to instinct [*Trieben*]" (Hegel 2006: 274; 1986c: 281). The stoic imperative is thus: be indifferent to everything but the immediate unity of self-consciousness. Or more precisely: maintain self-equality through treating everything else as of equal value, that is no value for self-equal subjectivity at all.[38] There is thus a conceptual point of connection between self-consciousness conceived in its immediacy and indifference: indifference is not an external expedient or instrument but is proper to self-consciousness so conceived. To see this, what has to be marked is that indifference is not a synonym for identity, nor is it mere difference. It is rather taking differences to be of no account. The commonsense understanding of indifference in English has this sense in certain contexts ("it's all the same to me"), and there is a German phrase which makes equality mean of no account or importance to the subject ("es ist mir egal," "I don't care"). The German word for indifference makes the moment of equality explicit: "*Gleichgültigkeit*," "Equal-validity," "being valid," or "counting" (*gelten*) as the same or equal (*gleich*). Above the immediacy of self-consciousness was parsed in terms of "self-cancelling difference." There is a difference between the I that knows and the I that is known, but that difference is immediately "taken back"—they are always already the same I—in order for the unity of self-consciousness to be graspable. Stoic indifference repeats this structure in the domain of the self-conscious subject's action: it "takes back" discriminable differences by arguing those differences to be of no account for the rational subject.

Hegel's aforementioned "according to reason" should be taken seriously: stoic indifference is both doxastic and practical. The stoic, on account of a determinist physics, *believes* pain and pleasure to be equally rational, in the sense that both physical states are explicable in terms of efficient causality, within a physical nature entirely thus explicable. In turn, the stoic *acts* as if pain and pleasure were identical, neither to be preferred. Pleasure is a "preferred indifferent" and pain a "dispreferred indifferent" only from a standpoint *outside* of stoic reason; there are no *rational* grounds to distinguish them from the standpoint of either theoretical or practical philosophy—if such a (Kantian) distinction between stoic physics and ethics can itself be meaningfully made.[39] Attendance to pleasure or pain *as if* that difference were a difference between a rational and a nonrational content would frustrate or undermine attendance to the proper site of this difference for the subject, that is, between self-identical harmony and episodes of sensation and desire. To put this is in the language of Robert Brandom's reading of Hegel's idealism (to which I will return briefly in Section 3), the stoic's doxastic and practical action are to be taken together as integrated, mutually supporting *commitments* (Brandom 2002: 21).

In the *Phenomenology*, the stoic labor of indifference has two sides. On the side of the subject, indifference is a *withdrawal*, "maintaining the lifelessness [*Leblosigkeit*] which consistently *withdraws* from the movement of existence, *withdraws* from actual doing as well as from something, and *withdraws* into *the simple essentiality of thought* [*in* die einfache Wesenheit des Gedankens zurückzieht]" (2018: §199/118; 1986a: 157). On the side of the object, "The freedom of self-consciousness is *indifferent* [gleichgültig] with respect to nature and for that reason has *likewise let go of natural existence, has let it be freestanding* . . . [dieses ebenso frei entlassen . . .]" (§200/119; 158). In reflecting on the self, in asserting and maintaining self-identity, we separate ourselves from objects at the same time as providing them with *their own* identity, a sphere distinct from that of the self. We have here in the *Phenomenology*'s narrative the distinction between oneself as a merely natural object (a body) and oneself as self-identical agent that is achieved at the end of the Anthropology, and in both cases, in terms of indifference. As a result of this two-sided labor we are left with two distinct, self-equal domains, about which nothing more can be said than they are *not* one another.[40] The connection—really, the mutual determination or constitution—of the freedom of thought and the external world is central to Hegel's philosophy. We read in the transition from "Subjective" to "Objective Spirit" in the *Philosophy of Mind* that for freedom to be *actual freedom* it must realize itself in the world (2007: §484/218; 1986b: 302).[41] That is, freedom cannot be coherently formulated as belonging to subjects alone; a proper understanding of the relationship of thinking and freedom involves a durable rational social order in which rational individuals can find themselves at home.

This point is put concretely in the *LHP* account and abstractly in the *Phenomenology*. To start with the former, Hegel claims that the "implication" of stoicism "is not that the world should be rational and just, but only that the subject as such should maintain its inner freedom [*seine Freiheit in sich behaupten*]." He goes on: "Here there is no demand for the real harmony of rationality as such with the existence of determinate being [*des Daseins*], nor is there anything that we can express as objective ethical life" (2006: 276–7; 1986c: 294). The critical counterpoint to this realized rationality for Hegel is Marcus Aurelius: "With regard to morality, strength of virtuous will [*des guten Willens*] and meditation upon oneself, nothing finer than [the *Meditations*] can be found. . . . But the circumstance of the Roman Empire was not altered by having this deep and fundamental thinker as its emperor" (277; 294–5). Stoicism goes wrong by figuring the labor of thought to consist of indifferent withdrawal from a world left to stand "freely" on its own—in the Roman case, in unfreedom. Again, for Hegel, "meditation upon oneself" is the *structure* of freedom, insofar as one (the observing I) is immediately with oneself in one's "other" (the observed I). But the "other" here must be put in scare quotes; it is not that freedom made actual in the world, being at home with really existing others in rational political community.

In the *Phenomenology*, the argument proceeds more abstractly: thinking self-consciousness is "initially"—that is, in its historical appearance in stoicism—

"only as the universal essence as such and not as this objective essence in the development and movement of its manifold being [*mannigfaltigen Seins*]" (2018: §197/118; 1986a: 156–7). By maintaining the immediate unity of self-consciousness by withdrawal from all particular contents, stoicism produces a one-sided ethical picture. It can neither offer a properly determinate, systematic thought nor determinate norms by which social relations may be judged. This line of critique is increasingly severe. At first, stoicism is simply said not to present thought in its "development and movement." This simple *not* becomes by the end of Hegel's discussion an *active* severing of thought from its actualization: "Yet in the way that the concept as an *abstraction* has here cut itself off from the manifoldness of things [*Mannigfaltigkeit der Dinge*], the concept *has in its own self no content* [Inhalt]; instead it has a *given* [gegebenen] content" (§200/119; 158). This givenness of content will be important when we turn to the Anthropology; indifference is a norm *given* to us as embodied beings (something we must do, even if some do it better than others), not a norm we determine for ourselves. Read in this light, the *Phenomenology* criticism seems to be that stoicism makes maintenance of the self-relating structure of self-consciousness in its immediacy to be *the* normative principle, to be the first and last word, an end in itself, the only guidance needed in the world (again, discounting the supplementary distinction between preferred and dispreferred indifferents). But so taken, such a principle lacks content, and stoicism "found itself in an embarrassing situation when it was asked . . . for *a content of thought itself.*" Hegel ends his account by taking pleasure in some sharp words:

> To the question put to it, "*What* is good and true?", its answer was once more that it was the abstract thinking *devoid of all contents itself* [*das* inhaltlose *Denken*], namely that the true and the good is supposed to consist in rationality. However, this self-equality [*Sichselbstgleichheit*] of thinking is only again the pure form in which nothing is determinate. The general terms, "true" and "good," or "wisdom" and "virtue," with which stoicism is stuck, are on the whole undeniably uplifting, but because they cannot in fact end up in any kind of expansion of content, they quickly start to become tiresome. (§200/119; 158–9)

The tedium of the stoic rhetoric of the good is the equivalent in thought of the master's tedious consumption of natural goods. As such, in Hegel's narrative, perhaps bizarrely, the laboring slave appears preferable to the stoic, who in making transformative labor the principle of thought alone is incapable of *genuinely* transforming themselves. As masters of thought inert in the world, stoics have willfully broken off the feedback loop between objectivity and self-consciousness operative for the laboring slave, and left themselves with nothing but empty edification. That is, the mutually determining relationship to material singularity ("I am the *one* who made *this*") and particularity ("I am the *kind* of being who makes *this kind* of object") has been lost; the stoic has only the purely universal insistence on self-identity: I am I, a singularity indistinguishable from universality; each I the same as all the others.[42] Such indistinguishability can provide no grounds for a determinate social order.

3. Indifference, Opinion, and Habit

The end of the Preface to the *Philosophy of Right*, although not only or even primarily addressing stoicism,[43] puts Hegel's critique of stoicism—and Hegel's alternative—clearly. Reason

> is little content with that cold despair which confesses that, in this temporal world, things are bad or at best indifferent [*mittelmässig*], but that nothing better can be expected here, so that for this reason alone we should live at peace with actuality [*Wirklichkeit*]. The peace which cognition [*Erkenntnis*] establishes with the actual world has more warmth in it than this. (1991: 22; 1986d: 27)

Rational individuals need not withdraw from sociopolitical reality, as it is possible to determine in existing social relations the outline of their rationality, the norms to which they hold themselves, even in their failure to meet them. And yet, only a paragraph later, Hegel suggests that indifference *is* in certain cases the appropriate attitude:

> If a content is to be discussed philosophically, it will bear only scientific and objective treatment; in the same way, the author will regard any criticism expressed in a form other than that of scientific [*wissenschaftliche*] discussion of the matter itself merely as a subjective postscript and random assertion and will treat it with indifference [*gleichgültig*]. (23; 28)

That the German for these two terms is different in this case (mittelmässig; gleichgültig) perhaps means that the seeming contradiction escaped his notice. But I want to suggest that there is no contradiction here, rather an element of the Hegelian counterpart to stoic ethics. Both would be about what we should and should not be indifferent to. To attend to reason means we *ought not* (contra stoicism) be indifferent to the rationality or otherwise of social and political institutions. But, more friendly to stoicism, we *ought* to be indifferent to mere opinion. I will say a little more about opinions now. I will then address the indifference as it is treated in the Anthropology section of the *Philosophy of Mind*, as habit. Indifference to sensation and natural desire is a capacity subjects acquire as a condition for agency, but should not be taken, as the stoics take it, to provide genuine normative guidance for such agency.

The simplest way to understand why Hegel thinks opinion is to be disregarded is that it is laden with *presuppositions*. As he says in the *Science of Logic*, "all too often and all too vehemently have I been confronted by opponents incapable of the simple consideration that their opinions and objections imply categories which are presuppositions (*Voraussetzungen*) and themselves in need of being criticized (*Kritik bedürfen*) first before they are put to use" (Hegel 2010a: 20; 1986e: 31). Stephen Houlgate's reading of the *Logic* takes this targeting of presuppositions to motivate the Hegelian enterprise as a whole (Houlgate 2006). On this reading, modernity is—as announced by the Reformation, the French Revolution, and given philosophical expression in Kant's critical project—the era of critique, in the sense that rational justification for belief and action is universally demanded, without exception. In turn, a rational justification of reason itself must be provided. Thinking back to Kant's discussion of indifferentism in Section 1 of this chapter, indifferentism to metaphysics—metaphysics understood as reason's self-clarification—would threaten the modern project as such. But for Kant

> it is pointless to affect *indifference* [Gleichgültigkeit] with respect to such inquiries [metaphysics], to whose object human nature *cannot* be *indifferent* [*nicht gleichgültig sein kann*] . . . these so-called *indifferentists* [*Indifferentisten*], to the extent that they think anything at all, always unavoidably fall back into metaphysical assertions, which they yet professed so much to despise. (Ax)

Given that the human being is a thinking being, the indifferentist unavoidably brings with them a metaphysics, but one laden with unexamined presuppositions.[44] Now, ancient philosophy in Hegel has an ambiguous relationship with this modern imperative.[45] Nonetheless, and even if for Hegel the stoics fail to provide ultimately satisfactory arguments, it is impossible, as I said in Section 1, to paint them as indifferentists in this sense: stoicism acknowledges that, as rational beings, we must provide reasons for our actions, ultimately grounded in an account of reason itself.[46]

The point I want to make here leans on Robert Brandom's reading of Hegel's *Phenomenology* and his inferentialist account of rational agency more generally. For Brandom, human beings are "essentially self-conscious," in that what such beings are is partly a function of their own self-conception.

Essentially self-conscious beings "enjoy the possibility of a distinctive type of *self-transformation: making* themselves be different by *taking* themselves to be different" (Brandom 2011: 26). This does not mean that "anything goes," that individuals just are whatever they merely say they are. Self-conscious beings are constitutively susceptible to having the consistency of their identifications (and corollary "commitments") tested by other self-conscious beings, what Brandom calls "deontic scorekeeping." Brandom takes Hegel's master-slave allegory to establish this structure. At the beginning of the master-slave dialectic, the two combatants initially take themselves (it might be said, have the "opinion" of themselves) as self-sufficient agents. This claim to self-sufficiency is put into question by the presence of another such claimant: one claimant—the master—proves themselves self-sufficient, that is, independent of the other; one claimant—the slave—has their claim to self-sufficiency, in their dependence on the other, shown up as illegitimate. Both combatants begin by taking self-sufficiency to be their *essential* identity, and their biological existence to be merely incidental: the slave, in yielding, in preferring to live, shows continued biological existence to be their essential identification, rather than self-sufficiency. As discussed earlier, this relation reverses itself. The master proves dependent, for their continuing claim to the status of master, on the acknowledgment or recognition of the slave, irreducible to the simple fact of domination, and entailing the slave's self-sufficient capacity *to* provide this recognition. The moral of the story on Brandom's account is that self-conscious beings must be *recognized* by others as having the status that they take themselves to have in order to actually have that status. In Brandom's view (and to telescope dramatically), being self-conscious means taking oneself to have certain statuses, which in turn means engaging in "the practice of giving and asking for reasons" (or with Sellars, the "space of reasons") in which one's entitlement to those statuses is tested by others entitled to so test. Hegel's argument for indifference to opinion, and a further deepening of his critique of stoic indifference, can be presented in this Hegelian-Brandomian framework.

Revision of an opinion to include reasons is something that self-conscious beings who identify as rational must be committed to, on pain of self-contradiction. In other words, rational agency consists in being *responsible* for rational justification of identifications and commitments, and for the compatibility of such justifications. Thus, the rational agent, if they are to live up to that identification, is not entitled to respond to a demand for justification with: "Well, that's just my opinion." If an agent is unable to provide a satisfactory rational justification for a belief or action, they must revise their position in an attempt to do so, or must qualify or abandon the previously held commitment to rational grounding of belief and action (itself a kind of rational act).[47] Justifiable *indifference* is approached from the other side: *if* an agent provides no reasons for their action or belief, and refuses to provide them, instead grounding their position in some extra-discursive, non- or a-conceptual content (Hegel paints his Romantic peers as intuitionist chest-thumpers of this kind)[48]—that is, if they do not take themselves to be responsive to reasons—the agent committed to rationality does not stand under a corresponding responsibility to rationally respond.[49] Hegel, in advocating justified indifference to opinion, is in a sense policing the boundary of the social practice, generalized in modernity, of giving and asking for reasons. What is determined in *this* indifference is the border of the space of reasons; mere opinions do not qualify for entry.

I argued in concluding Section 2 that the stoic, in indifferent withdrawal into thought, severs the link between subjectivity and material particularity established by the figure of the laboring slave. Here it appears that the stoic in their particular conception of reason is also severed from the space of reasons in Brandom's sense. From a certain perspective, the stoic takes themselves to be something (they "essentially identify" with freedom) other than what they actually are. A stoic may pronounce themselves free even in chains, and freedom is framed in such a way that the stoic does not take themselves to be susceptible to the obvious objection: that one is, essentially, living in fantasy, a freedom of the void, and so on. The stoic can always reply: but I am *essentially* free, insofar as freedom just *is* the freedom of self-consciousness, a freedom verifiable by the self. Stoicism in this way renders itself *immune* to rational contestation of the type Brandom considers, and so shuts down, in its attempt to divide the self from everything else, the difference between merely having an opinion of oneself, and actually legitimately possessing that status via the recognition of others. This severs the relationship between subjectivity and particularity in another, perhaps deeper sense: in refusing any contestation of one's self-conception, one would refuse the particularization of one's identity. On Hegel's version of the stoic position, one cannot actualize any particular identity in society (to take oneself to be *this kind* of person and be recognized as such), for any social role one takes up is different in kind from one's essential identification (any social status is an indifferent, not reflective of the virtue of the self).

This line of argument is contestable for at least two reasons. First, the freedom the stoic identifies is in an important sense verifiable by self-conscious beings: self-coincidence is immediately present to introspection.[50] Secondly, the stoic obviously is a *kind* of person, the kind who considers any identification other than "stoic" as an inessential one. The consistency of stoic commitments *can* be tested by others: if an agent makes an epistemic claim for the indistinguishability of pain and suffering, failure to act on that indifference—by, say, actively seeking pleasure—would provoke a justified challenge to the coherency and consistency of that agent's ensemble of commitments. The goal of stoicism is of course to be *actually* virtuous—that is, indifferent—when the time comes to prove it.[51] Stoicism thus appears undecidable, inside and outside of the space of reasons as Brandom formulates it. Hegel provides an explanation here: stoicism is ambiguous on this point because it *does* conceive of rationality, but only in its immediacy, as undeveloped into social relations.

Before moving on to the discussion of indifference as habit, I just want to try to make clear the normative status of indifference to opinion: *if* one takes oneself to be rational, that is, if one is committed to the giving of and asking for rational justifications, then one *must* (in the deontic sense) disregard opinion, treat it with indifference. But this is not natural necessity: one *ought* not have opinions but one *may* nonetheless express them.[52] The normative status of indifference to sensation and natural desire (as habit) is different: habituation is a norm embodied beings must first satisfy to engage in, or fail to engage in, the space of reasons in the first place. Put simply: for there to be reasons tested by others, there must be a self-same I to have them.

Hegel's discussion of habit effects the transition in the *Philosophy of Mind* from the "Anthropology" (the "animal soul") to "Phenomenology of Spirit" sections. The latter is the Encyclopedia version of the trajectory traced in the first half of the *Phenomenology of Spirit*, that is, in which immediate empirical consciousness proves to be conditioned by self-consciousness and, further, by the unity of subject and object ("Reason" proper).[53] At stake in the account of habit (§§409–10) is the subject's transition from immersion in bodiliness into simple self-relation:

> Self-feeling [*Das Selbstgefühl*], immersed in the particularity of the feelings (of simple sensations, and also desires, urges, passions, and their gratifications), is not distinguished from them. But the self is implicitly a simple relation of ideality to itself [*Aber das Selbst is an sich einfache Beziehung der Idealität auf sich*], formal universality . . . thus it is the *universality* that distinguishes itself from particularity, the universality that *is for itself* [für sich seiende Allgemeinheit]. (2007: §409/130; 1986b: 182)

After the aforementioned quote, Hegel adds that "the particular being of the soul is its *bodiliness*"—that which has been the subject of the Anthropology—but that "here [in habit] it breaks with this bodiliness [*mit welcher sie hier bricht*]" (§409/130; 183). This should put in mind the discussion of stoicism in the *Phenomenology*. There, self-consciousness, as thinking self-consciousness, asserted the difference between itself as simple unity and natural being, that is, the sensations and desires of the body. This difference was installed by the labor of indifference in its two-sidedness (a *withdrawal* into thought that left the natural world *free-standing*). In the Anthropology, indifference is again the operator, but understood as habit. Habit enables the movement from the subject's "impotence [*Ohnmacht*]," its "childlike unity" (§413Z/143; 201) with its body, to the capacity to take the body as an object for it. It is the emergence of this difference between the I and its objectivity that conditions the Encyclopedia's account of knowing in the following "Phenomenology of Spirit" section, which, like the *Phenomenology* itself, begins with the relation between the knowing subject and objectivity in general.[54]

This line of argument is prima facie strange. Habit is something that tends to be thought of negatively—bad habits that ought to be broken because in them the agent is an automaton, acting unconsciously, unfree. Let me make two points on this. First, Hegel does not mean "habit" in only this everyday sense. "We are habituated [*gewöhnt*] to the *representation* [Vorstellung] of habit [*Gewohnheit*]; nevertheless to determine the *concept* [*die Bestimmung des* Begriffs] of habit is difficult" (§410Z/133; 187). Rather, "habit is a form that embraces all kinds and stages [*Arten und Stufen*] of mind's activity" (§410R/132; 186). Hegel will discuss memory as habitual, and indeed, the being at home with others that constitutes ethical life is "the habit of right in general, of the ethical . . . [*die Gewohnheit des Rechten überhaupt, des Sittlichen . . .*]" (§410R/131; 185).[55] What is of concern here (surprise, surprise) is habit in its *immediacy*, habit as it first appears in the Hegelian account, again, as a point of transition. Hegel's examples of habit in this sense are of the order of learning to walk (to move the legs in a measured way without thinking about them) and to speak (to consistently modulate the vocal chords without thinking of them). Indeed, once habits of *this* order are acquired, they go worse the more they are thought about. "Bad" habits don't stutter in the same way when made conscious. They rather induce *shame*. A bad habit is bad because it does not accord with a subject's self-conception, forces the subject to acknowledge the kind of inconsistency or incompatibility discussed earlier: a gap between what they are and what they take themselves to be, or, at least, an inconsistency between one commitment and another. Habit in the sense discussed in §§409–10 is more fundamental than "bad" or "good" habits and the self-conception to which they belong. Habits of this fundamental kind are both temporally and logically prior to being able to distinguish what is bad and good "for me," just because they help to individuate subjects in the first place.

Secondly, Hegel the dialectician wants to point to habit as a kind of hinge between unfreedom and freedom.[56] It is *because* habits are automatic or "mechanical"—that they carry on regardless of, indifferent to, the sensations or desires of the moment—that they afford *freedom from* the relentless data of sensation and desire. Habits are thus a necessary condition for the rational pursuit of ends, the concern of the later "Psychology" section of the *Philosophy of Mind*. As elsewhere in Hegel, mechanism is not opposed to freedom, but a moment of it.[57] Hegel puts the relation of unfreedom and freedom here as follows:

> In habit man's mode of existence is natural, and for that reason he is unfree in it; but he is free in so far as the natural determinacy of sensation is by habit reduced to *his* mere being, he is no longer different from it, is indifferent to it, and so no longer interested, engaged, or dependent with respect to it [*er nicht mehr in Differenz und damit nicht mehr in Interesse, Beschäftigung und in Abhängigkeit gegen dieselbe ist*] ... The essential determination is the *liberation* [*Befreiung*] from sensations that man gains through habit, when he is affected by them. (§410R/131; 184)

While the German original does not mention indifference, the English translation makes explicit the presence here of the structure of indifference unpacked in Section 2. An indifference is a difference of no account. Via habit the subject no longer attends to the perceptible differences of sensations and desire; attendance to these differences would mean taking sensible particulars as an object for thought, as exerting some fascination or distraction. Self-identity for Hegel arises when differences of this kind are experienced as inessential, as *not* the essential self.[58] In other words, habitual indifference is a moment of freedom ("*liberation*") because in it the embodied agent is longer engaged by (immersed in) sensation but withdraws identification from it.[59] In so doing, in effecting this withdrawal from particularity, identity is *constituted* in its self-equality and abstract universality: I am the same I that is *not this* sensation as much as I am *not that* sensation.[60] The first chapter of the *Phenomenology* puts this relation between universality and indifference clearly. A "simple"—like stoicism's simple unity of self-consciousness discussed later in the *Phenomenology*—is "through negation; neither this nor that, it is both a *not-this* [Nichtdieses] and is just as indifferent [*gleichgültig*] to being this or that ... such a simple is what we call a *universal*" (Hegel 2018: §96/62; 1986a: 85).

Hegel goes on to isolate three forms of habit: (a) sensation, (b) desire, and (c) dexterity. In habit "(a) The *immediate* sensation is posited as negated, as indifferent [*als gleichgültig gesetzt*]" (2007: §410R/131; 1986b: 185). This is not to say that the contents of sensation disappear; they are rather preserved for the subject *in* their negation, as of no importance. Hegel's example reminds one of typical "stoic" virtues: indifference to "frost, heat, weariness of the limbs, etc., pleasant tastes, etc." These are "of course sensed by man . . . just reduced to an externality [*Äusserlichkeit*]" (§410R/131; 185). That is, they *can* be discriminated, there *is* a difference between these sensations, but discrimination is withdrawn. Habit also achieves "(b) Indifference towards *satisfaction* [*Gleichgültigkeit gegen die* Befriedigung]; desire, urges are dulled by the *habit* of their satisfaction. This is the rational [*vernünftige Befreiung*] liberation from them; monkish renunciation and forcible repression do not free us from them" (§410R/131; 185). Note in passing the Aristotelian position taken up by Hegel: indifference is not achieved through abstinence, but through regular satisfaction. Siding with Aristotle on this indicates what Hegel would take to be a critique of stoicism, but such a criticism—and its fairness to historical Stoicism—must be left aside here.

The point I want to make is that the content in both of these cases appears straightforwardly normative: one *ought* to be indifferent to sensations of frost, heat, weariness, pleasantness; one *ought* to regularly satisfy one's natural desires, rather than repress them. But the position of this discussion in the Encyclopedia system and awareness Hegel's developmental explanatory model should give us pause. Strictly speaking, the later Psychology section of the *Philosophy of Mind* is the place in which Hegel deals with fully fledged normative questions, the relationship between "urges and wilfulness" [*Die Triebe und die Willkür*] in terms of the "ought" [Das Sollen] (§473/210; 295). Indifference takes a more immediate, more primitive place in the *Philosophy of Mind*. As mentioned earlier, habit allows subjects, on Hegel's account, to install a gap or break between the agent and the objectivity—initially their own objectivity, their body. This is clear in Hegel's discussion of "(c) . . . habit as dexterity [*Gewohnheit als Geschicklichkeit*]." Here habit enables the body to be *used* as an instrument by the I. The example is, neatly, the playing of an instrument. "In dexterity bodiliness is then rendered pervious, made into an instrument, in such a way that as soon as the representation (e.g., a sequence of musical notes) is in me, the physical body too, unresistingly and fluently, has expressed it correctly [*richtig geäussert hat*]" (§410/132; 186). The separation between universal and particular, between the I and its body, enables the latter to be an object *used* by the former, an instrument of its ends.

The capacity for this separation clearly prefigures and is a moment of the distinction between the natural (what just happens to be the case for us, including bodily affects) and the normative (what ought to be, regardless). Importantly, however, indifference as habit is not a self-determined norm (a standard subjects set themselves) but a condition of there being such self-determination. Habit is a norm *given* to human beings as *natural* rational beings, something that *must* be mastered.[61] Habitual indifference is normative in the sense that indifference to sensations and desires can go more or less well; one can be better or worse at withdrawing from the arising and passing of sensations and natural desires. But just as the "norm" or "concept" of animal is typically noticed in its decline (the aging wolf is no longer capable of fully satisfying the conceptual form of "wolfness"),[62] rational agents only notice the norm of habitual indifference during malfunction, when they are incapable of maintaining a habit like standing up straight, or when hands now habituated to typing force one's attention back to the details of writing, making writing, not the thought being worked on through it, our conscious object. Nevertheless, the capacity, even shaky, to regard oneself as the same regardless of (indifferent to) the contingent sensations and desires one happens to feel indicates for Hegel the crossing of a certain threshold. For Hegel, as for stoicism, indifference to sensation and natural desire *is* the achievement *of* self-conscious agency, but the genitive for Hegel has a different sense and tense: such indifference is not something that agents ought to self-consciously *do*, but something *done* in the development of fully fledged self-conscious agency.

As such, and to sum up, for both Hegel and the stoics, to be free requires some distance from sensation and natural desire, and some position on what objects, practices, and experiences ought to be valued by rational agents, and which can be justifiably disregarded. Hegel's stoics offer one way to draw this boundary, Hegel himself another, but indifference is operative in both. Hegel integrates the stoic theme of indifference *and* his critique of it into his system by "downgrading" its status and significance. Per the *Phenomenology*, indifference is not an appropriate norm for rational agents insofar as of itself it provides indeterminate guidance; per the Anthropology, it is nonetheless a necessary condition of possibility for agents to take themselves as self-identical, and so ultimately a condition of agents taking themselves as normatively responsive and responsible. What emerges from the aforementioned reading of Hegel is that rational agents ought to be *morally* indifferent to the *habitual* indifference to sensation and natural desire; that they should pay indifference no further attention is just the point of habit in the first place.[63]

I am not in a position to determine the relation between the Hegelian line of thinking reconstructed here and the historical Stoics. But the aforementioned reading has perhaps further implications for Hegel interpretation, which I can here only suggest. Contrary to "belly-turned mind" readings of Hegel, not everything can or ought be included in the domain of reason.[64] Secondly, the explanatory power of the concept of immediacy in Hegel's thought itself requires further elaboration.

Notes

1 See, for example, Shklar (1976: 62–3), Ure (2016: 287–9), and Chiereghin (2009: 55–71). A recent exception is Redding (2017), discussed in note 3.

2 Hegel does demonstrate some engagement with the stoic tradition and its terminology in the *LHP*, including a brief account of stoic logic and physics, as well as ethics. His account in the *Phenomenology* (three dense and important pages) is a higher altitude conceptual take, written entirely in Hegel's own idiosyncratic vocabulary. While the critical position developed in the *Phenomenology* is substantially repeated in concluding the *LHP* account of stoic ethics (see Section 2), Hegel's more positive assessment (of stoic logic in particular) provides grounds for an alternative tracing of their relationship. See note 3.

3 Redding (2017) has recently presented a convincing account of stoicism's value for Hegel. Redding's emphasis on the *LHP* account of stoic logic leads to issues of logical form treated in the third book of Hegel's *Science of Logic* (the "Doctrine of the Concept"); my emphasis on the *Phenomenology* account leads to questions of agency in the "Anthropology" section of the *Philosophy of Mind*. The strategy of my chapter is similar to Redding's: Hegel does not mention the stoics by name in either the Anthropology or the Doctrine of the Concept, but Hegel's engagement with stoicism is nonetheless legible. However, it may be that our respective emphases on the *LHP* and the *Phenomenology* point up an inconsistency in Hegel's own thinking: in the *Phenomenology* account, stoicism is presented as conceptually indeterminate; Redding's line of argument from the *LHP* presents stoicism as *advancing* determinate accounts of representation. A consideration of this potential inconsistency cannot be undertaken here.

4 "An indifferent matter." Hegel uses the term in *LHP* (2006: 277). My focus on the term here continues the line of thinking begun in my PhD dissertation, which considers indifference in Kant's first *Critique* and Hegel's *Science of Logic* as an epistemic and ontological question (Flenady 2018).

5 In contemporary Hegel scholarship, Spirit (*Geist*) is by "naturalist," "non-metaphysical" or "Kantian" readers understood as human mindedness, not a

substantial transcendent entity (Pinkard 2012: 18). The appropriateness of the "human mindedness" formulation is contested by other deflationary readers, broadly on grounds that it draws Hegel too close to Kant. See Lumsden (2009) and Ikäheimo (2013).

6. Hegel's original German is for each quotation taken from the corresponding volume and passage in the Suhrkamp *Werke in zwanzig Bänden* (1986).

7. Hegel's Anthropology account of the role of habit in subject individuation is very clearly treated in Novakovic (2017: 32–9), and a full reconstruction is not provided here. The contribution of Section 3 of this chapter is rather to link the Anthropology to the discussion of stoicism and indifference in the *Phenomenology*.

8. The particular instance of Hegel's criticism of opinion treated in Section 3 is from the *Philosophy of Right* (1991: 17). See also the *Science of Logic* (2010a: 20) and the *Phenomenology* (2018: §110/67).

9. Hegel, tellingly, does not mention the stoic doctrine of preferred and dispreferred indifferents, discussed in Section 1.

10. Ultimately, for Hegel, fully *self-grounding* reasoning, that is, in Stephen Houlgate's language, the uniquely "presuppositionless" philosophy practiced in the *Science of Logic* (Houlgate 2006: 29–53). But see also Sedgwick's (2017) recent problematization of claims for this kind of foundationalism in Hegel.

11. Doyle and Torralba cite the numerous acknowledgments of this overlap (2016: 270).

12. "Kant uses the Stoic notion of virtue to develop his understanding of duty as the source of moral value. Having a good will is always in our power and, thus, is the only thing required by morality" (Doyle and Torralba 2016: 271).

13. Hegel similarly opposes Stoicism and Epicureanism via the rational/sensible opposition (2006: 264). How accurate (and useful) this is I leave aside.

14. In Doyle and Torralba's gloss, "since human beings are finite and have a sensible nature, Kant finds the Stoic understanding of happiness unsatisfactory. Even though happiness, according to Kant, should always be subordinated to duty, it is an inevitable component of our willing and, thus, of human fulfillment" (2016: 271).

15. See also Sellars (2006: 110–14).

16. Robert Pippin's work in and since *Hegel's Idealism* (1989) demonstrates the complexity of the Kant-Hegel relation. For a concise account, see Sedgwick (2000).

17. I rely here on Dicker (2004) and Sacks (2005).

18. These terms in Hegel have a Kantian pedigree. "Immediacy" and "mediation" are logical components of Kantian intuitional and conceptual representations, respectively (A320/B377). I consider this Kantian background in slightly more detail when treating immediacy and indifference in Section 2.

19. Hegel's term for this simultaneous negation and preservation is "Aufhebung," translated customarily as "sublation" (Hegel 2010a: 81–2).

20. In the *Phenomenology*, the tension is officially announced as that between (subjective) certainty and (objective) truth. For a reconstruction of these terms,

see Edmundts (2017). Stern (1990) is however able to economically track the movement of the *Phenomenology* as a whole in terms of universality and singularity.

21 This section of the *Phenomenology* mirrors the movement in the first *Critique* from the Transcendental Aesthetic to the presentation of transcendental unity of apperception (the "I think" that must accompany all objective representations) in the Transcendental Deduction section of the Transcendental Logic.

22 I am using "reason" here broadly to mean the characteristic activity of thinking, discursive beings. Though Kant and Hegel do use the term in this ordinary sense, they have their own technical understandings of the term. For Kant, "Reason" does not determine empirical objects through judgments (the work of the "Understanding") but rather is concerned with the grounds of and consistency between judgments (A298-309/B356–66). Hegel similarly contrasts "Understanding" (*Verstand*) with "Reason" (*Vernunft*). For Hegel, the former presupposes (among other things) a distinction between subject and object of consciousness, while the latter does not. As such, in Hegel's *Phenomenology* and *Philosophy of Mind*, "Reason" is a shape or moment Spirit in which thought comes to understand itself as actual in both consciousness and its object, and is thus a further development of self-conscious thought (2007: §438–9/164). Strictly speaking, stoicism for Hegel makes explicit the principle of self-consciousness, but does not adopt the standpoint of Reason proper. For an extended reflection on Hegelian Reason as the overcoming of the dualisms of the Understanding, see Ferrarin (2019).

23 Hegel emphasizes this stoic commitment in *LHP* (2006: 273).

24 The shift is legible on the page of contents: to the initially planned three-part structure ("A. Consciousness. B. Self-Consciousness. C. Reason") is added "C.(BB) Spirit. C.(CC) Religion. C(DD). Absolute Knowing," such that the Reason section has to be labeled "C.(AA) Reason."

25 As also noted by Shklar (1976: 62) and Chiereghin (2009: 58–9).

26 The conceptual reconstruction of the experience of consciousness meant implicit references to Aristotle, Locke, Hume, Kant, and so on, none of whom are mentioned by name. See Westphal (1998).

27 But see Buck-Morss (2009), which argues convincingly for Hegel's subterranean reference to the Haitian revolution.

28 This is interesting, given that a common assumption is that Roman stoicism "dilutes" the Greek original. This assumption is critically tested in Gretchen Reydams-Schils (2016). Hegel's account of the Roman world in the *Lectures on World History* is complex, and cannot be treated here. Hegel links stoicism to the "private" character of Roman individuality in *LHP* (2006: 278). For a related discussion, see the account of Roman law in the *Philosophy of Right* (Hegel 1991: 29–34).

29 It would be possible to suggest something similar regarding the contemporary fascination with "mindfulness."

30 There is a great deal of literature on master-slave. For a clear and concise reconstruction, see Stephen Houlgate (2013: 83–102). I provide a brief summary of Robert Brandom's influential interpretation in Section 3.

31 The conceptual resources for this distinction, between a "bad infinity" and "true infinity," have been developed at the end of the *Phenomenology*'s third chapter ("Force and the Understanding") and the start of the fourth on Self-Consciousness as such. They are *logically* treated in the "Existence" chapter of the first book of the *Science of Logic*. For a brief account vis-à-vis master and slave, see Chiereghin (2009: 56–7).

32 Hadot (1995) and Foucault (1986).

33 This point is suggested by Houlgate's reconstruction (2013: 102–7).

34 Salient here is Kant's "togetherness principle," in which immediate contents (paradigmatically for Kant, empirical intuitions, "appearances") are determinable as such only under certain conceptual ("mediating") conditions (A51/B75). On my understanding—indebted in particular to Pippin (2019)—Hegel's philosophy is a developmental rethinking of this Kantian principle: the dialectic discovers or unpacks the conceptual conditions of immediate contents. The critical question is how this discovery or unpacking is to be characterized. See Flenady (forthcoming).

35 See, for example, Hegel's explicit association of the historical progression from Parmenides to Heraclitus as coinciding with the development of the first moments of the *Science of Logic*, that is, "being" and "becoming" (2010a: 60).

36 The structure of "a difference that is no difference" is established in the previous chapter of the *Phenomenology*, "Force and the Understanding" (2018: §161/97–98), and then explicitly linked to the structure of self-consciousness (§163/99–100).

37 As Chiereghin points out, "thinking" (*Denken*) only emerges in the *Phenomenology* with the stoic expression of self-consciousness. Hegel wants to reserve the term for explicitly positing of "unity of the being and of the knowledge of it, of the subject and the object, and the multiplicity of the parts within a totality which is articulated in itself and by itself" (2009: 55). This is not the case in empirical knowledge claims, characterized by opposition between knowing subject and known object, which the *Phenomenology* begins by considering.

38 While I do not wish to claim that this is necessarily the position of historical Stoics, it bears some resemblance to Hadot's account: "There is thus a radical difference between what depends on us and can therefore be good or bad . . . and what depends not on us but on external causes and fate which is therefore indifferent. The will to do good is an unbreakable fortress which everyone can construct within themselves. It is there that we can find freedom, independence, invulnerability, and that eminently Stoic value, coherence with ourselves" (2002: 127).

39 Importantly, for the stoics the belief does not ground the action; rather, the belief is developed to strengthen the lived capacity to act in such a way. See J. Sellars (2006: 42–54) and Hadot (2002: 128).
40 This is the logical structure of being-for-itself elaborated in the third chapter of the first book of the *Logic* (Hegel 2010a: 126–51).
41 For an extended discussion of this idea of thought or concepts "actualising themselves," see Pippin (2008). The relationship between pure thought, actuality, and freedom in Hegel is a challenging one. Hegel suggests, in the Introduction to the *Science of Logic*, that thought thinking itself is a kind of freedom (2010a: 37). Leaving aside the influence of Aristotle's *noeseos noesis*, the difference of Hegel's *Logic* from Hegel's account of stoic thought would be that the labor of *Hegelian* thought produces of itself (actualizes itself in) contentful, individuated thought-determinations (Hegel's equivalent to the Kantian categories). In Redding's account (2017), however, stoicism in fact renders Aristotelian thought more determinate, by advancing logic as an analysis of representations (with linguistics arguably a stoic invention). Redding's position is convincing as a reading of the *LHP*, which spends time on stoic logic. It is harder to square with stoicism as a fixation on the immediacy of self-consciousness in the *Phenomenology*. But again, Hegel's possible inconsistency on this point will not be discussed here. See note 3.
42 As such, the stoic position represents a sliding back in the uncontrolled vanishing of singularity into universality (and vice versa) that Hegel diagnoses in the *Phenomenology*'s first chapter on Sense-Certainty.
43 His attempt here is to deflect criticisms of his political philosophy as an apology for the actually extant state, a reading that persists. See Pippin (2019: 87) and Allen Wood's editor's introduction to Hegel (1991).
44 Hegel broadly shares Kant's "rational animal" anthropology (Hegel 2010a: 96).
45 In the narrative of the Encyclopedia *Logic*'s "Preliminary Conception" (*Vorbegriff*), Ancient philosophy *is* the demand for rational justification, but in a one-sided way, requiring correction by modern empiricism, in turn requiring correction in Kant – and completion in Hegelian philosophy (Hegel 2010b).
46 Again, Hegel's *LHP* account acknowledges these lines of argument in stoic physics (Hegel 2006: 273).
47 On Houlgate's account, this structure opens onto the Kant-Hegel relationship as whole: in a philosophically very fruitful case of Brandom's "deontic scorekeeping," Hegel suggests that Kant, committed as he is to the critical examination of our presuppositions, fails to satisfy this commitment, and thus Kantian Idealism must be revised as Hegelian Idealism (Houlgate 2006: 16).
48 See for example *The Phenomenology* (Hegel 2018: §69/43).
49 Chomsky puts the point very nicely: "It's possible to respond to arguments. It is not possible to respond to opinions. If someone makes an assertion saying, 'Here's what

I believe,' that's fine—he can say what he believes but you can't respond to it. You can ask, what is the basis for your belief . . ." (2012: 66).

50 I leave aside the thorny question of whether this immediacy constitutes an "intellectual intuition." See the brief discussion of the problem in Flenady (forthcoming).

51 As Sellars puts it: "The real stoic must be able to translate [stoic] doctrines into concrete behavior. It is not enough to say one can be virtuous, and thus happy, regardless of circumstances; one must actually *be* happy regardless of circumstances, whether one is in danger, disgraced, sick or dying" (2006: 32).

52 See Hegel's ironic discussion of this kind of permissibility in the *Phenomenology* (2018: §9/8) and the *Logic* (2010a: 75–6). We under modern social conditions can of course become habitually indifferent to mere opinion, in the sense that we would not need to explicitly provide our reasons for that indifference at each exercise, but I cannot pursue that nuance here.

53 See note 21. That the *Encyclopedia* version does not include the *Phenomenology*'s explicitly *historical* half is further indication of the two-part structure of the work. See note 23.

54 This is not to say that bodiliness is simply left behind for the subject, that habit installs for Hegel a mind-body dualism. It is rather that habit enables or opens a moment of difference within mind-body identity that allows us to act in a different way within and with regard to our bodies. As always, Hegel is seeking to provide an account of the "identity of identity and difference" between terms ordinarily take to exclude one another, in this case, "mind" and "body." As Simon Lumsden has argued, "habit is more than just a transition point, dissolving itself and nature with it in the move from nature to spirit. The way Hegel conceives habit, particularly his characterization of it as second nature, challenges the dualism of nature and spirit" (2013: 121).

55 For an account of the status and function of habit in Hegel's *Philosophy of Right*, see Lumsden (2012).

56 This double-sided nature of habit is often approached in terms of "second nature," and Hegel uses this formula the *Philosophy of Mind* (2007: §410). This concept was influentially discussed in McDowell (1996). For a systematic account, see Novakovic (2017).

57 See the argument developed in the "Objectivity" section of the third book of the *Science of Logic* (2010a: 625–69).

58 Brandom, as we saw earlier, reads the master-slave dialectic as establishing the difference between essential and inessential identifications. My putting habit in these terms might make it sound as if the habit section can do the work of the master-slave dialectic. Again, however, habit is a necessary but insufficient condition for embodied rational agency, only a moment in a longer, more comprehensive Hegelian account. Our satisfaction of the given norm of habitual indifference would be susceptible to the kind of testing by others initially staged in

master and slave, though in a different, more primitive way (one would not revise reasons in response, but correct one's posture or clear one's throat).

59 Stekeler-Weithofer's reading of §410 makes the same point, though without explicit reference to indifference: "*Habitualisation* relieves the individual of having to check too many differences and make too many decisions in the course of 'running the programme' of an acquired generic action; it opens up the horizon for focusing on more general points" (2016: 46).

60 This fits neatly with the section immediately preceding habit, the "derangement" of "self-feeling" (2007: §§407–8/114–5). Habit liberates the subject from pathological identification with *one* particular affect, the "madness" that for Hegel accompanies self-feeling, by enabling a distinction between the subject and bodily feelings (Novokovic 2017: 32–3).

61 Lumsden's suggestion is that habit problematizes the natural/normative (or "space of causes" / "space of reasons") distinction foundational to Brandom's Sellarsian reading of Hegel. Such a reading for Lumsden "ignores or underplays is that there might in fact be a source of practices, norms, and values that one cannot understand as self-consciously authorized (owned) or natural and yet are part of human identity" (2013: 123). I am here suggesting that habit is a norm, but not a self-consciously authorized one. Rather it is given to us as embodied beings as a condition of self-conscious authorization. Habit would thus occupy the excluded middle as neither simply natural nor simply normative. I think the natural/normative distinction has *relative* explanatory purport, is necessary to make sense of certain kinds of self-conscious subjective action, though I agree that what it "ignores or underplays" must be acknowledged and elaborated. In other words, the distinction between nature and norm is not the whole story about action and value, but a moment of it.

62 The example is drawn from Pippin (2019: 154).

63 This is not to suggest agreement (or disagreement) with Novakovic's suggestion that Hegel is "suspicious" about reflection on habit in the *Philosophy of Right* sense, that is, habituation to social norms themselves (2017: 4). See note 54.

64 The claim is Adorno's (1973: 22–4). For Hegel, famously, the rational is the actual (1991: 20), but this does not mean everything is actual—some entities simply exist. "Existence" and "Actuality" are two distinct categories in the *Science of Logic*. See the discussion in Pippin (2019: 86–7).

Works Cited

Adorno, T. W. (1973), *Negative Dialectics*, trans. E. B. Ashton, London: Routledge.
Annas, J. (1996), "Aristotle and Kant on Morality and Practical Reasoning," in S. Engstrom and J. Whiting (eds.), *Aristotle, Kant, and the Stoics*, 237–60, Cambridge: Cambridge University.

Brandom, R. (2002), *Tales of the Mighty Dead: Historical Essays in the Metaphysics of Intentionality*, Cambridge, MA: Harvard University.

Brandom, R. (2011), "The Structure of Desire and Recognition: Self-Consciousness and Self-Constitution," in H. Ikaheimo and A. Laitinin (eds.), *Recognition and Social Ontology*, 25–51, Leiden: Brill.

Buck-Morss, S. (2009), *Hegel, Haiti and Universal History*, Pittsburgh: University of Pittsburgh.

Chiereghin, F. (2009), "Freedom and Thought: Stoicism, Skepticism, and Unhappy Consciousness," in K. Westphal (ed.), *The Blackwell Guide to Hegel's Phenomenology of Spirit*, 55–71, Oxford: Wiley-Blackwell.

Chomsky, N. (2012), *Occupy*, London: Penguin.

Dicker, G. (2004), *Kant's Theory of Knowledge: An Analytic Introduction*, Oxford: Oxford University.

Doyle, D. and Torralba, J. M. (2016), "Kant and Stoic Ethics," in J. Sellars (ed.), *The Routledge Handbook of the Stoic Tradition*, 270–85, Abingdon: Routledge.

Edmundts, D. (2017), "Consciousness and the Criterion of Knowledge in the *Phenomenology of Spirit*," in D. Moyar (ed.), *The Oxford Handbook of Hegel*, 61–80, Oxford: Oxford University Press.

Ferrarin, A. (2019), *Thinking and the I: Hegel and the Critique of Kant*, Evanston: Northwestern University.

Flenady, G. (2018), "Indifference and Determination: Kant's Concept/Intuition Distinction in Hegel's Doctrine of Being," PhD diss., Monash University, Melbourne, and The University of Warwick, Coventry.

Flenady, G. (forthcoming), "That Great Foe of Immediacy? Intellectual Intuition in Pippin's Reading of Hegel," *Australasian Philosophical Review*.

Forster, M. N. (1998), *Hegel's Idea of a Phenomenology of Spirit*, Chicago: Chicago University.

Foucault, M. (1986), *The Care of the Self: Volume 3 of The History of Sexuality*, trans. R. Hurley, New York: Pantheon.

Hadot, P. (1995), *Philosophy as a Way of Life: Spiritual Exercises from Socrates to Foucault*, ed. A. I. Davidson, trans. M. Chase, Oxford: Blackwell.

Hadot, P. (2002), *What Is Ancient Philosophy*, trans. M. Chase, Cambridge, MA: Belknap.

Hegel, G. W. F. (1986a), *Phänomenologie des Geistes*, eds. E. Moldenhauer and K. M. Michel, Frankfurt am Main: Suhrkamp Verlag.

Hegel, G. W. F. (1986b), *Enzyklopädie der philosophischen Wissenschaften III: Die Philosophie des Geistes*, eds. E. Moldenhauer and K. M. Michel, Frankfurt am Main: Suhrkamp Verlag.

Hegel, G. W. F. (1986c), *Vorlesungen über die Geschichte der Philosophie II*, eds. E. Moldenhauer and K. M. Michel, Frankfurt am Main: Suhrkamp Verlag.

Hegel, G. W. F. (1986d), *Grundlinien der Philosophie des Rechts*, eds. E. Moldenhauer and K. M. Michel, Frankfurt am Main: Suhrkamp Verlag.

Hegel, G. W. F. (1986e), *Wissenschaft der Logik I*, eds. E. Moldenhauer and K. M. Michel, Frankfurt am Main: Suhrkamp Verlag.

Hegel, G. W. F. (1991), *Elements in the Philosophy of Right*, trans. H. B. Nisbet, ed. A. W. Wood, Cambridge: Cambridge University.

Hegel, G. W. F. (2006), *Lectures in the History of Philosophy*, Vol. II, trans. R. F. Brown, Oxford: Clarendon Press.

Hegel, G. W. F. (2007), *Philosophy of Mind*, trans. W. Wallace and A. V. Miller, ed. M. Inwood, Oxford: Oxford University.

Hegel, G. W. F. (2010a), *The Science of Logic*, trans. G. di Giovanni, Cambridge: Cambridge University.

Hegel, G. W. F. (2010b), *The Encyclopedia of the Philosophical Science in Basic Outline: Part I, Science of Logic*, trans. and ed. K. Brinkmann and D. O. Dahlstrom, Cambridge: Cambridge University.

Hegel, G. W. F. (2018), *The Phenomenology of Spirit*, trans. T. Pinkard, Cambridge: Cambridge University.

Houlgate, S. (2006), *The Opening of Hegel's Logic*, Evanston: Northwestern University.

Houlgate, S. (2013), *Hegel's Phenomenology of Spirit: A Reader's Guide*, London: Bloomsbury.

Ikäheimo, Heikki (2013), "Hegel's Concept of Recognition—What Is It?", in C. Krijnen (ed.), *Recognition—German Idealism as an Ongoing Challenge*, 11–38, Leiden: Brill.

Kojeve, A. (1980), *An Introduction to the Reading of Hegel*, Ithaca: Cornell University.

Lumsden, S. (2009), "Philosophy and the Logic of Modernity: Hegel's Dissatisfied Spirit," *The Review of Metaphysics*, 63 (1): 55–89.

Lumsden, S. (2012), "Habit, Sittlichkeit, and Second Nature," *Critical Horizons*, 13 (2): 220–43.

Lumsden, S. (2013), "Between Nature and Spirit: Hegel's Account of Second Nature," in D. S. Stern (ed.), *Essays on Hegel's Philosophy of Subjective Spirit*, New York: SUNY.

McDowell, J (1996), *Mind and World*, Cambridge, MA: Harvard University.

Novakovic, A. (2017), *Hegel on Second Nature in Ethical Life*, Cambridge: Cambridge University.

Pinkard, T. (2012), *Hegel's Naturalism*, Oxford: Oxford University.

Pippin, R. (1989), *Hegel's Idealism: The Satisfactions of Self-Consciousness*. Cambridge: Cambridge University.

Pippin, R. (2008), *Hegel's Practical Philosophy: Rational Agency as Ethical Life*, Cambridge: Cambridge University.

Pippin, R. (2019), *Hegel's Realm of Shadows: Logic as Metaphysics in Hegel's Science of Logic*, Chicago: University of Chicago.

Redding, P. (2017), "Aristotelian Master and Stoic Slave: From Epistemic Assimilation to Cognitive Transformation," in R. Zuckert and J. Kreines (eds.), *Hegel on Philosophy in History*, 71–87, Cambridge: Cambridge University.

Reydams-Schils, G. (2016), "Stoicism in Rome," in J. Sellars (ed.), *The Routledge Handbook of the Stoic Tradition*, 17–28, Abingdon: Routledge.

Sacks, M. (2005), "The Nature of Transcendental Arguments," *International Journal of Philosophical Studies*, 13 (4): 439–60.

Schneewind, J. B. (1996), "Kant and Stoic Ethics," in S. Engstrom and J. Whiting (eds.), *Aristotle, Kant, and the Stoics*, 285–302, Cambridge: Cambridge University.

Sedgwick, S. (2000), "Metaphysics and Morality in Kant and Hegel," in S. Sedgwick (ed.), *The Reception of Kant's Critical Philosophy*, 306–24, Cambridge: Cambridge University.

Sedgwick, S. (2017), "Remarks on History, Contingency, and Necessity in Hegel's *Science of Logic*," in R. Zuckert and J. Kreines (eds.), *Hegel on Philosophy in History*, 33–49, Cambridge: Cambridge University.

Sellars, J. (2006), *Stoicism*, Chesham: Acumen.

Sellars, W. (1997), *Empiricism and the Philosophy of Mind*, Cambridge, MA: Harvard University.

Shklar, J. (1976), *Freedom and Independence*, Cambridge: Cambridge University.

Stekeler-Weithofer, P. (2016), "From Satisfaction of Desire to Fulfilment of Intentions: Hegel on the Bodily Basis of Higher Intelligence," in S. Hermann-Sinai and L. Ziglioli, *Hegel's Philosophical Psychology*, 37–54, New York: Routledge.

Stern, R. (1990), *Hegel, Kant, and the Structure of the Object*, London: Routledge.

Ure, M. (2016), "Stoicism in Nineteenth-Century German Philosophy," in J. Sellars (ed.), *The Routledge Handbook of the Stoic Tradition*, 287–302, Abingdon: Routledge.

Westphal, K. (1998), "Hegel and Hume on Perception and Concept-Empiricism," *Journal of the History of Philosophy*, 36 (1): 99–123.

Stoicism and the Development of the Human Sciences

Wilhelm Dilthey's Reception of Stoicism

Angus Nicholls[1]

1. Introduction: Dilthey and Nineteenth-Century Debates on the Natural and Human Sciences

Wilhelm Dilthey (1833–1911) is arguably the most important European theorist of the human sciences (*Geisteswissenschaften*) of the second half of the nineteenth century (see Gadamer 1989 [orig. 1960]: 6–7; Habermas 1972 [orig. 1968]: 140–86; Mazlish 2007: 91–4; Smith 2007: 150–63; Kindt 2000: 53).[2] Precisely because Dilthey's knowledge and treatment of the tradition of Western letters—incorporating at once philosophy, descriptive psychology, literary studies, historiography, and theology—is so sweeping, he is not normally regarded as a specialist in any of these individual fields, but rather as a generalist whose ideas have methodological implications for all of them. Indeed, as a leading specialist on Dilthey has noted, there is considerable "difficulty in relating the many disciplines to which Dilthey contributed and estimating their theoretical implications" (Makkreel 1975: 5). As a generalist of vast historical range, it is not surprising that Dilthey also has important things to say about the Stoics. But in keeping with his status as a generalist, Dilthey's statements on the Stoics would be unlikely to contribute to any specialist understanding of Stoic doctrines; they are, however, extremely instructive concerning how elements of the popular academic understanding of Stoicism were important for the self-conception of the modern human sciences during a crucial period of their development: that of the late nineteenth century. Most crucially, my claim here will be that Dilthey's reception of Stoicism helped him eventually to conclude that scientific knowledge of human cultural artifacts is of an entirely different order to knowledge generated by the natural sciences.

Having assumed the Chair of Philosophy at Berlin University in July 1882—a post previously held by Johann Gottlieb Fichte, Georg Wilhelm Friedrich Hegel, and Hermann Lotze—Dilthey was uniquely well placed to understand the challenges facing the human sciences during the final two decades of the nineteenth century.[3] An instructive example lies in the figure of Lotze (1817–81), Dilthey's immediate predecessor in Berlin, whose career has been characterized as having involved the managed decline of Hegelian idealism and the related attempt to "integrate philosophical speculation and modern natural science" (Schnädelbach 1984: 169). With the speculative thought-systems of Fichte, Hegel, and Schelling experiencing a marked collapse in their credibility following the so-called crash or cracking up (*großer Krach*) of German idealism as a philosophical project (see Vaihinger 1876: 1), the human sciences in general, and philosophy in particular, were faced with the task of rebuilding their epistemological foundations in such a way that they could compete with the rising success of the natural sciences. In his study of Dilthey's philosophical development, Michael Ermarth notes that during the 1870s and 1880s

> real knowledge was conceived to be rigorously scientific knowledge. Previous claims for speculative knowledge, intuitive knowledge, poetic knowledge, and knowledge of faith were seen as riddled with contradictions. Some, like Dilthey [...] looked forward to the rebirth of philosophy through cooperation with the positive sciences and acceptance of their results. (1978: 64)

This perceived need of the human sciences to collaborate with and adopt the methods of the natural sciences was further intensified by the appearance of prominent "men of science" such as Thomas Henry Huxley in Great Britain and Hermann von Helmholtz in Germany. Both Huxley and Helmholtz were concerned with demonstrating the methodological superiority of the natural sciences in comparison with the human sciences, as part of a broader attempt to call into question the hegemony of the classical humanist model of education among the European elite (see, for example, Huxley 1882; for context: White 2003).

Already in the 1860s, Helmholtz (1821–94), who would later be Dilthey's colleague in Berlin, was drawing a sharp methodological dividing line between the methodologies of the natural and human sciences, a highly political demarcation designed for the consumption of generalist academic audiences. Speaking in 1862, in a prominent public lecture delivered at the University of Heidelberg entitled "Über das Verhältniss der Naturwissenschaften zur Gesammtheit der Wissenschaft" (On the Relation of the Natural Sciences to the Totality of Science), Helmholtz makes the following general observation:

> If we [. . .] conduct an overview of the different sciences according to the method by which they must arrive at their results, we are confronted with a thorough-going difference between the natural and human sciences [*Natur- und Geisteswissenschaften*]. The natural sciences are for the most part in a position to derive sharply-defined general rules and principles from their inductions; the human sciences, on the other hand, are predominantly concerned with making judgements arrived at by a psychological sense of tact [*Urtheilen nach psychologischem Tactgefühl*]. [. . .] The philological sciences, insofar as they are concerned with the interpretation and emendation of texts passed down to us, with literature and the history of art, must attempt to intuit [*herauszufühlen*, literally: feel out] the meaning that the author intended [. . .] to this end, they must know how to proceed according to a correct intuition [*Anschauung*] not only of the individuality of the author but also of the genius of the language in which he wrote. These are all cases of artistic and not entirely logical induction. [. . .] The opposite extreme to the philological and historical sciences is presented by the intellectual work of the natural sciences [. . .] The essential difference of these [natural] sciences is based, it seems to me, upon the fact that in them it is comparatively easy to unite individual cases of observation and experience with general laws that have unconditional validity and extreme comprehensiveness, while it is precisely this activity which, in the former [human] sciences, presents us with insurmountable difficulties [. . .] Here [i.e., in the natural sciences] we see the conscious and logical activity of our intellect in its purest and most developed form. (Helmholtz 1896 [orig. 1862]: 172, 175–6)

When Helmholtz delivered this public lecture, Dilthey was a twenty-nine-year-old researcher based in Berlin, studying for his doctoral thesis in the field of philosophy. It is not an overestimation to suggest that the central issue alluded to by Helmholtz in his lecture—that of the relations between the natural and human sciences—would also come to be the central philosophical problem of Dilthey's entire academic career.

Dilthey's well-known contributions to hermeneutics can be seen as having developed out of the central question which looms large over all of his work, especially in its early phases, namely: How can the human sciences develop a method which, in its exactness and rigor, could compete with the precise results of the natural sciences? The importance for Dilthey of the issues raised by Helmholtz has been pointed out in recent scholarship on the relation between these two giants of nineteenth-century German academia (see Mezzanzanica 2011); indeed, Dilthey once referred to Helmholtz as the German scientist whose "comprehensive genius" seemed to represent "the entire scientific spirit" of the nineteenth century (Dilthey 1936: 263).

What, then, is the scientific spirit of Helmholtz's lecture? The underlying historical context, outlined at some length by Helmholtz, is the increasing specialization of knowledge in all academic disciplines. Johann Wolfgang Goethe (1749–1832)—who had died only some thirty years prior to Helmholtz's lecture, and who had made contributions to both the humanities and the natural sciences— embodied the scientific spirit of the late eighteenth century, in which educated private citizens could become Renaissance men by dabbling in any number of diverse areas of study, in Goethe's case: optics, botany, geology, and comparative anatomy, in addition to his literary productions (see Richards 2002: 325–502). But with the increasing professionalization, institutionalization, and specialization of the scientific disciplines in the middle of the nineteenth century, the very concept of *Wissenschaft*—a concept which had formerly been seen as uniting diverse fields of knowledge, including the human sciences—was itself undergoing fragmentation and transformation (for an overview, see Diemer 1968).

The origins of this transformation go back to the late eighteenth century and to Kant's third *Critique*, the *Kritik der Urteilskraft* (Critique of the Power of Judgement, 1790). In that text, Kant aimed to draw limits around what kind of knowledge claims could be regarded as applying to external nature, or what he called nature "in itself" or *an sich*. A particular issue was the role played by teleology, or what Kant referred to as "reflective judgments," in science (see Kant 2000 [orig. 1790]: §§ 61, 66, 75). These types of judgments are, thought Kant, commonly used in biology, since biology requires us to think of organisms as organized beings which suggest a design or plan at work in nature. Kant held that although teleological ideas could find a legitimate regulative use in science, according to which the scientist might proceed *as if* nature were organized according to a grand design, such a teleology could at the same time not be proven to exist in the mechanistic terms of modern science as laid down by Newton and others.

Here Kant revealed a certain similarity between teleological judgments in science and in aesthetics. Just as the flower might suggest to the botanist a design in nature which may guide their research, so too does the beautiful artwork create the impression that the artist has some either conscious or unconscious access to a design which the artwork brings to expression. For the romantic poets and philosophers who preceded the generation of Helmholtz and Dilthey, Kant's third *Critique* had intimated that science and art could be united as one grand project under the guise of a very general conception of *Wissenschaft*; an idea expressed most notably in Fichte's *Wissenschaftslehre* (Science of Knowledge) of 1800. Yet these later idealist thinkers went much further than Kant, by insisting that teleological ideas are not just regulative constructs designed to assist science. Rather, post-Kantian thinkers such as Schelling and Hegel held that there is an inherent teleology either in nature (early Schelling) or in history (Hegel); by this they meant not only nature and history as they *appear* to humans but also nature and history "in themselves" (see Richards 2002: 11, 64–71, 137–9; Hühn, Meiser-Oeser and Pulte 2004: 915–17).

First and foremost, then, Helmholtz's lecture is a complete rejection of this type of teleology in the sciences, and also a complete rejection of post-Kantian German idealism in general. At the same time, however, Helmholtz was also interested in *rehabilitating* Kant—but not his idealist successors in Schelling and Hegel—by providing a physiological grounding for Kant's theorization of subjectivity, a program which came to be known as "physiological neo-Kantianism" (see Helmholtz 1855; for context Beiser 2014: 196–201, this quote: 198). Within this context, Helmholtz's public lecture of 1862 is a professional statement designed to draw a clear line between the natural and human sciences, and to underline the superiority of the natural sciences in terms of their methodological exactness. Helmholtz demanded of the natural sciences a highly professionalized form of science, which relied purely on empirical inductions and experimental results to verify its hypotheses, and which ruthlessly abandoned any sense of speculative teleology.

This was a demand that the young Dilthey by and large shared, and which he also sought to extend to the *Geisteswissenschaften* or human sciences. As I will demonstrate, during the 1870s, Dilthey endeavored to outline a psychophysical form of literary criticism that recast textual interpretation within the frame of a descriptive psychology heavily informed by the methods of the natural sciences (see Kindt 2000: 55–6). But by the early 1880s, Dilthey began to realize that an objectively descriptive *Geisteswissenschaft*—a *Geisteswissenschaft* free of values— could not succeed, and this led him to differentiate the human sciences from the natural sciences. The result of this differentiation was Dilthey's philosophical magnum opus (or perhaps better: magnum opus manqué): a volume entitled *Einleitung in die Geisteswissenschaften* (Introduction to the Human Sciences), published in 1883.

The *Introduction to the Human Sciences* was a fragmentary project that preoccupied Dilthey for his entire career, and which he expanded upon continually up until his death in 1911, with his late and mature hermeneutics being found in the 1910 volume *Der Aufbau der geschichtlichen Welt in den Geisteswissenschaften* (The Formation of the Historical World in the Human Sciences).[4] In *Introduction to the Human Sciences* (1883), Stoicism is only briefly mentioned in relation to the theory of the state and to natural law, but does not constitute a major component of Dilthey's argumentation (Dilthey 1914a [orig. 1883]: 244, 342).[5] But in volume two of Dilthey's *Gesammelte Schriften*, in texts written during the 1890s and in the first decade of the twentieth century, one can find an extended and extremely important contribution to the late nineteenth-century German reception of Stoicism. This is because Dilthey sees Stoicism as having contributed to the origins of the modern human sciences.

An excellent article by Larry Frohman has already treated Dilthey's reception of Stoicism at some length, and much of the initial analysis offered here is based on Frohman's solid insights (see Frohman 1995). According to Frohman, "Dilthey argued that the recovery of Stoic philosophy in the later sixteenth and early seventeenth centuries played a central—in fact, nearly constitutive—role in the formation of the modern individual and, more generally, the transition to modernity" (1995: 263). Frohman also demonstrates that an assessment of Dilthey's reception of the Stoics involves not only an internal examination of his writings on them but also a consideration of how later authorities—chief among them Hans Blumenberg and Günter Abel—criticized this reception (1995: 264-5). Of special importance for the present chapter is Frohman's claim that Dilthey's reception of Stoic ideas concerning commonly held perceptions, ideas, and values—in other words, the notion of the *sensus communis*, particularly as propagated by Seneca—was crucial to his developing theorization of how understanding (*Verstehen*) in the human sciences differs from causal explanation (*Erklären*) in the natural sciences (Frohman 1995: 277-8).[6] It is this last insight in particular that this chapter seeks to explore at greater length than was possible in Frohman's fine contribution.

2. Dilthey's Reception of Stoicism and Its Critics

The second volume of Dilthey's *Schriften* is entitled *Weltanschauung und Analyse des Menschen seit Renaissance und Reformation* (Worldview and Analysis of Man since the Renaissance and the Reformation), and includes a series of long essays written between 1891 and 1904, three of which are my focus here, and none of which have been translated into English: "Das natürliche System der

Geisteswissenschaften im 17. Jahrhundert" (The Natural System of the Human Sciences in the Seventeenth Century, 1892–3); "Die Autonomie des Denkens, der konstruktive Rationalismus und der pantheistische Monismus nach ihrem Zusammenhang im 17. Jahrhundert" (The Autonomy of Thought, Constructive Rationalism and Pantheistic Monism in Their Seventeenth-Century Context, 1894); and "Die Funktion der Anthropologie in der Kultur des 16. und 17. Jahrhunderts" (The Function of Anthropology in the Culture of the Sixteenth and Seventeenth Centuries, 1904).[7] In all three of these essays, Dilthey refers directly to both individual Stoic thinkers of antiquity and early modern Neo-Stoic mediators of what he calls "the Roman worldview." Most prominent among this latter group is Justus Lipsius (1547–1606), who offered "the first systematic revival of Roman Stoicism since antiquity" (Morford 1991: xiii). Lipsius's *De Constantia* (see Lipisus 1584) is often regarded as the foundational text of Neo-Stoicism, and he also produced two handbooks on Seneca (Lipsius 1604a and 1604b), as well as an extended edition of Seneca's writings (see Lipsius 1605; for context: Sellars 2006: 6; Lagrée 2006).

The following quotation from the final of these three essays by Dilthey is characteristic of his sweeping and at times vague historical approach to the question of Stoicism's influence upon modernity. Referring to the sixteenth and seventeenth centuries, he writes:

> The relation of this time to the Stoics, and to the Roman worldview conditioned by them, rests principally on the fact that here [i.e., in Stoicism] a context was given in which, out of the teleological character of the world's interconnectedness as mediated by teachings concerning the human being, an essence of universal and unchangeable rules was derived, to which every organisation of society in law, the state, and religious belief is bound. This was what the time needed: the founding of new regulations, independent from the pre-existing authorities; the autonomy of the mind in the regulation of its practical activities in civic life; unassailable principles for the regulation of society according to its new requirements. These principles for the rational creation of law, the state, and religion as the forms of spiritual life could, however, only be founded upon the recognised law-like interconnectedness of the spirit [*Geist*]. They therefore required the development [*Fortbildung*] of an anthropology. (1914b [orig. 1904]: 441)

In short, and as Frohman already notes, Dilthey regards the Stoics as having provided European thought of the sixteenth and seventeenth centuries with an anthropology or "theory of the human being," as well with a "theory of living" (1914b [orig. 1904]: 416).[8] This bold historical argument can be unpacked into three distinct but related propositions elaborated across the three essays named earlier.

First: Dilthey maintains that the Stoic view of the world as a grand organism ordered by the indwelling *logos* offered a key point of departure for early modern science and philosophy, since it allowed for religious dogma to be questioned, it emphasized the importance of empirical observation and the autonomy of reason, and it enabled nature to be regarded as a rational system of laws. Dilthey refers to this worldview as both "constructive rationalism" and "pantheistic monism," and sees the Italian philosopher Bernadino Telesio (1509–88) as being one of the main sixteenth-century mediators of this tradition, underlining Telesio's influence on Spinoza, Hobbes, and Descartes (1914b [orig. 1894]: 283–96).

Second: Dilthey argues that the Stoic concept of *Selbsterhaltung* or self-preservation, according to which the thoughts of wise individuals are seen as being aligned with the grander scheme of the *logos*, exerted an important influence upon early modern ethics, especially the ethics of Spinoza. "The entire underlying ethics of Spinoza," writes Dilthey, "is founded on the Stoa, indeed to such an extent and with such correspondences in matters of detail, that the assumption that he used one of the most widely read Dutch humanistic writings dealing with the antique tradition, [. . .] Lipsius's *De Constantia*, seems unavoidable" (1914b [orig. 1894]: 285). Here an important feature of Dilthey's account of the transition to scientific modernity is his claim that the Stoic teleological worldview concerning the *logos* later reappears in a mechanistic guise in Spinoza:

> In general, the Stoa and Spinoza correspond with one another in the deepest way by conceiving of the totality of the world [*Weltall*] and also of the human being as a system of force [*Kraftsystem*]; herein lay that which essentially bound Stoic thought to the thinking of this epoch [i.e., the seventeenth century], the only difference being that the teleological context of the Stoa had transformed itself, since Galileo, into a mechanistic context. (1914b [orig. 1894]: 287)

The chief mediators of ancient Stoicism for these purposes were, according to Dilthey, Telesio and Lipsius (1914b [orig. 1894]: 285–9).

Third: Dilthey maintains that the Stoic idea of the *sensus communis*, a common or universal ground of natural truths and values, played a key role in overcoming the sectarian religious controversies of the sixteenth century, while also paving the way for modern hermeneutics. Dilthey sees the Swiss theologian Huldrych Zwingli (1484–1531) as having been the main mediator of these Stoic ideas, which he attributes chiefly to Seneca (1914b [orig. 1892–3]: 153–61), but important passages on them, which are likely to have been read by Dilthey, also appear in Lipsius (1604a), in particular §2.16 (for context, see Lagrée 2006: 162–3). I will return to the importance of the *sensus communis* for Dilthey shortly.

For now, and as Frohman has noted, it is important to observe that the first two of Dilthey's propositions—that concerning the influence of Stoic *logos*-philosophy on the early modern scientific worldview, and that concerning the importance of Stoic self-preservation for early modern ethics—have been extensively discussed and critiqued in the secondary literature, most notably by Hans Blumenberg and Günter Abel. The interventions of Blumenberg and Abel require close attention here, because by calling Dilthey's first two propositions into doubt, they throw into relief what may be of lasting historical significance in Dilthey's reception of Stoicism.

Blumenberg's critique of Dilthey emerges from his major contribution to intellectual history of 1966, *Legitimität der Neuzeit* (The Legitimacy of the Modern Age), and from a closely related long essay published in 1969 entitled *Selbsterhaltung und Beharrung. Zur Konstitution der neuzeitlichen Rationalität* (Self-Preservation and Persistence: On the Constitution of Early Modern Rationality). In *The Legitimacy of the Modern Age*, Blumenberg argues that intellectual history is not necessarily constituted by the substance of thought-traditions being handed down from one epoch to another, but rather by what he calls the "reoccupation" (*Umbesetzung*) of existing philosophical questions with entirely new answers (Blumenberg 1983 [orig. 1966]: 65). These reoccupied philosophical questions may determine the *function* of philosophical ideas in subsequent epochs, but not necessarily their *content*. Here Blumenberg's position stands in polemical opposition to that of Karl Löwith in *Meaning and History* (1949), in which Löwith argues that modern ideas about progress are never wholly enlightened or rational, because they retain within their structure the Judeo-Christian idea of salvation, in particular the "secularization of its eschatological pattern" (1949: 2).[9]

According to Blumenberg, early modern philosophy inherited from the Middle Ages the philosophical problem of contingency described by nominalism: a world which could at any moment be transformed by the incalculable agency of an omnipotent God. In Blumenberg's account,

> only after nominalism had executed a sufficiently radical destruction of the humanly relevant and dependable cosmos could the mechanistic philosophy of nature be adopted as the tool of self-assertion. (1983 [orig. 1966]: 151)

The key term here is "self-assertion" (*Selbstbehauptung*), which bears an obvious relation to the word that appears in the title of Blumenberg's essay on Dilthey: "self-preservation" (*Selbsterhaltung*). The semantic difference is important here, since—according to Blumenberg, who is in turn affirmatively quoting Dieter Henrich on this subject—self-assertion involves the upending of tradition by inserting something entirely new into the world: namely, the subjective agency of human rationality as expressed in the modern scientific method (Blumenberg 1969: 3; Henrich 1960: 91). Stoic self-preservation, by contrast, intimates the protection and continuation of something already in existence: the relation between human beings and the immanent *logos* of the cosmos.

In Blumenberg's view, the philosophical question faced by early modern thinkers—How to preserve oneself from the arbitrary dictates of an incalculable and omnipotent God?—could not have been resolved by way of recourse to the content of Stoic *logos*-philosophy, since that *logos*-philosophy had no resources for addressing the radical contingency expressed by nominalism; rather, it reposed in the belief that divine volition, natural events, and human thinking shared the same purposeful rationality (1969: 13, 21). As Blumenberg writes:

> There are concepts which have the same meaning for an historical formation that guiding fossils [*Leitfossilien*] do for a geological formation. The concept of self-preservation [*Selbsterhaltung*] has such a significance for the early modern period. Wilhelm Dilthey has already [...] emphatically pointed to its central role in the natural system of the seventeenth century, but the thesis concerning its origin in the reception of Stoicism obstructed his view of its possible authenticity. (1969: 3)

In Blumenberg's account, and here again he follows Henrich, early modern self-preservation is radically anti-teleological (1969: 3). For this reason, Blumenberg proposes that although the formal question of *Selbsterhaltung* may well have been inherited from the Stoics, the answer to it provided by early modern philosophy was entirely different to that found in Stoicism. The main characteristic of the early modern period is, according to Blumenberg, self-preservation through human-constructed rationality—in other words, self-preservation through self-assertion—and not self-preservation through the apprehension of the already-existing natural order of the immanent *logos* as in Stoicism. For these reasons, Blumenberg accuses Dilthey of having misunderstood the truly modern character of Spinoza's ethics, which he argues was entirely mechanistic and therefore not Stoic in its essential features (1969: 40–1). This accusation is made notwithstanding the fact that, as noted earlier, Dilthey himself registers that the early modern context in which Stoic ideas were received was a mechanistic one (1914b [orig. 1894]: 287).

Günter Abel, in his 1978 book *Stoizismus und Frühe Neuzeit* (Stoicism and the Early Modern Period), initially agrees with Blumenberg's claim that far from being teleological in the manner of the Stoics as suggested by Dilthey, early modern natural philosophy is a response precisely to the "loss of an unquestionable and teleological basis in nature," and the replacement of this basis with a "causal-mechanistic" worldview (1978: 8, 30). But Abel also criticizes Blumenberg for outlining an overly abstract epochal transition to an early modern period from which all remnants of Stoic thinking have purportedly been excised by the need to respond to the radical contingency of late medieval nominalism (1978: 23). Abel points out that even with respect to natural philosophy, Stoic and Neo-Stoic teleological thought patterns were never entirely dispensed with; rather, they were incrementally *adapted* to a predominantly mechanistic worldview, as is attested by their continued regulative use, even as late as Kant's third *Critique* of 1790 (1978: 33–4). Similarly, Abel alleges that Blumenberg's predominant focus on early modern natural science causes him to overlook the ways in which elements of Stoicism persist in the ethics and political thought of the period (1978: 20–1). Hobbes's theory of the state as a form of rational self-preservation is, for example, presented by Abel as an artificial and second-order version of Stoic *logos*-philosophy (1978: 36).

As Frohman argues (1995: 265), Abel's more nuanced view of how Stoicism may have influenced early modern thought actually places him closer to the position of Dilthey than to that of Blumenberg. According to Frohman,

> Dilthey argues that [. . .] natural law theorists such as Johannes Althusius and Hugo Grotius all turned to the Stoic idea of natural law to help them articulate this increasingly urgent belief in moral and political precepts which were so clear and evident to natural reason that they could be shared by all men. (1995: 266)

Crucially, in Frohman's view, Dilthey did not believe that these "clear and evident" ideas were grounded in the "teleological harmony of man and nature in antique Stoicism"; rather, their basis was much more contingent, and lay in "public opinion, the *sensus communis*, and the desire to find a basis for religious tolerance and understanding" (1995: 266). Further to this, the contingency of such ideas also pointed to the importance of understanding their *historicity*, one of the primary tasks of Dilthey's new method for the human sciences: philosophical hermeneutics. Dilthey famously saw philosophical hermeneutics as supplementing a deficiency in Kant's three *Critiques*, namely Kant's tendency to see time only as an ideal intuition, rather than as the medium in which lived historical experience takes place (see Makkreel and Rodi 2002: 9). Dilthey's self-proclaimed "Kritik der historischen Vernunft" (Critique of Historical Reason) would, he argued, remedy this problem in Kant by pointing to "temporality" as the "first categorical determination" of lived experience, the "one that is fundamental for all others" (2002 [orig. 1910]: 213–15).

3. Dilthey and the Stoic *Sensus Communis*

Before proceeding to Dilthey's discussion of the Stoic *sensus communis* and its early modern reception, it is necessary briefly to return to Hermann von Helmholtz's sharp differentiation between the natural and human sciences. By associating the natural sciences with what he called "the logical activity of the human intellect in its purest and most developed form," Helmholtz set a certain standard of rigor for all academic disciplines in modern German research universities (1896 [orig. 1862]: 176). As I have shown, Dilthey took this challenge seriously, and during the 1870s, he tried to incorporate it into his own developing conception of philology as a form of science.

The clearest example of this can be found in an essay by Dilthey published in 1878 in the *Zeitschrift für Völkerpsychologie und Sprachwissenschaft* (*Journal of Folk-Psychology and Language Science*). This journal, edited by Moritz Lazarus and Heyman Steinthal, was at the vanguard of a new approach to the human sciences that was informed by the natural scientific psychology of Johann Friedrich Herbart and Gustav Theodor Fechner (for context, see Trautmann-Waller 2004). In this essay, entitled "Über die Einbildungskraft der Dichter" (On the Imagination of the Poets, see Dilthey 1878), Dilthey attempts to outline a philological method of interpretation based on the emerging sciences of psychology and physiology. His background reading for this project included the pioneers of modern academic physiology in Germany: Helmholtz and Johannes Müller. Another key source was Fechner, the founder of psychophysics, which held that all psychological states arise from scientifically measurable physiological states (Fechner 1860; for context: Heidelberger 2004 [orig. 1993]). Dilthey's self-prescribed program of research into physiology and psychology has been summarized by Michael Ermarth under the heading of "The Naturalization of the Spirit": namely, the attempt to understand the mind—in German: *Geist*, a word heavily laden with the baggage of idealism—in natural scientific terms (1978: 62–79).

Arguing for an "inductive" philology securely based in what he calls "psychological facts," Dilthey's essay proposes that the intensity of a poet's "visual sense" (*Gesichtssinn*) stands in direct relation to the power of their poetic productions (Dilthey 1878: 43, 47, 57–8; for context, see Nicholls 2011). In this way, Dilthey elaborates a psychological theory of poetic causation, according to which the "apperception" of "organic stimuli" precedes their later "recollection" and "reproduction" in literary compositions (Dilthey 1878: 58, 61–2). The way to secure an objective and scientific interpretation of a particular work is apparently to trace the work back to the so-called organic stimuli which produced it, which effectively means carrying out exhaustive research into the author's lived experience. This heavily biographical and positivist approach to literature was influential during the early phases of professional academic criticism in Germany, and was most influentially adopted by Dilthey's friend and colleague Wilhelm Scherer (see Kindt 2000; Müller 2000; Kaltenbrunner 2010).

At stake in Dilthey's essay is the attempt to demystify and naturalize a concept which had been central to Kant's aesthetics in the third *Critique*: that of genius, which, in Kant's view (see §§46–9), requires us to assume a "subjective purposiveness" or teleology that cannot be cashed out conceptually or proven empirically (Kant 2000 [orig. 1790]: 195). Dilthey's case study for the demystification of genius was—unsurprisingly—Goethe, whom he regards as "*the* case of the first order," because he demonstrates the "power" (*Gewalt*) of "the poetic capacity" (*das dichterische Vermögen*) in its clearest and most transparent form (Dilthey 1878: 42). Goethe, Dilthey argues, possessed a special "poetic eye" (*Dichterauge*)—an ability to capture the vibrancy of life in poetic form (1878: 100–1). This capacity to register, recall, and transpose into language a vibrant lived experience is, argues Dilthey, more apparent in "outstanding people" such as Goethe, who are endowed with a heightened "visual sense," a purportedly scientific insight which Dilthey attributes to the research of Fechner and Müller (1878: 57).

Yet despite the natural scientific language and sources invoked by Dilthey, his argumentation ultimately rests on a neo-romantic conception of lived experience (*Erlebnis*), which he sees as underlying great works of literature, and which would later stand at the centre of his major work of criticism of 1906: *Das Erlebnis und die Dichtung* (Poetry and Experience, see Dilthey 1985a [orig. 1906]). The crucial distinction here is that between two words used for experience in German: *Erlebnis* and *Erfahrung*. The former suggests something that is immediate, sensuous, vibrant, and prerational (see Dilthey 1924 [orig. 1907/8]: 313–16), while the latter is associated predominantly with conscious and rational cognition.[10] Dilthey's implication in this 1878 essay—a position that would later undergo extensive theoretical elaboration between 1880 and 1910—is that the most powerful literature involves the transposition of a vibrant and primordial *Erlebnis* into language. Interpreting such *Erlebnis*-based texts, Dilthey would eventually argue, requires the reader to somehow transport themselves back into the emotional and cultural world of the author in order empathetically to relive the original experience that gave rise to the text.

Five years after "On the Imagination of the Poets," in the *Introduction to the Human Sciences* (1883), this notion of inner experience—referred to in German as both *innere Erfahrung* and as *Erlebnis* in order to underline its internal and therefore nonempirical status—is further emphasized, but now as a means sharply to *differentiate* the human sciences from the natural sciences rather than to unify them. For Dilthey in 1883, inner experience cannot be measured or subjected to laws of mechanistic causation, and thus it becomes the particular field in which the human sciences specialize:

> As a first step towards the independent constitution of the human sciences [...] it suffices to distinguish between those processes which have as their material what is given in the senses and is produced by means of connections of thought, and processes that concern a range of facts which are given originally in inner experience [*in der inneren Erfahrung*] and without the cooperation of the senses. Processes of this second kind are constituted from material originally given in inner experience [*Material innerer Erfahrung* . . .] Thus there arises a special realm of experiences [*Erfahrungen*] which has its independent origin and its own material in inner experience [*im inneren Erlebnis*] and which is, accordingly, the subject matter of a special science of experience [*Erfahrungswissenschaft*]. And so long as no one can claim to make Goethe's life more intelligible by deriving his passions, poetic productivity, and intellectual reflection from the structure of his brain or the properties of his body, the independent position of such a science cannot be contested. (1989 [orig. 1883]: 60–1, translation altered)

The philosophical problem for Dilthey's new and independent justification for the human sciences thus becomes the following: How do we understand the "life-expressions" (*Lebensäusserungen*) of other people—people from whom we may be separated by cultural and especially historical distances?

Dilthey entered into his fullest theorization of this problem in *The Formation of the Historical World in the Human Sciences* (1910), a text in which the term "life-expression" undergoes stringent discussion and definition (see Dilthey 2002 [orig. 1910]: 226–40).[11] The intervening years between *Introduction to the Human Sciences* and the *Formation of the Historical World*, namely those between 1883 and 1910, were those that saw Dilthey's most intensive engagement with

Stoic ideas, and it is at this point in Dilthey's career—that is, after he has given up the project of a descriptive-causal human sciences, and while he was developing the *Erklären / Verstehen* distinction during the mid-1890s—that the Stoic idea of *sensus communis* becomes important for him.

The term *sensus communis* has two essential meanings that emerge from the classical sources. In Aristotle's *De Anima* (III.1 425a27), *koinē aisthēsis* is referred to as the sixth sense which coordinates the other five senses, endowing them with order and unity. In Aristotle and in most of his early commentators, the *sensus communis* is therefore confined to the theory of perception, and has no direct relevance to the subject of interpersonal or intercultural understanding (Neumann 2007: 841–2; Leinkauf et al. 1995: 622–7). But from the first century BC onward, the idea of *sensus communis* is transformed by Roman thinkers, particularly by Cicero and Seneca. In these thinkers, it is used to describe feelings, ideas, thoughts, and perceptions which are common to a group people, and which may provide a basis for shared ethical, social, and political values; this basis is described in the secondary literature as being "pre-rational" and "pre-philosophical," and as involving appeals that may be capable of achieving consensus (Leinkauf et al. 1995: 629).

This later Stoic provenance of "common sense" has been carefully explored by Charles Brittain (2005), to whose excellent article I am deeply indebted. Brittain surveys the difficult and fragmentary evidence for Stoic doctrines about "preconceptions" (*prolēpseis*) and "common conceptions" (*koinai ennoiai*), which the Stoics claim are "natural" for all human beings, and whose aggregation converts each child's animal soul into a human mind (Brittain 2005: 175–9). Brittain argues that it is Cicero who first conceptualizes what we now call "common sense," which anglicizes the Latin phrase *sensus communis* (Brittain 2005: 207 n. 133). Cicero is an Academic Skeptic rather than a Stoic, but in this, as in many other respects, he borrows and adapts Stoic ideas. As an advocate and legal theorist, his primary concern is a practical one. He advises that speakers define contested terms in accordance with the "common opinion" (*communis opinio*), "common mentality" (*communis mens*), or "common sense" (*communis sensus*) shared by all jurors (see Brittain 2005: 206–7). But this practical advice rests upon an expanded and modified Stoic theory of concept acquisition, which holds that everyone in a community naturally acquires inchoate "delineations" of many ideas (Brittain 2005: 202–4). This pre-philosophical shared intellect is what makes effective courtroom arguments possible.

In *De Oratore* (2.68), for example, Cicero refers to "common sentiments of humanity" (*in sensu hominis communi*) and to "natural inclinations and morals" with which speakers on matters of public life must be familiar in order to convince their audiences (2.68, trans. 1942: vol. 1, 249). Similarly, in the *Moral Epistles*, Seneca sees the *sensus communis* as referring to a kind of comportment which philosophers must master if they are to communicate effectively with their fellow men. "The first thing," he writes, "which philosophy undertakes to give is fellow-feeling with all men [*sensum communem*]; in other words, sympathy and sociability. We part company with our promise if we are unlike other men" (5.4, trans. 1925: vol. 1, 20–1). Similar sentiments are found in *On Benefits*, where Seneca invokes the phrase *sensus communis* as a form of politeness associated with the giving of gifts, remarking that one should not, for example, give winter clothing during summer: "common sense [*sensus communis*] should be used in bestowing benefit; there must be regard for time, place and the person" (1.12.3, trans. 1935: vol. 3, 39–41). Rather than an ambitious philosophically grounded ethics, these passages would seem to suggest a much more modest and pragmatic theory of living.

The text in which Dilthey invokes the notion of *sensus communis* is entitled "The Natural System of the Human Sciences in the Seventeenth Century," written in 1892–3. Here he attributes the development of theology, jurisprudence, and political theory in the seventeenth century to this "natural system," in which there lies

> the answer to the needs of the seventeenth century. Its basis [. . .] was the teachings concerning common concepts, inborn concepts or elementary insights, upon which a rational theology, jurisprudence and statecraft, and finally also a rational natural science, could be founded. In order correctly to understand this great doctrine, which dominated the seventeenth century, and in which a natural system of religion and morals, of law and scientific truth is contained, we must first of all clarify the influence of the Roman Stoics since the emergence of humanism. (1914b [orig. 1892–3]: 153–4)

The sweeping claim made by Dilthey in this passage cannot entirely be separated from those positions that both Blumenberg and Abel subject to stringent critique: namely, the idea that both early modern natural science and ethics are heavily influenced by the Stoics. Yet here the subject at issue is a "natural system of the human sciences" founded on "inborn concepts and elementary insights," which seems to suggest a method for how humans might attempt to understand one another at a very basic and practical level. It sounds, in other words, like a proto-hermeneutics in Dilthey's sense of the term.

What would such a hermeneutics involve? Perhaps the best way to answer this question is to see where Dilthey ended up, in his mature hermeneutics, which emerged after his heaviest engagement with Stoic ideas during the years spanning roughly from the early 1890s to 1904 (see, for example, Dilthey 1914b [orig. 1892-3]: 153-61; 1914b [orig. 1894]: 283-96; 1914b [orig. 1904]: 439-52). The key text here is *The Formation of the Historical World in the Human Sciences* (1910), which outlines a theory of understanding (*Verstehen*) for the human sciences, and which departs quite radically from Dilthey's earlier attempt of 1878 to explain (*Erklären*) how a poetic text comes into being through the methods of descriptive psychology. For the late Dilthey, the most elementary form of understanding arises "through interests of practical life where persons rely on interchange and communication." In such settings, people must "make themselves understandable to each other" and "know what the other wants" (2002 [orig. 1910]: 228). Dilthey seems to recall here the "elementary insights" of Cicero and Seneca: namely that a speaker should know the commonly held values of their audience or that a giver of gifts should be aware of what people may wish to receive in particular contexts.

Dilthey does not, however, claim that these common ideas or expectations are universal or transhistorically valid; rather, they are always marked by their historicity and cultural specificity: their location in a particular time, place, and language. As Jürgen Habermas has observed in *Knowledge and Human Interests*, Dilthey's common ideas are both context-dependent and pragmatic, being part of what Habermas refers to as "the practical life relation of hermeneutics" (1972 [orig. 1968]: 176). As Habermas notes in his extended discussion of Dilthey:

> Dilthey introduces the concept of the "common" in a specific sense. Being common means the intersubjectively valid and binding quality of the same symbol for a group of subjects who communicate with each other in the same language [. . .] I understand myself only in the sphere of "what is common" in which I simultaneously understand the other in his objectivations. (1972 [orig. 1968]: 155-6)

This contingent situatedness of common ideas was in fact the key to Dilthey's project of a "Critique of Historical Reason," and it is here where Dilthey returns, in this late text, to post-Kantian philosophy and to the Hegelian notion of "objective mind" or "objective spirit" (*objektiver Geist*). By this Hegel means the way in which the values of spirit objectify themselves in extra-subjective institutions such as morality, the family, religion, and the state (Hegel 1970 [orig. 1830]: 366-94). Dilthey's use of the term is stripped of Hegel's historical metaphysics,[12] and operates on a more empirical level, referring to

> the manifold forms in which a commonality existing among individuals has objectified itself in the world of the senses [. . .] Its scope extends from lifestyles

and forms of social intercourse to the system of purposes that life has created for itself. It also encompasses custom, law, state, religion, art, the sciences, and philosophy. (2002 [orig. 1910]: 229)

Because, in Dilthey's view, all "life-expressions" are situated historically, understanding them necessarily involves familiarizing oneself with the cultural context—in other words, the "objective spirit"—which informs them, since "even the work of a genius will reflect a common stock of ideas, attitudes and ideals characteristic of an age and a region" (2002 [orig. 1910]: 229).

This task of interpretation becomes more complicated when a historical or geographical gulf exists between the interpreter and his or her object of interpretation: "the greater the inherent distance between a given life-expression and the one who seeks to understand it, the more frequently uncertainties will arise" (Dilthey 2002 [orig. 1910]: 231, translation altered). Here interpretation must involve assiduous historical and cultural research, combined with the ability to empathetically place oneself into the position of the author (*sich hineinversetzen*) in order to re-create (*nachbilden*) and re-experience (*nacherleben*) the original lived experience (*Erlebnis*) that gave rise to the text or artifact (Dilthey 2002 [orig. 1910]: 234). Hermeneutics, as Dilthey understands it, involves the training of such historical and cultural sensitivity, and is based on the apprehension of the differences between one's own historically conditioned values and those of the text. "Re-creating and re-experiencing what is foreign and from the past," he writes, "shows clearly how understanding is based on a special, personal kind of talent." This "technique," according to Dilthey, "emerges with the development of historical consciousness [. . .] The science of this art is hermeneutics" (2002 [orig. 1910]: 237–8, translation altered).

From this we can conjecture that the "natural system of the human sciences" that Dilthey finds in the sixteenth- and seventeenth century reception of the Stoics seems to have informed his own approach to hermeneutics as a distinct methodology for humanistic inquiry. Descriptive causation and explanation (*Erklärung*), which the early Dilthey, under the influence of Helmholtz, favored as a superior method of scientific explanation, has been replaced here with a science that attempts to understand (*Verstehen*) cultural artifacts through a consideration of the historically determined values which inform them. Stoic ideas about the *sensus communis* function here as way of thinking about the values that humans may share during a particular period or within a particular culture, with the crucial difference being that Dilthey *historicizes* these values, thereby making them relative, rather than universal. Thus, even if

Hans Blumenberg and Günter Abel may be correct in their claims that Dilthey misunderstood the radically non-teleological features of early modern natural science and ethics—leading him mistakenly to posit a Stoic influence upon them—this criticism does not touch upon the contribution which the Stoic notion of *sensus communis* made to Dilthey's conception of hermeneutics as a distinct method for the human sciences.

4. Postscript: The Stoic *Sensus Communis* in Philosophical Hermeneutics After Dilthey

The most immediate inheritor of Dilthey's tradition of philosophical hermeneutics is Hans-Georg Gadamer (1900–2002). In *Wahrheit und Methode* (Truth and Method, 1960), Gadamer addresses the role played by the Roman Stoic *sensus communis* in the German tradition of philosophical hermeneutics, thereby rendering more explicit an influence which is by and large only implicit in Dilthey's writings. In tracing this history, Gadamer identifies the Italian philosopher Giambattista Vico (1668–1744) as the principal early modern mediator of Roman ideas about the *sensus communis*.[13] In Vico's attempt to theorize a new science of the human, according to Gadamer,

> there is a positive ethical motif involved that merges into the Roman Stoic doctrine of the *sensus communis*. The grasp and moral control of the concrete situation require subsuming what is given under the universal—that is, the goal that one is pursuing so that the right thing may result [. . .] Vico's return to the Roman concept of *sensus communis*, and his defense of humanist rhetoric against modern science, is of special interest to us, for here we are introduced to an element of truth in the human sciences that was no longer recognizable when they conceptualized themselves in the nineteenth century. (Gadamer 1989 [orig. 1960]: 21–3)

These passages, and the larger section of *Truth and Method* to which they belong, present Gadamer's scarcely veiled polemic against his main precursor in the tradition of the human sciences: Dilthey. After citing Helmholtz's famous essay on the differences between the natural and human sciences, Gadamer claims that "Dilthey let himself be profoundly influenced by the model of the natural sciences," and for that reason "did not really progress very far beyond the simple statements made by Helmholtz" (1989 [orig. 1960]: 7). While this is partially true of the early Dilthey, it is completely incorrect when applied to Dilthey's mature hermeneutics from 1883 onward, and especially as found in the *Formation of the Historical World* of 1910. Nonetheless, Gadamer implies here that revisiting Vico on the *sensus communis* will help us to understand where Dilthey went wrong in his alleged attempts to conform too closely to the requirements of the natural sciences as laid down by Helmholtz. In particular, Gadamer's comment seems to suggest that Dilthey did not sufficiently understand the roles played by prejudice, authority, and tradition in the human sciences.

In the *Scienza Nuova* (New Science, 1725), Vico defines "common sense" as "judgement without reflection shared by an entire class, an entire people, an entire nation, or the entire human race." For Vico, this constitutes a form of natural law, since "the common sense of the human race" functions as "the criterion taught to the nations by divine providence to define what is certain in the natural law of nations" (Vico 1948 [orig. 1725]: 57). Gadamer interprets this to mean that in judging a particular case of human action, "a conclusion based on universals, a reasoned proof, is not sufficient, because what is decisive is the circumstances [. . .] The sense of the community mediates its own positive knowledge" (1989 [orig. 1960]: 23). This is because, for Gadamer, the *sensus communis* does not represent the "abstract universality of reason"; rather, it constitutes "the concrete universality represented by the community of a group, a people, a nation, or the whole human race. Hence developing this communal sense is important for living" (1989 [orig. 1960]: 21).

The conservative implications of the idea that a "communal sense" can possess a "concrete universality" may be less surprising when one recalls Gadamer's rehabilitation of prejudice, tradition, and authority in opposition to what he calls the Enlightenment's "prejudice against prejudices," an argument partially directed at Kant's critique of prejudice in his famous essay on the Enlightenment (Gadamer 1989 [orig. 1960]: 271–7, especially, 272; see also Kant 1970 [orig. 1784]). This argument is also aimed at Dilthey, since Gadamer claims that Dilthey remained preoccupied with the standards of the natural sciences in his alleged attempt to "legitimate the knowledge of what was historically conditioned as an achievement of objective science, despite the fact that the knower is himself conditioned" (Gadamer 1989 [orig. 1960]: 231). Writing under the influence of Heidegger's claim that to be human is to be "thrown" (*Geworfen*) in history (Heidegger 1962 [orig. 1927]: 174–6), Gadamer disputes the idea that the prejudices arising from one's position in history can ever be overcome by the critique of tradition, or by a self-reflexive examination of one's own historical consciousness (Gadamer 1989 [orig. 1960]: 265–71).

To be fair, Gadamer does correctly point out that Vico's *New Science* was a reassertion of the power of tradition in the face of the rise of Cartesian method (see Mali 1992: 16–73). Yet here an apparent contradiction lies in the fact that, according to Vico's own definition, the *sensus communis* is a form of *"judgement without reflection"* (italics mine); in other words, a procedure that we would normally think of as conscious and rational (i.e., judgment) takes place "without reflection," in what is presumably a prerational procedure. At the same time, however, it also carries a universal validity by virtue of its sanction by divine providence and tradition, a position which quickly loses its credibility in secular contexts and appears, at least for modern audiences, to resemble decisionism.

Gadamer attempts to resolve this problem by de-politicizing and aestheticizing it, a familiar move of classical German culture since Thomas Mann's *Reflections of a Non-Political Man* (Mann 1983 [orig. 1918]). He does so by associating this prerational form of judgment with Kant's discussion of the *sensus communis* in §20 of the third *Critique* (Gadamer 1989 [orig. 1960]: 34). Here the context is of course not moral or legal judgment, but rather aesthetic judgment or taste, which, according to Kant,

> must [. . .] have a subjective principle, which determines what pleases or displeases only through feeling and not through concepts, but yet with universal validity. Such a principle, however, could only be regarded as common sense [. . .] only under the presupposition that there is a common sense (by which, however, we do not mean any external sense but rather the effect of the free play of our cognitive powers) [. . .] can the judgment of taste be made. (2000 [orig. 1790]: 122)

The paradox of something which seems to have universal validity, but which is based only on subjective feeling, raises once again the problems associated with Kant's legacy in the tradition of German idealism. The existence of a common sense can only be a presupposition for Kant, because the phenomenon with which it is associated—namely, the beautiful—is something which Kant holds to be universal on the one hand and yet only subjectively grounded and therefore not transposable into concepts on the other (Kant 2000 [orig. 1790]: §6). This radically subjective moment in Kant's aesthetics was, in Gadamer's opinion, "truly epoch-making," because in "discrediting any kind of theoretical knowledge except that of natural science, it compelled the human sciences to rely on the methodology of the natural sciences in conceptualizing themselves" (1989 [orig. 1960]: 41).

As we have seen, this was indeed the position in which Dilthey found himself in the second half of the nineteenth century, following in the wake of the more rampantly speculative systems propagated by post-Kantian thinkers such as Fichte, Schelling, and Hegel. But Gadamer's account of Dilthey's role in developing a method for the human sciences does not do justice to Dilthey's reception of the Stoic *sensus communis*. Indeed, in *Truth and Method*, Gadamer completely ignores Dilthey's reception of the Stoics. As has been argued here, Dilthey does not remain confined to the natural scientific model of positivist causation in his mature theorization of the human sciences, and he does not, in the manner of Gadamer, suggest that the *sensus communis* can hold a concrete universal validity vouchsafed by tradition.

Dilthey's decisive move is to claim that the *sensus communis* is never universal, but only historically contingent, being based on the "objective spirit" of a particular people at a particular point in history. The task of hermeneutics as the "Critique of Historical Reason" thereby becomes that of understanding the *difference* between one's own historically conditioned values and those of the text or artifact. This, admittedly, is a more skeptical understanding of Dilthey's project than Dilthey himself may have favored, since it emphasizes precisely the difference and discontinuity between historical contexts, rather than their potential coming together in acts of transhistorical understanding, a possibility which is always left open by Dilthey's claim that the reader can "re-experience" (*nacherleben*) the "lived experience" (*Erlebnis*) which gave rise to the text (see Dilthey 2002 [orig. 1910]: 234–7). This notwithstanding, a reexamination Dilthey's reception of the Stoic *sensus communis* helps us to discover him anew and even read him against the grain as I am doing here. Such readings are necessary, precisely because the critical potential of Dilthey's hermeneutics has been eclipsed by the more powerful legacy of Gadamer, and is therefore yet to be fully realized.

Notes

1 My thanks to Kurt Lampe and Larry Frohman for their advice on earlier drafts of this chapter, as well as to participants at the symposium on *Stoicism and German Philosophy: From Dilthey to Sloterdijk* held at the University of Miami in August 2016. All translations from works in German are my own unless otherwise noted. Some of the arguments presented here can also be found in other contexts in Nicholls (2006, 2011).

2 Throughout, I translate the German *Geisteswissenschaften* as *human sciences* rather than as *humanities*, since Dilthey's use of this term includes not only traditional humanities subjects such as literary criticism, philosophy, and history but also

other fields—such as psychology and sociology—which, at least in the Anglophone world, extend beyond the bounds of the humanities as they have traditionally been conceived. As Roger Smith notes (2007: 122–7), this translation is also not without its problems, since the English prefix *human* fails to capture the complexity of *Geist* in German, which essentially refers, for Dilthey, to any "socio-historical reality" to have emerged from the human *Geist*, meaning *both* mind and spirit (see Dilthey 1989 [orig. 1883]: 56–8).

3 For context surrounding Dilthey's appointment to this Chair, see Thielen (1999: 40–1).
4 For the German original, see Dilthey (1927 [orig. 1910]); the English translation is Dilthey (2002 [orig. 1910]).
5 I cite here the German edition of Dilthey's *Einleitung in die Geisteswissenschaften* (Dilthey 1922), because the English translation by Makkreel and Rodi (Dilthey 1989) is a truncated version from which some parts are missing.
6 The distinction between *Verstehen* and *Erklären* is first developed in Dilthey (2010 [orig. 1894]: 115–210).
7 The relevant texts are as follows: Dilthey (1892–3, 1894, 1904). All are reprinted in Dilthey (1914b). These texts do not appear in the multivolume edition of the *Selected Works* edited and translated into English by Rudolf Makkreel and Frithjof Rodi. In order to give the reader a historical sense of when they were published and in which journals, I have given separate entries for them in the list of works cited.
8 I refer here to the title of one of the essays in volume two of Dilthey's *Schriften*: "Die Funktion der Anthropologie in der Kultur des 16. und 17. Jahrhunderts" (The Function of Anthropology in the Culture of the 16th and 17th Centuries). The first section title of this essay is "Menschenkunde und Theorie der Lebensführung im Zeitalter der Renaissance und Reformation" (Theory of the Human Being and Theory of Living in the Age of the Renaissance and Reformation), see Dilthey (1914b [orig. 1904]: 416).
9 For a contextualized analysis of this debate, see Flasch (2017: 471–82), Gordon (2019).
10 The literature on this distinction in Dilthey's works is extensive. See, for example: Cramer (1972), Sauerland (1972), Rodi (1969: 80–92; 2003: 100), Jay (2005: 222–34), Nicholls (2006: 72–4). The 1907/8 reference is to Dilthey's "Fragmente zur Poetik," collected in Dilthey (1924).
11 Makkreel and Rodi translate *Lebensäusserung* as "life manifestation"; I favour "life-expression," which is used by Kurt Mueller-Vollmer in his translation of a short piece from *The Formation of the Historical World* (see Dilthey 1985b).
12 On this, see Makkreel and Rodi (2002: 3).
13 For an overview of Vico's and Gadamer's positions on the *sensus communis* and their interrelation, see Schaeffer (1990: 80–126).

Works Cited

Abel, Günter (1978), *Stoizismus und frühe Neuzeit. Zur Entstehungsgeschichte modernen Denkens im Felde von Ethik und Politik*, Berlin: De Gruyter.

Beiser, Frederick C. (2014), *The Genesis of Neo-Kantianism 1796-1880*, Oxford: Oxford University Press.

Blumenberg, Hans (1969), *Selbsterhaltung und Beharrung. Zur Konstitution der neuzeitlichen Rationalität*, Wiesbaden: Verlag der Akademie der Wissenschaften und der Literatur in Mainz.

Blumenberg, Hans (1983 [orig.1966]), *The Legitimacy of the Modern Age*, trans. Robert M. Wallace, Cambridge, MA: MIT Press.

Brittain, Charles (2005), "Common Sense: Concepts, Definition and Meaning in and out of the Stoa," in Dorothea Frede and Brad Inwood (eds.), *Language and Learning: Philosophy of Language in the Hellenistic Age*, 164-209, Cambridge: Cambridge University Press.

Cicero (1942), *De Oratore*, 2 vols., trans. E. W. Sutton, London: Heinemann.

Cramer, K. (1972), "Erleben, Erlebnis," in Joachim Ritter, Karlfried Gründer and Gottfried Gabriel et al. (eds.), *Historisches Wörterbuch der Philosophie*, vol. 2, 702-11. Basel: Schwabe.

Diemer, Alwin (1968), "Die Differenzierung der Wissenschaften in die Natur- und Geisteswissenschaften und die Begründung der Geisteswissenschaften als Wissenschaft," in Alwin Diemer (ed.), *Beiträge zur Entwicklung der Wissenschaftstheorie im 19. Jahrhundert*, 174-221, Meisenheim am Glan: Anton Hain.

Dilthey, Wilhelm (1878), "Über die Einbildungskraft der Dichter," *Zeitschrift für Völkerpsychologie und Sprachwissenschaft*, 10: 42-104.

Dilthey, Wilhelm (1892-93), "Das natürliche System der Geisteswissenschaften im 17. Jahrhundert," published in five parts in *Archiv für Geschichte der Philosophie*, 5 (4): 480-502; *Archiv für Geschichte der Philosophie*, 6 (1): 60-127; *Archiv für Geschichte der Philosophie*, 6 (2): 225-56; *Archiv für Geschichte der Philosophie*, 6 (3): 347-79; *Archiv für Geschichte der Philosophie* 6 (4), 509-45; (all reprinted in Dilthey 1914b: 90-245).

Dilthey, Wilhelm (1894), "Die Autonomie des Denkens, der konstruktive Rationalismus und der pantheistische Monismus nach ihrem Zusammenhang im 17. Jahrhundert," *Archiv für Geschichte der Philosophie*, 7 (1): 28-92 (reprinted in Dilthey 1914b: 246-96).

Dilthey, Wilhelm (1904), "Die Funktion der Anthropologie in der Kultur des 16. und 17. Jahrhunderts," *Sitzungsberichte der Preußischen Akademie der Wissenschaften* 1904, 2-12; 316-47 (reprinted in Dilthey 1914b: 416-92).

Dilthey, Wilhelm (1906), *Das Erlebnis und die Dichtung. Lessing, Goethe, Novalis, Hölderlin*, Leipzig: Teubner.

Dilthey, Wilhelm (1914a [orig. 1883]), *Gesammelte Schriften*, vol. 1, *Einleitung in die Geisteswissenschaften. Versuch einer Grundlegung für das Studium der Gesellschaft und die Geschichte*, ed. Georg Misch, Leipzig: Teubner.

Dilthey, Wilhelm (1914b), *Gesammelte Schriften*, vol. 2, *Weltanschauung des Menschen seit Renaissance und Reformation*, ed. Georg Misch, Leipzig: Teubner.

Dilthey, Wilhelm (1922), *Gesammelte Schriften, 1. Einleitung in die Geisteswissenschaften: Versuch einer Grundlegung für das Studium der Gesellschaft und der Geschichte*, Leipzig and Berlin: Teubner.

Dilthey, Wilhelm (1924), *Gesammelte Schriften*, vol. 6, *Die Geistige Welt. Einleitung in die Philosophie des Lebens*, ed. Georg Misch, Leipzig: Teubner.

Dilthey, Wilhelm (1927 [orig. 1910]), *Gesammelte Schriften*, vol. 7, *Der Aufbau der geschichtlichen Welt in den Geisteswissenschaften*, ed. Bernhard Groethuysen, Leipzig: Teubner.

Dilthey, Wilhelm (1936), *Gesammelte Schriften*, vol. 11, *Vom Aufgang des geschichtlichen Bewusstseins. Jugendaufsätze und Erinnerrungen*, ed. Erich Weninger. Leipzig: Teubner.

Dilthey, Wilhelm (1985a [orig. 1906]), *Selected Works*, vol. 5, *Poetry and Experience*, eds. and trans. Rudolf A. Makkreel and Frithjof Rodi, Princeton, NJ: Princeton University Press.

Dilthey, Wilhelm (1985b [orig. 1910]), "The Understanding of Other Persons and Their Life-Expressions," trans. Kurt Mueller-Vollmer, Kurt Mueller-Vollmer (ed.), *The Hermeneutics Reader: Texts of the German Tradition from the Enlightenment to the Present*, 152–64, New York: Continuum.

Dilthey, Wilhelm (1989 [orig. 1883]), *Selected Works*, vol. 1, *Introduction to the Human Sciences*, eds. and trans. Rudolf A. Makkreel and Frithjof Rodi, Princeton, NJ: Princeton University Press.

Dilthey, Wilhelm (2002 [orig. 1910]), *Selected Works*, vol. 3, *The Formation of the Historical World in the Human Sciences*, eds. and trans. Rudolf A. Makkreel and Frithjof Rodi, Princeton, NJ: Princeton University Press.

Dilthey, Wilhelm (2010), *Selected Works*, vol. 2, *Understanding the Human World*, eds. and trans. Rudolf A. Makkreel and Frithjof Rodi, Princeton, NJ: Princeton University Press.

Ermarth, Michael (1978), *Wilhelm Dilthey: The Critique of Historical Reason*, Chicago: University of Chicago Press.

Fechner, Gustav Theodor (1860), *Elemente der Psychophysik*, 2 vols., Leipzig: Breitkopf und Härtl.

Flasch, Kurt (2017), *Hans Blumenberg. Philosoph in Deutschland: Die Jahre 1945–1966*, Frankfurt am Main: Klostermann.

Frohman, Larry (1995), "Neo-Stoicism and the Transition to Modernity in Wilhelm Dilthey's Philosophy of History," *Journal of the History of Ideas*, 56 (2): 263–87.

Gadamer, Hans-Georg (1989 [orig. 1960]), *Truth and Method*, trans. Joel Weinsheimer and Donald G. Marshall, New York: Continuum.

Gordon, Peter E. (2019), "Secularization, Genealogy, and The Legitimacy of the Modern Age: Remarks on the Löwith-Blumenberg Debate," *Journal of the History of Ideas*, 80 (1): 147–70.
Habermas, Jürgen (1972 [orig.1968]), *Knowledge and Human Interests*, trans. Jeremy J. Shapiro, Boston: Beacon Press.
Helmholtz, Hermann von (1855), *Über das Sehen des Menschen*, Leipzig: Leopold Voss.
Helmholtz, Hermann von (1896 orig. 1862]), "Über das Verhältniss der Naturwissenschaften zur Gesammtheit der Wissenschaft," in *Vorträge und Reden*, 4th ed., vol. 1, 157–85, Brauchschweig: Viehweg.
Hegel, Georg Wilhelm Friedrich (1970 [orig. 1830]), *Enzyklopädie der philosophischen Wissenschaften III*, eds. Eva Moldenhauer and Karl Markus Michel, Frankfurt am Main: Suhrkamp.
Heidegger, Martin (1962 [orig. 1927]), *Being and Time*, trans. John Macquarrie and Edward Robinson, Oxford: Blackwell.
Heidelberger, Michael (2004 [orig. 1993]), *Nature from Within: Gustav Theodor Fechner and His Psychophysical Worldview*, trans. Cynthia Klohr, Pittsburgh, PA: University of Pittsburgh Press.
Henrich, Dieter (1960), "Der Begriff der sittlichen Einsicht und Kants Lehre vom Faktum der Vernunft," in Dieter Henrich, Walter Schultz and Karl-Heinz Volkmann-Schluck (eds.), *Die Gegenwart der Griechen im neueren Denken. Hans-Georg Gadamer zum 60. Geburtstag*, 77–115, Tübingen: Mohr.
Hühn, H., S. Meier-Oeser, and H. Pulte (2004), "Wissenschaft," in J. Ritter, K. Gründer and G. Gabriel (eds.), *Historisches Wörterbuch der Philosophie*, vol. 12, 902–47, Basel: Schwabe.
Huxley, Thomas Henry (1882), *Science and Culture and Other Essays*, London: Macmillan.
Jay, Martin (2005), *Songs of Experience: Modern American and European Variations on a Universal Theme*, Berkeley, CA: University of California Press.
Kaltenbrunner, Wolfgang (2010), "Literary Positivism? Scientific Theories and Methods in the Work of Saint-Beuve (1804–1869) and Wilhelm Scherer (1841–1886)," *Studium*, 3: 74–88.
Kant, Immanuel (1970 [orig.1784]), "An Answer to the Question 'What Is Enlightenment?'" in Hans Reiss (ed.) and H. B. Nisbet (trans.), *Political Writings*, 54–60, Cambridge: Cambridge University Press.
Kant, Immanuel (2000 [orig. 1790]), *Critique of the Power of Judgement*, trans. Paul Guyer and Eric Matthews, Cambridge: Cambridge University Press.
Kindt, Tom (2000), "Wilhelm Dilthey (1833–1911)," in Christoph König, Hans-Harald Müller and Werner Röcke (eds.), *Wissenschaftsgeschichte der Germanistik in Porträts*, 53–68, Berlin: De Gruyter.
Lagrée, Jacqueline (2006), "Justus Lipsius and Neostoicism," in John Sellars (ed.), *The Routledge Handbook of the Stoic Tradition*, 160–73, Abingdon: Routledge.

Leinkauf, T., T. Dewender, A. von der Lühe, and K. Grünepütt (1995), "Sensus Communis," in J. Ritter, K. Gründer, G. Gabriel (eds.), *Historisches Wörterbuch der Philosophie*, vol. 9, 622–75, Basel: Schwabe.

Lipsius, Justus (1584), *De constantia libri duo qui alloquium praecipue continent in publicis malis*, Antwerp: Plantin.

Lipsius, Justus (1604a), *Manuductionis ad stoicam philosophiam libri tres, L. Annaeo Senecae aliisque scriptoribus illustrandis*, Antwerp: Plantin-Moretus.

Lipsius, Justus (1604b), *Physiologiae Stoicorum libri tres, L. Annaeo Senecae aliisque scriptoribus illustrandis*, Antwerp: Plantin-Moretus.

Lipsius, Justus (1605), *L. Annaei Senecae philosophi opera quae exstant omnia a Justo Lipsio emendata et scholiis illustrata*, Antwerp: Plantin-Moretus.

Löwith, Karl (1949), *Meaning in History: The Theological Implications of the Philosophy of History*, Chicago: University of Chicago Press.

Makkreel, Rudolf A. (1975), *Dilthey: Philosopher of the Human Studies*, Princeton, NJ: Princeton University Press.

Makkreel, Rudolf A. and Frithjof Rodi (2002), "Introduction to Volume III," in Wilhelm Dilthey, *Selected Works*, vol. 2, *Understanding the Human World*, eds. and trans. Rudolf A. Makkreel and Frithjof Rodi, 1–20. Princeton, NJ: Princeton University Press.

Mali, Joseph (1992), *The Rehabilitation of Myth: Vico's New Science*, Oxford: Oxford University Press, 1992.

Mann, Thomas (1983 [orig.1918]), *Reflections of a Non-Political Man*, ed. and trans. Walter D. Morris, New York: Ungar.

Mazlish, Bruce (2007), *The Uncertain Sciences*, New Brunswick, NJ: Transaction.

Mezzanzanica, Massimo (2011), "Philosophie der Erfahrung und Erneuerung des Apriori: Dilthey und Helmholtz," in H. Lessing, R. A. Makkreel and R. Pozzo (eds.), *Recent Contributions to Dilthey's Philosophy of the Human Sciences*, 59–82, Stuttgart: Frommann-Holzboog.

Morford, Mark (1991), *Stoics and Neostoics: Rubens and the Circle of Lipsius*, Princeton, NJ: Princeton University Press.

Müller, Hans-Harald (2000), "Wilhelm Scherer (1841–1886)," in Christoph König, Hans-Harald Müller and Werner Röcke (eds.), *Wissenschaftsgeschichte der Germanistik in Porträts*, 80–94, Berlin: De Gruyter.

Neumann, F. (2007), "Sensus Communis," in Gert Ueding et al. (eds.), *Historisches Wörterbuch der Rhetorik*, vol. 8, 841–7, Tübingen: Niemeyer.

Nicholls, Angus (2006), "The Subject-Object of *Wissenschaft*: On Wilhelm Dilthey's Goethebilder," *Colloquia Germanica*, 39 (1): 69–86.

Nicholls, Angus (2011), "Scientific Literary Criticism in the Work of Wilhelm Dilthey and Matthew Arnold," *Comparative Critical Studies*, 8 (1): 7–31.

Richards, Robert J. (2002), *The Romantic Conception of Life: Science and Philosophy in the Age of Goethe*, Chicago: University of Chicago Press.

Rodi, Frithjof (1969), *Morphologie und Hermeneutik: Diltheys Ästhetik*, Stuttgart: Kohlhammer, 1969.
Rodi, Frithjof (2003), *Das strukturierte Ganze. Studien zum Werk von Wilhelm Dilthey*, Weilerswist: Velbrück.
Sauerland, Karol (1972), *Diltheys Erlebnisbegriff*, Berlin: De Gruyter.
Schaeffer, John D. (1990), Sensus Communis: *Vico, Rhetoric and the Limits of Relativism*, Durham, NC: Duke University Press.
Schnädelbach, Herbert (1984), *Philosophy in Germany, 1831–1933*, trans. Eric Matthews, Cambridge: Cambridge University Press.
Sellars, John (2006), "Introduction," in John Sellars (ed.), *The Routledge Handbook of the Stoic Tradition*, 1–14, Abingdon: Routledge.
Seneca (1925), *Ad Lucilium Epistulae Morales*, trans. Richard Gummere, 3 vols., London: Heinemann.
Seneca (1935), *Moral Essays*, trans. John W. Basore, 3 vols., London: Heinemann.
Smith, Roger (2007), *Being Human: Historical Knowledge and the Creation of Human Nature*, New York: Columbia University Press.
Thielen, Joachim (1999), *Wilhelm Dilthey und die Entwicklung des geschichtlichen Denkens in Deutschland im ausgehenden 19. Jahrhundert*, Würzburg: Königshausen & Neumann.
Trautmann-Waller, Céline (2004), "La *Zeitschrift für Völkerpsychologie und Sprachwissenschaft* (1859–1890): entre Volksgeist et Gesamtgeist," in Céline Trautmann-Waller (ed.), *Quand Berlin pensait les peuples. Anthropologie, ethnologie et psychologie (1850–1890)*, 105–20, Paris: CNRS.
Vaihinger, Hans (1876), *Hartmann, Dühring und Lange. Zur Geschichte der deutschen Philosophie im XIX. Jahrhundert. Ein kritischer Essay*, Iserlohn: Baedecker.
Vico, Giambattista (1948 [orig. 1725]), *The New Science of Giambattista Vico*, trans. Thomas Goddard Bergen and Max Harold Fisch, Ithaca, NY: Cornell University Press.
White, Paul (2003), *Thomas Huxley: Making the "Man of Science"*, Cambridge: Cambridge University Press.

4

Nietzschean Stoicism

An Ascetic Strategy in Pursuit of Knowledge

Hedwig Gaasterland

1. Introduction

Nietzsche's famous concept of *amor fati* is often conceived to be a form of therapy resembling one of the Stoic exercises in the pursuit of happiness.[1] Peter Groff (2004: 154), for instance, finds it "illuminating to read Nietzsche as a kind of late modern neo-Stoic, providing us with a veritable banquet of spiritual exercises aimed at the cultivation of the self and the affirmation of fate." Michael Ure's book *Nietzsche's Therapy* discusses in great detail Nietzsche's turn to the Stoics, claiming that "what looms large in Nietzsche's thinking is the question of psychological health and sickness [...]. In the middle period, [...] he conceives the patient, piecemeal labour of psychological self-observation as a therapy of the soul" (2008: 3). Ure's article "Nietzsche's Free Spirit Trilogy and Stoic Therapy" further explores the implications of Nietzsche's adoption of Stoic therapy for the notion of *amor fati* (2009: 60–84). Although it is claimed that *amor fati* is set up as an alternative to those elements of Stoicism that Nietzsche is discontent with, it is stated throughout that it remains faithful in many respects to the basics of Stoic therapy. In short, Nietzsche's suggestion to love one's fate mirrors, according to Michael Ure, Epictetus's advice: "Do not seek to have events happen as you wish, but *wish* them to happen as they do happen, and all will be well with you" (*Ench.* 8, trans. by Boter 1999).[2]

The aim of this chapter is to challenge two of the main assumptions instructing this view. First, I will trace Nietzsche's engagement with Stoicism in the Middle Works, or the so-called Free Spirit Trilogy, which include *Human, All Too Human* (*HAH*), *Daybreak* (*D*), and *The Gay Science* (*GS*) through Book IV. I intend to show that Nietzsche's motivation for turning to the Stoics is not, at least not exclusively, the question of psychological health and sickness, or self-observation as a therapy of the soul. Parallel to this interest, and closely related, runs Nietzsche's fascination for truth and the scientific practice aimed at the increase of knowledge. I will argue that Nietzsche's passion for knowledge (or *Leidenschaft der Erkenntnis*) shapes the engagement with Stoicism in a stronger sense than his quest for health.

Secondly, after showing how Nietzsche's stance toward Stoicism starts out sympathetic in *HAH* yet ends fiercely critical in *GS*, I will make the case that *amor fati* is not only un-Stoic but even anti-Stoic. *Amor fati* occurs only ten times in the totality of Nietzsche's works, including his notes (henceforward referred to as the *Nachlass* or *NL*[3]) and his letters, and its first published occurrence is in the first aphorism of *GS* IV. I will argue that the timing of this first occurrence is not coincidental: the introduction of *amor fati* follows from Nietzsche's growing dissatisfaction with Stoicism. This also has an impact on our understanding of *amor fati*, at least of its meaning in *GS*.[4] My point is that it is informed by Nietzsche's struggle with the desire for truth, one that Nietzsche gradually came to understand in *GS* in close relation to the encouragement of pain and other sensations, and to the future enhancement of the human species.

2. The Contrast between the Opening of *GS* Book IV and Section 306

Nietzsche's attitude toward Stoicism in general is characteristically ambiguous. This can hardly come as a surprise, since most of Nietzsche's responses to important philosophical schools or figures are ambivalent: some aphorisms betray clear admiration, while others—sometimes even within the same book—are written in a tone of aversion, revealing a highly polemical attitude. Moreover, not many texts explicitly mention the philosopher who is admired or attacked. The reader is expected to be so familiar with the philosophical tradition that one is capable of recognizing Nietzsche's implicit opponent or ally. Developing a consistent account of Nietzsche's relation to Stoicism therefore faces these two difficulties: we have to take into account that those whom Nietzsche fights in one text might be admired in another and we have to be aware that Nietzsche might discuss Stoicism in an aphorism lacking explicit signs of it.

Book IV of *GS* serves as a good example. This Book shows both difficulties. Nietzsche seems to be critical and appreciative of Stoicism, both implicitly and explicitly. It contains one of the most explicit evaluations of Hellenistic Ethics in the totality of Nietzsche's published oeuvre, namely aphorism 306 entitled "Stoics and Epicureans." Nietzsche clearly prefers the Epicureans over the Stoics in this text. But several other aphorisms reveal an implicit dialogue with the Stoic philosophers as well. The Opening of Book IV, for instance, bears a remarkable yet implicit resemblance to the Stoic therapy of affirming fate, that is, according to several commentators (Ure 2008; 2009: 60–84; Groff 2004: 139–73; Sellars 2006: 157–71; Brobjer 2003: 429–32). We read:

> *For the new year.* I'm still alive; I still think: I must be still alive because I still have to think. *Sum, ergo cogito: cogito, ergo sum.* Today everyone allows himself to express his dearest wish and thoughts: so I, too, want to say what I wish from myself today and what thought first crossed my heart—what thought shall be the reason, warrant, and sweetness of the rest of my life! (GS 276)

Nietzsche playfully transforms the Cartesian saying that we can only know for certain that we exist, because we think: "cogito, ergo sum." For Nietzsche, the connection goes both ways, which makes the intimacy between thinking and living even stronger. "I must be alive, because I still have to think": there is no living without thinking. Moreover, the thought he wishes to express "for the new year" is "his dearest." To think a particular thought, it appears, has the power to have a lasting impact on one's life: it can become one's "reason, warrant," and even one's "sweetness," changing drastically its taste, sensation, or quality. There is no thinking without living; there is no living well—for Nietzsche—without thinking this particular thought.

This intimate connection is taken as a clue pointing toward the idea that Nietzsche is engaged in a dialogue with Hellenistic philosophy. That is: the Stoic tradition in particular has introduced us to the idea that the way we think affects the way we feel.[5] Secondly, it is not just the fact that our thinking affects our well-being, but it is rather a specific thought that will turn out to be therapeutic, namely that of affirming fate. For the Stoics, the entire universe is determined by an "all-embracing ineluctable fate" (Hankinson 1999: 526)—yet we can achieve happiness (*eudaimonia*) and psychological health by accepting and embracing our fates, even if they seem to be horrendous.[6] The "dearest wish" that Nietzsche expresses in the first aphorism, after loosely introducing it in the "motto" preceding Book IV[7] is the following:

> *Amor fati*: let that be my love from now on! I do not want to wage war against ugliness. I do not want to accuse; I do not even want to accuse the accusers. Let *looking away* be my only negation! And, all in all and on the whole: some day I want only to be a Yes-sayer!

Nietzsche sees in *amor fati* a thought that can become a "sweetness," making "all things well." Even though he does not explicitly name a Stoic philosopher, the concept of loving fate can be and has been interpreted as one that draws on Stoicism.

The apparent attitude of agreement with Stoic doctrines does not last throughout the Book, however. Aphorism 306, where Nietzsche explicitly compares and evaluates Stoic and Epicurean ways of living, is radically different in tone. He portrays a Stoic as someone who "trains himself to swallow stones and worms, glass shards and scorpions without nausea," and as one who "wants his stomach to be ultimately insensible to everything the chance of existence pours into him." Nietzsche explicitly prefers the more selective attitude of the Epicurean, who "seeks out the situation, the persons, and even the events that suit his extremely sensitive intellectual constitution."

Nietzsche thus mocks the Stoic aim to be completely open to whatever fate may bring here.[8] Yet on first sight, he does not seem to have different Stoic doctrines in mind: in both *GS* 276 and 306 the Stoic idea is central that we are dependent on fate somehow and that we should "wish the events as they happen" instead of "making the events happen as you wish." Yet in contrast to the Opening of Book IV, Nietzsche firmly rejects this idea in 306. We should not become "ultimately insensible to everything the chance of existence pours into us" he suggests there; rather, we should actively select the things that are to our taste and reject the things that are not. How then to explain the wish expressed in *GS* 276 to be "a Yes-sayer only," someday?

It is this puzzle that will be addressed in this chapter. As we will see, a more thorough account of Nietzsche's long and complex engagement with Stoicism will shed some light on both aphorisms and how they relate.

3. Science and Knowledge 1: Nietzsche's Appreciation of the Stoic Approach to Emotions

It is crucial to distinguish between two major concerns in the "Free Spirit Trilogy": *health* and *science* (science taken in the broad sense of German *Wissenschaft*). My approach concurs with that of Melissa Lane (2007: 25–51), who, different from commentators like Michael Ure (2008: 2009), Peter Groff (2004: 139–73), Martha Nussbaum (1994: 139–67), and Keith Ansell-Pearson (2011: 179–204; 2010: 137–63), does not evaluate Nietzsche's engagement with Stoicism merely from the angle of ethics and therapeutic self-cultivation.

Whereas Peter Groff claims that Nietzsche is "committed to the task of banishing or overcoming sorrow" arguing that he "appropriate[s] many of the Stoics' therapeutic techniques toward this end" (Groff 2004: 154), Melissa Lane's point is that "while self-fashioning has become a leading theme of the 'post-modern' reading of Nietzsche, [. . .] there has been little discussion of [. . .] the extent to which Nietzsche marks out a virtue of honesty named *Redlichkeit* from *Daybreak* (1881) onward" (2007: 25). Yet, whereas her analysis reveals "the extent to which honesty and intellectual adequacy came to weigh for him on the side of Stoicism" (Lane 2007: 26), my conclusion shall be that Nietzsche increasingly criticizes the Stoics, precisely for their misapprehension of the value of rationality in the pursuit of truth.

It is clear from the beginning of Nietzsche's philosophical project that the interests in truth and health do not complement each other.[9] As the first Book of *HAH* reveals, for instance in the title of aphorism 33 ("*Error regarding life necessary to life*"), the search for truth might uncover things that do not sit well with our "human, all too human" constitution. In aphorism 34, this thought is developed as follows:

> Will truth not become inimical to life, to the better man? A question seems to lie heavily on our tongue and yet refuses to be uttered: whether one *could* consciously reside in untruth? or, if one were *obliged* to, whether death would not be preferable?

This same aphorism reveals how Nietzsche, be it implicitly, has a Stoic philosopher in mind who can set us an example of how to deal with a devastating yet desired truth (even if the Stoics do not recognize the idea that truth and health may be opposed). This text reveals the presence of Stoicism in at least three ways. One: the temperament that is recommended is one "by virtue of which a life could arise much simpler and emotionally cleaner," reminding us of the Stoic idea that life is lived more effectively without the burden of great emotions:

> I believe that the nature of the after-effect of knowledge is determined by a man's *temperament*: [. . .] I could just as easily imagine a different one, quite possible in individual instances, by virtue of which a life could arise much simpler and emotionally cleaner than our present life is: so that, though the old motives of violent desire produced by inherited habit would still possess their strength, they would gradually grow weaker under the influence of purifying knowledge. [. . .] For this to happen one would, to be sure, have to possess the requisite temperament, as has already been said: a firm, mild and at bottom cheerful soul.

The description of "a firm, mild and at bottom cheerful soul" is similar to the state of *eupatheia* the Stoics envision; it resembles their ideal of a calm and rational temperament, well balanced, in which all extreme passions are held in check.[10]

Two: this state is traditionally achieved through adopting an attitude of "detachment." One should be able to perceive most things as "indifferent" and "forgo much":

> [He] must, rather, without envy or vexation be able to forgo much, indeed almost everything upon which other men place value; that free, fearless hovering over men, customs, and the traditional evaluations of things must *suffice* him as the condition he considers most desirable.

The idea is simple. Dismissing as indifferent the things that we would instinctively value means to be able to remain cheerful and calm, also when these are taken away or fundamentally questioned. This attitude of "detachment" is illustrated in this aphorism as "free, fearless hovering over men, customs, and the traditional evaluations of things," a description that is almost identical to what we find in Marcus Aurelius's *Meditations*:

> One who would converse about human beings should look on all things earthly as though from some point far above, upon herds, armies, and agriculture, marriages and divorces, births and deaths, the clamour of law courts, deserted wastes, alien people of every kind, festivals, lamentations, and markets, this intermixture of everything and ordered combination of opposites. (7.48)

Three: the relation between temperament and truth is double. On the one hand, Nietzsche acknowledges that the response to knowledge depends on one's "temperament": a nature whose life is "emotionally cleaner" might react more calmly and rationally. On the other hand, it is *because* of the effects of knowledge that the passions lose their strength and weaken, for knowledge can be "purifying" as we have seen earlier: "though the old motives of violent desire [. . .] would still possess their strength, they would gradually grow weaker under the influence of purifying knowledge." The implicit idea seems to be that it is not the things themselves that are threatening or disturbing, rather it is our *opinion* or reaction to it—an idea that we find recurring in Epictetus (e.g., *Ench.* 5) and Marcus Aurelius (e.g., 4.7). We should, thus, use the purifying workings of this knowledge in order to calm down our passions.

Consequently, we can see how a form of Stoicism is taken on board by Nietzsche as part of a therapy that will not only prepare us to face a hostile truth by adopting a calm attitude of passion-free detachment but that moreover changes our expectations of that truth: it may be devastating at first, but it may, in the long run, purify and even liberate us. This idea can be found explicitly in *HAH* 170: "To perceive all this can be very painful, but then comes a consolation: such pains are birth-pangs. The butterfly wants to get out of its cocoon."

4. Science and Knowledge 2: Nietzsche's Rejection of the Stoic Approach to Emotions

Nevertheless, this hopeful attitude concerning the relation between knowledge and psychological health changes in *Dawn*. Correspondingly, the appreciative stance toward the Stoics develops into one of rejection, the most explicit example of which is *GS* 306, as we have seen. *GS* 305 reveals in more detail what exactly Nietzsche's disappointment with Stoicism entails.

> *Self-control.* Those moralists who command man first and above all to gain control of himself thereby afflict him with a peculiar disease, namely, a constant irritability at all natural stirrings and inclinations and as it were a kind of itch. [. . .] [N]o longer may he entrust himself to any instinct or free wing-beat; instead he stands there rigidly with a defensive posture, armed against himself, with sharp and suspicious eyes, the eternal guardian of his fortress, since he has turned himself into a fortress. [. . .] [H]ow impoverished [he has become] and cut off from the most beautiful fortuities of the soul! And indeed from all further *instruction*! For one must be able to lose oneself if one wants to learn something from the things that we ourselves are not.

The fact that this aphorism is immediately followed by 306, "Stoics and Epicureans," suggests that Nietzsche sees at least the Stoics (perhaps the Epicureans, too) as examples of sick "moralists who command man first and above all to gain control of himself." They are described here as those who rigidly defend their own "fortresses," a very familiar image within the writings of Marcus Aurelius.[11] But interestingly, Nietzsche's objection to this kind of attitude is not just that it is unhealthy ("a peculiar disease"); it is also inappropriate for those who wish to *learn*. Nietzsche's desire in this time is still (partly at least) to find truth, which is confirmed by *GS* 309: "This penchant and passion for what is true, real, non-apparent, certain—how it exasperates me!" *GS* 305 shows Nietzsche's awareness that if one wishes to grow, to *learn*, one must have faith in one's own instincts. Only if we "lose ourselves," "entrust ourselves to any free wing-beat," will we not be cut off "from further *instruction*" and actually come to discover new things.

This preoccupation with learning can also be recognized in *GS* 306, where Nietzsche prefers the Epicureans over the Stoics because the Epicurean attitude fits a learning attitude (formulated as "the work of the spirit") better:

> But someone who more or less *expects* fate to allow him to spin *a long thread* does well to take an Epicurean orientation; people engaged in the work of the spirit have always done so! For it would be the loss of all losses, for them, to forfeit their subtle sensitivity in exchange for a hard Stoic skin with porcupine spines.

What insight made Nietzsche change his mind between *HAH* and *GS* concerning the right attitude for dealing with truth? Whereas *HAH* obviously regards Stoic *eupatheia*, an attitude with calmed and purified passions, as the right preparation for uncovering even these truths that are inimical to life, *GS* encourages us to adopt a selective, Epicurean attitude instead, one that protects its "subtle sensitivity" and deems the Stoic attitude "insensible," "inflexible," "defensive," "suspicious," having a hard skin "with porcupine spines," reminiscent of what he would later, especially in *GM* III, come to term "asceticism"—a term to which I will return later.

In *Dawn*, a shift occurs concerning the role of the passions in the quest for knowledge. Even though *Dawn* is mostly read in the context of therapy and self-cultivation, it also contains many aphorisms showing an involvement with *Wissenschaft* and objective judgment. On that subject, we find on the one hand texts in which the Stoic attitude of rational detachment, even of hovering over all things, is appreciatively adopted, for instance in the following aphorism:

> To view our own experiences with the eyes with which we are accustomed to view them when they are the experiences of others—this is very comforting and a medicine to be recommended. [. . .] [This] maxim is certainly *more in accord with reason and the will to rationality*, for we adjudge the value and meaning of an event more objectively when it happens to another than we do when it happens to us [. . .]. (*D* 137)

This text resembles what we saw in *HAH*. It strongly recalls a passage in Epictetus[12] and stresses the importance of reason: arguably, it is more rational to regard one's experiences through the eyes of others, leading to a more "objective" evaluation of the event—being untroubled by passions that stand in the way of a clear and rational judgment. Also, in *D* 497, we find the suggestion that men with "true geniuses" are those who possess "the *pure, purifying* eye which seems not to have grown out of their temperament and character but, free from these and usually in mild opposition to them, looks down on the world as on a god and loves this god," again hinting at the importance of a kind of rational strength functioning detached from one's emotional humors. It even has the potential to hover over them: "the spirit seems to be only *loosely attached* to the character and temperament, as a winged being who can easily detach itself from these and then raise high above them."

On the other hand we find examples that reveal a slowly dawning awareness of truth being such that it will not be uncovered by adopting a detached and rational point of view. *D* 539: "Have you never been plagued by the fear that you might be completely incapable of knowing the truth? The fear that your mind may be too dull and even your subtle faculty of seeing still much too coarse?" And this is not the only fear; slowly its possible implication is explored, namely that we may not have *any* access to a truth outside. We may be imprisoned by our deceptive senses, as *D* 117 holds: "it is by these horizons, within which each of us encloses his senses as if behind prison walls, that we *measure* the world [. . .] and it is all of it an error!" And, further: "The habits of our senses have woven us into lies and deception of sensation: these again are the basis of all our judgements and 'knowledge'—there is absolutely no escape, no backway or bypath into the *real world!*" This line of thought, then, leads to a kind of despair expressed in *D* 483: "Learn to know! Yes! But always as a man! What? [. . .] Never to be able to able to see into things out of any other eyes but *these*? [. . .] What will mankind have come to know at the end of all their knowledge?—their organs! And that perhaps means: the impossibility of knowledge! Misery and disgust!"

The conclusion then must be that "truth," if possible at all, will not reveal itself to those who are engaged in purely rational activity: "Or do you believe that today, since you are frozen and dry like a bright morning in winter and have nothing weighing on your heart, your eyes have somehow improved? Are warmth and enthusiasm not needed if a thing of thought is to have *justice* done to it?" (*D* 539) Rather, we are constantly presented with the results of our own inner sensitive movements: "when you are tired you will bestow on things a pale and tired coloration; when you are feverish you will turn them into monsters" (*D* 539). Hence, it is acknowledged that passions and drives should not be left out of the process of acquiring knowledge—rather, they may possibly be the only thing we will ever get to know, or at least they provide us with the only method that perhaps enables us to acquire small amounts of knowledge:

> Before knowledge is possible, each of these impulses [to laugh, lament, and curse] must first have presented its one-sided view of the thing or event; then comes the fight between these one-sided views, and occasionally out of it a mean, an appeasement, a concession to all three sides, a kind of justice and contract. (*GS* 333)

It should not come as a surprise, therefore, to find Nietzsche in *GS* encouraging the stimulation of as many impulses, passions, and "views" as possible—which is quite opposite to the idea of the possibility of a "detached genius" we encountered in *D*, and of the adoption of a Stoic, calm, rational attitude we saw Nietzsche defending in *HAH*. *GS* 12 reveals explicitly how Nietzsche had not forgotten about the Stoics; here he formulates very precisely and in a tone of respect how he has come to disagree.

> But what if pleasure and displeasure are so intertwined that whoever *wants* as much as possible of one *must* also have as much as possible of the other [. . .]? And that may well be the way things are! At least the Stoics believed that this is how things are, and they were consistent when they also desired as little pleasure as possible in order to derive as little pain as possible from life. (*GS* 12)

This aphorism conveys appreciation for the Stoic doctrine of passions as communicating vessels (it is impossible to have more pleasure without an increase of pain[13]). But importantly, it is entitled "*On the aim of science,*" suggesting that its focus again is science, not well-being. It finishes as follows:

> With *science* one can actually promote either of these goals! So far it may still be better known for its power to deprive man of his joys and make him colder, more statue-like, more stoic. But it might yet be found to be the *great giver of pain*!— And its counterforce might at the same time be found: its immense capacity for letting new galaxies of joy flare up!

This aphorism once more describes the Stoic attitude in terms of stiffness and inflexibility, adding "cold" and "statue-like" to the list of adjectives. But it also shows how the Stoic denunciation of pain and pleasure, like all passions—still adopted in *HAH* as the only attitude available for those attempting to uncover truth—is now rejected. Instead of encouraging us to "purify" all our passions Nietzsche reaches the conclusion that the practice of science rather involves their full engagement and stimulation.

5. The Importance of Pain for the Future: The Need for an Un-Stoic Kind of Heroism

Now that we have traced the importance of the quest for knowledge in Nietzsche's growing dissatisfaction with the Stoic approach to emotions, let us return to the other issue at work in *The Free Spirit Trilogy*: health. For although it must be conceded that *D* contains several aphorisms that draw on Stoicism in the context of health, be it physical or psychological, it is from this perspective also that Nietzsche grows more and more discontent with Stoicism. In two respects in particular is this the case: Nietzsche comes to alter his view on the importance of pain for health in itself, and the meaning of health becomes more and more embedded in a view for the future of humanity.

As we have seen already, Nietzsche diverges from the Stoics on the meaning and significance of pain and suffering. This should not be understood from the angle of the development of science only, for according to a Primavera-Lévy (2011: 130–55), the medical achievements of the nineteenth century may have been an influence as well. Because of the production of several narcotics, among them morphine, the question to what extent suffering really was necessary gained renewed interest in Nietzsche's days and led to a discussion on the meaning of suffering in itself. Primavera-Lévy distinguishes between two typically nineteenth-century interpretations of *Schmerz* that are at work in Nietzsche's philosophy but are essentially at odds. One is part of a heroic vitalism, a kind of interpretation initiated by Hippokrates and Galen and taken up by Kant and Fichte, approaching suffering as a necessary ingredient for health; the other is part of an "epistemological critique," and aims rather to "de-substantiate" pain. It is inspired by Léon Dumont, and regards *Schmerz* as the outcome of interpretation: it is not substantive (as it is in the first account) but relative, and always the outcome of a process of the mind.

We can find many examples of the second notion of pain in *Daybreak*. What is more, Nietzsche explicitly points to Marcus Aurelius as a guide for diminishing pain through a process of the mind.[14] Yet, it is the first interpretation that gains more and more momentum in Nietzsche's thought. In line with Kant, Nietzsche comes to understand pain as one of the most indispensable stimuli of life, without which a more passive, even morbid state would occur. Both Nietzsche and Kant associate a life lacking *Reiz*, the painful stimulus leading to action, with a state of moral and mental lethargy (*Trägheit*, literally denoting a kind of "slowness"). In the *Nachlass* fragments written in the time of GS, we can see the connection both between the addition of pain and a kind of heroism and between a lack of heroism and *Trägheit*. Moreover, Nietzsche comes to evaluate the Stoics explicitly by these criteria:

Heroism is the strength to suffer and to *add* pain. (*NL* 9 12[140])

The attitude of *Stoicism* in what is taken to be suffering is a sign of paralyzed power, one places a slowness (*Trägheit*) on the balance—lack of heroism [. . .]. (*NL* 9 12[141])

According to Nietzsche, the Stoics do not seek pain; they rather do everything to reduce it. One note, written in the fall of 1881, constitutes one of the most lengthy passages on Stoicism in his entire oeuvre and reproaches the Stoics on a similar basis. After defining as its "essential feature" "its comportment toward pain," Nietzsche indicates as the principal aim of Stoic edification "to hate the passions themselves as if they were a form of disease or something entirely unworthy."

> I am very antipathetic to this line of thought. It undervalues the value of *pain* (it is as useful and necessary as pleasure), the value of stimulation and suffering. It is finally compelled to say: everything that happens is acceptable to me; nothing is to be different. There are *no emergencies* (Nothstände) *to be averted* because it has killed the perception of emergencies. (NL 9 15[55])

We recognize in these lines the Stoic attitude of calm acceptance of GS 306, preparing one's "stomach to be ultimately insensible to everything the chance of existence pours into him." GS 318's title "*Wisdom in pain*," which implicitly seems to continue the dialogue with the Stoics, further elaborates the use of "pain" in two ways. First, it is said that being sensitive to its messages (informing us of the presence of a *Nothstand*, to which the Stoics are said to have become insensitive in NL 15[55]) gives us the chance to make sure we will be safe, averting a certain death:

> *Wisdom in pain.*—There is as much wisdom in pain as in pleasure. [...] In pain I hear the captain's command: "Pull in the sails!" The hardy seafarer "Man" must have learned to adjust the sails in a thousand ways; otherwise he would have gone under too quickly and the ocean would have swallowed him too soon. (GS 318)

Being awake to the subtle indications hidden in pain that one's life might be in danger has prevented many unwelcome deaths in the past and will continue to do so; it reintroduces the awareness that the self and survival is important. A Stoic would ignore these signals, it is suspected, and stubbornly continue his quest for knowledge, stiffly choosing death over "adjusting the sail."[15] At the same time, secondly, pain gives the opportunity for humanity to grow, this time not by obeying to its message of self-protection, but by adding even more pain to the situation:

> True, there are people who hear exactly the opposite command when great pain approaches and who never look as proud, bellicose, and happy as when a storm is nearing—yes, pain itself gives them their greatest moments! They are the heroic human beings, the great *painbringers* of humanity, those few or rare ones

who need the same apology as pain itself—and truly, they should not be denied this! They are eminently species-preserving and species-enhancing forces.

The suggestion is that pain is not something to be avoided, but a necessary ingredient for growth: heroic people who are strong enough not only to take in pain but also as "*painbringers*" to provoke their fellow human beings should be seen as "eminently species-preserving and species-enhancing forces." This perspective on pain fits the description of *Wissenschaft* of *GS* 12 quoted earlier; *Wissenschaft* understood by Nietzsche as a practice that stimulates rather than silences the passions could be such a "*painbringer.*" We noticed already that the effects of this new concept of science are opposite to what we have understood as science thus far in terms of Stoicism (it made humanity "colder, more statue-like, more stoic"), making apparent that Nietzsche regards the Stoic attitude toward pain and science as that which needs to be overcome.

The importance of pain and the adding of pain, therefore, is that it both increases the amount of knowledge, at least specifically related to one's very own situation, for instance in the case of a dangerous situation, and stimulates the development of oneself and humanity. Yet it should be noted that the two effects reinforce each other. It is only if one has sufficient knowledge of one's own constitution that one knows when adding pain will lead to growth and in what cases it will lead to death—so knowledge is required for the enhancement of humanity; and, vice versa, the stimulation of all passions, that is, the enhancement of a human being, is required for the pursuit of more knowledge. We should, in this context, keep in mind that Nietzsche slowly but steadily develops the insight that the content of all knowledge redirects us to our human, all too human perspectives. The clearest expression of this awareness is *D* 483, quoted already: "Never to be able to able to see into things out of any other eyes but *these*? [. . .] What will mankind have come to know at the end of all their knowledge?—their organs!"

It is, in other words, important both for the development of knowledge and for the enhancement of oneself and humanity that an element of danger is kept in place. Nietzsche concludes:

Preparatory human beings.—[. . .] For—believe me—the secret for harvesting from existence the greatest fruitfulness and the greatest enjoyment is—*to live dangerously*! Build your cities on the slopes of the Vesuvius! Send your ships into uncharted seas! (*GS* 283)

The danger of living "on the slopes of Vesuvius" and sending your ships "into uncharted seas" is the only way in which "the greatest fruitfulness and the greatest enjoyment" can be "harvested," formulations indicating the state of human beings who are "more fruitful, more endangered, happier." They are preparatory for a new age, one that "will carry heroism into the search for knowledge," emphasizing once again the interconnectedness of the addition of pain ("heroism") and knowledge.

Although Nietzsche's project of increasing knowledge involves, indeed, an intensification of pain and suffering by living in danger, it simultaneously amounts therefore to a more refined understanding of one's limitations, which limits the chances of perishing—it is a matter of *knowing* when to "adjust the sail." Precisely this knowing is, again, the outcome of the project of the pursuit of knowledge, which amounts to living dangerously, and heroically exercising both the painful and the joyful passions. It is this knowledge that his age lacks, but the Stoics as well, which Nietzsche attributes to their petrifying diet. These observations lead to an understanding of the dealing with pain and suffering as a subtle game of constant self-observation: which cases must be considered too dangerous, causing death or Stoic petrification, and should be avoided by "adjusting one's sail," and which must be welcomed instead, as chances to take both knowledge and humanity to a next level.

Nietzsche sometimes refers to this game as an "experiment for the knowledge-seeker" or as a "dance" or "play"; all these expressions we find in *GS* 324.[16] Understanding life as an experiment for the knowledge-seeker is, for Nietzsche, a "great liberator." Ever since this thought "overcame him," life appeared to him "truer, more desirable and mysterious." Knowledge is to Nietzsche a "world of dangers and victories," in which "heroic feelings have their dance- and playgrounds."[17] The effect of this new perspective on the relation between life, knowledge, danger, pain, and suffering is that life appears as a place of experiment, constantly testing and challenging one's limits; but it can appear this way only after developing enough understanding of one's own *Organe* and the workings of knowledge in general to have gathered the health, energy, and courage to continue without perishing or petrifying. What is more, the old perspectives on suffering now appear in a different light. Whereas pain used to indicate something to be simply averted or diminished (a position still defended in *D*), it can now be conceded that those who defended this view perhaps purposively exaggerated its unbearableness.

> *Soul-doctors and pain.*—[. . .] What fantasies about the inner "miseries" of evil persons the preachers of morals have concocted! How they have even *lied* to us about the unhappiness of passionate people! Yes, "lied" is here the proper

term: they knew very well about the superabundant happiness of this type of person, but kept a deathly silence about it, since it constituted a refutation of their theory on which happiness arises only with the annihilation of passion and the silencing of the will! Finally, concerning these doctors' prescription and their praise for a severe, radical cure, one may ask: is our life really so painful and burdensome that it would be advantageous for us to trade it for a fossilized Stoic way of life? Things are *not bad enough* for us that they have to be bad for us in a Stoic style! (*GS* 326)

The question with which the aphorism ends must now be answered with an unequivocal *no*. Not only is our life, even without Stoicism, full of tricks to extract the thorn of pain and unpleasantness, we have also seen that the taking away of "pain" will go hand in hand with the loss of many kinds of "joys"—which would be a true impoverishment. There is no "greatness" in the mere endurance of pain (even women and slaves can do it, as we read in *GS* 325 entitled "What belongs to greatness"), which makes this attitude weak in comparison to the heroic one; but first and foremost, there is no "advantage" in this kind of approach of suffering. Only the heroic stance has the potential to take us to a higher level—in the development of knowledge as well as in the enhancement of the humankind.

6. Stoic Asceticism versus *Ja-sagen* in GS 276's *amor fati*

Having traced the development of Nietzsche's stance toward the Stoic treatment of the passions in the context of health and the desire for truth—from one of appreciation to its opposite—it is time to return to the initial question: How to understand the apparent incompatibility between *GS* 276 and 306 on the affirmation of fate? Although it seems clear by now that Nietzsche's rejection in *GS* 306 is the result of a long and intricate dialogue with Stoicism, we still need to develop an idea of the meaning of *amor fati* as introduced in the Opening of Book IV in a way that explains its apparent similarity to one of the typically Stoic doctrines. Yet following the line we developed so far, *amor fati* too, may best be read in the light of this development.

We could say that the story as established thus far begins with a reflection on the past in *GS* 306 and ends with a future-oriented perspective in *GS* 276. That is: we have seen that Nietzsche's desire for truth leads him in *HAH* to go along with the typically Stoic idea that the best method of acquiring knowledge is to "calm down" one's emotions by developing a "purified," rational outlook. We also saw how Nietzsche slowly comes to change his mind, realizing how indispensable the stimulation of passions, drives, and impulses is for knowledge. In *On the Genealogy of Morality* (*GM*), he looks back upon this earlier phase as follows:

> Perhaps I am too familiar with all this: [...] that stoicism of the intellect which, in the last resort, denies itself the "no" just as strictly as the "yes," that *will* to stand still before the factual, the *factum brutum*, that fatalism of "*petits faits*" (*ce petit fatalisme*, as I call it) [...]—on the whole, this expresses the asceticism of virtue just as well as any denial of sensuality (it is basically just a *modus* of this denial). (*GM* III 24)

It is in this context that I believe we should place *GS* 306, for it seems that Nietzsche there, too, looks back at the ascetic attitude he used to adopt in *HAH* and *D* (a kind of fatalism indeed, as *GM* III has it[18]) but now rejects it. Instead, the proper attitude toward truth should hold a combination of adopting as many emotional perspectives as possible on the one hand, balanced on the other by the game of experimenting with the knowledge one has developed of oneself.

In *GS* 276, the aspects of both danger and hope for the future can be recognized, as *amor fati* is introduced as a "dearest wish," a thought that shall be "the reason, warrant and sweetness" of the rest of his life. Read against *GS* 324, a text that expresses Nietzsche's vision of a life that has become "truer," "more desirable and mysterious every year" because of "the thought that life could be an experiment for the knowledge-seeker," it seems that *amor fati*, too, should be read in this light.[19] At least the opening of *GS* 276, in which the intimate Cartesian connection is made between life and thought, life and the intellectual quest for truth, suggests that we may read *amor fati* as the expression of Nietzsche accepting or even affirming his fate as a thinker, who necessarily dedicates his life to knowledge ("I *must* still be alive because I still *have* to think"; italics mine).

The fate to be loved in this context must therefore concern Nietzsche's own identity, which is, as a result of the quest for knowledge, based upon self-knowledge. This leaves unconvincing the suggestion made earlier, that Nietzsche's *amor fati* may reflect Epictetus's advice to "not seek to have events happen as you wish, but *wish* them to happen as they do happen, and all will be well with you." It now appears as though the fate that Nietzsche has in mind in *GS* 276 is not a fate that is concerned with "events," or with external things which "the chance of existence" pours into us, as *GS* 306 describes it; rather, it is a form of "yes-saying" to the inner process that has everything to do with the *Leidenschaft der Erkenntnis*, which shapes so much of Nietzsche's thought in these years.

What is more, as a final argument against the idea that *amor fati* in *GS* 276 reflects a Stoic sense of coming to terms with external events, let me focus on the different kinds of negation that are at play in the final sentences of GS 276. Recall how Nietzsche exclaims, "I do not want to wage war against ugliness. I do not want to accuse; I do not even want to accuse the accusers. Let *looking away* be my only negation!" Even if we must acknowledge that "looking away," too, is presented as a form of negation (one that is allowed before the ultimate goal, "only to be a Yes-sayer," will be attained), it is clearly a kind of negation that is distinguished from "waging war" and "accusing." In what follows I will argue that Nietzsche's analysis of asceticism, which is associated with both *Ja-* and *Nein-sagen*, reveals how he has come to understand Stoic asceticism as the kind of negation that he wishes to distance himself from.

We only have to take a look at text GS 304, the aphorism that along with GS 305 seems to be the introduction to GS 306, in order to find what kind of negation Nietzsche criticizes. We have seen earlier how GS 305 points out that there is something wrong with "those moralists who command man first and foremost to take control of himself"; for they leave their students "impoverished and cut off from the most beautiful fortuities of the soul! Indeed from further *instruction!*" The preceding aphorism GS 304 introduces the topic of "negative virtues" such as "self-denial" as follows:

> *by doing we forgo.*—Basically I abhor every morality that says: "Do not do this! Renounce! Overcome yourself!" But I am well disposed towards those moralities that impel me to do something again and again from morning till evening [. . .]. When one lives that way, one thing after another that does not belong to such a life drops off: without hate or reluctance one sees this take its leave [. . .]. "What we do should determine what we forgo; in doing we forgo"—that's how I like it. (GS 304)

This text does not imply that *Ja-sagen* is all we should do; the negative must also have its place (at least for now). The difference between how Nietzsche likes it and the taste of the moralists who recommend "self-denial" (of which the Stoics and the Epicureans provide the best example in GS 306) is that they have eyes only for what is *not* welcome: "negation and self-denial"; Nietzsche, on the other hand, focuses on the positive, the goal, that for which the "negation" is exercised. The elements that have to be denied will disappear in a natural way "without hate or reluctance," so Nietzsche asserts—which is utterly different from the "waging war" and "accusing" in GS 276. GS 307 makes the same point in another way: "We negate and have to negate because something in us *wants* to live and affirm itself, something we might not yet know or see!" The fact that this aphorism immediately succeeds the one on Stoicism suggests that its procedure betrays the opposite course: as it is described in *GS* 305, a moralist like the Stoic "stands there rigidly with a defensive posture, armed against himself, with sharp and suspicious eyes." There is no expectation of a greater future or a higher world there; the motivation for (self-)denial is merely out of a defensive fear that "his self-control" may be "endangered."

Asceticism, understood as a disciplining of one's drives by withholding their satisfaction (or a "denial of sensuality" as it is expressed in *GM* III), is therefore not something Nietzsche rejects tout court. There is a subtle difference between "renunciation" out of a positive aim and one that is merely negative. *GS* 27 explains how renunciation can be an indication that one is a *Ja-sagende* still:

> *The renouncer.*—What does the renouncer do? He strives for a higher world, he wants to fly further and higher than all affirmers—*he throws away much* that would encumber his flight, including some things that are not valueless, not disagreeable to him: he sacrifices it to his desire for heights. [. . .] Yes, he is cleverer than we thought [. . .], this affirmer! For he is just as we are even in his renunciation. (*GS* 27)

Yet it is clear that this kind of asceticism, this kind of sacrifice and self-negation, is utterly different from the direct war that he sees the Stoics undertake against the "natural stirrings and inclinations" (*GS* 305). We only have to recall what Nietzsche accused the Stoics of in his *Nachlass* note: they "*hate* the passions themselves as if they were a form of disease or something entirely unworthy" (italics mine). We must therefore conclude, first, that the future prospect of being "a Yes-sayer only" in *GS* 276 cannot be equated to the attitude ascribed to the Stoics in *GS* 306 of swallowing "stones and worms, glass shards and scorpions without nausea," or of having a stomach that is "ultimately insensible to everything the chance of existence" pours into us; rather, it seems that Nietzsche recognizes in Stoicism a negating rather than an affirming philosophy. Secondly, the negation that Nietzsche allows himself still is one that has a future ideal as purpose, one that includes the enhancement of humanity through the development of science and knowledge—again something he finds utterly lacking in ascetic Stoicism.

7. Conclusion

Amor fati is not to be understood as resembling the Stoic therapy to embrace all events, fortunate as well as unfortunate. This chapter has attempted to challenge the assumption made by Ure, Nussbaum, Ansell-Pearson, and Groff that Nietzsche's reflection on Stoicism takes place for the most part in the context of psychological health and therapy. I have argued instead how Nietzsche's stance toward Stoicism in the context of the desire for truth shifts from being appreciative in *HAH* to fiercely critical in *GS*. The difference between the two approaches concerns the role of passions and drives in this quest. Whereas *HAH* still concurs with the Stoic idea that one should be calmly rational, allowing as little emotion as possible in the practice of *Wissenschaft* (in which also our emotions will be "purified"), *GS* holds the opposite: we need all the drives and passions we have in order to increase the amount of perspectives on things. Hence Nietzsche's preference in *GS* 306 for the Epicurean "selectivity": only this attitude can safeguard our sensitivity. Losing contact with our emotional inner life would be "the loss of all losses" (*GS* 306), leaving us "cut off from the most beautiful fortuities of the soul! And indeed from all further *instruction!*" (*GS* 305). The merely ascetic stance toward truth is one that Nietzsche is "too familiar with" (*GM* III 24)—but it is abandoned nevertheless.

The idea that *amor fati* in *GS* 276 draws inspiration from a Stoic source is therefore not plausible. What is more, now that we have investigated in more detail what Nietzsche's relation to the Stoics entails, we may even conclude that *amor fati* is *anti*-Stoic. It is an expression of hope for a future ("some day I want only to be a Yes-sayer!") in which the practice of science may ultimately be a preparation for a new future for humanity. The loving of fate, that is, the project of being a thinker for whom the quest for knowledge entails a dangerous dance and game, is the attitude Nietzsche considers most fruitful with respect to the realization of health as well as the future attainment of knowledge (hence the significance of *amor fati* appearing for the first time in a book called *GS*). It is the expression of a heroically joyful, healthy, *and* scientifically promising perspective for a future *away* from a stiff and rational, that is, ascetic, Stoicism.

Notes

1 A different version of this chapter has been published in *Pli. The Warwick Journal of Philosophy*, 2016. We are grateful to *Pli* for permission to publish this revised version.
2 See Ure: "Nietzsche develops a quintessentially Stoic ethic, anchored in the complete affirmation of natural necessity" (2009: 76).
3 Translations from the *NL* are mine, based on the *KSA* (Nietzsche 1980).

4 I agree with Tom Stern (2013: 145–62), who argues that the meaning of *amor fati* changes between *GS* and its last appearances in 1888. He rightly argues (Stern 2013: 157–8): "Nietzsche scholars are far too relaxed about picking and choosing from his different books to construct a version of Nietzsche that suits their particular interests. [...] This would be unobjectionable if his views about some of the key notions associated with *amor fati* (in *The Gay Science*) were not subject to change in the coming years. As it happens, they were."

5 See Pierre Hadot (1995) as one of the most prominent works in this field. Also John Sellars (2003: 3–4) suggests that Nietzsche's notion of philosophy as an "art of living" is influenced by Stoicism.

6 See, for example, MA 5.8. On the topic of the Stoic doctrine of fate, determinism, and free will, there is a lot of literature. See, for instance, Susanne Bobzien (2001) and Hankinson (1999). For more on the relation between Nietzsche and fatalism, see Solomon (2002).

7 Motto *GS* IV: "Ever healthier it rises, Free in fate most amorous."

8 Curiously, within contemporary analyses of Stoicism this idea of being "completely open" to fate without being selective is absent. The image is rather that the Stoics seek out persons and situations and events suitable for themselves, and have elaborate theories about precisely those details. (I thank Kurt Lampe for pointing this out to me.) I cannot dwell here on this difference in understanding Stoicism; I only wish to emphasize that, clearly, Nietzsche's understanding of Stoicism cannot and should not be simply equated to our contemporary knowledge. It has only been in the twentieth century that Stoicism was fully studied in its own right: Nietzsche did not have access to, for instance, the *Stoicorum Vetera Fragmenta* (as Hans von Arnim composed these a few years after Nietzsche's death [1903–5]), and was probably influenced by Hegel and Schopenhauer in his view on Stoicism. For more on this historical background of Nietzsche's reception of Stoicism, see Gaasterland (2017: 13–19, 95–120).

9 The development of Nietzsche's thought on the relation between health, happiness, and the destructive desire for truth is eloquently and in full detail worked out by Marco Brusotti (1997).

10 This similarity is also identified by Michael Ure (2008: 126). *Eupatheia* literally means a "state of good passion." In Stoic psychology, a passion is understood to be a "mistaken opinion" or as the "result of a mistaken opinion" (Inwood 1999: 699). It is often stated that the ultimate Stoic goal is to reach *apatheia*, a state without mistaken judgments, hence of emotionlessness. But a life in which impulses are rational, moderate, and held in check leads, according to Seneca for instance to a state of calm joy: *eupatheia* (*Ep. Mor.* 25). For more on *eupatheia*, see *Inwood (1999: 701), Brennan (2005, 97–100)*.

11 See Pierre Hadot (2001) on the writings of Marcus Aurelius; moreover, we can find in in *Meditations* 8.48 an explicit example by Marcus Aurelius himself: "Remember

that your ruling center becomes invincible when it withdraws into itself and rests content with itself, doing nothing other than what it wishes, even where its refusal to act not reasonably based; and how much more contented will it be, then, when it founds its decision on reason and careful reflection. By virtue of this, an intelligence free from passions is a mighty citadel."

12 *Ench.* 26: "The will of nature may be learned from things upon which we are all agreed. As when our neighbor's boy has broken a cup, or the like, we are ready at once to say, 'These are casualties that will happen'; be assured, then, that when your own cup is likewise broken, you ought to be affected just as when another's cup was broken. Now apply this to greater things. Is the child or wife of another dead? There is no one who would not say, 'This is an accident of mortality.' But if anyone's own child happens to die, it is immediately, 'Alas! how wretched am I!' It should be always remembered how we are affected on hearing the same thing concerning others."

13 For the Stoics, all emotions can be defined either as "mistaken opinion" or as the "result of a mistaken opinion" (Inwood 1999: 699). Typically, they place all emotions within four categories: "pleasure," "pain," "fear," and "desire." (Brennan 2005: 93) Since the basis for all these four is the underlying cognitive mistake, those who continue to have mistaken opinions will continue to experience all four emotions more or less equally. It may be the case that Nietzsche kept this knowledge at the back of his mind, also in *GS* 338: "happiness and misfortune [*Glück und Unglück*] are two siblings and twins who either grow up together or—as with you—*remain small* together!"

14 *D* 54 for instance explicitly mentions Marcus Aurelius as an example of how to take away actual pain by taking away the accompanying phantasy of pain.

15 The Stoically inspired exclamation that can be found frequently in the Notes of *D* "Was liegt an mir?" highlights the climax of rational restraint, the neglect of the importance of the self, and self-sacrifice in the pursuit of knowledge: "what is up to me?" "what is in my power?" See *NL* 15[59], *KSA* 9.655, *D* 494, *D* 547, Gaasterland (2017: 138–45). Moreover, several Stoics, Seneca being one of them, are known for their rather benevolent attitude regarding suicide.

16 We are also reminded of the description of "Two happy ones," portrayed in *GS* 303. The second of the two lives is the life of danger described earlier, and claims: "I know more about life because I have so often been on the verge of losing it; and precisely therefore do *I get* more out of life than any of you!"

17 Also the expression *Nierenprüfer* is relevant in this context, literally denoting someone who examines one's own kidneys; it appears in *GS* 308: "for you who scrupulously examine the inside of things and *know about conscience*!" and in *GS* 335 "*Long live physics!*," in the context of self-knowledge.

18 Which can also be well connected to what Nietzsche describes several years later in *Ecce Homo* as "Russian Fatalism" ("why I am so wise" 6).

19 Brusotti (1997: 455) also connects this aphorism explicitly with *amor fati*.

Works Cited

Ansell-Pearson, K. (2010), "For Mortal Souls: Philosophy and Therapeia in Nietzsche's *Dawn*," *Royal Institute of Philosophy Supplement*, 66: 137–63.
Ansell-Pearson, K. (2011), "Beyond Compassion: On Nietzsche's Moral Therapy in *Dawn*," *Continental Philosophy Review*, 44 (2): 179–204.
Bobzien, S. (2001), *Determinism and Freedom in Stoic Philosophy*, Oxford: Oxford University Press.
Boter, G. (1999), *The Encheiridion of Epictetus and Its Three Christian Adaptations*, Leiden: Brill.
Brennan, T. (2005), *The Stoic Life. Emotions, Duties, and Fate*, Oxford: Clarendon Press.
Brobjer, T. (2003), "Nietzsche's Reading of Epictetus," *Nietzsche-Studien*, 32: 429–32.
Brusotti, M. (1997), *Die Leidenschaft der Erkenntnis: Philosophie und ästhetische Lebensgestaltung bei Nietzsche von Morgenröthe bis Also sprach Zarathustra*, Berlin: W. de Gruyter.
Gaasterland, H. L. J. (2017), "Nietzsche's Rejection of Stoicism. A Reinterpretation of *Amor fati*," PhD diss., Leiden University.
Groff, P. (2004), "Al-Kindī and Nietzsche on the Stoic Art of Banishing Sorrow," *Journal of Nietzsche Studies*, 28 (1): 139–73.
Hadot, P. (1995), *Philosophy as a Way of Life. Spiritual Exercises from Socrates to Foucault*, trans. Michael Chase, Oxford: Blackwell.
Hadot, P. (2001), *The Inner Citadel. The Meditations of Marcus Aurelius*, trans. Michael Chase, Cambridge MA: Harvard University Press.
Hankinson, R. J. (1999), "Determinism and Indeterminism," in K. Algra, J. Barnes, J. Mansfield and M. Schofield (eds.), *The Cambridge History of Hellenistic Philosophy*, Cambridge: Cambridge University Press.
Inwood, B. (1999), "Stoic Ethics," in K. Algra, J. Barnes, J. Mansfield, and M. Schofield (eds.), *The Cambridge History of Hellenistic Philosophy*, Cambridge: Cambridge University Press.
Lane, M. (2007), "Honesty as the Best Policy. Nietzsche on *Redlichkeit* and the Contrast between Stoic and Epicurean Strategies of the Self," in Mark Bevis, Jill Hargis, and Sara Rushing (eds.), *Histories of Postmodernism*, 25–51, New York: Routledge.
Marcus Aurelius (2011), *Meditations*, trans. Robin Hard, Oxford: Oxford University Press.
Nietzsche, F. W. (1980), *Sämtliche Werke. Kritische Studienausgabe in 15 Bänden*, eds. Giorgio Colli and Mazzino Montinari, Munich and Berlin: W. de Gruyter.
Nietzsche, F. W. (1996), *Human, All Too Human. A Book for Free Spirits*, trans. R. J. Hollingdale, Cambridge: Cambridge University Press.
Nietzsche, F. W. (1997), *Daybreak*, trans. R. J. Hollingdale, eds. Maudemarie Clark and Brian Leiter, Cambridge: Cambridge University Press.
Nietzsche, F. W. (2001), *The Gay Science*, trans. Josephine Nauckhoff, ed. Bernard Williams, Cambridge: Cambridge University Press.

Nietzsche, F. W. (2005), *The Anti-Christ, Ecce Homo, Twilight of the Idols*, trans. Judith Norman, ed. Aaron Ridley, Cambridge: Cambridge University Press.

Nietzsche, F. W. (2007), *On the Genealogy of Morality*, trans. Carol Diethe, ed. Keith Ansell-Pearson, Cambridge: Cambridge University Press.

Nussbaum, M. (1994), "Pity and Mercy, Nietzsche's Stoicism," in Richard Schacht (ed.), *Nietzsche, Genealogy, Morality; Essays on Nietzsche's "On the Genealogy of Morality,"* 139–67, Berkeley and Los Angeles: University of California Press.

Primavera-Lévy, E. (2011), "'An sich gibt es keinen Schmerz.' Heroischer und physiologischer Schmerz bei Nietzsche im Kontext des späten 19. Jahrhunderts," *Nietzsche-Studien*, 40: 130–55.

Sellars, J. (2003), *The Art of Living. The Stoics on the Nature and Function of Philosophy*, Burlington, VT: Ashgate.

Sellars, J. (2006), "An Ethics of the Event, Deleuze's Stoicism," *Angelaki: Journal of the Theoretical Humanities*, II (3): 157–71.

Solomon, R. C. (2002), "Nietzsche on Fatalism and 'Free Will'," *Journal of Nietzsche Studies*, 23: 63–87.

Stern, T. (2013), "Nietzsche, *Amor Fati*, and *The Gay Science*," *Proceedings of the Aristotelian Society*, CXIII (2): 145–62.

Ure, M. (2008), *Nietzsche's Therapy; Self-Cultivation in the Middle Works*, Lanham, MD: Lexington Books.

Ure, M. (2009), "Nietzsche's Free Spirit Trilogy and Stoic Therapy," *Journal of Nietzsche Studies*, 38: 60–84.

5

Sovereign/Creature

Neostoicism in Benjamin's *Origin of the German Trauerspiel* and His Response to Carl Schmitt's *Political Theology*

Paula Schwebel

Walter Benjamin's analysis of the German *Trauerspiel*, or mourning play, owes a significant, and as yet unexplored, debt to Neostoicism. Neostoicism, which was popularized in the seventeenth century by Justus Lipsius, involved the synthesis of Roman Stoicism with Christian beliefs.[1] Benjamin makes numerous references to Stoicism and Neostoicism in his *Trauerspiel* book.[2] Nevertheless, the significance of Neostoic ideas for his analysis of the baroque plays has been almost entirely overlooked.[3] This may be due to the general neglect of Neostoicism in our reception of modern philosophy and political theory. But there was a revival of research into Neostoicism among German scholars of the Baroque in the period following the First World War, and Benjamin's *Trauerspiel* book draws on this scholarship.[4] As the scholarship shows, Neostoicism exerted a considerable influence on early modern natural and political philosophy (Dilthey 1914) and on cultural and literary works, including the German *Trauerspiele* (Welzig 1961; Stalder 1976; Schings 1966, 1971; Hoyt 1983).

Uncovering the influence of Neostoicism on Benjamin's idea of the *Trauerspiel* would be of significant interest in its own right. But my focus in this chapter is on the importance of Neostoicism for Benjamin's analysis of the representation of sovereignty in the baroque plays. Benjamin's discussion of the sovereign hero in the *Trauerspiel* has attracted considerable attention, since it is the primary locus of his engagement with Carl Schmitt.[5] Benjamin prominently references Schmitt's *Political Theology* (1922) in the section on sovereignty in his *Trauerspiel* book ([1928] 2009: 65–6). He also sent Schmitt a copy of his *Origin of the German Trauerspiel*, along with a letter professing the depth of the latter's influence on his presentation of the seventeenth-century concept of sovereignty (Benjamin 1997: vol. 3, 558).[6] Benjamin's evident debt to Schmitt has been the subject of much controversy.[7] Schmitt had enthusiastically embraced Nazism during the Third Reich, and was considered an unsavory correspondent for Benjamin, a left-wing Jewish intellectual, who ultimately took his own life while fleeing Nazi-occupied France. Seeking to save Benjamin from this "dangerous liaison,"[8] much of the literature on Benjamin's relationship to Schmitt has sought to demonstrate that Benjamin subtly but significantly subverts Schmitt's ideas.[9] I agree that Benjamin's conception of sovereignty differs in important ways from Schmitt's. Indeed, by uncovering the Neostoic elements in Benjamin's analysis of the *Trauerspiel*, I aim to demonstrate that Benjamin's portrait of the baroque sovereign rests on a fundamentally different metaphysical idea than Schmitt's concept of sovereignty.

Schmitt draws his concept of sovereignty from Jean Bodin's analysis of absolute power in his *Six livres de la république* (Schmitt [1922] 2006: 8–10). As I show in detail elsewhere, Bodin's account of sovereignty is laden with an underlying metaphysical voluntarism, which also colors Schmitt's conception of sovereignty.[10] According to the voluntarist, God's omnipotence is unconstrained by any independent necessity, apart from the logical principle of noncontradiction, and this is revealed in God's absolute freedom to suspend or alter the ordinary laws established in the creation. Bodin's voluntarism is prominently on display in his 1596 compendium of natural philosophy, the *Theatrum Universae Naturae* (Theater of Universal Nature) (Blair 1997: 116–52; Engster 2001: 47–81). Bodin argues that, by his "extraordinary" providence, God can suspend or alter the "ordinary" laws of nature at will, as is revealed in miracles.[11] In the *République* (1576), Bodin characterizes the sovereign's absolute power in similar terms, as the power to unilaterally repeal or alter the "ordinary" (i.e., positive) laws of the state, should the exigencies of the situation require it.[12] Schmitt employs the same distinction between the system of ordinary laws and the sovereign's absolute, or unlimited, power to suspend these laws in the state of exception ([1922] 2006: 5, 12). Confirming the voluntarist underpinnings of his idea of sovereignty, Schmitt points to the structural analogy between the sovereign's suspension of normal laws in the state of exception and God's suspension of the laws of nature in miracles ([1922] 2006: 36).[13]

Lipsian Neostoicism is diametrically opposed to voluntarism.[14] According to Lipsius, God's nature is immutable, and his providential plan for the universe is fixed and necessary. In other words, Lipsius acknowledges no "state of exception." Moreover, while Bodin and Schmitt depict the sovereign as a secular redemptive power, Lipsius conceives of the political sovereign as emphatically a creature. Lipsius argues that all creaturely life is governed by the necessary law of mutability—that is, all created things must decay and perish. Only God is exempt from the effects of transience; even the highest earthly power—the sovereign—falls under its sway. As a countermeasure to the transience of all things, Lipsius argues for the Stoic virtue of constancy, or the capacity to be unmoved by the fluctuations of external circumstances. Constancy, which has its seat in reason and its governance over the emotions, is the only genuine form of sovereignty available to human beings. In attaining constancy, the Stoic sage aspires to the immutability of God's nature.

In the *Trauerspiel*, according to Benjamin, sovereignty is represented by two extremes, both of which have their roots in Neostoicism: on the one hand, the monarch appears as a Stoic martyr, who is constant even in torments. On the other hand, the monarch appears as a tyrant, who falls prey to his conflicting emotions, demonstrating his subjection to creaturely mutability and a distinct failure of sovereignty.[15] The Neostoic association of mutability with a failure of sovereignty reveals the crux of Benjamin's disagreement with Schmitt. For Schmitt, the very mark of sovereignty resides in the sovereign's absolute freedom to change the law (or to change his mind, when the law emanates from his own command). But, for Benjamin, this is symptomatic of the tyrant's inconstancy, or his subservience to the flux of his desires.[16]

Two prefatory remarks are warranted before I launch into my argument: first, as much as I am reading Benjamin's *Trauerspiel* book through the lens of Lipsian Neostoicism, I am also reading Lipsius through a Benjaminian lens. While I argue that Benjamin's idea of the *Trauerspiel* has its roots in Neostoicism, I am equally convinced that there are also elements of the *Trauerspiel*, as Benjamin understands it, in Lipsius's dialogue *On Constancy*. I acknowledge that this is an unorthodox—albeit textually grounded—reading of Lipsius.

Second, it must be made clear from the outset that Benjamin is not endorsing the Neostoic position. It is characteristic of Benjamin's method for the interpretation of art that he rarely pronounces an evaluative judgment on his material. True to form, he delves into Neostoic ideas, not in order to affirm or reject them, but to give concrete expression to a historical idea. Nevertheless, in the details of Benjamin's presentation, he raises a potent critique of the Neostoic idea of reason's sovereignty over the emotions. Benjamin suggests that this idea of sovereignty is premised on the presumption of the guilt of creaturely life, which leads to reason's dictatorial repression of the creature's spontaneous impulses and feelings. The damming up of emotions in the name of reason's sovereignty leads, in Benjamin's analysis, to a pervasive mood of mourning. This is the broader significance of the trope of sovereignty in Benjamin's analysis of the mourning play, and it takes us beyond the strict confines of political philosophy.

1. Divine Providence in History: Natural Necessity, Mutability, and Fate

The resurgence of Stoicism in early modern Europe took place—contemporaneously with the rise of the baroque *Trauerspiel*—during a period of devastating religious wars. In face of the terror caused by warring religious factions, the revitalization of Stoicism exercised an intense appeal, since Stoicism offered a secular model of the virtuous life (Oestreich 1982: 8, 17; Cassirer 1961: 166–70). Neostoicism presents stoic thought, particularly that of Seneca, as the precursor to a Christian idea of virtue.[17] However, since stoic philosophy is grounded in natural reason, rather than religious dogma, it appealed to moderates of both confessions as well as to the *politiques*, who prized the security of the state above religious differences. While Neostoicism is secularizing in this sense, it does not banish God from the world; on the contrary, divine providence plays a fundamental role in the Neostoic conception of nature and history (which are synthesized in an idea of creation).

If I begin with an elucidation of Lipsius's account of the role of divine providence in the creation, it is because Benjamin's analysis of the *Trauerspiel* hinges around an idea of creaturely life—an idea that I see as grounded in Neostoicism. Benjamin presents the significance of the "creaturely" for the idea of the *Trauerspiel* through a comparison of the *Trauerspiel* to the medieval Passion play (Benjamin [1928] 2009: 76). What these two forms of drama have in common, according to Benjamin, is that they both perceive the "tragic" mournfulness of life to be immediately graspable in the events of history—that is, in temporal life, depicted as a play of insuperable despair (Benjamin [1928] 2009: 77–8). But whereas the medieval drama, like medieval historiography, regards temporal life as a fleeting stage within a narrative of salvation, Benjamin argues that, in the aftermath of the schisms of the church, a unified redemptive framework was radically called into question (Benjamin [1928] 2009: 77–8). Hence, the baroque drama, like the baroque understanding of historical life, turned its full attention to the state of creation, understood as a spatial totality—a sublunary *world*—rather than as a temporal phase to be suffered through on the way to redemption (Benjamin [1928] 2009: 81, 84; cf. Benjamin [1923] 2004: 378).

Benjamin argues that the question of salvation remained an enduring preoccupation throughout the Baroque, but that access to the divine had ceased to be direct. Such glimmers of revelation as there were could only be grasped indirectly from the reflected light of divine providence in profane creation (Benjamin [1928] 2009: 79). On this point, Benjamin distinguishes between the Spanish mourning plays of Calderón and the German *Trauerspiele*. The Spanish plays presented the sovereign as a secularized redemptive power ([1928] 2009: 81), which is consistent with Schmitt's representation of the sovereign in *Political Theology*. The German plays, however, stand out for their "rash flight into a nature deprived of grace" ([1928] 2009: 81). The sovereign hero in these plays is not presented as a God on earth, but is emphatically a creature; indeed, he is the representative figure of creaturely life ([1928] 2009: 85). As such, he is "driven along to a cataract" with the rest of creation ([1928] 2009: 66). Benjamin argues that it is the sovereign's downfall, rather than his status as sacrosanct, that exercised fascination in the German plays ([1928] 2009: 70). The fall of the highest earthly power not only reinforced the image of historical life as an endless play of mourning—literally, a *Trauerspiel*—the sovereign's downfall also provided an indirect confirmation of God's providence, since it was interpreted as evidence of divine justice in punishing guilty creation.

Benjamin's representation of the sovereign hero of the *Trauerspiel* is thus diametrically opposed to Schmitt's sovereign: While Schmitt's sovereign is a transcendent and redemptive figure, Benjamin portrays the baroque sovereign as confined to creaturely immanence. The fall of the sovereign epitomizes the fallen state of creation (Benjamin [1928] 2009: 85). The political theology of the sovereign-*creature* differs starkly from that of the sovereign-*God*. The marks of the sovereign-creature are subjection to divine providence, submission to divine judgment, and necessary downfall, as punishment for the guilt of creaturely life.

I find the philosophical basis for Benjamin's political theology of creaturely life in Lipsian Neostoicism, particularly in Lipsius's dialogue *On Constancy*.[18] *On Constancy*, which bears the subtitle *in publicis malis* (constancy in times of public evil), begins with a description of the turmoil, instability, and despair caused by the religiously fueled civil wars in the Netherlands. The so-called public evils, referred to in Lipsius's title, include these wars, as well as pestilence, tyranny, slaughter, and famine ([1595] 2006: 42). This litany of "evils"—which admit of no nuance in degree, and which give rise to bitter lament—provides insight into how historical life was experienced at the time. On this point, *On Constancy* converges with the German dramas of Benjamin's study.[19]

Written as a dialogue in two books, *On Constancy* depicts a conversation between a young "Lipsius" and his wise and older friend, "Langius."[20] The dialogue begins with "Lipsius" lamenting to his friend that the civil war in Belgium at the time makes him wish to flee his homeland. He seeks peace, stability, and security, and he can no longer find these in the Netherlands. "Langius" responds by directing "Lipsius" to the ideas of the Roman Stoa.[21] According to "Langius's" counsel, external events are, in themselves, neither good nor bad; it is our opinions and emotional reactions that color these events as negative or positive.[22] The troubles afflicting "Lipsius" are internal rather than external—the product of a diseased mind, rather than realities in themselves.

Through the character of "Langius," Lipsius presents a series of arguments intended to show that the subjective experience of historical life—as an endless parade of "evils"—is rooted in false and distorting opinions and emotions ([1595] 2006: 54). The first of these arguments is that everything that happens—including the so-called evils—has its source in divine providence. Providence gives rise to a fixed and immutable necessity. In his second argument, "Langius" discusses two forms of necessity: the natural necessity that all created things will decay and perish, and the immutable series of causes dictated by fate. In his third argument (which I discuss in §2), "Langius" offers his version of a theodicy, arguing that God sends the "evils" to strengthen the virtuous and punish the guilty.[23] Ultimately, since everything that comes from God is both necessary and good, the perception of these events *as evils* must be cleared away and replaced with true understanding.

Lipsius's overarching argument—that these "evils" have no objective character, but that they stem from the subjective torments of a mind in the grips of distorting thoughts and feelings—resonates with Benjamin's argument about the ultimately phantasmagorical character of evil for the Baroque: "[Evil] means precisely the non-existence of what it presents.... There is no evil in the world. It arises in man himself" ([1928] 2009: 233). *On Constancy* ends with "Lipsius" declaring, "I have escaped the evil, and found the good" ([1595] 2006: 129). Benjamin attributes a similar arc to the *Trauerspiel*, which ends with a radical *shift in perspective*—a reversal from melancholy immersion in everything sorrowful and corrupt in history, to a beatific vision in which the whole phantasmagoria of evil abruptly *vanishes* ([1928] 2009: 232). According to Benjamin, the source of dramatic tension in the *Trauerspiel* should not be sought in the endless scenes portraying the stoic constancy of martyrs, or the downfall of tyrants; rather, it derives from a deeper question about the salvation of humankind ([1928] 2009: 78–9). These dramatic stakes are revealed in the reversal, from the depths of depraved feeling to right reason, which is anchored in God's vision of the world.

The lynchpin of Lipsius's positive conception of history is the notion of divine providence—namely, God's governance and foresight over everything that transpires in the universe. By appealing to providence, "Langius" endeavors to show not only that the so-called public evils are sent by God but also that they are necessary and unavoidable. Both the necessity that inheres in the nature of things and the necessity of fate, or destiny, issue from providence.[24] Since God's providential plan for the universe is fixed, nothing in nature and history is contingent, or alterable in its course, and there is no "state of exception."

Taking on natural necessity first, "Langius" argues that it is an inherent property of all created things to "fall into mutability and alteration" (Lipsius [1595] 2006: 58). Only God is firm and stable (Lipsius [1595] 2006: 59), whereas all of creation must inevitably decay and perish (Lipsius [1595] 2006). The necessity of generation and decay encompasses both natural and political entities. Just as natural creation decays and dies, so too do great cities and kingdoms fall into ruin (Lipsius [1595] 2006: 60). Ruins—especially the ruins of great civilizations—are a source of *wonder*, since they simultaneously manifest the irresistible transience of created things, and also point, indirectly, to the divine law that necessitates the downfall of creation.[25] It is tempting to speculate that ruins have an equivalent significance in the natural theology of Neostoicism as miracles do within voluntarism.[26]

The notion that all created things must perish and decay encapsulates what Benjamin means by baroque natural history. History and nature are synthesized in the idea of transience. On the one hand, the historical process, understood in terms of a continuous cycle of generation and corruption, is absorbed back into nature. Political upheavals, such as the religious wars, are analyzed as the expression of a periodically destructive natural force, rather than as the result of human agency. As Benjamin puts it, "The constantly repeated drama of the rise and fall of princes, the steadfastness of unshakeable virtue, appeared to the writers as less a manifestation of morality than as the natural aspect of the course of history, essential in its permanence" ([1928] 2009: 88). On the other hand, nothing in the created world is deemed immune from the ravages of time. Since transience demarcates creation from the timelessness of God, the historical process afflicts profane nature as much as the world of human artifice. History is thus "imprinted" on nature in the characters of transience, or as Benjamin puts it, "it is fallen nature which bears the imprint of the progression of history" ([1928] 2009: 180).

Underlying this woeful spectacle of the "casual and inconstant variableness of all things," "Langius" argues that true understanding will discern the underlying necessity of God's providence, which arranges "all things . . . in a steady and immovable order" (Lipsius [1595] 2006: 62). From providence, "Langius" now derives the second aspect of necessity: namely, fate. Fate refers to the "steady and immovable" order of causes, which seems to suggest a strict causal determinism that leaves no room for chance events, miracles, or acts of free will.[27] "Langius" acknowledges the need to tread carefully at this juncture in his argument, since the Stoic idea of fate appears to come into conflict with Christian belief (Lipsius [1595] 2006: 62). Most seriously, fate seems to bind God's will, subjecting God to the fixed necessity of what he preestablished when he created the world (Lipsius [1595] 2006: 65). Lipsius draws a subtle distinction between Stoic fate and "true fate," which harmonizes with Christian beliefs. But what he refers to as "true fate" bears more than a passing resemblance to the Stoic idea of fate, provided that the latter is carefully interpreted (Sellars 2014b). Properly understood, God's will is not bound by fate. Rather, a fatal necessity results from the *immutability* of God's nature. God is "stayed, resolute, and immutable, always one, and like himself, not wavering or varying in those things which he once willed and foresaw" (Lipsius [1595] 2006: 63). The immutability of God's nature is due to his perfection, rather than the limitation of his freedom. Since God is supremely good and rational, he has already chosen the best and most rational course of events, and therefore has no reason or desire to change his mind (Sellars 2014b: 665).

The argument that God's will is immutable highlights the polar contrast between Neostoicism and voluntarism. Neostoicism decisively rejects the voluntarist's identification of absolute power with God's freedom to contravene his own decrees. Indeed, Lipsius associates changeability with the imperfection of creaturely life. Alteration, as we have seen, is what divides the creation most sharply from God.

2. The Suffering of the Constant Martyr and the Madness of the Tyrant in Lipsius's Theodicy

To his argument about divine providence and the fatal necessity to which it gives rise, Lipsius adds a third argument about divine justice and its mysterious workings in the world. According to "Langius," what we perceive to be "evil" cannot actually be evil, since these things proceed from God, and whatever emanates from God must be good (Lipsius [1595] 2006: 85–6). Lipsius's theodicy holds particular interest for us, since it is here that two figures are introduced—the Stoic martyr and the tyrant—which, according to Benjamin, form the stock representations of sovereignty in the *Trauerspiel* ([1928] 2009: 69).

Lipsius argues that there are three main ways that God utilizes suffering for our benefit: first, he uses adversity to test and prove the virtue of innocent people; second, he sends calamities to chastise and correct sinners; and third, he makes use of "evils" to punish the incorrigibly wicked ([1595] 2006: 89).[28] The idea that virtue is tested and confirmed through adversity gives rise to the image of the Stoic martyr, who remains constant throughout torments. The martyr is a "mirror" of virtue, since "the Constancy and Patience of good men in miseries is a clear light to this obscure world" ([1595] 2006: 91).

Despite the Christian trappings of martyrdom, the torments of the Stoic martyr are decidedly of the flesh. Lipsius gives several examples, which intend to show that the loss of material possessions, bodily integrity, and even life, cannot destroy the hero's virtue:

> Bias lost both his goods and his country, but his words sound in the ears of men at this day: "that they should carry all their goods about them." Regulus was unworthily put to death by torments, but his worthy example of keeping his promise lives yet. Papinianus was murdered by a tyrant, but the same butcherly axe that cut off his head emboldens us to suffer death for justice's sake. Finally, so many notable citizens we see violently and injuriously either banished or murdered; but out of rivers of their blood we do, as it were, drink Virtue and Constancy every day. ([1595] 2006: 91)

The Neostoic variation on martyrdom involves the capacity to patiently endure bodily pain.[29] Benjamin thus refers to the martyr figure in the baroque dramas as a *radical stoic*: "the perfect martyr is no more released from the sphere of immanence than is the ideal image of the monarch. In the drama of the baroque he is a radical stoic, for whom the occasion to prove himself is a struggle for the crown or a religious dispute ending in torture and death" (Benjamin [1928] 2009: 73).

At the other extreme, Lipsius singles out the figure of the tyrant, whose downfall exemplifies God's justice in punishing the wicked:

> These punishments upon tyrants and spoilers of the whole world must necessarily be inflicted sometimes, that they may be mirrors to admonish us, "that it is the eye of justice which beholds all things," which also may cry out to other princes and people, "learn justice now by this, and God above despise no more." (Lipsius [1595] 2006: 93)

The tyrant's downfall serves as a sign and confirmation of divine justice. Note, however, that it is impossible to tell, from the degree of suffering alone, whether one is witnessing the testing of a martyr or the punishment of a tyrant: both are set on the rack and drowned in blood. The only difference—and it is a significant one—is that the martyr exhibits the Stoic virtue of constancy, or equanimity. His mental composure remains unscathed while his property and bodily integrity are destroyed. The tyrant, on the other hand, falls into mental disarray as a symptom of the disordered nature in him. Lipsius writes: "Do you see a tyrant breathing out threatenings and murders, whose delight is in doing harm, who could be content to perish himself, so he may persecute others? Let him alone; he strays from his right mind. And God, as it were, by an invisible string leads him to his destruction" (Lipsius [1595] 2006: 87).[30] Benjamin confirms that what fascinated the baroque audience was the image of the tyrant, as "the summit of creation, erupting into madness like a volcano and destroying himself and his entire court" ([1928] 2009: 70; cf. Benjamin [1923] 2004: 368).

Despite the extreme representations of God's justice in the testing of constant martyrs and the punishment of raving tyrants, Lipsius's theodicy makes it impossible to distinguish between innocence and guilt on strictly moral grounds. According to Lipsius, it is a measure of our ignorance and finitude that we tend to atomize the world into distinct individuals, whereas God, in his higher wisdom, perceives nature as one integral whole: "know this, that God joins together those things which we through frailty and ignorance do separate and put asunder, and that he beholds families, towns, kingdoms, not as things confused or distinguished, but as one body and entire nature" (Lipsius [1595] 2006: 108–9). Because God perceives each individual as participating in the guilt-context of the whole, he may *transfer* punishments, afflicting an entire community for an individual's crimes, or else sacrificing an individual for the crimes of the community. "Lipsius" raises the concern that innocent people are thus unjustly punished, but "Langius" reassures him that no one is completely free from error or vice ([1595] 2006: 106–7). This belief resonates with the Stoic idea that the perfect sage is a rarity, and that anyone who is not a sage exists in a state of madness, folly, and corruption.[31] It also recalls the doctrine of original sin, which is how Lipsius's Christian readership would have received this idea.[32] In both the Neostoic discourse of transferred punishments, and the Christian discourse of original sin, guilt is distributed throughout the field of creation, rather than concentrated in individuals.

The pervasive guilt of all creaturely life is a central theme in Benjamin's analysis of the *Trauerspiel*. Benjamin qualifies this guilt as *natural*, rather than *moral*, since the corruption of creaturely life is less a matter of moral agency than of the periodic stirring of destructive nature, which shapes historical events ([1928] 2006: 129). Echoing Lipsius's argument that punishments can fall on an entire community, Benjamin argues that "in the *Trauerspiel* [death] frequently takes the form of a communal fate, as if summoning all the participants before the highest court" ([1928] 2006: 136).

According to Benjamin, the inevitable downfall of creaturely life is atonement for natural guilt (Benjamin [1928] 2009: 131; cf. Benjamin [1923] 2004: 378). But, above all, it is the downfall of the sovereign—the representative of creaturely life—that displays the subjection of creation as such to divine judgment. The efficacy of divine justice in history is most evident when the sovereign falls prey to the necessity of the divine law: "At the moment when the ruler indulges in the most violent display of power, both history and the higher power, which checks its vicissitudes, are recognized as manifest in him" ([1928] 2009: 70). Thus, if the baroque sovereign appeared to the age as "the principal exponent" and "representative of history," it is primarily because the age saw its historical predicament represented in the sovereign's downfall ([1928] 2009: 62; 65). The sovereign's downfall registers as a judgment on the guilt of creation as a whole: "For if the tyrant falls, not simply in his own name, as an individual, but as a ruler and in the name of mankind and history, then his fall has the quality of a judgment, in which the subject too is implicated" ([1928] 2009: 72).

3. The Sovereignty of Reason, or Political Psychology

According to the voluntarism of Bodin and Schmitt, the state of exception is a metaphysical reality. Because the voluntarist considers the entire order of creation to be contingent on God's will, which is changeable, a political philosophy that takes voluntarism seriously must presuppose that there will be circumstances that have not—and could not have been—anticipated within the system of normal laws. Following Bodin, Schmitt's answer to the contingency and changeability of the situation is to invest the sovereign with power that is discretionary, flexible, and not bound by positive laws. By contrast, the state of exception has no objective reality for the Neostoic. While Lipsius does not deny that the experience of historical life is dominated by continual flux—an impression cemented by the cataclysmic religious wars—he contends that the reality underlying this experience is a fixed and necessary order, grounded in the immutability of God's will. Lipsius thus locates the source of volatility in the subject's *inner life*—in the false and distorting opinions and emotions.

As a countermeasure against the subject's emotional turbulence, Lipsius champions the sovereignty of reason. Reason's sovereignty—which Lipsius considers to be the only genuine form of sovereignty possible for human beings—involves bridling the opinions and emotions and aligning one's beliefs and behavior with the immutability of divine and natural law: "To obey [reason] is to bear rule, and to be subject to it is to have the sovereignty in all human affairs. Who so obeys her is lord of all lusts and rebellious affections" (Lipsius [1595] 2006: 39). To be sovereign over one's lusts and affections is to attain a state of constancy, in which one is indifferent to the vicissitudes of changing circumstances (Lipsius [1595] 2006: 37). The association of sovereignty with constancy is radically opposed to Schmitt's notion of sovereignty as an elastic power, which responds to the flux of historical circumstances by suspending or altering the law.

The concept of reason's sovereignty is at the heart of Benjamin's analysis of the *Trauerspiel*. Although Benjamin acknowledges the significance of Schmitt's insight that sovereignty reveals itself in the decision on the state of exception ([1928] 2006: 65–6), his discussion of the motif of sovereignty revolves around the "state of emergency in the soul, the rule of the emotions" ([1928] 2006: 74). Indeed, Benjamin argues that the particularities of the *Trauerspiel* as a genre are essentially connected to the Neostoic project of overcoming the emotions. As he argues, the authors of the *Trauerspiel*—who purported to be following in the footsteps of ancient authorities, but who distorted these ideas beyond recognition—replaced Aristotle's notion of the *catharsis* of fear and pity with the Neostoic virtue of *apatheia*[33]:

> The *Trauerspiel* should fortify the virtue of its audience. And if there was a particular virtue which was indispensable in its heroes, and edifying for its public, then this was the old virtue of ἀπάθεια. The association of the stoic ethic with the theory of modern tragedy was effected in Holland; and Lipsius had remarked that Aristotelian 'ἔλεος' [pity] should be understood exclusively as an active impulse to alleviate the physical and mental suffering of others, and not as a pathological collapse at the sight of a terrifying fate, not as *pusillanimitas* but as *misericordia*. (Benjamin [1928] 2009: 61)[34]

In the pursuit of *apatheia*, the violent emotions of fear and pity are aroused in the *Trauerspiel*, not simply to be purged, but to be stripped naked and humiliated—revealed in the light of reason to be the symptoms of a diseased and corrupted mind. The dramatic reversal of the baroque plays—which run their course from the depths of terror and mourning to the evaporation of these emotions in blessed reason—is thus tied to the extirpation of these emotions.

Benjamin links the emotions of fear and pity to the drama of the tyrant and the martyr-drama, respectively ([1928] 2009: 69). Indeed, the tyrant and the Stoic martyr find their particular significance in the "state of emergency in the soul" and the possibility of its overcoming: the tyrant is ruled by his emotions, while the Stoic martyr succeeds in overruling them. This suggests that when tyrants and martyrs appear as *types* within the *Trauerspiel*, it is not only as the representative figures of political life. Rather, they appear primarily as personifications of distinct psychological states, or as allegories for virtue and vice (Benjamin [1928] 2009: 91).

In *On Constancy*, Lipsius applies the political concepts of "sovereignty" and "tyranny" to his discussion of the subject's psyche. This is why I refer to Lipsius's argument as a *political psychology*. In politicizing the psyche, Lipsius conceives of the human soul as a battleground between two opposing forces: reason, on the one hand, and opinion and the emotions, on the other ([1595] 2006: 38). According to Lipsius, both of these forces vie for sovereignty ([1595] 2006: 38), but only the sovereignty of reason is legitimate, whereas the rule of the emotions is tyrannical.[35]

The war between reason and the emotions is rooted, for Lipsius, in a division within our natures: we are both embodied and rational beings ([1595] 2006: 38–9). Our souls are not purely rational, since they are also responsive to our bodies, as is attested to by our feelings and sensations ([1595] 2006: 39). Appealing to Seneca's idea of the sparks of divine reason within us, Lipsius argues that the purely rational part of our minds emanates from the divine, and orients us toward God's eternal laws ([1595] 2006: 38–9).[36] Reason's sovereignty is thus by *divine right*. Lipsius maintains that reason, as an indwelling remnant of God, is the seat of constancy and virtue ([1595] 2006: 39).

On the other hand, our opinions and emotions derive from the impure mixture of the soul with the body, whereby the soul is "infected and a little corrupted with the filth of the body and the contagion of the senses" ([1595] 2006: 39). Whereas Lipsius considers reason to have its source in God, he argues that the body has its source in the earth. As the offspring of the body, the opinions and emotions also resemble the earth in their mutability and corruption. Opinion, "whose seat is the senses, whose birth is the earth . . . tends downwards and savours nothing of high and heavenly matters. It is vain, uncertain, deceitful, evil in counsel, evil in judgment" ([1595] 2006: 40). Since opinion is immersed in the ebb and flow of creaturely life, its telltale sign is flux: "Today it desires a thing, tomorrow it defies the same. It commends this, it condemns that" ([1595] 2006: 40). Opinion is thus the seat of inconstancy and vice ([1595] 2006: 40).

Lipsius not only identifies the rule of opinion and emotions with a state of tyranny, he also portrays the tyrant himself as overcome by the rule of his emotions. Citing Sallust in the *Politica*, he represents the tyrannical prince as someone "whose desires are as fluctuating as they are strong, and often contradictory" ([1589] 2004: 381). The figure of the tyrant thus personifies the tyranny of the emotions over the soul. This personification resonates with Benjamin's typology of the tyrant in the *Trauerspiel*: "In the course of the action [the tyrant's] will is increasingly undermined by his sensibility: and he ends in madness" ([1928] 2009: 99).[37]

The image of the tyrant suffering, to the point of madness, under the rule of his emotions reveals to Benjamin the dialectical proximity of the tyrant to the figure of the martyr ([1928] 2009: 73). (Note that Benjamin also discerns an element of tyranny concealed in the martyr-drama—particularly in the martyr's *dictatorial* repression of her emotions—as I will discuss later). With respect to the element of martyrdom in the drama of tyranny, Benjamin refers to the common baroque perception that to rule is to bear a heavy burden: "Just as Christ, the King, suffered in the name of mankind, so, in the eyes of the writers of the baroque, does royalty in general" ([1928] 2009: 73). But the suffering of the tyrant is described in a particularly Stoic fashion: he is depicted as *inwardly tortured* by his perturbing and violent emotions. According to Benjamin, the insanity that accompanies the tyrant's downfall springs from an excess of *fear*. This characterization comes straight out of Lipsius,[38] who observes that tyrants are constantly tormented by fear and suspicion, which leads to the eventual overthrow of their minds: "Add to this the mental agony and torment," he writes—citing Tacitus in the *Politica*—for "if the minds of tyrants were opened, wounds and slashes would be visible: just as when bodies are wounded with the whip, so their minds are wounded by cruelty, lust and bad decisions" ([1589] 2004: 693). Lipsius construes this mental torture as an "internal punishment" sent by God ([1595] 2006: 101–3).

The dialectical martyrdom of tyranny culminates with the representation of the prince as the paradigm of a melancholy man (Benjamin [1928] 2009: 142). Benjamin's portrayal of the melancholy prince bears a striking, yet unstated resemblance to Lipsius's characterization of the tyrant as assailed by his emotions, especially fear: "melancholy, whose domination over man is marked by shudders of fear, is regarded by scholars as the source of those manifestations which form the obligatory accompaniment when despots meet their end. It is taken for granted that serious cases culminate in violent insanity" ([1928] 2009: 143-4). The baroque theory of melancholy, which Benjamin outlines, is profoundly Lipsian. Consider the "physiology" of melancholy that Benjamin finds in Gryphius's *Leo Armenius*. Like Lipsius, Gryphius describes the oppressive rule over the mind by that part of the soul that is affected by the body: "Or is it only the imagination that oppresses the tired spirit, which, because it is in the body, loves its own affliction?" (Benjamin [1928] 2009: 146; cf. Gryphius 1991: 77). Recall that, for Lipsius, the body is born of the earth, which explains why the emotions and opinions, as the offspring of the body, are mutable and corrupt. The earth has the same significance in Benjamin's discussion of melancholy: "For all the wisdom of the melancholic is subject to the nether world; it is secured by immersion in the life of creaturely things, and it hears nothing of the voice of revelation. Everything Saturnine points down into the depths of the earth" ([1928] 2009: 152). The mutability of earthbound and creaturely life gives rise to the inconstancy of the melancholic, and in the tyrant, this manifests itself as indecisiveness: "The indecisiveness of the prince, in particular, is nothing other than saturnine *acedia*. . . . The fall of the tyrant is caused by indolence of the heart" ([1928] 2009: 152).

For Benjamin, it is evident that Schmitt's idea of sovereignty must culminate in tyranny: "The theory of sovereignty which takes as its example the special case in which dictatorial powers are unfolded, positively demands the completion of the image of the sovereign, as tyrant" ([1928] 2009: 69). However, what stands out in Benjamin's characterization of the tyrant is not the unfolding of "dictatorial powers," but the inadequacy of the sovereign-*creature* to perform his fundamental task. Whereas Schmitt makes the monarch's *decision* on the exception constitutive of sovereignty, Benjamin portrays the monarch as mired in *indecisiveness* due to the tyranny of the emotions, which overrule his mind:

> The prince, who is responsible for making the decision to proclaim the state of emergency, reveals, at the first opportunity, that he is almost incapable of making a decision. . . . What is conspicuous . . . is not so much the sovereignty evident in the stoic turns of phrase, as the sheer arbitrariness of a constantly shifting emotional storm. (1928] 2009: 71)

Measured against the rational sovereignty of the Stoic sage, whose constancy mirrors the immutability of God's nature, the tyrant's continuously changing impulses are evidence of a distinct failure of sovereignty. In keeping with the Neostoic view of the emotions as earthbound and creaturely, Benjamin contends that in the figure of the tyrant, "the supreme creature, the beast can re-emerge with unsuspected power" (1928] 2009: 86). Thus, far from identifying the mutability of the monarch's will with transcendence, Benjamin follows Lipsius in conceiving of the tyrant's emotional flux as a mark of the corruption of his nature, which, as we recall, is representative of the natural guilt of creation as such.

Benjamin's deduction of the element of tyranny within the drama of martyrdom also stems from his interpretation of Neostoicism. Recall that, according to Benjamin, the baroque martyr is "a radical stoic," who exhibits virtue by patiently enduring agonies ([1928] 2009: 73). Benjamin finds an aspect of tyranny concealed within the stoic virtue of constancy, insofar as it involves the dictatorial rule of reason over the emotions:

> The function of the tyrant is the restoration of order in the state of emergency: a dictatorship whose utopian goal will always be to replace the unpredictability of historical accident with the iron constitution of the laws of nature. But the stoic technique also aims to establish a corresponding fortification against a state of emergency in the soul, the rule of the emotions. It too seeks to set up a new, anti-historical creation . . . which is no less far removed from the innocent state of primal creation than the dictatorial constitution of the tyrant. ([1928] 2009: 74)

According to Benjamin's analysis, the "stoic technique" leads to the creation of a *second nature* ("a new, anti-historical creation"), constituted by the rule of reason over the emotions. This second nature is insulated from the vicissitudes of external circumstances (it is "anti-historical").[39] But fortification against the rule of the emotions is only possible as a result of the subject's tyrannical treatment of *first nature*.

This passage is significant, since it reveals Benjamin's critical stance toward the Neostoic ideal of reason's sovereignty. As Benjamin suggests, the "stoic technique" does violence to the immediacy of creaturely life. Lipsius justifies this violence by casting the emotions as tyrannical usurpers of reason's legitimate rule. For him, the emotions are not only inimical to peace and stability; they are also vile and base, rooted in *guilty* creation. Reason thus fights on God's side in its holy war against the emotions. But Benjamin rebukes this position when he characterizes the spontaneous immediacy of first nature as "the *innocent* state of primal creation" (my emphasis). Here we can see that Benjamin sides with suffering nature. He rejects both the Neostoic designation of creaturely life as guilty as well as the repressive restraint of the emotions in the name of reason's sovereignty.

In discerning an aspect of tyranny within the Neostoic ideal of reason's sovereignty, Benjamin characterizes Stoic "virtue" as *culpable* for its violence to first nature, while he recasts Stoic "vice" as the *innocent* expression of creaturely life. He thus reverses the valences of guilt and innocence as they appear in Neostoicism. In a corresponding reversal, which overturns the Baroque association of melancholy with the tyrannical rule of the emotions, Benjamin discerns the root of mournfulness in reason's repression of creaturely life. He insinuates that Stoic *apatheia*, or its early modern revival, is itself the source of a profound mood of mourning, caused by the "deadening of the emotions" ([1928] 2009: 140). He amplifies this theme, albeit in somewhat different terms, in his discussion of baroque allegory in the latter part of the *Trauerspiel* book. Benjamin finds a dichotomy in allegorical language between the creaturely voice, on the one hand, and the rule of signification, or meaning, on the other ([1928] 2009: 201–2). This division within language reflects the duality that Neostoicism discerns within the subject between creaturely emotions and divine reason. For Benjamin, the root cause of mournfulness is the repressive rule of meaning, which blocks the creature's spontaneous expression of feeling:

> And the spoken word is only afflicted by meaning, so to speak, as if by an inescapable disease; it breaks off in the middle of the process of resounding, and the damming up of the feeling, which was ready to pour forth, provokes mourning. Here, meaning is encountered, and will continue to be encountered as the reason for mournfulness ([1928] 2009: 209).[40]

Much of Benjamin's *Trauerspiel* book is devoted to the exposition of a historically concrete idea; indeed, my work in this chapter has been to unfold this idea, which reveals its particular debt to Neostoicism in the baroque typology of sovereignty. However, Benjamin's own philosophical commitments are revealed in his idea of the mournfulness of creation, which results from reason's "dictatorial" repression of the spontaneous expression of feeling.[41] Although Benjamin does not explicitly voice this critique of Neostoicism (nor is it the intention of his text to engage with Neostoicism in this way), his solidarity with suffering creation is antithetical to Lipsius's idea of reason's sovereignty. Nevertheless, Benjamin's recourse to Neostoicism reveals Schmitt's conception of sovereignty in a new light. As the contrast between Schmitt's voluntaristic sovereign and the constancy of the Stoic sage suggests, the rationalization of human life makes a certain idea of governance tangible: one that is linked to self-discipline and calculative control. Without the discipline of reason, Benjamin implies that the monarch's rule can only be arbitrary and tyrannical.

Notes

1. The Belgian humanist, Justus Lipsius, is the author most prominently associated with the revival of Stoic thought in seventeenth-century Europe. Other Neostoics who followed in Lipsius's footsteps include Guillaume Du Vair and Pierre Charron of France, and Francisco de Quevedo of Spain. For studies of Lipsius's life and thought, see Jason Lewis Saunders (1955) and Mark Morford (1991). For works focusing on Neostoicism and the history of political thought, see Gerhard Oestreich (1991), Nannerl O. Keohane (1980), Richard Tuck (1993), and Christopher Brooke (2012).
2. Benjamin makes numerous references to Stoicism and Neostoicism ([1928] 2009: 61, 71, 73–4, 78, 88–9, 112, 140 and 158). He refers to Lipsius once by name ([1928] 2009: 61). He also refers to the "pseudo-antique" Stoicism of the Baroque ([1928] 2009: 140) and Seneca's influence on the German Baroque ([1928] 2009: 50–1, 59, and 218).
3. At least this is the case in English-language scholarship, with the exception of Beatrice Hanssen, who briefly mentions the significance of Dilthey's interpretation of the Roman Stoa for Benjamin's idea of natural history in the *Trauerspiel* book (2000: 52). In the German scholarship, there has been more awareness of Neostoic ideas in the *Trauerspiel*, and of their significance for illuminating Benjamin's theory of the baroque dramas. See, for instance, Achim Geisenhanslüke (2016: 76) and Hans-Jürgen Schings (1971).
4. One of the key texts that reintroduced the ideas of Neostoicism into the history of philosophy was Wilhelm Dilthey's *Weltanschauung und Analyse des Menschen seit Renaissance und Reformation* (1914). Benjamin makes reference to Dilthey's text, as well as the body of scholarship on the Baroque that Dilthey inspired.
5. The literature devoted to understanding Benjamin's engagement with Carl Schmitt is extensive. Some important recent works, which discuss Benjamin's engagement with Schmitt on the concept of sovereignty, include Horst Bredekamp (1999), Giorgio Agamben (2005), Samuel Weber (2008), Marc de Wilde (2011), and Annika (Yannik) Thiem (2013).
6. Bredekamp (2016) gives a thorough account of how—after years of being repressed or ignored—Benjamin's letter to Schmitt (dated December 9, 1930) gradually became public between 1956 and 1974, following Schmitt's reference to it in an appendix to his 1956 book, *Hamlet or Hecuba* (ibid.: 680–1; cf. Schmitt [1956] 2009: 62).
7. Giorgio Agamben writes that, since its publication, Benjamin's letter "has always appeared scandalous" (2005: 52), and in Jacob Taubes's words, Benjamin's letter was nothing less than "a ticking bomb," which "comprehensively shatters our preconceptions regarding the intellectual history of the Weimar period" (2013: 16).

8   In a 1934 letter to Gretel Adorno, Benjamin reflects on the importance of "dangerous liaisons"—that is, encounters between extreme positions—for his work (Benjamin 1997: vol. 2, 1369). "Dangerous liaisons" is also the title of Susanne Heil's 1996 monograph on the relationship between Benjamin and Schmitt.
9   Marc de Wilde (2011) chronicles the different stages in the secondary literature that has emerged since Benjamin's letter to Schmitt was first published in 1974. According to de Wilde, the earliest responses were split between those who saw the letter as indicating a disturbing proximity between far left- and far right-wing positions during the Weimar period (Ellen Kennedy 1987; Taubes 2013) and those who regarded the affinity expressed by Benjamin in his letter to Schmitt as superficial and misleading (Martin Jay 1987; Ulrich Preuss 1987). De Wilde observes a more nuanced approach in recent interpretations of the Benjamin-Schmitt relationship, citing Samuel Weber (2008), and Giorgio Agamben (2005), among others. These more recent positions have emphasized that, while borrowing Schmitt's concepts and method, Benjamin injected new meaning into these concepts by transposing them into a different context (de Wilde 2011: 365).
10 See Chapter Two in my forthcoming book *The Political Metaphysics of Sovereignty in Carl Schmitt and Walter Benjamin: "The Prince is the Cartesian God."* Several scholars have noted Bodin's underlying voluntarism, and have commented on the correspondence between Bodin's sovereign and the voluntaristic God, including Margherita Isnardi Parente (1973) and Daniel Engster (2001: 47–81).
11 Bodin employs a variation of the Scholastic distinction between God's "absolute" and his "ordained" power. This distinction was originally used—for instance, by St. Thomas Aquinas—to differentiate between what it is logically possible for God to do (i.e., God's power considered absolutely), and what God actually decreed in the creation (whereby his will is ordained in accordance with the common laws of nature). A new meaning of this distinction emerged in the last quarter of the thirteenth century, which had its source in papal law. The canonists referred to the pope's plenitude of power (*plenitudo potestatis*) to suspend or alter particular laws, on a discretionary basis, when the common good of the church was deemed to be at stake. This prerogative came to be referred to as the Pope's "absolute" power (Mika Ojakangas 2012: 512–13). Duns Scotus—a voluntarist—was the first to use this particular idea of absolute power with reference to God's omnipotence. When Bodin discusses God's absolute power in his *Theatrum Universae Naturae*, he means precisely the "extraordinary" power to suspend or alter the "ordinary" laws of nature. Thus, he distinguishes between God's "extraordinary" and his "ordinary" providence. By God's ordinary providence, Bodin means the order and plan for the universe that God established in the creation. By God's "extraordinary" providence, he means God's alteration or suspension of the normal order of nature, as revealed in miracles and wonders (Blair 1997: 118–21).

12 In the *République*, Bodin contrasts the sovereign's "absolute power" to a power that is bound by "ordinary" (i.e., positive, human) laws ([1576] 1992: 13; cf. Francis Oakley 1984: 110). Bodin argues that the sovereign's power is absolute, since even when the sovereign condescends to rule in accordance with given, positive laws, he does not require the consent of the people, or their representatives, to suspend or alter these laws (Bodin [1576] 1992: 11).

13 For further discussion of the voluntarist underpinnings of Schmitt's conception of sovereignty, see Agata Bielik-Robson (2016) and Gwenaëlle Aubry (2017).

14 The opposition between Bodin and Lipsius extends to Lipsius's political philosophy. Whereas the core notion of Bodin's political philosophy is legislative sovereignty—or the sovereign's freedom to make and repeal laws—Lipsius enjoins the monarch to strictly adhere to inherited customs and laws, even if these laws are not the best (Lipsius [1589] 2004: 429). Instead of granting the sovereign the freedom to alter or repeal the laws, Lipsius offers an idea of the sovereign's "mixed prudence," arguing that sovereigns may derogate from the strict path of virtue, using deception and manipulation to maintain order and control over the population. Lipsius's *Politica* draws primarily on Tacitus (among the ancients) and Machiavelli (among the moderns). Because it is not "Neostoic" in any robust sense, a discussion of its ideas goes beyond the scope of this chapter. However, I take up Lipsius's political philosophy in my forthcoming book, where I argue that the central themes of Lipsius's political philosophy—that is, the sovereign's "mixed prudence" and the "reason of state"—inform Benjamin's analysis of the figure of the "sovereign intriguer" in the baroque plays. With the figure of the intriguer, Benjamin highlights the rise of calculative and instrumental reasoning in the early modern idea of governance ([1928] 2009: 95–8).

15 As noted earlier (note 12), Benjamin's typology of baroque sovereignty also includes the figure of the intriguer (Benjamin [1928] 2009: 95).

16 Throughout the early modern period, the starkness of the contrast between voluntarism and Stoicism was obvious, so much so that it was popular to contrast an idea God's arbitrary freedom with Stoic fatalism (Oakley 1984: 90).

17 Due to a series of letters between Seneca and St. Paul (now considered forged), church fathers and Renaissance humanists embraced Seneca as a pagan philosopher whose ideas could be reconciled with Christianity (Sellars 2014a: 13).

18 Benjamin's familiarity with Neostoicism was almost certainly mediated—both through the permeation of Christianized Stoicism in the *Trauerspiele* themselves and through the early twentieth-century scholarship, which threw a spotlight on the Stoic revival in the Renaissance and Baroque. Tracing these mediations would be a worthwhile project; but since I am interested in uncovering the philosophical resonances between Neostoicism and Benjamin's idea of the *Trauerspiel*, I find it congenial to go back to primary sources. I draw primarily

on Justus Lipsius's influential dialogue *On Constancy* (*De Constantia Libri Duo*) (1584), and I support my reading with occasional references to Lipsius's *Politica* (Politicorum sive Civilis Doctrinae Libri Sex) (1589). These were Lipsius's most famous and influential texts. *De Constantia* was so popular in the seventeenth century that it went through thirty-two Latin editions between 1584 and 1705 (Sellars 2007: 342).

19 Consider the similarity between Lipsius's catalogue of "public evils," and Opitz's definition of the *Trauerspiel*, as a work that concerns itself with "the commands of kings, killings, despair, infanticide and patricide, conflagrations, incest, war and commotion, lamentation, weeping, sighing and suchlike." For Benjamin, the significance of Opitz's definition is that it reveals that the *Trauerspiel* was immediately graspable in the representation of historical life ([1928] 2009: 62; cf. Martin Opitz [1658]: 30–1).

20 When speaking of the characters in the dialogue *On Constancy*, I use quotation marks (i.e., "Lipsius" and "Langius") to mark the distinction from Lipsius the author.

21 The title of Lipsius's dialogue is modeled after Seneca's *De Constantia Sapientis* (Sellars 2007: 341).

22 Lipsius recasts the ancient Stoic argument that all external harms and goods are "indifferent" ([1595] 2006: 42).

23 In a fourth argument, Lipsius combs through history to demonstrate that the "evils" afflicting the Netherlands at the time are neither particularly grievous nor unusual. Since this argument is primarily based on historical examples, I do not discuss it.

24 The dependency of necessity on providence is crucial for Lipsius's Christianized Neostoicism. The ancient Stoics tended to identify providence with fate and necessity (Sellars 2014a: 99–104), but this led to the interpretation—anathema to Christians—that even God's will is bound by a fatal necessity. To deflect the non-Christian implications of this argument, Lipsius makes a point of establishing God's priority over necessity, referring to God as *the first cause of causes* ([1595] 2006: 56).

25 According to "Langius," the ruins of great empires are cause for wonder, since they deliver insight into the necessary and divine law of transience: "our elders saw the ruins of Carthage, Numantia, Corinth, and wondered at them. And we ourselves have beheld the unworthy relics of Athens, Sparta, and many renowned cities, and even that Lady of all things and countries [Rome], falsely termed everlasting, where is she? Overwhelmed, pulled down, burned, overflowed" (Lipsius [1595] 2006: 60). Compare this to Benjamin's discussion of ruins as the paradigmatic expression of baroque natural history ([1928] 2009: 177–8).

26 Especially significant in the context of my argument is Benjamin's citation from Karl Borinski, which establishes a connection between miracles and ruins in the Baroque imaginary ([1928] 2009: 178; cf. Borinski 1914: 193–4).

27 Lipsius does acknowledge God's free will, and argues that human free will also plays a role in the "secondary causation" of things ([1595] 2006: 69).
28 As John Sellars notes in his "Introduction" to *On Constancy*, Lipsius's theodical arguments are modeled on similar arguments in Seneca's *De Providentia* ([1595] 2006: 17n40).
29 Thomas S. Freeman notes that "the differences between ideals of martyrdom in the late Middle Ages and the Reformation . . . arose from the revival of classical and patristic martyrological virtues, such as *apatheia* and the stoic endurance of suffering" (2001: 699).
30 The image of God leading the tyrant on an invisible string is strongly reminiscent of the puppet theater, which Benjamin sees anticipated in the precise relationship between mourning and play in the *Trauerspiel* ([1928] 2009: 83, 124–5). The play element in the German Baroque manifests itself in variations on the theme that we are but playthings of the Gods; that is to say, there is an overarching necessity that shapes our lives, which deprives our purposes of their ultimate seriousness. The medium of the puppet theater appears as a variation of the theme that we are playthings of the Gods, with the added nuance that we are drawn, puppetlike, on the invisible strings of our desires and ambitions. In Benjamin's words: "Such play need not be thought of as accidental, it might just as easily be planned and calculated and might therefore be seen as a puppet-play, with ambition and desire holding the strings" ([1928] 2009: 82–3).
31 According to John Sellars, "given how rare the perfect sage is, practically all humankind are in a state of imperfection, being 'madmen and fools, impious and lawless, at the extremity of misfortune and utter unhappiness'" (2007: 353; cf., Plutarch, *De Stoicorum Repugnantiis:* 1048e).
32 Lipsius refers to the Christian idea of original sin in his discussion of inherited punishment ([1595] 2006: 108). Geoffrey Aggeler finds the source of the connection between the doctrine of original sin and the Stoic belief that most of humanity exists in a condition of depravity in Calvin's commentary on Seneca's *De Clementia* (Aggeler 1990: 224–5).
33 Benjamin seems to equate Stoic *apatheia* with Lipsius's idea of constancy. But these are not identical concepts. Whereas the ancient Stoics advocated the *extirpation* of the emotions, Lipsius argues for a softer *harnessing* of the emotions ([1595] 2006: 49). Moreover, Lipsius identifies constancy with the "voluntary endurance without complaint of all things that can happen to or in a man" ([1595] 2006: 37), which contributes to the association of constancy with martyrdom. As Sellars has pointed out, this association was forged in early modernity. The ancient Stoic is not a martyr, since he "suffers nothing, for he knows nothing bad can happen to him, no matter what fate can bring" (2007: 345).
34 Lipsius does not discuss Aristotelian tragedy in *On Constancy*. Benjamin seems to be referring to Lipsius's discussion of pity as a "malady" and a "dangerous

contagion," which ought to be eradicated. Instead of pity, Lipsius argues that the virtuous person ought to have an active impulse to help others: "I permit mercy, but not pitying. I call mercy an inclination of the mind to succor the necessity or misery of another" ([1595] 2006: 52–3).

35 Lipsius identifies subjection to the opinions and emotions with tyranny: "Therefore, as they which would banish tyranny out of a city do above all things overthrow castles and forts therein, so if we would bear an earnest desire to have a good mind, we must cast down even by the foundation this castle of opinions" ([1595] 2006: 40).

36 According to Geoffrey Aggeler (1990), Seneca's idea of the divine sparks was taken up in early modern Protestant discourse as an indwelling God, which constitutes the seat of conscience within us. Aggeler argues that this led the English Protestants, William Perkins (1560–1603) and Joseph Hall (1574–1656), to formulate a radical and subversive idea of the sovereignty of conscience against tyrants. While this subversive implication is perhaps anticipated in Lipsius's argument for reason's sovereignty, Lipsius does not openly endorse active resistance against tyrants.

37 In a curious reversal, which demonstrates the close affinity among the Baroque authors between emotional unruliness and tyranny, Benjamin notes that Aegidius Albertinus wanted people suffering from melancholy to be kept in chains, lest they become tyrants ([1928] 2009: 145; cf. Albertinus 1617: 414).

38 I do not wish to imply that Benjamin derived this idea from Lipsius directly. Rather, he discovers the association of the monarch with fearfulness in the *Trauerspiele* themselves, for instance, in Andreas Gryphius's 1646 *Trauerspiel, Leo Armenius* ([1928] 2009: 143–4; cf. Gryphius 1991: 30, 96).

39 Benjamin implies that the "anti-historical" second nature of the Stoic sage involves an abstract negation in its fortification against external circumstances. Thus, according to Benjamin, the constant martyr is unable to modulate her response to changing historical circumstances and appears on stage in a rigid or frozen posture. For instance, Benjamin writes: "The sovereign alone reflects any kind of moral dignity, and even here it is the totally unhistorical moral dignity of the stoic" ([1928] 2009: 88).

40 In an earlier fragment, "Language in the *Trauerspiel* and Tragedy" (1916), Benjamin suggests that the allegorical significance of the sovereign in the *Trauerspiel* ought to be located in the human being's capacity to bestow meaning on the rest of creation: "whereas the created world wished only to pour forth in all purity, it was man who bore its crown. This is the significance of the king in the mourning play.... These plays represent a blocking of nature, as it were an overwhelming damming up of the feelings that suddenly discover a new world in language, the world of signification, of an impassive historical time; and once again the king is both man (the end of nature) and also the king (the symbol and bearer of significance) ... sorrow fills the sensuous world in which nature and language meet" ([1916a] 2004: 60).

41 There is evidence of this motif in Benjamin's thought from as early as 1916. It harkens back, not only to the fragment on "Language in the *Trauerspiel* and Tragedy" (see note 39) but also to his discussion of the "lament" of nature in "On Language as Such and on the Language of Mankind," also from 1916. The passages in the *Trauerspiel* book that reference the mournfulness of nature read almost as paraphrases of Benjamin's earlier essay " On Language" ([1928] 2009: 224–5; cf. [1916b] 2004: 72–3).

Works Cited

Agamben, Giorgio (2005), *State of Exception*, trans. Kevin Attel, Chicago: University of Chicago Press.

Aggeler, Geoffrey (1990), "'Sparkes of Holy Things': Neostoicism and the English Protestant Conscience," *Renaissance and Reformation/ Renaissance et Réforme*, 14 (3): 224–5.

Albertinus, Aegidius (1617), *Lucifers Königreich und Seelengejaidt, oder Narrenhatz: in 8 Theil abgetheilt*, Augspurg: N. Hainrich / Aperger.

Aubry, Gwenaëlle (2017), "'Miracle, Mystery and Authority': A Deconstruction of the Christian Theology of Omnipotence," *MLN*, 132 (5): 1327–50.

Benjamin, Walter (1997), *Gesammelte Briefe*, 4 vols., eds. C. Gödde and H. Lonitz. Frankfurt am Main: Suhrkamp.

Benjamin, Walter ([1916a] 2004), "Language in *Trauerspiel* and Tragedy," in *Selected Writings: Volume One, 1913–1926*, eds. M. Bullock and M. W. Jennings, trans. R. Livingstone, 59–61, Cambridge, MA: The Belknap Press of Harvard University Press.

Benjamin, Walter ([1916b] 2004), "On Language as Such and on the Language of Man," in *Selected Writings: Volume One, 1913–1926*, eds. M. Bullock and M. W. Jennings, trans. R. Livingstone, 62–74, Cambridge, MA: The Belknap Press of Harvard University Press.

Benjamin, Walter ([1923] 2004), "Calderón and Hebbel," in *Selected Writings: Volume One, 1913–1926*, eds. M. Bullock and M. W. Jennings, trans. R. Livingstone, 363–86, Cambridge, MA: The Belknap Press of Harvard University Press.

Benjamin, Walter ([1928] 2009), *The Origin of the German Tragic Drama*, trans. John Osborne, London and New York: Verso.

Bielik-Robson, Agata (2016), "Beyond Sovereignty: Overcoming Modern Nominalistic Cryptotheology," *Journal for Cultural Research*, 20 (3): 295–309.

Blair, Ann (1997), *The Theater of Nature: John Bodin and Renaissance Science*, Princeton: Princeton University Press.

Bodin, Jean ([1576] 1992), *On Sovereignty: Four Chapters from the Six Books of the Commonwealth*, ed. and trans. Julian H. Franklin, Cambridge, UK: Cambridge University Press.

Borinski, Karl (1914), *Die Antike in Poetik und Kunsttheorie von Ausgang des klassischen Altertums bis auf Goethe und Wilhelm von Humboldt, Vol. 1*, Leipzig: Dieterich'sche Verlagsbuchhandlung.
Bredekamp, Horst (1999), "From Walter Benjamin to Carl Schmitt, via Thomas Hobbes," *Critical Inquiry*, 25 (2): 247–66.
Bredekamp, Horst (2016), "Walter Benjamin's Esteem for Carl Schmitt," in *The Oxford Handbook of Carl Schmitt*, trans. Melissa Thorson Hause, Jackson Bond, and Katharina Lee Chichester, 679–704, Oxford: Oxford University Press.
Brooke, Christopher (2012), *Philosophic Pride: Stoicism and Political Thought from Lipsius to Rousseau*, Princeton: Princeton University Press.
Cassirer, Ernst (1961), *The Myth of the State*, New Haven: Yale University Press.
De Wilde, Marc (2011), "Meeting Opposites: The Political Theologies of Walter Benjamin and Carl Schmitt," *Philosophy and Rhetoric*, 44 (4): 363–81.
Dilthey, Wilhelm (1914), *Weltanschauung und Analyse des Menschen seit Renaissance und Reformation. Abhandlungen zur Geschichte der Philosophie und Religion (Gesammelte Schriften*, vol. 2), Leipzig: B.G. Teubner.
Engster, Daniel (2001), *Divine Sovereignty: The Origins of Modern State Power*, Dekalb: Northern Illinois University Press.
Freeman, Thomas S. (2001), "Early Modern Martyrs," *Journal of Ecclesiastical History*, 52 (4): 696–701.
Geisenhanslüke, Achim (2016), *Trauer-Spiele: Walter Benjamin und das europäische Barockdrama*, Paderborn: Wilhelm Fink.
Gryphius, Andreas (1991), *Dramen*, ed. Eberhard Mannack, Frankfurt am Main: Deutscher Klassiker Verlag.
Hanssen, Beatrice (2000), *Walter Benjamin's Other History: Of Stones, Animals, Human Beings, and Angels*, Berkeley: University of California Press.
Heil, Susanne (1996), *"Gefährliche Beziehungen": Walter Benjamin und Carl Schmitt*, Stuttgart/Weimar: Metzler.
Hoyt, Giles T. (1983), "Vanity and Constancy," in *German Baroque Literature*, ed. Gerhart Hoffmeister, 211–32, New York: Frederick Ungar.
Jay, Martin (1987), "Reconciling the Irreconcilable? Rejoinder to Kennedy," *Telos*, 71: 67–80.
Kennedy, Ellen (1987), "Carl Schmitt and the Frankfurt School," *Telos*, 71: 37–66.
Keohane, Nannerl O. (1980), *Philosophy and the State in France: The Renaissance to the Enlightenment*, Princeton: Princeton University Press.
Lipsius, Justus ([1589] 2004), *Politica: Six Books of Politics or Political Instruction*, ed. and trans. Jan Waszink, Assen: Royal Van Gorcum.
Lipsius, Justus ([1595] 2006), *On Constancy*, ed. John Sellars, trans. Sir John Stradling, Exeter: Bristol Phoenix Press of the Exeter Press.
Morford, Mark (1991), *Stoics and Neostoics: Rubens and the Circle of Lipsius*, Princeton: Princeton University Press.

Oakley, Francis (1984), *Omnipotence, Covenant, and Order: An Excursion in the History of Ideas from Abelard to Leibniz*, Ithaca: Cornell University Press.

Oestreich, Gerhard (1982), *Neostoicism and the Early Modern State*, Cambridge: Cambridge University Press.

Ojakangas, Mika (2012), "*Potentia absoluta et potentia ordinata Dei*: On the Theological Origins of Carl Schmitt's Theory of Constitution," *Continental Philosophy Review*, 45 (4): 505–17.

Opitz, Martin (1658), *Prosodia Germanica, Oder Buch von der Deudschen Poeterey*, Frankfurt am Main.: Christian Klein.

Parente, Margherita Isnardi (1973), "Le Voluntarisme de Jean Bodin: Maimonide ou Duns Scot?" in *Jean Bodin*, ed. Horst Denzer, 23–38, Munich: C.H. Beck.

Preuss, Ulrich (1987), "The Critique of German Liberalism: Reply to Kennedy," *Telos*, 71: 97–109.

Saunders, Jason Lewis (1955), *Justus Lipsius: The Philosophy of Renaissance Stoicism*, New York: The Liberal Arts Press.

Schings, Hans-Jürgen (1966), *Die Patristische und Stoische Tradition bei Andreas Gryphius: Untersuchungen zu den Dissertationes funebres und Trauerspielen*, Cologne/ Graz: Böhlau Verlag.

Schings, Hans-Jürgen (1971), "Consolatio Tragoediae: Zur Theorie des barocken Trauerspiels," in *Deutsche Dramen-Theorien: Beiträge zu einer historischen Poetik des Dramas in Deutschland*, ed. Reinhold Grimm, Frankfurt am Main: Athenäum Verlag.

Schwebel, Paula (forthcoming), *The Political Metaphysics of Sovereignty in Carl Schmitt and Walter Benjamin: "The Prince Is the Cartesian God"*, London: Palgrave Macmillan.

Sellars, John (2007), "Justus Lipsius's *De Constantia*: A Stoic Spiritual Exercise," *Poetics Today*, 28 (3): 339–62.

Sellars, John (2014a), *Stoicism*, London: Routledge.

Sellars, John (2014b), "Stoic Fate in Justus Lipsius's *De Constantia* and *Physiologia Stoicorum*," *Journal of the History of Philosophy*, 52 (4): 653–74.

Schmitt, Carl ([1922] 2006), *Political Theology: Four Chapters on the Concept of Sovereignty*, Chicago: University of Chicago Press.

Schmitt, Carl ([1956] 2009), *Hamlet or Hecuba: the Intrusion of Time into the Play*, trans. David Pan and Jennifer Rust, New York: Telos Press Publishing.

Stalder, Xaver (1976), *Formen des barocken Stoizismus: der Einfluss der Stoa auf die Deutsche Barockdichtung—Martin Opitz, Andreas Gryphius und Catharina Regina von Greiffenberg*, Bonn: Bouvier.

Taubes, Jacob (2013), *To Carl Schmitt: Letters and Reflections*, trans. Keith Tribe, New York: Columbia University Press.

Thiem, Annika (Yannik) (2013), "Theological-Political Ruins: Walter Benjamin, Sovereignty, and the Politics of Skeletal Eschatology," *Law and Critique*, 24 (3): 295–315.

Tuck, Richard (1993), *Philosophy and Government 1572-1651*, Cambridge: Cambridge University Press.
Weber, Samuel (2008), "Taking Exception to Decision: Walter Benjamin and Carl Schmitt," in *Benjamin's -Abilities*, 176-94, Cambridge, MA: Harvard University Press.
Welzig, Werner (1961), "Constantia und barocke Beständigkeit," *Deutsche Vierteljahrsschrift*, 35 (3): 416-32.

6

From *Oikeiōsis* to *Ereignis*
Heidegger and the Fate of Stoicism

Josh Hayes

1. Introduction

This chapter aims to explore an unthought debt in the philosophy of Martin Heidegger. Such a debt demands a certain rethinking of his philosophical corpus by returning to the origins of metaphysics. It is well established that Heidegger exclusively engages the Pre-Socratic inheritance (Anaximander, Heraclitus, and Parmenides) for the sake of interrogating the foundations of Platonic and Aristotelian metaphysics. During the 1920s, Heidegger consistently returns to Plato and Aristotle as an indication of the closure of the first Greek beginning. However, might another beginning commence if we are to retrieve those Greco-Roman thinkers effectively occluded from Heidegger's thought? Here one would be remiss to neglect the untold influence of the Stoic tradition. Indeed, the *opinio communis* that has arisen often holds Stoicism in abeyance on behalf of Heidegger's critique of humanism. By beginning with Heidegger's later works after the turn (*die Kehre*), we shall be better able to trace the influence of Stoicism upon the entire trajectory of his thinking.[1] If we are to honor Heidegger's intentions about how his works should be read, thereby affirming his claim that the truth of being (*alētheia*) is to be understood as the locality (*topos*) of being, where does Heidegger most comprehensively attend to the multiple iterations of *oikos* (home) and *oikeiōsis* (appropriation) in his thought by reference to their Stoic affiliations?

The chapter proceeds by investigating three primary "*topoi*" within Heidegger's corpus where the correspondence between *oikos* and *oikeiōsis* fundamentally articulates itself as critical to his understanding of the truth of being (*alētheia*) and the event of appropriation (*Ereignis*). In what follows, I shall attempt to articulate this preoccupation in Heidegger's thinking, beginning with *oikos* to designate the truth of being (*alētheia*) and *oikeiōsis* to designate the event of appropriation (*Ereignis*). First, we shall examine the "Letter on Humanism" (1947), the most comprehensive "public" statement of his later thinking, by considering how the truth of being (*alētheia*) and the event of appropriation (*Ereignis*) are consonant with the Stoic concepts of *oikos* and *oikeiōsis*, the appropriation or familiarization with oneself as echoed by both Chrysippus and Hierocles. Second, we shall aim to trace Heidegger's retrieval of *oikos* and *oikeiōsis* to the origins of his project of fundamental ontology by returning to *Sein und Zeit* (1927), namely Heidegger's account of authenticity (*Eigentlichkeit*) and inauthenticity (*Uneigentlichkeit*) and the being of Dasein as care (*Sorge*) from the Roman myth of Hyginus that bears its name. Third, we shall conclude with an early lecture course, *Introduction to the Phenomenology of Religion* (1920–1), where Heidegger's engagement with the Stoic and Pauline tradition reveals *oikeiōsis* to be a hidden enigma in his thinking. Heidegger's retrieval of the Stoic concepts of *oikos* and *oikeiōsis* critically frames his thinking from his earliest engagement with the Stoic and Pauline tradition to the "Letter on Humanism." Heidegger's unsaid retrieval of both *oikos and oikeiōsis* reveals the ontic ground of his own account of the truth of being (*alētheia*) and the event of appropriation (*Ereignis*), and therefore demand a rethinking of both the foundations of his fundamental ontology and his thinking after the turn.

2. "Letter on Humanism"

The "Letter on Humanism" (*Brief über den Humanismus*) remains exceptional among Heidegger's works for its avowedly public character as the first mature expression of his later thought.[2] Written in 1946 and published in 1947, the "Letter on Humanism" is composed in light of the tradition of humanism that Heidegger identifies most explicitly with the demise of thinking. With the inauguration of the Roman epoch, the multiple origins of being constituting the advent of Pre-Socratic thought have withered away and become replaced by the dominance of human reason *tout court*. The "Letter on Humanism" intends to retrieve the meaning of the human being from its mistaken path. Heidegger is clear to avoid an *explicit* definition of the human being since humanism problematically categorizes and defines the nature or essence of the human being as a rational animal (*zōon logon ekhon*). With Heidegger's refusal to define the human being, the problematic character of the relation between animal and the rational first comes to light. By gesturing toward a path beyond the simple correspondence of the human with the rational, the relationship between contemplation and action is to be thought anew, "thinking acts insofar as it thinks" (*Das Denken handelt, indem es denkt*) (Heidegger 1967: 313). The *act* of thinking is by no means caused by thinking itself as *causa sui*, rather thinking arises only in its relation (*Bezug*) to being.[3]

In what portends to be a reversal of *Sein und Zeit*, where Dasein lays claim to its being by its own appropriation, Heidegger's turn in the "Letter on Humanism" reveals that it is language (*logos*) that most authentically expresses the relation between being and Dasein. Thinking assumes an intimate familiarity (*Innigkeit*) with being:

> thinking brings [*bringt*] this relation to being solely as something handed over to thought itself from being. Such an offering [*Darbringen*] consists in the fact that in thinking being comes to language [*im denken das Sein zur Sprache kommt*]. Language is the house of being [*Die Sprache ist das Haus des Seins*]. (Heidegger 1967: 313)

Heidegger's admission of thinking as that which brings being to language is clearly influenced by the Stoic emphasis on relationality as an alternative to the metaphysics of substance and teleology.[4] The relationality between thinking (*Denken*) and being (*Sein*) is intimate enough for Heidegger to conclude that "language is the house of being. In its home human beings dwell [*In ihrer Behausung wohnt der Mensch*]" (Heidegger 1967: 313). With this decisive gesture, the tradition of humanism becomes inverted whereby being *claims* our Dasein.

Heidegger's decision to privilege the Stoic emphasis on relationality has long-standing consequences for his own critique of the history of being (*Seinsgeschichte*), as Agamben has previously demonstrated.[5] This handing over of thought and thinking to being is a prelude to the inception of releasement (*Gelassenheit*) in his later thinking: "thinking, in contrast, lets itself be claimed by being so that it can say the truth of being" (*Das Denken dagegen lässt sich vom Sein in den Anspruch nehmen, um die Wahrheit des Seins zu sagen*, Heidegger 1967: 313). Heidegger's retrieval of the Stoic concept of *oikos* anticipates this inversion where "language *as* the *house* of being," one's own home, property (*ousia*) where one dwells, needs to be guarded and preserved: "Those who think and those who create with words are guardians of this home [*die Wachter dieser Behausung*]. Their guardianship accomplishes the manifestation of being [*der Offenbarkeit des Seins*] insofar as they bring this manifestation to language and preserve it in language through their saying [*in der Sprache aufbewahren*]" (Heidegger 1967: 313). Indeed, *our* destiny (*Geschick*) is to shepherd and guard the truth of being. The destiny of being, where being claims our Dasein, is *epochal* and hence outside of our control insofar as we are appropriated by it. The movement (*Bewegung*) of this appropriation demands that we understand it beyond the simple distinction between activity and passivity.[6] To appropriate the destiny of being is to be appropriated by it. Therefore, Heidegger's claim that our destiny is to be at home with being might be taken in the most rigorous sense as a retrieval of the Stoic concept of *oikos*, an appropriation that is at once the origin of ethics if *oikeiōsis* (familiarization or appropriation of oneself) may be said to be *both* the founding principle (*arkhē*) of ethics and its reversal or *anarchic* withdrawal back into ontology. Indeed, as Heidegger reminds the reader near the conclusion of his "Letter on Humanism," "If the name, ethics, in keeping with the basic name of the word, '*ethos*,' should now say that ethics ponders the abode of the human being [*den Aufenthalt des Menschen bedenkt*], then that thinking which thinks the truth of being as the primordial element of the human being [*das anfängliche Element des Menschen*], as one who ek-sists, *is* in itself originary ethics [*die ursprüngliche Ethik*]" (Heidegger 1967: 356).

3. *Ereignis*

If we are to proceed anarchically, whereby the relationship between thinking and acting loses its foundation, we must retrieve the role of *Ereignis* as determining the most decisive direction in Heidegger's later thinking.[7] In contrast to the explicitly public declaration of the "Letter on Humanism," the inception of *Ereignis* requires a brief admission of the private significance of *Beitrage zur Philosophie: Vom Ereignis* (Contributions to Philosophy: On Enowning), composed between 1936 and 1938, a work that Heidegger did not plan to publish until his death. Conceived as the most fundamental concept of his thinking throughout the 1930s, *Ereignis* originates in the most pre-theoretical sense as an encounter with one's own sense of self and hence one's own lived experience (*Erleben*).[8] Prior to the epistemological break between the subject and the world, *Ereignis* as a coming into one's own sense of self assumes a certain kind of pre-theoretical awareness of oneself and those things that constitute the world, and thereby a *reciprocity* whereby I am first taken up by lived experience and the world is given to me. As the phenomenological key to his later thinking, *Ereignis* overturns the foundational categories of Western metaphysics—namely, the Platonic distinction between being and nonbeing, existence and essence—in the most destructive way so as to retrieve what lies at its origins.

We must effectively accomplish the same task within the Stoic tradition to discover anew the foundations of *oikeiōsis* as a principle of Stoic ontology and ethics. Here it may be appropriate to turn to the Stoic doxographical tradition to at least begin to ponder in the most preliminary sense the semantic resonance between *Ereignis* and *oikeiōsis*. In a well-known report of Chrysippus's account of *oikeiōsis*, Diogenes Laertius writes:

> A living thing's first impulse [*hormē*] is to self-preservation, because nature from the outset has rendered it familiar to itself [*oikeiousēs autōi tēs phuseōs ap'arkhēs*], as Chrysippus affirms in the first book of his work *On Ends*, affirming that for every living thing the first familiar thing [*prōton oikeion*] is its own constitution [*sustasin*] and the awareness of itself. For it was not likely that nature should estrange the living thing from itself [*allotriōsai*] or that the nature which has generated it could render it extraneous and not familiar to itself. We are forced then to conclude that nature in constituting the living thing has rendered it familiar to itself [*oikeiōsai pros heauto*]; for so it comes to repel all that is injurious and to give free access to all that is familiar [*ta oikeia*]. (7.85 [=LS 57A], trans. Hicks)

Chrysippus's account of *oikeiōsis* privileges the constitution (*sustasin*) of the living thing and its awareness of this constitution as that which remains most familiar (*prōton oikeion*) to it. Self-perception thus enables the organism to arrive at an awareness of its own constitution. However, such self-perception is always dependent upon *how* the organism finds itself in the world according to both temporal and environmental conditions. Seneca's own treatment of *oikeiōsis* confirms that the natural constitution of the organism always has a certain history, "Each period of life has its own constitution, one for the baby, and another for the boy, another for the youth, and another for the old man. They are all related appropriately to that constitution in which they exist" (*Ep.* 121.15, trans. LS 57B). In light of the accounts of *oikeiōsis* presented earlier by both Chrysippus and Seneca, the earliest stages of Heidegger's own thought allude to the fact that Dasein does not experience itself as a subject that has established any kind of absolute identity with itself. Rather, Dasein primordially ex-sists *as* nothing other than a relation in the having or possessing of itself (*ein Wie des Sichhabens*) (Heidegger 2004: 181ff). Since relationality is anterior to the being of the Stoic subject, the ex-sistence of Dasein as *oikeiōsis* marks the appropriation (*Ereignis*) of that which remains radically in-appropriable, the expropriation (*Enteignis*) of its own facticity.[9]

In what portends to be a radical shift away from the metaphysics of essence, the relation of Dasein to its there and hence to itself and to the world is identified with facticity:

> the concept of "facticity" compromises within itself the being-in-the-world of an "innerworldly" entity [*innerweltlichen Seienden*] such that this entity can understand itself as, in its "destiny" [*Geschick*], bound up with the entities [*verhaftet mit dem Sein des Seienden*] which it encounters within its world. (Heidegger 1993: 56)

Heidegger privileges the factuality (*Tatsache*) of facticity as Dasein's most definite way of being (*Seinbestimmtheit*). The factuality of Dasein is most importantly divorced from the factual occurrence (*tatsächlichen Vorkommen*) of Dasein since the factuality of Dasein is disclosed as something that is owned by Dasein as its presence-at-hand: "Dasein understands its ownmost Being in the sense of a certain factual Being present-at-hand [*tatsächlichen Vorhandenseins*]" (Heidegger 1993: 56). The familiarization with its presence-at-hand (*Vorhandensein*) only further emphasizes an innate awareness conducive to the Stoic account of *oikeiōsis*. Returning to Seneca's naturalism, we might claim that this familiarization with the self determines how Dasein relates to the world:

> For even if there is in store for him any higher phase into which he must be changed, the state in which he is born is also according to nature. It is with itself that the animal is first of all familiarized [*primum sibi ipsum conciliatur animal*], for there must be a pattern to which all other things may be referred. . . . This inheres in all living beings, and is not added to them at a second time, but is innate. (Sen. *Ep.* 121.17-18, trans. Gummere [modified])

If facticity is to be divorced from any metaphysical projection that undertakes to hypostatize it as something innate to Dasein, facticity is the relation that Dasein has with itself and its world. In an implicit gesture to the role of *oikeiōsis* within the Stoic tradition, Heidegger consistently privileges the language of dwelling (*oikos*) and appropriation (*oikeiōsis*): "By its very nature, Dasein brings its there home with it" (*Das Dasein bringt sein Da von Hause aus mit*, Heidegger 1993: 133). Dasein remains bound to its there. The there *is* the disclosedness by which Dasein relates to itself and to the world.

Although Da-sein is bound to its there (*Da*) and develops an attunement to it, the there remains an enigma (*ein Rätsel*): "mood or attunement brings Dasein before the 'that-it-is' of its 'there,' which as such it stares in the face with the inexorability of an enigma [*unerbittlicher Rätselhaftigkeit entgegenstarrt*]"

(Heidegger 1993: 136). Indeed, Dasein finds itself suspended between its own appropriation (*Ereignis*) and its own expropriation (*Enteignis*). Dasein is thrown into the there but cannot retrieve itself from the there. The there remains impenetrable to Dasein as a *burden* whereby "the whence and the whither remain in darkness" (*das Woher and Wohin bleiben im Dunkel*, Heidegger 1993: 134), and a *gift* whereby the there illuminates: "To say that it is illuminated [*erleuchtet*] means that as Being-in-the-world it is cleared [*gelichtet*] in itself, not through any other entity, but in such a way that it *is* itself the clearing [*dass es selbt die Lichtung ist*]" (Heidegger 1993: 133). The presence-at-hand (*Vorhandensein*) of Dasein will become disclosed in terms of how Dasein naturally *uses* itself as a relation to itself and the world.[10] Being-thrown open into the world, Dasein remains affected and hence afflicted by the world. Heidegger's discussion of moods thereby frames his discussion of facticity as expropriation (*Enteignis*). Moods assail us, overcome us, and estrange us. In our consignment to moods by virtue of their uncanninesss (*Unheimlichkeit*), moods determine our relation to facticity since we only understand ourselves and the world in and through them:

> In having a mood, Dasein is always disclosed moodwise [*ist immer schon stimmungsmässig*] as that entity to which it has been delivered over in its Being [*dem das Dasein in seinem Sein überantwortet wurde als dem Sein*]; and in this way it has been delivered over to the Being, which, in existing, it has to be. (Heidegger 1993: 134)

The insistent pervasiveness of moods imposes a demand upon Dasein. Dasein can "be" no other way than *open* to and *in* its moods.

Being-open to and in its moods constitutes the ontological affectivity of Dasein. This fundamental openness to moods thus always already entails a certain kind of *oikeiōsis*, since the Stoic familiarity with one's own constitution is equiprimordial with the impulse (*hormē*) that tends to self-preservation. This impulsive disposition to self-preservation may even be deemed to be originary to Dasein's own ontological affectivity. Therefore, the role of impulse (*hormē*) should not be displaced but instead becomes foundational to Heidegger's account of the structure of care. Like *oikeiōsis*, Heidegger's engagement with impulse (*hormē*) precedes the composition of *Sein und Zeit*. Beginning with the 1925 lecture course, *History of the Concept of Time*, Heidegger describes how urge or impulse (*Hang*) suppresses the tendency (*Drang*) to fall into and become dispersed by the world, "for urge only cares about the 'towards,' and this is at any price, in blind disregard of everything else. The blind state of only being 'towards and nothing else' [*Hin zu sonst nichts*] is a modification of caring" (Heidegger 1979: 410). The blindness of urge accords with the impulse to preserve oneself at all costs. The instinct for self-preservation so natural to the constitution of the organism performs a decisive role throughout the Stoic account of *oikeiōsis*. It is no coincidence that Chrysippus's own juxtaposition between pursuit (*hairesis*) and avoidance (*phugē*), "so that it comes to repel all that is injurious and to seek all that is familiar to itself" (DL 7.85), is later echoed by Seneca in terms of the care of oneself:

> I seek pleasure: for whom? For myself. I am therefore taking care of myself [*mei curam ago*]. I shrink from pain; on behalf of whom? Myself. Therefore, I am taking care of myself. Since I do everything for care of myself, therefore care of myself is prior to everything [*ante omnia est mei cura*]. (*Ep.* 117.17)

As we shall see later, Seneca's distinction between pleasure and pain will only reappear in Heidegger's own account of affectivity (*Befindlichkeit*) in the existential analytic where Dasein is confronted with the same possibility of flight and pursuit: "the way in which the mood discloses is not one in which we look at thrownness, but one in which we turn towards or turn away" (*An und Ab-kehr*) (Heidegger 1993: 135). In what follows, we shall now trace how Heidegger's appropriation of this distinction becomes apparent in terms of his account of authenticity (*Eigentlichkeit*) and inauthenticity (*Uneigentlichkeit*) in *Sein und Zeit*.

4. Authenticity (*Eigentlichkeit*) and Inauthenticity (*Uneigentlichkeit*)

Throughout *Sein und Zeit*, Dasein's being-thrown into the world constitutes not only the possibility of factical givenness but ultimately the Stoic possibilities of pursuing that which remains familiar to oneself and evading the injurious. Heidegger develops both directions of the Stoic account by projecting facticity as the pivotal choice for pursuing or evading one's ownmost possibility of being. If we are to read Heidegger retrospectively, *Eigentlichkeit* is most originally a manifestation of *Ereignis*. We should therefore resist the temptation to interpret *Eigentlickeit* as a singular event of appropriation that finalizes one's ownmost possibility as an individual by resolutely anticipating and being-toward-death. Instead, *Eigentlichkeit* should be conceived as a movement that dynamically unfolds throughout the span of life from natality to mortality whereby Dasein becomes more familiar and indeed at home with itself. This progressive familiarity with oneself is warranted by the inauthenticity (*Uneigentlichkeit*) that constitutes our thrown condition as mortals: "authenticity is only a modified way in which such everydayness is seized upon [*ein modifiziertes Ergreifen dieser*]" (Heidegger 1993: 179). Dasein is burdened by an inauthenticity, the ruinance of its own nullity, that cannot be overcome. Thus, authenticity is only a modification of inauthenticity.[11] Even in the resoluteness of authenticity, Dasein remains an enigma since the appropriation of oneself by becoming familiar with oneself is to choose its nullity. The nullity of Dasein thereby assumes that appropriation is always already an expropriation (*Enteignis*) or becoming other than oneself.

Although Heidegger's emphasis upon inauthenticity might be said to depart from the Stoic account of *oikeiōsis*, Chrysippus does not completely rule out the possibility that nature may estrange the organism from itself: "For it was not likely that nature should estrange the living thing from itself [*allotriōsai*] or that the nature which has generated it could render it extraneous and not familiar to itself" (DL 7.85 [LS 57A]). This estrangement or alienation (*Enteignis*) drives Dasein to become familiar with itself by resolutely choosing its facticity. The urgency to resist the temptation of falling frees Dasein for the possibilities that become available by resolutely appropriating the untruth of the They (*das Man*): "Resolution does not withdraw itself [*entzieht sich*] from actuality [*Wirklichkeit*], but discovers first what is factically possible; and it does so by seizing upon it in whatever way is possible for it as its ownmost potentiality-for-being in the 'they' [*eigenstes Seinkommen im Man*]" (Heidegger 1993: 299).

By undertaking to reverse the direction of *oikeiōsis* from familiarity with oneself to familiarity with that which is most uncanny or unfamiliar (*unheimlich*), Heidegger privileges our ownmost nullity as what remains incapable of appropriation. The conceptual distinction between authenticity and inauthenticity remains tenuous for Heidegger. Although his account of resoluteness (*Entschlossenheit*) is presented as a modification of the They (*das Man*), the familiarity with oneself is always already implicated by an incipient and originary awareness of oneself. Following Chrysippus, who first emphasizes familiarity with oneself and with one's own constitution as primary to the organism, the second-century Stoic Hierocles develops an account of *oikeiōsis* beginning with sense-perception (*aisthēsis*): "From birth, the living thing has sensation of itself and familiarity with itself and with its constitution [*aisthanesthai te hautou kai oikeiousthai heautōi kai tēi heautou sustasei*]" (Ramelli and Konstan 2009: 20, 45–50). *Oikeiōsis* or familiarity with oneself is a condition of the co-sentiment or co-feeling of oneself (*sunaisthēsis*) and one's own constitution. This conjunction between one's own awareness and one's own constitution not only reveals the organism to itself but ultimately demonstrates its affectivity to the world.[12]

Such a feeling of oneself or what we might deem to call "auto-affection" might also be said to entail a distancing from oneself and thereby make possible the estrangement or alienation identified with inauthenticity. Perhaps Heidegger's own introduction of this estrangement or alienation (*allotriōsis*) back into the Stoic tradition may be conceived by retrieving his account of the genesis of care (*Sorge*) as the being of Dasein.

5. The Myth of Care (*Sorge*)

In section 42 of *Sein und Zeit*, Heidegger presents a genetic account of care (*Sorge*) by introducing the myth of Cura authored by the Roman poet Hyginus. As the only myth introduced by Heidegger to frame the genesis of Dasein, the myth purports to explain how care arises out of the earth (*humus*).[13] By introducing the Myth of Care as a pre-ontological way of interpreting the genesis of Dasein, Heidegger concedes that the content of the myth is merely historical (*nur geschichtlich*). However, its fundamental historical character may assist us in understanding the temporal structure of Dasein as care:

> Once when Care was crossing a river, she saw some clay; she thoughtfully took up a piece and began to shape it. While she was meditating on what she had made, Jupiter came by. "Care" asked him to give it spirit, and this he gladly granted. But when she wanted her name to be bestowed upon it, he forbade this, and demanded that it be given his name instead. While "Care" and Jupiter were disputing, Earth arose and desired that her own name be conferred on the creature, since she had furnished it with part of her body. They asked Saturn to be their arbiter, and he made the following decision, which seemed a just one: "Since you, Jupiter, have given its spirit, you shall receive that spirit at its death, and since you, Earth, have given its body, you shall receive its body. But since 'Care' first shaped this creature, she shall possess it as long as it lives. And because there is now a dispute among you as to its nature, let it be called '*homo*,' for it is made out of *humus* (earth)."[14] (Heidegger 1993: 197–8, translating Hyginus *Fabulae* 220)

Heidegger translates a line from Seneca's *Moral Epistle* 124 to explain its ontic significance:

> unius bonum natura perficit, dei scilicet, alterius cura, hominis.
> Man's *perfectio*—his transformation into that which he can be in Being-*free for his ownmost possibilities* (projection)—is "accomplished" by "care" [*eine Leistung der Sorge*]. (Heidegger 1993: 199, italics my own).

Heidegger privileges the role of projection as an existential structure that enables Dasein to avail itself *as* a possibility. In conjunction with the Stoic understanding of *perfectio*, Heidegger understands *perfectio* as presenting the possibility for transformation (*Werden*). If we are to identify care with the transformation of the human essence, the possibility of Dasein as projection in its coming into that which it *can* be is accomplished by care. However, this accomplishment stands as something potentially outside of Dasein's power, "If the Good of the one, namely God, is fulfilled by his Nature; but that of the other, man, is fulfilled by care" (Sen. *Ep.* 124.14). Although care is responsible for determining the essence of Dasein, this essence should not mistakenly be deemed as substantial. Rather, the essence of Dasein as an event of appropriation (*Ereignis*) or an occurrence of the truth of being (*alētheia*) is nothing other than the event of its surrender and withdrawal. After highlighting the role of projection, Heidegger returns to thrownness as that which is responsible for instituting this withdrawal and hence its surrender to the world of limited possibilities: "But with equal primordiality, care 'determines' what is basically specific in this entity [*bestimmt sie aber die Grundart dieses Seienden*] according to which it has been *surrendered* to the world of its concern (thrownness) [*die besorgte Welt ausgeliefert ist (Geworfenheit)*]" (Heidegger 1993: 199). Therefore, to be free for one's ownmost possibilities is at once an admission that these possibilities only *provisionally* remain within our power.[15] Heidegger's translation of human *perfectio*—as "*the transformation into that which he can be in being-free (Freisein)*" (italics mine)—echoes Chrysippus's own account of *oikeiōsis* as—in Hick's suggestive translation—"*giving free access [prosietai] to all that is familiar [ta oikeia]*." (DL 7.85, italics mine).[16] Such a granting or giving of these possibilities does not remain with the realm of mortals, but resides only with the plan of Zeus:

> "*Cura prima finxit*": in care this entity has the "source" of its Being. "*Cura teneat, quamdiu vixerit*"; the entity is not released from this source, but is held fast, dominated by it through and through as long as this entity "is in the world." (Heidegger 1993: 198)

If "this source" (*Ursprung*) is in fact an allusion to Zeus, Heidegger establishes a possible connection between the mortal life of the organism and its reliance upon divine providence.[17] The possibility that care may perfect the good of the human being affirms *oikeiōsis* as an act of appropriating one's own nature as an organism, what is most good for the individual and what is most good for the species. Since the impulse (*hormē*) that drives *oikeiōsis* is fundamental to the preservation of the organism, Dasein's projection to realize its ownmost (*eigentlich*) possibilities also remains fundamental to our condition as mortals.

Heidegger's interpretation of Dasein as a mere mortal throughout the Myth of Care thereby anticipates his treatment of both fate (*Schicksal*) and destiny (*Geshick*) in Sein und Zeit.

6. Fate (*Schicksal*) and Destiny (*Geschick*)

In his retrieval of Stoic cosmology, Heidegger develops an account of *oikeiōsis* as affirming our thrown condition through the activity of resolutely choosing one's own fate. Following his account of the basic constitution of historicality, choice always already entails that one is beholden to a certain fate (*Schicksal*):

> Fate is that powerless superior power [*die ohmächtige, den Widrigkeiten sich bereitstellende Übermacht*] which puts itself in readiness for adversities—the power of projecting oneself upon one's own Being-guilty [*eigene Schuldigsein*] and of doing so reticently, with readiness for anxiety. As such, fate requires as the ontological condition for its possibility, the state of Being of care, that is to say, temporality.[18]

By engaging the power of fate as a readiness which resides in the resolute anticipation of authenticity, Dasein is compelled by anxiety toward one's ownmost possibility, namely being-toward-death. In this sense, we are all guilty or fallen (*Verfallenheit*) if we fail to recognize this possibility as the fate of Dasein. Within Stoic cosmology, fate (*heimarmenē*) is identified with the concatenation, order, and conjunction of spatial bodies. The overarching power of fate extends from the concatenation of spatial bodies that exist far beyond us in the cosmos to those bodies that inhere within us. In accordance with Chrysippus's account of fate as the power of breath (*pneuma*) that holds the universe together (LS 55J-N), Heidegger contends that "man's *perfectio*—his transformation into that which he can be in Being-*free for his ownmost possibilities* (projection)—is 'accomplished' by 'care'" (Heidegger 1993: 199). If we are to establish a preliminary parallel between the world-arranging power of *pneuma* and the accomplishment (*Leistung*) of care, fate accords with the *natural* perfection of Dasein since such a transformation of oneself always occurs within a finite horizon of individual possibilities. However, Heidegger also takes a step beyond the Stoic account of fate as the power of *pneuma* and the projection of care by introducing the collective destiny (*Geshick*) of the "we" through being-with-others:

> If Dasein, by anticipation, lets death become powerful in itself, then, as free for death, Dasein understands itself in its own *superior power* [*eigenen Übermacht*],

the power of its finite freedom, so that in this freedom, which "is" only in its having chosen to make such a choice, it can take over the powerlessness of abandonment [*die Ohnmacht der Überlassenheit*] to its having done so, and can thus come to have a clear vision for the accidents of the Situation that has been disclosed. But if fateful Dasein, as Being-in-the-world, exists essentially in Being-with-Others, its historizing [*Geschehen*] is a co-historizing [*Mitgeschehen*] and determinative for it as destiny [*Geschick*]. (Heidegger 1993: 384)

Since we are individually thrown into a collective historical destiny (*Geshick*) insofar as our being-in-the-world is always being-with-others, how might we strive to live in Chrysippus's sense in accordance with the *pneuma* that reflects the rational order of the universe? Here we might turn to Cicero's rejection of the commonsense understanding of fate, whereby fate is understood as simply the inaction of predetermination. Indeed, Cicero supports Chrysippus in rejecting this account of fate:

> Nor will we be blocked by the so called "Lazy Argument" (the *argos logos*, as the philosophers entitle it). If we gave in to it, we would do nothing whatever in life. They pose it as follows: "If it is your fate to recover from this illness, you will recover, regardless of whether or not you call the doctor. Likewise, if it is your fate not to recover from this illness, you will not recover, regardless of whether or not you call the doctor. And one or the other is your fate. Therefore, it is pointless to call the doctor." (LS 55S)

Echoing Chrysippus, Cicero claims that my recovery from the illness is partly caused by my prudent decision to call the doctor (LS 55S). Fate thus operates through us as the primary causal responsibility for our actions and hence as the *pneuma* that binds the universe together. Heidegger remains rightly suspicious of the inaction of predetermination that accompanies the Lazy Argument. His account of the equiprimordiality of thrownness and projection might thereby be said to replicate Cicero's claim that fate operates through us, since projection always occurs within a given horizon of possibilities that we may choose to act upon. If the facticity of being born and hence "thrown into the world" exists as our collective destiny, "being in the world is essentially being-with others," our individual fate is nothing other than this possibility, this powerless superior power, of *projecting* ourselves upon our ownmost being-guilty as a symptom of our fallen inauthenticity. Although neither Chrysippus nor Cicero addresses the existential themes of guilt, fallenness, authenticity, and inauthenticity, their presentation of fate as something that temporally unfolds within us in accordance with our *pneuma* may only serve as a further provocation to investigate

Heidegger's interpretation of *oikeiōsis* through the lens of his engagement with Pauline Stoicism. Hence, we can only come to terms with the abandonment of our own thrownness and the fallen estrangement from ourselves through an act of conversion (*metanoia*) by choosing to live according to fate.[19]

7. Pauline Stoicism

In what follows, I shall illustrate how Heidegger retrieves the Stoic accounts of fate and *oikeiōsis* by returning to his earliest engagement with the Helleno-Christian tradition, namely his phenomenological explication of the letters of Paul in the 1920 lecture course, "Introduction to the Phenomenology of Religion." Heidegger specifically highlights three directions to his phenomenological explication of Paul:

> What is phenomenology? What is phenomenon? Here this can be itself indicated only formally. Each experience—as experienc*ing*, and what is experi*enced*—can "be taken in the phenomenon," that is to say, one can ask: 1. After the original "*what*," what this is experienced therein (*content*). 2. After the original "*how*," in which it is experienced (*relation*). 3. After the original "*how*," in which the relational meaning is *enacted* (*enactment*). (Heidegger 2004: 43)

Heidegger chooses to focus on Paul's Letter to the Galatians, "a historical report from Paul about the story of his conversion," to make phenomenologically apparent "the fundamental comportment of Christian consciousness—according to the sense of its content, relation, and enactment" (Heidegger 2004: 48). Heidegger claims that the *content* of Paul's communal world is to be seen in its determination in connection with the *how* of his relation to this communal world (Heidegger 2004: 61). If Paul's Letter to the Galatians tells the story of Paul's conversion, Paul's Letter to the Thessalonians, addressed to his congregation, is explicitly concerned with evangelization. Heidegger returns to both themes of conversion and evangelization to demonstrate the intersection between Paul's establishment of a congregation in Thessalonica through the freedom of realizing his own possibilities (*projection*) and the historically situated facticity leading to his own conversion (*thrownness*). Thus, Paul concretely epitomizes Heidegger's later account of "thrown projection" (*geworfene Entwurf*) in *Sein und Zeit*. In his Letter to the Thessalonians, Paul is first confronted with his own anguish in determining how such an evangelization is to be enacted given the painful separation from his congregation and the failure of previous efforts to return to Thessalonica. Paul's anguish becomes the struggle of the congregation to survive as a congregation despite persistent persecution. The letter is marked by the specific attunements of anxiety and despair demonstrating how Paul relates to his congregation. Heidegger explicitly emphasizes 1 Thess 1:6, where Paul proclaims *how* his congregants have become (*Gewordensein*) examples to all believers by "welcoming the word in affliction much with joy." Such a having-become (*genesthai*) is an acceptance or welcoming of the word (*dekhesthai ton logon*): "the *dechesthai* brought the despair with it, which also continues, yet at the same time, a 'joy' (*meta charas*) which comes from the Holy Spirit (*pneumatos agiou*) is alive—a joy which is a gift, thus not motivated from out of one's own experience" (Heidegger 2004: 66). This acceptance of the intermingling of joy and despair constitutive of the anguish of life remains pivotal to Heidegger's account of anticipatory resoluteness in *Sein und Zeit*. As a possibility hidden in resoluteness, anticipation attests to the sober understanding of the possibilities inherent within facticity:

> neither does anticipatory resoluteness [*vorlaufende Entschlossenheit*] stem from "idealistic" exactions soaring above existence and its possibilities; it springs from a sober understanding [*nüchternen Verstehen*] of what are factically the basic possibilities for Dasein. Along with the sober anxiety [*nüchternen Angst*] which brings us face to face with our individualized potentiality-for-Being, there goes an unshakeable *joy* [*gerüstete Freude*] in this possibility. (Heidegger 1993: 310)

Paul's conversion and evangelization thus presents the possibility of a radical interrogation of his own facticity. Since Paul's facticity cannot be substantially transformed or changed, all that can be accomplished is a kind of expropriation by *using* one's facticity in a new way.[20] Here Heidegger turns to Cor 1:7 where Paul's admonition to the Corinthians to heed their factical situation becomes most apparent:

> I mean, brothers and sisters, time has grown short; what remains is so that those who have wives many be *as not* [*hōs me*] having, and those who mourn *as not* mourning, and those who rejoice *as not* rejoicing, and those who buy *as not* possessing, and those who use the world *as not* abusing. For the present form this world is passing away. I want you to be without care. (1 Cor 7: 29–32)

Paul's admonition importantly demonstrates the Stoic influence of *oikeiōsis* as a category of relationality in his illustration of how believers should reflectively detach themselves from the dominant economic and social forms in the remaining moments preceding the *eschaton*. *Oikeiōsis* is fundamentally *enacted* in the resolute anticipation of authenticity (*Eigentlichkeit*) as the "fact which must not be denied and which we are forced to grant; it must be conceived in its *positive necessity*" (Heidegger 1993: 358).

In his attempt to phenomenologically explicate the original experience of Paul's conversion, Heidegger also highlights Gal 2:19 ("through the law, I died to the law/ *apethanen nomo dia nomu* [sic]") as the most "concentrated form of the entire Pauline dogmatic" (Heidegger 2004: 49).[21] Paul's conversion can be conceived in a similar way as a movement of the individual away from oneself for the sake of a normative identification with the collective self, the person of Christ. This form of *oikeiōsis* presented in Heidegger's reading of Gal 2:19 might in some way be responsible for the inception of authenticity (*Eigentlichkeit*) in *Sein und Zeit*. Authenticity is not merely a recognition of one's own finitude, but a recognition of the destiny of a people, thus making possible a kind of shared life. In an allusion to Stoic providence, Paul's proclamation in Gal 2:19 construing the law as Christ himself, "through the law/I died to the law— through Christ/I died to Christ" resonates with Heidegger's own proclamation in the "Letter on Humanism," "that the law or injunction (*nomos*) always and everywhere determines the abode (*oikos*) of Dasein" (Heidegger 1967: 274). If *nomos* is the condition for *oikos*, the law of finitude as the nullity that constitutes our own being also presents the possibility of *being-at-home* with ourselves by *being-toward-death*. The realization of this fact of our existence in our being-toward-death grants us "free access to all that is familiar" and gives us a life that transcends our individuality as mortals. Such a destiny constitutes the shared life of Stoic community.[22]

8. Conclusion

In conclusion, I shall now return to the "Letter on Humanism" where Heidegger accuses metaphysics of privileging the role of *animalitas*: "Metaphysics thinks the human being on the basis of its *animalitas* and does not think in the direction of his *humanitas*" (Heidegger 1967: 246–7). If metaphysics indeed privileges the role of *animalitas*, including the tradition of Stoic naturalism, *oikeiōsis* as an event of appropriation constituting the impulse to self-preservation that arises with the organism cannot be disassociated from the domain of metaphysics. However, as I have attempted to demonstrate earlier, Heidegger nevertheless implicitly retrieves and appropriates *oikeiōsis* as essentially ontological. Heidegger's ontological appropriation of *oikeiōsis* remains misconceived and problematic for the project of his fundamental ontology. This misconception can only be resolved by returning to the Stoic ethical tradition to discern if another beginning can be breached. This other beginning would begin not with the event of appropriation identified with *oikeiōsis* but rather with the event of expropriation identified with *allotriōsis*. Such an expropriation discloses an estrangement and alienation unique to the ontological essence of Dasein. Indeed, appropriation (*oikeiōsis*) cannot be severed from expropriation (*allotriōsis*). Stoic ethics thus presents the possibility of an unexplored region of fundamental ontology. Its originary "ontological" nature *belies* its ontic roots. By returning to the ontic basis of the fundamental ontology, we are presented with the possibility of reviving the theme of life throughout Heidegger's corpus as not a theme that is to be occluded from his thinking of being, but rather as a theme that constitutes Heidegger's understanding of being as such. The Greek and Roman legacy of Stoicism marks not the decline of the originary Pre-Socratic Greek beginning as merely another stage in the history of Platonism, but rather its denouement, where the life of the organism (*zōē*) in its most nascent and incipient sense is both revived and survives as a seminal contribution to Stoic ethics, psychology, and metaphysics. The truth of being (*alētheia*), the disclosure or presencing and withdrawal of being as a dynamic movement of appropriation and expropriation, thus remains indebted to the Stoic understanding of life. Even the inception of *Ereignis* as an event of appropriation, an encounter with one's own self and hence one's own lived experience, may be originally conceived by the Stoic account of *oikeiōsis*. If *oikeiōsis* frames Heidegger's discourse on authenticity, then the conceptual apparatus framing the existential analytic of Dasein throughout *Sein und Zeit* must be called into question.[23]

A primary aim of this chapter has been to investigate this daimonic core (*zōē*) of Dasein as yet another iteration within the Stoic tradition in order to fundamentally disclose the possibility of understanding Heidegger's ontology as corresponding not only to Stoic metaphysics but ultimately to Stoic ethics. In closing, if we are to develop a more robust account of Heidegger's moral ontology, perhaps it might be best *not* to focus exclusively on the Aristotelian inheritance, but rather return to his investigation of early Christian sources where Heidegger is engaging with the intersection between the Stoic and Pauline traditions. How does Paul extend the Stoic account of *oikeiōsis* away from *animalitas* and toward *humanitas*? How is Paul responsible for opening a new path in Heidegger's thought, a path that begins not with the animal but with the human?[24] An investigation of this nature would require a return to the *vexata relatio* between *zōē* and *anthropos*. Within the Stoic tradition, there remains a certain zone of indiscernibility between *zōē* and *anthropos* whereby human nature is a reflection of animal nature; indeed the organization of the organism is a reflection of the organization of the cosmos *writ large*. The retrieval of the theme of the organism throughout the legacy of Stoic naturalism bears careful consideration. If the organic cannot be severed from the artificial and the distinction between *phusis* and *tekhnē* remains a mere fiction, then we are presented with a cosmos that takes life to be at the center of being.[25] Hence, the Greco-Roman heritage of Stoic naturalism haunts Heidegger's philosophical oeuvre and provides a new horizon for rethinking both the ethical and the cosmological implications of his ontology for our time.

Notes

1 Schürmann (1987: 1–21). Schürmann cites the 1969 Le Thor seminar where Heidegger indicates how he should be read: "After *Being and Time*, my thinking replaced the expression 'meaning of being' with 'truth of being.' And so as to avoid any misapprehension about truth, so as to exclude its being understood as conformity, 'truth of being' has been elucidated as 'locality of being'—truth as the locus-character of being. That presupposes, however, an understanding of what a locus is. Hence the expression—*topology of being*" (Heidegger 2012: 46–7).

2 Conceived as a reply to Jean Beufret on the topic of humanism, Skocz (2008) notes that the proper interlocuters are Heidegger and Sartre. Indeed, Heidegger is not replying to the questions posed by Beufret as much as he is replying to Sartre's controversial essay "Existentialism is a Humanism" (1945). I shall not address Heidegger's critique of Sartrean existentialism here. Rather, I shall highlight its problematic affiliation for Heidegger's account of the history of being.

3 What shall remain integral to our account of the Stoic inheritance is Heidegger's gesture toward the relationality of being. This relationality of being to beings and hence their presencing as things through language remains a preoccupation of Heidegger's later thinking. See Mitchell (2015).

4 The Stoic account of *oikeiōsis* opposes the category of relationality to activity (*energeia*) and the actualization of substance (*entelekheia*) implicit to Platonic and Aristotelian metaphysics. Agamben (2015) performs his own genealogy of the Stoic notion of *oikeiōsis* from Chrysippus to Plotinus, affirming that *oikeiōsis* is nothing other than a relation of the self to itself. Agamben cites the application of *oikeiōsis* in Stoic thought as the appropriation or familiarization of the self to the self: "If one accepts this relational and non-substantial interpretation of the Stoic self, then— whether it is a matter of self-sensation, of *sibi conciliatio*, or of use-of-oneself—the

self coincides each time with the relation itself and not with a predetermined telos" (Agamben 2015: 54).

5 Here, one might pause if only to consider the history of philosophy as a history of the will, a history of appropriation and hence the domination of the metaphysics of presence ranging from Plato to Nietzsche (with the possible exception of Plotinus and Meister Eckhart). To be claimed by being echoes Plotinus (and later Eckhart) in admitting to a passivity, how one finds oneself, as only provisionally related to being itself. Such a provisional expression can only be used to identify the mode of the being of the One: "Well then, suppose, he did not come to be, but is as he is and not of his own substance. And if he is not a master of his substance [*ouk ōn tēs autou ousias kurios*], but is who he is, not hypostatizing himself but using himself as what he is [*ouk hupostēsas heauton, khrōmenos de heautōi hoios estin*], then he is what he is of necessity, and could not be otherwise" (Plot. 6.8.10 [trans. Armstrong]). Agamben (2015) claims that this non-hypostatic, non-substantializing use of oneself is first conceived by Chrysippus and later reiterated by Plotinus.

6 On the phenomenon of the middle voice, see Sheehan (1995).

7 Since I have pejoratively translated *Ereignis* as the event or event of appropriation, it is imperative that the semantic range of *Ereignis* not be lost upon us. Whereas the prefix *er-* "carries the sense of a beginning motion or of an achievement," *eignis* referring back to *eigen*, usually means "own." Although a number of neologisms have developed out of attempts to translate *Ereignis*, including en-owning, appropriation, or event of appropriation" Vallega Neu (2010: 141).

8 In his 1919 lecture course, *Zur Bestimmung der Philosophie* (*The Idea of Philosophy*), Heidegger hyphenates the word to indicate its importance to the originary lived experience of one's own self, *er-leben*: "*Er-leben* ['lived experience'] does not pass by me, like a thing that I would posit as an object; rather I *er-eigne* ['en-own' or 'appropriate'] it to myself and it *er-eignet sich* [it happens, appropriates itself, or en-owns itself] according to its essence. And if, looking at it, I understand lived experience in that way, then I understand it-not as a process [*Vor-gang*], as a thing, object, but rather as something totally new, as *Ereignis*" (Heidegger 2000: 63).

9 Even in the resoluteness of authenticity, Dasein remains an enigma since the appropriation of oneself by becoming familiar with oneself is to choose its nullity. The nullity of Dasein thereby assumes that appropriation is always already an expropriation, a "becoming other" than oneself. Heidegger will frame such a "becoming other" by the language of inauthenticity.

10 Agamben especially privileges the role of use in his reading of Seneca, "And if use in the sense that we have seen, means being affected, constituting oneself insofar as one is in relation with something, then use-of-oneself coincides with oikeiōsis, insofar as the term names the very mode of being of the living being" (Agamben 2015: 54).

11 The event of appropriation (*Ereignis*) is always an expropriation (*Enteignis*). Yet, the question remains, why does Heidegger's respect for the proper/improper remain so fundamental to his philosophical concerns? What does this tension between propriety and impropriety disclose about the originary belonging/non-belonging to Being? Can Dasein ever be at home with itself (*heimlich*) other than being not-at-home (*umheimlich*) in the inexorable enigma of its own essence? If the there (*Da*) of Da-sein remains impenetrable, we are confronted with an originary conflict between appropriation and expropriation, a *polemos* that threatens any fundamental pretense of tranquil interiority. Dasein is at war with itself. The war that Dasein wages against itself is a war that occludes the human being from the essence of Dasein. It is precisely this occlusion of the human being as a *zōon logon ekhon* that remains decisive to Heidegger's account of the meaning of being from his earliest lecture courses to *Sein and Zeit* to the alleged turn in his thinking.

12 If the living being is nothing other than an essential relation to itself and the world, then Agamben's assessment of Stoic *oikeiōsis* remains true to Heidegger's own intentions for the ontological constitution of Dasein: "the living being uses itself, in the sense that in its life and in entering into relationship with what is other than the self, it has to do each time with its very self, feels the self, and familiarizes itself with itself. *The self is nothing other than use of oneself*" (Agamben 2015: 54).

13 Heidegger conspicuously remarks that he "ran across the myth in an article by Karl Burdach" who calls attention to the double meaning (*Doppelsinn*) of the term "cura," "according to which it signifies not only 'anxious exertion'[*ängstliche Bemühung*] but also 'carefulness'[*Sorgfalt*] and 'devotedness' [*Hingabe*] before declaring that the content of the myth is pre-ontological or rather an ontic interpretation [*ontischen Auslegung*] as opposed to any existential-ontological interpretation [*existenzial-ontologische Interpretation*]" (Heidegger 1993: 1999).

14 Stanley Rosen and his student, Drew Hyland, observe the affinity between Heideggerian care and Platonic *erōs*. However, they neglect to develop an interpretation of care that arises from the Stoic account of *oikeiōsis*. How are we to understand the twofold structure of care if not by reference to facticity and transcendence, thrownness and projection, what Heidegger will refer to as "thrown projection" (*geworfene Entwurf*)? See Hyland (1997).

15 As Kurt Lampe notes, "Heidegger would probably not consider the Stoics open to the insight that thrownness is also fundamental to Dasein . . . . Thrownness appears in the Stoic's careful handling of *what is in her power*. For example, she tries to choose the beautiful and appropriate way to have breakfast, commute to work, perform her job, treat her family, and generally undertake every action. Inasmuch as she chooses prudently (and provisionally [*meth' hupexaireseos*]), her anxious care is as it were sublated and validated by the firm purposefulness of Providence. But it's vital to recognize that this does not abolish her initiative or responsibility

for choosing values and pathways to their realization. Because even the sage cannot know the mind of God (and nobody ever becomes a sage), human care is eternally estranged from the plan of Zeus. Or perhaps we should say instead that even the sage only brushes against the transcendental meaningfulness of Zeus, which she must renew in each present moment; while for us non-sages, asymptotic ascent toward this horizon—like the proverbial Stoic 'progressor' who drowns an inch below the surface—is the best we can do. Thus something *like* Heideggerian thrownness remains in Stoic ethics." To return to Lampe, "Goldschmidt's point is that we should not rush to call this form of care 'inauthentic.' Rather, we should look at it as a different way of organizing the structures of care identified by Heidegger and situating them in a cosmology" (2014; cf. Lampe, 2020: Section 3).

16 Although Heidegger's language of "being free" echoes Chrysippus's language of "giving free access," Diogenes's Greek does not directly correspond to Heidegger's *Freisein*. One must also resist the temptation to hypostasize Care as a substance even though Heidegger's interpretation of Care in accordance with the Stoic understanding remains woefully similar to Zeus. Here we would not be remiss if we were to invoke the role of Zeus in Hesiod's *Theogony*. In this sense, it may be important to trace the role of Zeus in Heidegger's thinking from the *Essays on Early Greek Thinking* to the *Parmenides* lecture.

17 "Even as early as the Stoics, *merimna* was a firmly established term, and it recurs in the New Testament, becoming '*sollicitudo*' in the Vulgate. The way in which 'care' is viewed in the foregoing existential analytic of Dasein, is one which has grown upon the author in connection with his attempts to Interpret the Augustinian (i.e., Helleno-Christian) anthropology with regard to the foundational principles reached in the ontology of Aristotle" (Heidegger 1993: 199).

18 Heidegger (1993: 385). Might we claim that *oikeiōsis* is also beholden to an individual fate (*Schicksal*) or collective destiny (*Geshick*) if necessity determines the future course of all things?

19 In Heidegger's preparations for a planned lecture course, "Philosophical Foundations of Medieval Mysticism" (1919), his investigations into the phenomenology of religion prompted his own kind of coming into oneself—the becoming of his own nature—as evident in a letter to Father Engelhart Krebs: "I believe that I have the inner calling to philosophy, and, through my research and teaching, to do what stands in my power for the sake of the eternal vocation of the inner man, and to do it for this alone, and so justify my existence and work ultimately before God" (Heidegger 2007: 96). Here, we might in a proto-Kantian vein recall Seneca's affirmation of autonomy: "What then? Shall I not follow in the footsteps of my predecessors? I shall indeed use the old road, but if I find one that makes a shorter cut and is smoother to travel, I shall open the new road. Men who have made these discoveries before us are not our masters, but our guides. Truth

lies open for all; it has not yet been monopolized. And there is plenty of it left even for posterity to discover. Farewell" (Sen. *Ep.* 33.11).

20 Agamben also observes the influence of *oikeiōsis* upon Paul: "The 'new creature' is only the capacity to render the old inoperative and use it in a new way" (Agamben 2015: 56).

21 As previously argued by Engberg Pedersen (2000), Paul's own relationship with Christ imitates the Stoic form of *oikeiōsis* whereby one shifts from seeing oneself as a particular individual to seeing oneself as a rational being.

22 "What we call the beginning is often the end / And to make and end is to make a beginning / The end is where we start from. . . . We shall not cease from exploration / And the end of all our exploring / Will be to arrive where we started / And know the place for the first time" (Eliot 1952: 144–5).

23 Krell (1992) has magisterially exposed the incipient daimonic core haunting the question of being by hearkening back to the latent Pre-Socratic beginnings in Heidegger's thinking.

24 Here we arrive at a juncture whereby Heidegger's engagement with Aristotle, especially his account of the *psyche*, becomes relevant since Heidegger's fundamental ontology might be said to retain the same impulse of *zōē* in Aristotle through his account of *orexis*. However, what we find in the Stoic tradition is perhaps a refinement of Aristotelian *orexis* by introducing the problem of self-consciousness in the organism for the first time.

25 This gesture is a radical decentering of the Aristotelian cosmos whereby it is not life, but the Unmoved Mover, and hence divine thinking, itself that will undergird his metaphysical enterprise. The Stoic legacy thus presents an apparent radicalization of the Aristotelian one back toward *zōē* and *animalitas* rather than the mistaken belief of a culmination in *humanitas* and the *animal rationale*.

Works Cited

Agamben, G. (2015), *The Use of Bodies*, trans. Adam Kotsko, Stanford: Stanford University Press.

Eliot, T. S. (1952), *The Complete Poems and Plays of T.S. Eliot 1909–1950*, New York: Harcourt Brace Jovanovich.

Engberg Pedersen, T. (2000), *Paul and the Stoics*, Westminster: John Knox Press.

Heidegger, M. (1967), *Wegmarken*, Frankfurt am Main: Vittorio Klostermann

Heidegger, M. (1979), *Prolegomena zur Geschichte des Zeitbegriffs*, Frankfurt am Main: Vittorio Klostermann

Heidegger, M. (1993), *Sein und Zeit*, Tubingen: Max Niemeyer Verlag

Heidegger, M. (2000), *Towards the Definition of Philosophy*, trans. Ted Sadler, London: Athlone Press.

Heidegger, M. (2004), *The Phenomenology of Religious Life*, trans. Matthias Fritsch and Jennifer Anna Gosetti-Ferencei, Bloomington: Indiana University Press.

Heidegger, M. (2007), *Becoming Heidegger: On the Trail of His Earliest Occasional Writings, 1910–1927*, eds. Theodore Kisiel and Thomas Sheehan, Evanston: Northwestern University Press.

Heidegger, M. (2012), *Four Seminars*, trans. Andrew Mitchell and Francois Raffoul, Bloomington: Indiana University Press.

Hyland, D. (1997), "Heidegger, Plato, and the Myth of Care", *Research in Phenomenology*, 27 (Fall 1997): 90–102.

Krell, D. F. (1992), *Daimon Life: Heidegger and Life Philosophy*, Bloomington: Indiana University Press.

Laertius, Diogenes (1925), *Lives of Eminent Philosophers*, VII, trans. R. D. Hicks, Cambridge: Harvard University Press.

Lampe, K. (2014), "Goldschmidt and Heidegger," *Continental Stoicisms*, https://stoicisms.wordpress.com. Accessed August 21, 2019.

Lampe, K. (forthcoming 2020), "Stoicism, Language, and Freedom," in K. Lampe and J. Sholtz (eds.), *French and Italian Stoicisms: From Sartre to Agamben*, London: Bloomsbury.

Long, A. A. and Sedley, D. N. (1987), *The Hellenistic Philosophers*, vol. 1, Cambridge: Cambridge University Press.

Mitchell, A. (2008), "Contamination, Essence, and Decomposition: Heidegger and Derrida," in D. Pettigrew and F. Raffoul (eds.), *French Interpretations of Heidegger: An Exceptional Reception*, 131–50, Albany: State University of New York Press.

Mitchell, A. (2015), *The Fourfold: Reading the Late Heidegger*, Evanston: Northwestern University Press.

Plotinus (1998), *Enneads*, 7. Vols. trans. A. H. Armstrong, Cambridge: Harvard University Press.

Ramelli, I. and Konstan, D. (2009), *Hierocles, the Stoic: Elements of Ethics, Fragments, and Excerpts*, Lexington: Society of Biblical Literature.

Schürmann, R. (1987), *Heidegger on Being and Acting: From Principles to Anarchy*, Bloomington: Indiana University Press.

Seneca (1917), *Ad Lucilium epistulae morales*, Books I–LXI, trans. Howard M. Gummere, Cambridge: Harvard University Press.

Seneca (1925), *Ad Lucilium Epistulae Morales*, Books XCIII–CXIIV, trans. Howard M. Gummere, Cambridge: Harvard University Press.

Sheehan, T. (1995), "Heidegger's New Aspect: On *In Sein, Zeitlichkeit*, and the Genesis of Being and Time," *Research in Phenomenology*, 25 (Fall 1995): 207–25.

Skocz, D. (2008), "Postscripts to the 'Letter on Humanism': Heidegger, Sartre, and Being Human," in D. Pettigrew and F. Raffoul (eds.), *French Interpretations of Heidegger: An Exceptional Reception*, 73–88, Albany: State University of New York Press.

Vallega-Neu, D. (2010), "Ereignis: The Event of Appropriation," in B. Davis (ed.), *Martin Heidegger: Key Concepts*, 140–54, Durham: Acumen.

Hans Jonas, Ancient Stoicism, and the Problem of Freedom

Emidio Spinelli

As Lore Jonas vividly recalls in her *Introductory Remarks* to the *Erinnerungen*, the autobiographical book that best brings out Hans Jonas's personality and intellectual standing, he "had received an education in the grand humanistic tradition that was typical of his generation, and which is almost unknown today. He could quote Homer in Greek and Cicero in Latin, learned Hebrew in secondary school, and was fond of the Prophets" (Jonas 2008: xv). It is undeniable, therefore, that in reconstructing the conceptual universe of Jonas's oeuvre a privileged place can, or indeed must, be reserved for his relationship with the classical heritage in antiquity. Certainly, it is far from easy to provide a clear and detailed outline of this relationship with the ancient philosophical past. Jonas is not the kind of author who peppers his writing with quotes, references, and footnotes. Often his engagement with the past is a silent one, and only a painstaking approach can reveal the presence of this or that ancient author. In the light of this premise, I shall limit myself to garnering some data in a systematic and orderly fashion; and above all I shall pay attention to the crucial role played by Hans Jonas and his particular attitude for a coherent interpretation of ancient Stoicism. Apart from some (maybe scattered, even occasional or only preparatory) observations about the role of Stoic ideas,[1] I shall focus especially (or better uniquely) on a course he offered twice at the New School for Social Research in New York (1966 and 1970), which I edited some years ago (see Jonas 2010).

If we want to identify the main structure of the course, we have to remember that it is devoted to a careful analysis of the roots of the concept of freedom, or better on a plurality of different, even conflicting concepts of freedom in the ancient world (from Plato to Augustine). It is impossible to deny, from a more comprehensive point of view, that the concept of freedom should be considered as a *"fil rouge"* of Jonas's overall philosophy, in each step of his production, always well attested not only in his published works but also and often in his didactic activity at the New School for Social Research.[2]

Before examining the originality of the role and function of freedom in ancient Stoicism, Jonas offers a survey of various positions held by previous thinkers: from Plato (to whom he honestly dedicates only a very short "spot," only few lines, restricted to the mention of a decisive passage in *Republic* 10.614ff.: see Jonas 2010: 271-2) to a sort of "running commentary' on Aristotle's *Nichomachean Ethics*, book 3, where he underlines the importance and the novelty of the Aristotelian distinction between voluntary and involuntary actions as well as the special weight given there to the notion of "deliberate choice" (Jonas 2010: 272-9). According to Jonas, it is possible and legitimate to highlight a common, distinctive trait of this "classical" idea of freedom: it concerns the power or capacity to positively do something, namely as a political feature of the Greek citizen (or *politēs*), who reaches his moral excellence or *aretē* by acting "outside," in the open field of political engagement linked to the everyday life of his *polis*.

After this historical reconstruction of the Greek (and maybe especially Athenian) concept of freedom, Jonas alters the perspective of his analysis and rather stresses, beyond the "practical" or "political" attitude of the classical discussion about free moral choices, the "theoretical" background of any possible debate in the ancient world about freedom. It is useful, in this case, to quote his actual words:

> <Practical problems of freedom[3]> In their classical form these problems were of a twofold nature: (a) Granted my power to act and granted the control of my will over my own immediate action, what is my power of action in the scheme of things? Will it make a difference in the outcome? By having control over my doings, do I control, or at least influence, my destiny with my doings? (b) Granted my doing what I just wished to do, was I in full control of myself in wishing to do so? Was my ego master in its own house? Was I, perhaps, more possessed, <more> carried away, than active in my actions? In other words, if an action is called free when willed, was the will also free in willing it? (Jonas 2010: 268)

Given this "theoretical" approach, Jonas indicates a major, decisive "turning point" in the history of ancient Greece: namely, the advent of the so-called Hellenistic Age after the extensive conquests of Alexander the Great, and the new political order established after his death. This is an exceptional, even exclusively peculiar, moment that especially affects and radically alters the idea of moral excellence or *aretē* and accordingly any ethical attitude for and inside the new Hellenistic schools of philosophy. Jonas's exact words can help us in this case too:

> The practical consequences of this are not our concern, but it took away one essential dimension from Greek life and from the possibilities of achieving perfection or excellence and self-fulfillment in terms of that dimension. Prominent individuals in the cities could become benefactors of their cities by way of donation, initiating a building program which would constitute a monument to themselves, and such activities shifted to the non-political sphere with enterprises such as civic improvement, building of gymnasia, baths, theaters, etc. With this <constriction> of the whole area open to individual communal enterprise (not individual *business* enterprise, which greatly expanded) the conception of *aretē* which had been developed in the classical period lost the very condition of its operation, the possibility of meaningful application. It had to be modified, therefore to fit the new conditions, and the major modification was what you might call the "invention" of the idea of the private individual. (Jonas 2010: 282)[4]

Among these schools, Jonas attributes a decisive role to Stoicism, because "Stoic philosophy reinterprets the position of man within his environment and ultimately within the universe. The major event in ancient history which brought about this transformation was the fall of the Greek polis" (Jonas 2010: 281).[5] Behind such a highly positive evaluation, there is the conviction that Stoicism (even more than Aristotle) can be considered as the first and best philosophical examination of the idea of freedom from a strong, systematic, holistic point of view. This is clear from the following:

> One may say that the Stoa is the first philosophical school to devote explicit attention to freedom as a problem and goal for man. Aristotle merely dealt with the fact that some of our actions are voluntary and some involuntary, some of mixed nature, and so on, and one cannot say that in Aristotle we encounter a *problem* of human freedom. What we do find is a description of types of human action which fall under one or the other class of acts; i.e., free actions, non-free actions, and actions partly free, partly unfree, etc. The *problem* of freedom may come about in connection with a conception of a universal law of all things. That is, it is in confrontation with a doctrine of universal determinism, or in confrontation with a universalizing of the concept of cause, that the problem of freedom first appears *as* a problem, in the sense of whether or not freedom is possible and if so *how* without violating a principle which is otherwise as firmly established as the principle of universal determination happened to be

<in the Stoic philosophy>. So in some respects the problem of freedom in Stoic philosophy is a self-created one in so far as the Stoics who set so high a price on human freedom were the same as those who also emphasized with such energy the principle of a universal and irrefragable causal law. (Jonas 2010: 295)

The problem of freedom in Stoicism cannot be restricted to a mere moral question, since one has at the same time to clarify some necessary aspects in logic and physics. Jonas rightly underlines the systematic or, if we prefer, the "holistic" character of Stoic philosophy[6]; and at the same time he rightly underlines that this Stoic approach is very different from our contemporary attitude, which tends to create isolated "departments" or "bits and pieces" of knowledge, not reciprocally and necessarily interrelated. (This, as all of us well know, is the normal way with modern specialisms.)

I think that the care with which Jonas's assertion is made should be noted, since it represents a strong lesson in methodology: he examines the Stoic notion of freedom without ignoring any of its logical, physical, theological, ethical aspects. Therefore, he insists on the physical structure of the Stoic world[7] as well as on the dialectical relationship between the whole (interpreted as a perfect, harmonious, ordered, beautiful *kosmos*, a material/corporeal entity, the divine Fire, not eternal but characterized by a cyclic development) and its parts (above all, human beings).

I would like to stress the deep philosophical interest of such a doctrine: one defending a strong idea of necessity, that however should not be identified (at least in case of human beings) with a form of "blind necessity" (Jonas 2010: 303), or better with too strict a form of constraint or even compulsion. In order to understand better the philosophical weight of the entire conceptual universe here evoked, Jonas insists on the technical use of the term *heimarmenē*:

> The universal necessity which rules all things and makes them conform to the interest of the whole is called *heimarmene*. This is an old name promoted by the Stoics to a central position in the canon of cosmological and philosophical terms. *Heimarmene* means destiny. This is not the same as *ananke*, which means compulsion. *Heimarmene* signifies distribution, <allotment>, as in a governmental system where functions, roles, rewards and punishments are meted out, distributed by lot. Whatever occurs is part of a universal dispensation.
>
> For the part that tries to resist the dispensation of the whole there is no difference between brute *ananke* and the *heimarmene* which is an expression of the universal reason of things. In other words, for the unreasonable or non-rational parts the universal law is a law of brute necessity. But to the extent that parts of the universal system are endowed with the capacity to determine their

> own inner attitudes towards the universal rule the subjection to it may turn from one of mere necessitation to one of assenting conformity. The secret of the Stoic cosmic piety and of their whole conception of freedom lies in the power of man to determine, if not his external destiny, at least his internal attitude towards what befalls him, what surrounds him, and ultimately towards the whole. (Jonas 2010: 302)

If this is the global picture of the Stoic idea of "destiny" and more generally of its notion of "determinism," it should always be remembered (against the background of a specific form of "immanentism," rather than pantheism: see Jonas 2010: 305) that such a form of *heimarmenē* also has a theological value, and thus must be identified with a specific form of "providence" or *pronoia*. This means that in the famous *infinita series causarum* (infinite series of causes) everything is pre-ordered toward what is the best condition of the universe, although the overall providential structure here described does not seem to exercise its power right down to single human lives in their minute, minimal details:

> Therefore, *heimarmene* is not merely the all-pervading necessity. It is also the principle of continual self-adjustment. [...]
>
> Thus it is evident that *heimarmene*, although a strict principle of causality, is not the same as mechanical causality. *Heimarmene* is a causality with an overall goal which <is> not an end toward which the cosmos strives but is rather the maintaining of the cosmos in the best self-adjusted condition. There is, then, a certain teleology. Therefore, *heimarmene*, which is best translated as "destiny," can be equated with *pronoia*, which means "providence."
>
> The identification of universal causal necessity with wise providence is one of the crucial points of Stoic philosophical theology, which means a theology of nature. The divine is totally immanent in the universe in the form of the divine *logos*, which is identical with the whole, and which is the ordering and governing principle of the whole. (Jonas 2010: 304–5)

Jonas deeply admires this Stoic doctrine (or at least he seems to do so *at this point of his course*), because it does not propose a blind form of determinism, but rather anticipates a global idea of "theodicy," according to the following, basic guidelines:

> Of course that whole is most perfect whose parts have the maximum perfection for themselves. But whenever it is a case of choosing between the continued perfection or the saving of a part and the continued perfection of the whole, then, of course, the perfection, life, and beauty of the whole prevails. This is the

reason why there is evil in the world. There are evils for the limited, partial self-interest of the parts, but what may be evil for a part—such as its own destruction or the impairment of its self-realization or happiness—may be necessary for the maintenance of the harmony and completeness of the whole.

This is the Stoic theodicy, the justification for the design, and the answer to the question of why there is evil in the world. No evil spirit, no contrary, anti-divine principle, is responsible for the existence of evil. Evil is a matter of perspective. Each of the parts of the universe, especially animate parts—and these are the parts that interest the Stoics, apart from man in particular—has a tendency to realize itself and to seek its own fulfillment, its own pleasure and happiness, and to perpetuate itself in being. Each has the drive for self-preservation. (Jonas 2010: 301)

Given such a perspective and such a strongly inclusive picture, Jonas does not play the role of a neutral historian of ancient philosophy. Rather, he feels the necessity of asking some very prickly questions, linked to his overall theoretical approach to the difficult theme of freedom. Once we have accepted this complex Stoic physical description of the world, questions arise: What is the space and the special role granted to human beings? What is the relationship between them as moral agents and the totality of events, that forms the "history" of the entire *kosmos*? And how should we understand the alleged virtue or *aretē* attributed to human beings as privileged members of the whole?

As to the Stoic answer, we can safely affirm that it makes use of a clear metaphorical model[8]: that of the organism, the organic body, where each part has a biologically vital function, not just for itself, but in order to guarantee the global and correct functioning of the whole body, inside a network of interrelated elements. Jonas's presentation of this doctrine has great acuity:

The model of a whole is, of course, an organic body, where there is the relation of parts to whole, the existence of the whole by means of its parts, with each part having a vital function, and being not for itself but for the whole. From Plato onwards this organic model served for the conception of the universe as a whole. It follows that the universe is finite, but this is not the crux at the moment. What matters is that the universe means an inter-relation of all the parts. It means, therefore, for each part, two things: (1) on the one hand, it is fully integrated into the network of interactions, inter-relations, which constitute the whole of the universe. No part can separate itself, make itself independent of the whole. It is what it is by virtue of the whole existence and in constant interdependence with all the other parts. (2) Each part has also a role in the whole. It is not merely determined by and dependent on the whole. In a certain sense the whole is dependent on it, at least in the sense that the wholeness of the whole requires the presence and continuous functioning of all of the parts. That does not mean that each individual part in its individual identity is indispensable to the whole. Each individual agent in this universe is perishable and therefore obviously expendable, but during the time that it is "on <stage" it> has its assigned role, which role may also include its leaving the scene when its assignment is over and it has played out its role. (Jonas 2010: 299)

But again: What about human beings? Jonas stresses the fact that for Stoicism their peculiar function is guaranteed not only by the special and creative use of their hands[9] but also and especially by the central role played by their reason or *logos*. Surely, this must be considered the main feature of their ethical approach to reality and one should always presuppose behind it the well-known Socratic attitude of a deep moral intellectualism, strongly defended by ancient Stoic thinkers too.

Be that as it may, and given also the stress the Stoics lay upon the function of the *hēgemonikon*, or the "leading part" of human beings,[10] Jonas raises an additional question (and maybe he also begins his critical engagement at this point): from a Stoic point of view, how is it possible to reconcile the rational use of our intellectual powers on the one side and the full achievement of our freedom on the other side? Under which conditions can we reach the goal of a complete *eudaimonia*, or better of that happiness intended and constantly presented as the *summum bonum*? Jonas maintains that the Stoic answer cannot open the space of a completely free choice,[11] because we are unable to modify and alter the determined course of things and the events in the network of the *heimarmenē*. Human *logos* can only limit itself to the knowledge of the whole, of its inner relations. Here the originality of Jonas's interpretation emerges, since this is a novel version (once again over and beyond the Aristotelian praise for the theoretical life) of the Greek love for contemplation or *theōria*, which the Stoics pursue "not so much for the service of the delight of contemplation in the strict theoretical sense, i.e. in the sense of a dialectical penetration into the structure of being, but more in the religious sense of being able to discern the identity of one's own innermost principle with the principle of the all" (Jonas 2010: 306).

This Stoic attitude is another, refined, highly intellectualistic form of assimilation to God,[12] although this does not mean that human beings can determine their own essence or the nature of other natural things, neither can they modify the infinite series of causes around them. Does this imply that they can only play a passive role and that the mental power of the best part of their soul (the so-called *hēgemonikon*) is inevitably limited? In one sense, the answer must be positive: human beings can only give their "assent" (*sunkatathesis*) to some "impressions" (*phantasiai*) that are absolutely true, namely in the technical Stoic jargon "graspable" (*kataleptikai*)[13]; we have here a mental mechanism of action/reaction valid at the same time from a logical, physical, and ethical point of view.

According to these philosophical premises and doctrines, the horizon of Stoic freedom is clear: it is depicted as a form of obedience, which acts in strong conformity to the universal law of the whole. The Stoic sage, indeed, who is the only actually free human being, submits himself to the order of the *Logos*,[14] since he comes to know thoroughly and therefore willingly accept the perfect plane of divine providence.

We can use here another metaphorical tool for describing this Stoic doctrine of a positive *eudaimonia* considered as a "good flow of life" (*euroia biou*).[15] We should always be "in tune" with the overall and necessary structure of the *kosmos*, since the highest peak of our morality cannot but be represented by our complete and total agreement with the harmonious course of the world. Quite appropriately, Jonas adds that this "is a Stoic trick by which the tragic aspect of man's condition in a powerful world is eliminated and everything is turned to the good. Whatever happens, can be accepted as being for the good by the wise man who has made the cause of the cosmos his own and has therefore made the cause of God his own" (Jonas 2010: 307).

Ancient Stoicism deploys an extensive range of metaphors to express this position, therefore another reference can be added here: the sage is like an actor, a good actor, who is able to play any role assigned to him on the great stage of the *kosmos*, without even trying to act outside the perfect plot written by the divine *Logos*.[16]

At the end of such a long and detailed reconstruction of the Stoic idea of freedom, Jonas begins to advance his objections and his critiques: given the Stoic acceptance of the universal and immutable law of the whole, are we still allowed to properly speak of "freedom" for human beings? According to Jonas, this is rather a radical form of fatalism; indeed, it risks destroying any autonomous power of moral agents, since it confines our allegedly free actions inside the restricted realm of the inner self and denies any possibility of changes, any modifications with respect to the strict rules imposed by *heimarmenē*. On this question, Jonas's polemical tone becomes very tough:

> The theoretical problem of the Stoics is how the freedom to assent or dissent, confirm or not confirm, struggle or not struggle, is compatible with the principle of universal determination, which *as* universal and all-encompassing

should extend to the very act of willing itself. This theoretical problem was not satisfactorily solved by the Stoa. The principle of their solution is that we have to distinguish between what happens in the corporeal concatenation of cause and effect and what happens in one innermost sphere of our being, the sphere of our rational self-determination. How can these two things be made sufficiently separate from one another to claim autonomy for the one while the other is completely under the universal necessity? (Jonas 2010: 307)

In conclusion, I think it is worth noticing that such a critique can be properly understood *if and only if* we put it against the wider and very well-known background of one of the crucial steps in Jonas's thought, namely his strong fight against any passive attitude and any form of resignation or quietism, to which he fiercely opposes his active idea of a widespread, conscious, strong kind of *Verantwortung* (responsibility). In sum, these pages about Stoicism in his *Problems of Freedom* (1970) can be rightly considered a clear anticipation and a sort of "prehistorical" chapter of his masterpiece *The Imperative of Responsibility* (Jonas 1984).

There Jonas offers a profound reflection on a renewed anthropology: a discourse on human being not weighed down by abstract rhetorical considerations, but driven by what are bound to be ethical requirements. He invites us to turn, then, to what is known as the sphere of morality in philosophy, in the awareness that a step in this direction immediately brings to the fore the need to examine the very concept of freedom, this risky peculiarity of ours whose breadth can only be measured when it allows itself to be guided by responsibility, against the background of a wider notion of necessity.

I would like to investigate further at least some of crucial elements related to such new anthropological reflections. It is worth noting that Jonas himself began his magnum opus by turning to the ancient world, to classical Greek tragedy, and in particular to the first *stasimon* of Sophocles's *Antigone*, in search of the original seed of this close attention to human beings: their potential, their achievements, but also their weaknesses and limits. For as Sophocles's chorus recites, "many [are the] the wonders but nothing more wondrous than man" (Sophocles, *Antigone* 332–3, Engl. tr. in Jonas 1984: 2; see also Spinelli 2014: 200–203).

These primordial anthropological insights are not enough, however. They do not throw sufficient light on the human condition, which is now faced with a completely different situation. As Jonas writes at the beginning of *The Imperative of Responsibility*, the present context is one in which

> modern technology, informed by an ever-deeper penetration of nature and propelled by the forces of market and politics, has enhanced human power beyond anything known or even dreamed of before. It is a power over matter,

over life on earth, and over man himself; and it keeps growing at an accelerating pace. Its unfettered exercise for about two centuries now has raised the material estate of its wielders and main beneficiaries, the industrial "West," to heights equally unknown in the history of mankind. (Jonas 1984: ix)

This is Jonas's rough diagnosis: what technological development promised, or promises, risks becoming—or, rather, has already become—a concrete, everyday threat to the very life of our planet. Hence, a strong need is felt for a new proposal, a powerful thesis that might cut to the root of our most important and ethically elevated behavior. In the light of all this, Jonas puts forward a very strong starting hypothesis, which theoretically verges on a new form of "practical reason" (following Kant, but obviously also going beyond him; see Theis 2008). Jonas sums up his thesis as follows:

> the altered, always enlarged nature of human action, with the magnitude and novelty of its works and their impact on man's global future, raises moral issues for which past ethics, geared to the direct dealings of man with his fellow men within narrow horizons of space and time, has left us unprepared. A new reflection on ethical principles—including such that, for lack of application, could hitherto remain silent—is required for coping with those issues. (Jonas 1984: ix–x)

The overflow of this unchecked technology—fueled by a science increasingly aware of its methods, yet at the same time committed to meeting the needs of an economy wholly bent on indiscriminate profit-making—requires a radical change, affecting the very essence of human agency. The enormity of this profoundly new (and, in Jonas's eyes, extremely dangerous) scenario makes even appeals for individuals to respect the law ineffective. Therefore, Jonas writes: "The *Antigone* chorus on the *deinotes*, the wondrous power, of man would have to read differently now [sic]; and its admonition to the individual to honor the laws of the land would no longer be enough" (Jonas 1984: 6).

Moreover, the new course to be imparted to moral prescriptions designed by and addressed to human beings cannot be limited to what we might term "the ethics of concern for one's fellow man," understood in evangelical (or Kantian) terms. We now have a wider space within which to exercise our freedom, and hence the burden of the responsibility attached to it has become far greater, as nature itself would appear to be emphatically asserting its rights. As Jonas writes,

> it is at least not senseless anymore to ask whether the condition of extrahuman nature, *the biosphere as a whole and in its parts*, now subject to our power, has become a human trust and has something of a moral claim on us not only for

our ulterior sake but for its own and in its own right. If this were the case it would require quite some rethinking in basic principles of ethics. It would mean to seek not only the human good *but also the good of things extrahuman*, that is, to extend the recognition of "ends in themselves" beyond the sphere of man *and make the human good include the care for them*. (Jonas 1984: 8, my italics)

The human and everything surrounding it, then, what we might call, in Stoic terms, the *kosmos*, now share the same destiny. Our very anthropological structure can no longer be self-enclosed and forget the intrinsic dignity of nature as a whole, to the point of reducing it to a mere object of utilitarian exploitation (see Jonas 1984: 137); rather, it must become "environmentally sustainable," to borrow a trendy expression. To phrase this in Kantian terms, the new man described by Jonas must be willing and able to fully obey an imperative that, while certainly still categorical, sounds different to everyone everywhere, "an imperative responding to the new type of human action and addressed to the new type of agency," and which ought to sound as follows:

> "Act so that the effects of your action are compatible with the permanence of genuine human life"; or expressed negatively: "Act so that the effects of your action are not destructive of the future possibility of such life"; or simply: "Do not compromise the conditions for an indefinite continuation of humanity on earth"; or, again turned positive: "In your present choices, include the future wholeness of Man among the objects of your will." (Jonas 1984: 11)

Ensuring this possibility of safeguarding the life of the whole biosphere (of the *kosmos*, again according to the Stoics) is not a task to be fulfilled by only one culture, be it humanistic or scientific: both these cultures must enter into dialogue in order to provide productive help to human beings in order to make conscious and responsible choices that will benefit the future integrity of the whole world. In this way—perhaps, *also* in this way—it will be possible to dispel the shadows and resume a serious reflection, capable of restoring the light of rational, conscious morality, so as to contain the dangers posed by climate change.

Notwithstanding his clear critique of some (unacceptable) Stoic conclusions, proposed in order to interpret freedom as the (more or less enthusiastic) acceptance of a universal and necessary form of determinism, I suggest that Jonas does not want to *completely* refuse the Stoic lesson concerning the (unavoidable) link between freedom itself and necessity. This becomes clear, again in *The Imperative of Responsibility*, as soon as he tries to fight against any unproductive and even dangerous philosophical form of "utopia," since, as he clearly writes, the fundamental error of the whole conception, already in Marx[17], is *the separation of the realm of freedom from the realm of necessity*, the belief that the one begins where the other ends, that freedom lies somewhere beyond necessity instead of in the meeting with it. (Jonas 1984: 196)

To find a stable equilibrium between freedom and necessity can be a difficult, a very difficult task: but it is something that should be at the top of the agenda of anyone who wants to understand the space of our free actions against the background of our existential (and duly necessary) relationship with the environment on the one side and other human beings on the other. This is the full moral meaning of our responsibility, and this is what Jonas always attempted in all his philosophical endeavors.[18]

Notes

1 One should quote, in this connection, both his early monography, first published in 1930 on *Augustin und das paulinische Freiheitsproblem* (see Jonas 1965), and his major work on Gnosticism (see Jonas 1988, 1993).

2 See especially Pinsart (2002) and Lenzig (2006); for other bibliographical references, see also Jonas (2010: xii–xiv) and notes.

3 Angular brackets indicate Jonas's handwritten additions to his typewritten lecture notes.

4 As to this very peculiar philosophical "invention" Jonas rightly insists on the "pre-historical" and decisive role played by the Cynics: see especially Jonas (2010: 287–90) and also Spinelli (2015).

5 The condition of Greek people in the Hellenistic Age is more adequately described by Jonas elsewhere, when he emphasizes the new dimension of "inwardness": "it is obvious that the source of one's strength and the power of one's possible happiness are transferred into the inwardness of the individual. From within must come those possessions or states of being which constitute happiness. With the loss of the legacy of the *polis* what happened was not so much the discovery of the dimension of inwardness like a new original independent vision, but rather the throwing back of man upon himself by the denial of that outwardness which had formerly offered the dimension for proving and fulfilling oneself. It was the loss of the political sphere as the relevant and essential which forced men to cultivate the inner life as the means and the dimension of self-realization. Self-realization was no longer possible in the sphere of objective action and relation. The external world had lost much of its relevance with the mere fact that it was no longer in the power of the individuals <which had been> making up the small commonwealth of <the>

classical <past>. So this external sphere was increasingly seen as the area of *tyche*, accident and Fate" (Jonas 2010: 293).
6   The best Stoic description of such a "holistic" approach to the entire field of the philosophical enterprise is maybe offered by Diogenes Laertius 7.39–40.
7   On Stoic physical and cosmological doctrines, Hahm (1977) remains essential.
8   More generally, the role of metaphorics in ancient Stoicism is also highly stressed by Hans Blumenberg: see Kurt Lampe's chapter in this volume.
9   This is maybe a sort of "privilege" already highlighted by Anaxagoras: see DK 59 A 102.
10 Regarding the "leading part" or "commanding-faculty," see LS 53.
11 For a complete and very stimulating reconstruction of the possible "compatibilist" attitude of ancient Stoicism (especially in the case of Chrysippus), see Salles (2005); on the relationship between freedom and determinism in Stoic philosophy, see also (although with qualifications and some doubts) Bobzien (2001).
12 On this very intriguing question, see now Reydams-Schils (2017).
13 Regarding graspable impressions, see LS 39-41.
14 Or better of Zeus, if we prefer to use the strong theological image defended by Cleanthes in his famous *Hymn to Zeus* (SVF I.537 = LS 54I; cf. LS 61G).
15 See for example, SVF III 16, LS 61A2.
16 One might even agree with Seneca, who strongly defends the idea that the Stoic sage is the best and most consistent of all actors in a world presented as a stage: see for example, *Ep.* 35.4; see also *On Benefits* 2.17.2.
17 One should note that, in the same passage of the German edition of this work, we do not find only Marx as the champion of this (wrong) principle, on which is based any utopian ideology, but also, and quite obviously, Ernst Bloch ("bei Marx wie bei Bloch," in Jonas (1979: 357).
18 Let me warmly thank Kurt Lampe, who kindly revised and improved my (more or less poor) English.

Works Cited

Bobzien, S. (2001), *Determinism and Freedom in Stoic Philosophy*, Oxford: Oxford University Press.

Hahm, D. E. (1977), *The Origins of Stoic Cosmology*, Columbus: Ohio State University Press.

Jonas, Hans (1965), *Augustin und das paulinische Freiheitsproblem. Eine philosophische Studie zum pelagianischen Streit*, ed. and Intro. M. Robinson, 2nd ed., Göttingen: Vandenhoeck & Ruprecht.

Jonas, Hans (1979), *Das Prinzip Verantwortung. Versuch einer Ethik für die technologische Zivilisation*, Franfurt am main: Insel Verlag.

Jonas, Hans (1984), *"The Imperative of Responsibility," in Search of an Ethics for the Technological Age*, trans. H. Jonas and D. Herr, Chicago: University of Chicago Press.

Jonas, Hans (1988), *Gnosis und spätantiker Geist. Erster Teil. Die mythologische Gnosis. Mit einer Einleitung Zur Geschichte und Methodologie der Forschung*, 4th ed., Göttingen: Vandenhoeck & Ruprecht.

Jonas, Hans (1993), *Gnosis und spätantiker Geist. Teil II.1–2*, ed. K. Rudolph, Göttingen: Vandenhoeck & Ruprecht.

Jonas, Hans (2008), *Memoirs*, trans. K. Winston, ed. and Annot. C. Wiese, Waltham, MA: Brandeis University Press.

Jonas, Hans (2010), *Problemi di libertà*, ed. E. Spinelli, trans. A. Michelis, Torino: Nino Aragno Editore (English text and Italian translation).

Lenzig, U. (2006), *Das Wagnis der Freiheit. Der Freiheitsbegriff im philosophischen Werk von Hans Jonas aus theologischer Perspektive*, Stuttgart: Kohlhammer.

Pinsart, M.-G. (2002), *Jonas et la liberté. Dimensions théologiques ontologiques, éthiques et politiques*, Paris: Vrin.

Reydams-Schils, G. (2017), "'Becoming Like God' in Platonism and Stoicism," in T. Engberg-Pedersen (ed.), *From Stoicism to Platonism: The Development of Philosophy, 100 BCE-100 CE*, 142–58, Cambridge: Cambridge University Press.

Salles, R. (2005), *The Stoics on Determinism and Compatibilism*, Aldershot: Ashgate.

Spinelli, E. (2014), "La filigrana filosofica di una tragedia: Sofocle e il primo stasimo dell'*Antigone*," *Scienze dell'antichità*, 20: 191–206.

Spinelli, E. (2015), "Die Rolle der Tyche: die kynische Provokation bei Hans Jonas," *Giornale critico di Storia delle Idee*, 14: 17–30.

Theis, R. (2008), *Jonas. Habiter le monde*, Paris: Michelon.

8

Dignity and Self-Making

Seneca, Pico della Mirandola, and Hannah Arendt

Andrew Benjamin

1. Introduction

What today is a critical engagement with Stoicism?[1] While the specific domain of investigation in this instance centers around Arendt's critique of Stoicism in *The Human Condition*, the force of that critique cannot be distinguished from her own attempt both to rethink and thus reposition what counts as the being of being human, while engaging critically with the implicit philosophical anthropology she takes to be located within Stoicism.[2] In other words, her encounter with Stoicism cannot be separated from the prevailing concerns of the development of a philosophical anthropology. For Arendt that project assumes the centrality of the world. Freedom occurs in the world. Thinking human being therefore has to involve not just a thinking of worldly being but the sustained continuity of worldly being as activity. Being, creating and beginning—creating and beginning as present as modes of continuity—are interarticulated from the start. To deploy her own formulation, the human

> *is* a beginning, man can begin; to be human and to be free are one and the same. God created man in order to introduce into the world the faculty of beginning: freedom. (1961: 166)

The question that attends this description of human being pertains to whether or not freedom is a predicate of an individual, or if freedom is descriptive of a plurality of activities and, thus, implicated in any conception of freedom, would be the space that such activities both presuppose and maintain. Activity as placed and place as the location of activity, two determinations that coalesce in her idea of the "space of appearance," would then have to form part of any definition of freedom.³ Clearly, her argument involves overcoming the centrality of the individual such that freedom is then connected to a space of activity. Not only is Stoicism identified with the earlier position, more significantly her conception of Stoicism is such that Stoicism is unable to think the predicament in which the world now finds itself. Thus, entailing that there is a clear tension between what it means to be free, which may be no more than the work of the imagination, and the possibility of enacting freedom.⁴ The imagination can never supplant the work of thought. Indeed, while what is to be developed here in terms of *enacted freedom* can be imagined, it remains unthinkable in Stoic terms if there were the need to connect thinking, acting, and the world's transformation.⁵ Even though Seneca locates human being within the world, insofar as the human has a collective "we" such that "membra sumus corporis magni" (we are parts of a great body, *Ep.* 95.52), that position does not yield the world as a locus in which there is an interconnection between freedom, acting, and possible transformations grounded in the discontinuous continuity of beginnings. A connection to the world would be essential however once freedom is enacted and thus not just a state of mind. Equally, and this despite Arendt's own insistence on the primacy of action, the space between thought and action, which is another configuration of the space of the political, will, in the end, pose problems for her overall argumentation. Though it should be noted that Arendt has a very clear conception of this space. Hence, she writes that the "political in the sense of the polis, its end or *raison d'etre*, would be to establish and keep in existence a space where freedom as virtuosity can appear" (1961: 153).⁶

There is an initial complex of concerns. The problem, on one level, is the connection between thinking and action. The limit of the imagination is straightforward. Imagining that one is free does *not* entail being free. Being free is inextricably connected to the actualization of a capacity to act. Once this position can be maintained and what matters is the interplay of capacity and actualization, then the concept of potentiality plays a central role. Freedom needs to be equated with *enacted freedom*. It follows therefore that central to freedom is the actualization of a capacity. Arendt is of course right when she argues in *On Revolution* that "political freedom . . . means the right to be a participator in government or it means nothing at all" (Arendt 1973: 218). And yet, fundamental to having that right is the possibility of its actualization. Actualization involves crossing a threshold. The key concept, even if its force remains unacknowledged by Arendt, continues to be potentiality.⁷ Participation is a coming to participate. It is therefore the actualization of the potential to participate. Even what she calls the "right to have rights" does not entail the enactment or realization of the possibilities afforded by the presence of that right as an original condition.[8] On the contrary, it merely acknowledges the presence of such a condition. Enactment is the movement from right to activity, the movement across a threshold, thus the actualization of a potentiality. Policing does not just occur at the threshold; policing names that which gives the threshold, now combining with the border, its own sense of continuity.[9]

Within this overall context, Stoicism, with its promulgation of an exigent "tranquility," that state in which the "soul" endures in "a peaceful state being never uplifted nor cast down," would be precipitate *now* because of the world's own exigency. In other words, it is *now* too early for tranquility. The world, the present stage of the world, the world as it is *now*, does not allow it. And yet, caution is necessary, since Stoicism cannot be equated with a single position. Its own history incorporates a diverse range of Greek and Roman thinkers, its transformation in the Renaissance, its endurance within Christianity—a project that attains its highest point in French seventeenth-century philosophy and literature—and its reappearance in Foucault's project linked to *souci de soi* (care of the self), all of which means that any single claim runs the risk of reducing Stoicism to a caricature.[10] Consequently, the level of engagement has to be specifically philosophical. Arendt's references in *The Human Condition* to Stoicism should not be read therefore as a series of claims about a specific historical doctrine in any direct sense. On the contrary, "Stoicism" names or identifies a set of philosophical positions against which she is writing. These conditions can be developed precisely because they are not directly reducible to the letter of Stoicism. The conjecture to be pursued here is that this set of positions, while compatible with defining aspects of Stoicism, has greater extension. Stoicism names a particular philosophical position with its own philosophical anthropology. It is equally the case, for example, that a similar conception of being human and thus a comparable philosophical anthropology is evident in Pico della Mirandola; specifically, in the *Oratio de Hominis Dignitate* (Oration on the Dignity of Man). Thus, by noting the interconnection between Pico and elements of Stoic thought, predominately in Seneca, it is possible to recover and make more explicit the object of Arendt's critique.

A further point should be added concerning Arendt. Precisely because of the centrality of the term "dignity" to her own project, its presence in Seneca and then its incorporation into Pico's thinking are significant. It should be added however that Pico's use of the term "dignity" distances the all-too-quick interconnection of *dignitas* and *otium* that occurs in Roman thought, with the attendant consequence of tying the dignity and leisure of a political elite to the retained necessity of slavery. It remains the case that dignity as a quality for Pico, a quality which, as will be suggested, is there to be "emulated," while severing the link to slavery, still does not have attributed to it the force that will in the end be demanded by Arendt.[11]

2. Pico

Both direct references and allusions to Seneca appear a number of times in Pico's *Oratio de Hominis Dignitate*. The most significant for these current concerns is the following:

> It is certainly ignoble [*ingenerosum*] as Seneca says to know only through books and, as though the discoveries of our ancestors had barred the way to our industriousness and the power of nature [*vis naturae*] were exhausted in us, to bring about from ourselves nothing that, even if it fell short of demonstrating the truth, might at least hint at it from afar. (§197, translation modified)[12]

In Seneca, there is indeed a refusal of preestablished delimitations. He claims in *De Vita Beata* 3.2 that "I do not bind myself" (*non alligo me*) to the history of Stoic doctrines.[13] As such, he is clear that there needs to be an opening to thought. Though, more significantly, that opening has to allow for activity. The activity in question is the creation of a life. The passage from *De Vita Beata* continues by outlining the project at hand.

> Wisdom is not straying from nature and then forming ourselves according to her law and pattern.[14]

The possibility of self-making or self-forming is essential. Wisdom is linked to a specific type of modeling. In the passage from *De Vita Beata* cited earlier, self-forming occurs as a response to the demands to which, while they are made by the tradition, the tradition itself cannot furnish an adequate reply. The true determining figure is nature.[15] While the language in which the position is advanced alters a number of times, the fundamental contention continues, namely that the soul is able to be molded. Hence, while *Epistulae Morales* 112.29 begins with the claim that a human being is "imperfect" (*imperfecto*), there is no necessity that the imperfect state endure. After its having been supplanted, Seneca adds—and it should be noted that the addition of the language of project is important—the person is "still not good, but is being molded to goodness" (*sed in bonum fingitur*). Molding as an activity produces "goodness." Again, in

De Vita Beata the one who has not been "corrupted," and thus the one with a "reliable spirit," can be the "moulder of his life" (*artifex vitae*, 8.3). Seneca asks in *De Beneficiis*, with a rhetoric that demands analysis in its own right: "Who will you admire more than the man who commands himself, than the one who has power over himself?" (5.7.5).[16] While terminology shifts, what continues is a conception of self as the one charged with its own project. It will be important to return to the ways self-making and self-molding occur in Seneca. At this stage however, it is vital to stay with what is at work in Pico's reference to Seneca.

What is identified by Pico as "our industriousness" (*nostrae industriae*) and the "power of nature" (*vis naturae*) indicates that there is an inherent capacity for human action. And yet, precisely, because any one act is free, there needs to be a sense of the regulative. In the context of the *Conclusiones nongentae* even though the "act of belief" (*actus credendi*) is described as a "free act" (*actus liber*), that freedom is quickly qualified (Mirandola 2013: 76). The qualification of freedom is the already-present concession not just to the presence of external forms of regulation but equally to the necessity that they exert force. (The necessity is in the exertion of force, not in the response. Sin and ignorance have to endure as possibilities.) Thus, what is important here is to pursue, firstly, the way that self-making, as an act, is understood by Pico and then, secondly, the extent to which what endures within all such acts is the regulative.

The presence of the regulative brings two further questions into play. How is the regulative to be understood, and who is regulated? The answer to the second part of this question is linked to the creation of the subject and thus the individuation of a specific subject position. What is at stake in the passages cited earlier, at least initially, concerns "being wise" (*sapere*). Knowledge, which in this context is the state of being wise, must come from within. It must involve the actualization of an inner power. There is a capacity. However, since there is a capacity, its actualization, the acts themselves, can always lead in a number of directions (at times, contrary directions). This position is compounded because of a claim made elsewhere that the human is a "creature of indeterminate image" (§18). Though more exactly, and this is the crucial point, the human is an entity "made neither of heaven nor of earth, neither mortal nor immortal" (*Nec te celestem neque terrenum, neque mortalem neque immortalem fecimus*, §22). Again, this act of creation is positioned by the question of limits. While nature is controlled by its laws, there is an opening since the human is "constrained by no limits" (*nullis angustiis cohercitus*), and more exactly the human can set the measure for itself. This opening threatens the surety of human being; hence, the problem to be addressed is how the absence of limits on the one hand, and a capacity to establish limits on the other, are to be understood. The setting in which to address this problem is not arbitrary. On the contrary, it is created by the claim that the human was "made neither of heaven nor of earth." There are no founding traces. Freedom occurs as a result. How, here, is being human to be understood?

While Pico would not have been aware of Hyginus's *Fabulae*—specifically the fable of Cura—since the manuscript was only edited and printed by Jacob Micyllus in 1535 (the text itself may have been composed around 34 BCE), it is important in this context because it continues a tradition that incorporates *Genesis* and in which fundamental to the origin and creation of human being is the presence of both different forms of earthly presence and the incorporation of an immaterial force into materials.[17] In Hyginus, the earth has two formulations. It is present both as a deity (*Tellus*) and as a material (*humo*). The fable in toto is the following:

> When Cura was crossing a certain river, she saw some clayey mud. She took it up thoughtfully and began to fashion a man [*et coepit fingere hominem*]. While she was pondering on what she had done [*Dum deliberat secum quidnam fecisset*], Jove came up; Cura asked him to give the image life, and Jove readily granted this. When Cura wanted to give it her name, Jove forbade, and said that his name should be given it. But while they were disputing about the name, Tellus arose and said that it should have her name, since she had given her own body. They took Saturn for judge; he seems to have decided for them: Jove, since you gave him life [take his soul after death; since Tellus offered her body] let her receive his body; since Cura first fashioned him, let her possess him as long as he lives [*quamdiu vixerit, Cura eum possideat*]; but since there is controversy about his name, let him be called homo, since he seems to be made from humus [*ex humo videtur esse factus*].[18]

Here, of course, is the creation of life as that which is, ab initio, irreducible to what Walter Benjamin identified as "mere life" (*das bloße Leben*) (1980: II.1 p. 201, 1996: 250). As a result, "mere life," which is the reduction of life to the bodily or the creaturely, is not an original setting, but is always produced; and thus the life produced is marked, and thus could never be just bare, as the marks of its production will always have to be borne. To ignore them is to remain oblivious to the always present particularity involved in the reduction of human being to "mere life." Irreducibility obtains since what is also there, at the same time, is "*Cura*."[19] *Cura* becomes the quality that allows for a different sense of measure.

In directly historical terms the extent to which Hyginus's fable is a retelling of *Genesis* 2.7 is an open question. In *Genesis* 2.7, God has formed the "human" from the "dust." Into "it" God breathes "life." Life is linked henceforth to the logic of breath. That act, the logic's work, transforms the merely human into what is identified in the verse as *nepes hayyah*, namely a human that has the quality of a "living soul." This addition, it can be argued, is that which allows for a differentiation to be made between "mere life" and the life that is proper to human being. What is named therefore is an excess. Once this sense of propriety is developed, it then becomes possible to see, in the first place, in what way there might be an overlap between "care," as a defining human quality, and "the living soul," and then in the second, the differing ways in which the human can be understood as having been created in the image of God.[20] What becomes important is that this additional quality, the one that allows for a differentiation of the "human" from the "creaturely," is both internal to human being and yet has an inherent fragility and thus demands to be defended. Were the quality to be named—remembering that what is named is intrinsic to human being and thus names a founding sense of propriety whose force is unconditional—it can be understood as dignity. The defense of that quality, it can then be argued, becomes a defense of human dignity and thus the defense of a quality that is intrinsic to human being.

Care for Hyginus, which results from the productive presence of the logic of breath, namely the transformation of simple matter, thus the strictly empirical, into that which has a sense of life that holds itself apart from mere life, is not just an account of life. Life is marked from the start by a doubling, a plurality, such that life cannot be reduced to bodily life, except in those circumstances in which identities are produced as coterminous with bodily presence. (As occurs, for example, in slavery.) As intimated earlier, it is an account of life in which what counts as life's propriety, that which sets the measure, is already internal to life. Care names another modality of excess. As an internal determination of human being, thus present as an intrinsic quality, it would be present prior to all creative acts by human subjects (including self-creation or self-fashioning). Moreover, that internal quality is constitutive of the propriety of human being and yet at any point may be disavowed. Precisely because of its precarity, it demands forms of defense. That demand, it needs to be conjectured, is another opening to the law, since it is only the law, the law as that which is open continually to the possibility of justice, that allows for the defense of the necessary precarity introduced by the logic of breath.[21] While the questions of what is meant by "care" and "law" demand detailed investigation, it is nonetheless clear that what both terms inscribe are limit conditions and thus criteria of judgment that are intrinsic to human being. Neither the ethical nor a concern with the nature of the subject's relation to the law, when taken together, comprises external considerations. There is what can be described as an always-already-present—thus, *anoriginal*—relation between the ontological and the ethical.[22] That relation delimits a certain modality of human being. The force of Pico's claim that the human was "made neither of heaven nor of earth" entails that the possibility of regulative action has to be found elsewhere. The conception of humanism that emerges from the *Oratio* suspends the already-present connection between the ontological and the ethical by locating that which guides and controls freedom and, moreover, allows activity to be judged, in the creation of limits that are necessarily extrinsic to human being. The refusal or suspension of the intrinsic opens up that which Pico's own position has then to maintain. As will become clear, not only is that suspension the opening connection between Pico and Seneca, it also provides Stoicism as a generalizable mode of thought rather than a mere historical doctrine, with another mode of endurance.

Having seen that against which Pico's version of humanism is staged, what has to be addressed is how the modality of freedom in his work is to be understood. There are three elements that are involved in answering this question. The first resides in the already-identified capacity for free action. While Kristeller describes Pico as stressing "man's freedom to choose his way of life," it needs to be noted that this freedom depends upon the forms of suspension noted earlier (Kristeller 1947: 100). The second is the recognition that despite this freedom there needs to be a sense of regulation. The "dual nature of souls" is such that one aspect or element of the soul will always, for Pico, "drag us down into the depths" (§85). The regulative however is not an intrinsic quality of the self. Hence, the third element involves the engagement with that predicament. The absence of an intrinsic quality becomes problematic. The argument here is that a resolution to the problem posed by the need for the regulative and the absence of intrinsic qualities and therefore the need for a sense of limits that are then imposed is furnished, in the *Oratio*, by connecting freedom to a structure of emulation. The emulated is both external and regulative, and it is essential that it be both; moreover, the possibility of self-fashioning depends upon the necessity of that connection and thus both on externality and a coterminous absence of intrinsic qualities.

One of the most exact formulations of self-fashioning occurs in the same section of text that begins with the claim that the human is made neither of "heaven" nor of "earth." The passage continues by noting the consequence of this positioning of human being: "so that you may, as the free and extraordinary shaper of yourself, fashion yourself in whatever form you prefer (§22)." However, neither self-fashioning nor self-making as modes of freedom involve pure openness. Both demand forms of delimitation. There is, in Pico, an important connection between self-making, the self that is then made (or being made), and emulation. It is not just that the human is a spirit "clothed in human flesh" (*humana carne circumvestitum*); that entity, as has been noted, has the capacity for self-creation and thus self-fashioning (§40). Moreover, Pico, citing Evanthes the Persian, then states that what is specific about human being is that there is no *nativam imaginem* (innate image). While Evanthes may not have actually existed, though there is some numismatic evidence, it is significant that Pico grounds this assertion in the tradition. The position thus acquires greater authority. The claim is clear: integral to the definition of human being is the absence of an internal image that would then appear externally. Intrinsic qualities do not appear because they are not there. The absence of the possibility for the projection of such an image is inextricably bound up with the way that self-making occurs. Self-fashioning is not just a possibility for human being; it is precisely that capacity that makes the human, for Pico, "admirable." The human "fashions, shapes and transforms [*effingit, fabricat et transformat*] his appearance into that of all flesh [*omnis carnis*], his own character in that of every creature" (*omnis creaturae*, §42).

What has to be addressed at the outset therefore is the inherent sense of the regulative that attends this capacity. This is provided not just by a structure of emulation but a reiteration of the actual language of emulation. The emulated are those who have a transcendent quality in relation to human being. They are closest to God. They are named in the text, inter alia, as the "seraphim" and the "cherubim." What matters here is not the ineliminability of emulation but what it is that is emulated. (There cannot be just emulation.) The text is unequivocal in this regard: "dignitatem et gloriam emulemur" (let us emulate their dignity and their glory, §49). The important point here is that dignity is not an intrinsic quality of human being.[23] Rather, it is the result of the emulation of the dignified. This is further clarified in the argument that the emulation of the "cherub" has, as its precondition, the movement to the "heights of love," which is the place of the cherub, and then a subsequent return to the world, "well taught and prepared for the duties of the active life" (§66). The "cherubic spirit animates" and allows for reasoned engagement (§82). In other words, here that which has transcendent qualities in relation to human being—transcendent and external— sets the measure. Emulation provides the means by which those qualities can organize and regulate being in the world. Worldly knowledge remains inspired and limits have been imposed.

Knowledge however cannot complete or be complete. There is always the counterforce of ignorance. Ignorance is acted out; it, too, is worldly. In regard to the question of worldly knowledge, ignorance has a specific formulation. Ignorance is linked not just to "vice" but equally to the creation of noise. Hence, Pico writes that "dogs always bark at strangers, in the same way they often hate and condemn what they do not understand" (*canes ignotos semper adlatrant, ita et ipsi saepe damnant oderuntque quae non intelligunt*, §233). What is at stake here is ignorance. Ignorance, "hatred," and "condemnation" are linked to a failure to comprehended. "Barking" names the sound that is occasioned by ignorance. The image is clear. Ignorance and cacophony combine.

There is a straightforward source for this combination. Pico refers elsewhere to Heraclitus, whom the Stoics acknowledged among their primary influences. Indeed, he would have had access to the fragments of Heraclitus in the Latin translation of Diogenes Laertius, which was published in 1472.[24] Fragment DK 97 of Heraclitus also invokes barking dogs: "Dogs bark at every one they do not recognize" (κύνες γὰρ καταβαΰζουσιν ὧν ἂν μὴ γινώσκωσι).[25] (There is, after all, an interesting affinity between *non intelligunt* and μὴ γινώσκωσι.) Ignorance cannot be equated with a simple mistake concerning the presence of an entity or an event. Ignorance is connected to understanding. Understanding the world, which has to be accompanied by the proposition that the world is understandable, means that it conforms to laws and principles which are discoverable. While reason is a quality of human being for both Heraclitus and Pico, the human, for Pico, is attributed an intrinsic yet inherently precarious quality that is, essentially "admirable." Human being is admirable because it can emulate and retains its self as locus of admiration as a result of processes of emulation. (The presence of an intrinsic quality that would allow for admiration occurs in the tradition that runs from *Genesis* to Hyginus and also occurs in Kant's evocation of the human capacity for "holiness" in the *Critique of Practical Reason*.[26])

Human imperfection is linked firstly to the absence of the knowledge of the presence of the regulative (or its content) and then, secondly, to a reluctance to concede that human life needs to be lived according to principles that have a necessary externality. The reluctance is also a consequence of human freedom. Overcoming the results of this freedom is provided by emulation. Pico writes that "emulation" of the "cherubic life" will limit the deleterious impact of the affective. Equally, the use of "dialectic" and "moral science" (*moralem scientiam*) will "purge" the soul of "ignorance and vice." Emulation has the effect, in sum, of curbing the possibility of emotional, moral and epistemological delirium (§71). The interarticulation of emulation and self-making opens the way, again, to Seneca.

3. Seneca

Seneca's own account of human being contains a commitment to a form of universalism. Virtue is available to all. All can act virtuously. Virtue and dignity are not just interconnected, that interconnection can be discerned. Hence the important claim linking virtue and dignity: "virtue, though obscured [*obscura*], is never concealed, but always gives signs [*signa*] of its presence; whoever has dignity [*dignus*] can trace her out by her footsteps" (*Tranq*. 3.7). Discerning its presence and then following virtue presupposes that there is a certain type of character formation. Moreover, there is a related claim. Connected to the recovery of virtue is the distancing or dismissing of the impact made by "chance" (*fortuna*). Chance, however, is not merely the unpredictable. Chance is part of a complex of concerns. As a beginning, chance is bound up with freedom. The unpredictable does not designate the exceptional. On the contrary, it can be equated with the necessary and thus ineliminable presence of the vicissitudes of life. The possibility of virtue occurs within this setting. As such, it gives rise to a specific formulation of the "highest good" and thus the presence of that "good" as situated within the passage of life. Seneca is clear: "The highest good is a mind that scorns the happiness of chance and rejoices only in virtue" (*Summum bonum est animus fortuita despiciens virtute laetus, Vit. Beat.* 4.2). The argument, in Seneca, continues with the link to "freedom" (*libertas*), in which freedom is obtained by a staged "indifference to chance" (*fortunae neglegentia, Vit. Beat.* 4.5). Indifference has, as its condition of possibility, not just the inevitability of "chance," but rather its hypostatization and thus its projected fixity. Seneca writes that "all of us are chained to fortune" (*omnes cum fortuna copulati sumus*, *Tranq*. 10.3). Fortune is given. As such, it is not itself a site of confrontation and activity. For Seneca, even death, as part of life, is accounted for in terms of "fortune." Cornelia, the mother of the Gracchi, gave birth to ten children, though "fortune reduced it to two" (*ad duos fortuna redegerat, Helv.* 16.6). Freedom, virtue, and chance continue to be positioned within the movement of life. However, virtue's condition is premised upon the response of "indifference" and thus the assertion of a preference not to be involved; this is an assertion that individuates while allowing for the world to be closed off. Moreover, there is a fundamental reciprocity between individuation and closure; that is, a reciprocity between the process of individuation, which here is the production of the subject, and what can be understood as the nonnecessity of relationality. This is the position that stands opposed to Arendt's claim that "not man but men live on the earth" (Arendt 1961: 164).

Seneca's position can be refined by focusing as much on the subject as on the conception of universalism at work within the subject's production—that is, the process of subjectivization—as a topos within his writings. The subject for Seneca stands alone. Note the formulation in *Epistulae Morales* 74.1, "(H)e who in every case has defined the good by what is honorable, is happy with inwards happiness" (*intra se est felix*). Again, subjectivization is individuation. The formulation in *Epistulae Morales* 92.2 is exact: "he keeps to the heights, leaning upon none but himself." To be propped up is to occasion the possibility of falling. Not only must the subject be alone, standing at the summit, this is a position that links honor and rectitude. Such a conception of being a subject (the process of subjectivization) has an affect on how relationality is then understood. Relationality, as a result, would then be connected to a form of moral undoing: falling as undoing.[27] Relationality would be either the deleterious aftereffect of the putative assertion of the primacy of individual particulars or the descriptive of that to which the response of indifference would be obligatory, were wisdom and virtue to be held as primary. Individuality or singularity has to be posited as an original possibility. Again, the nature of the logic at work here needs to be noted. The move, the one to a self which, in caring for itself, is able to stand alone and apart, does not just amount to the assertion of a form of individuality. Such an assertion is equally premised on relationality's nonnecessity. Relationality is conceived as secondary. As a consequence, this positioning can lead to the denial or refusal of relationality. Even emulation, which is central for Seneca, can be understood in terms of forms or processes of individuation within relationality that can lead to relationality's eventual refusal.[28] The imitation of God, which is the making oneself as God, *deum effingas*, a setup proposed in *De Vita Beata*, always occurs in singular terms for an individual (*Vit. Beat.* 16.1). Virtue, thus the virtuous individual, as understood in this overall context, cannot be separated, once again, from the refusal of relationality. Indeed, it could be argued that it is predicated on such a refusal. There is an important and constitutive reciprocity at work. The consequence of that reciprocity is that virtue is already implicated in the refusal of chance, which is the refusal of an openness to the insistence of negotiation that the presence of others as comprising an integral part of the vicissitudes of life demands. Others will always be there, always already there, there demanding. Relationality exerts demands. Activity and negotiation combine. (It is vital in such a context to recognize that *negotiation* is *nec otium*.)

Virtue is universal and therefore universalizes. Virtue however has to be thought as bound to the form of refusal noted earlier. Virtue, as based on the refusal of an already-present form of relationality, would then be marked, marked inevitably, by its having been, if not premised on that refusal, concomitant with it. The subject position that pertains to this sense of virtue is addressed within the movement of "benefits" outlined by Seneca in *De Beneficiis*.

> Moreover, he who denies that a slave can sometimes give a benefit to his master is ignorant of the rights of man [*Praeterea servum qui negat dare aliquando domino beneficium, ignarus est iuris humani*]; for, not the status, but the intention, of the one who bestows is what counts. No one is precluded from virtue [*Nulli praeclusa virtus est*]; it is open to all, admits all, invites all, the freeborn and the freedman, the slave and the king, and the exile; neither family nor fortune determines its choice—it is satisfied with the naked human being [*nudo homine contenta est*]. . . . It is possible for a slave to be just, it is possible for him to be brave, it is possible for him to be magnanimous; therefore, it is possible also for him to give a benefit, for this also is one part of virtue. So true is it that slaves are able to give benefits to their masters that they have often caused their benefit to be their masters themselves. (*Ben.* 3.18.2–4)

The key point is the claim that virtue is all-inclusive. Not only does the conception of virtue present here have direct implications, virtue takes on a specific condition. A slave can be virtuous insofar as what counts is the "intention" and not the "status." As a result, virtue pertains solely to the universalized yet individuated individual. And here it is important to recognize that the individual is not a given entity that would have priority in either a temporal or an evaluative sense. Even though individualism understands the presence of the individual in that precise way. The contrary is the case. The individuated individual is the singular or the individual as produced. Thus never strictly individual, and thus always predicated on the denial of anoriginal relationality.

Virtue is, initially, the expression of a particular state of mind, or more accurately, a state of the soul. Hence, "the freeborn and the freedman, the slave and the king" can all act virtuously. However, as has been suggested, virtue is not just the expression of a particular state of mind (or soul) since virtue equally and simultaneously involves a complex form of individuation. Thus, virtue is also implicated in—if not constituted by—a simultaneous refusal of relationality, a refusal that marks the subject. Virtue's presence within that setting means that the question of relationality as itself constituting a possible locus of virtue cannot arise. Thus, what is withdrawn from consideration is the possibility that the distinction between "slave" and "king," or "freeborn and freedman" could themselves ever be subject to a form of philosophical scrutiny in which either virtue or dignity were at stake. While within the limits of Stoicism there will always be that which is determinative of correct actions (*orthōmata*), this occurs without any consideration being given to relationality. Hence, questions pertaining to whether dignity or virtue could be undone because of the nature of a relation rather than because of individual actions have to remain unaddressed. The neutrality of the "naked human being" (*nudo homine*) endures. For this precise reason, virtue needs a guarantee. Once linked to the centrality of self-molding as the creation of self that takes "nature" as providing both "pattern" and "law," then self-creation has identified its externally regulated force. (What emerged in Pico is therefore recalled.) Moreover, this is a claim that must extend over all subject positions. The conclusion to be drawn is that the conception of self-molding coupled to the way virtue is understood in Seneca continues to reinforce the primacy of the individuated subject. It is not just that there is the continual possibility of a withdrawal from the world, a withdrawal that has tranquility as its end state; it is that within such a setting, both world and subject cannot be thought other than in terms of the relationship between macrocosm and microcosm that structures the God/world relation in Seneca. In *De Otio*, Seneca writes of "two republics" (*duas res publicas*, 4.1).[29] However, more significantly, in *Epistulae Morales* 5 there is the important claim that "God's place in the universe corresponds to the soul's relation to man. World-matter corresponds to our mortal body" (5.25).[30]

While this relation indicates the human's share in the soul of God, what is significant is that it cannot allow for the emergence of the world as the place of human being either as a domain of activity or as constituting a site of philosophical thought in its own right. Even though there may be a conception of self-care in Seneca, such a possibility has to be interpreted in terms of the self/world relation that sustains it. Marcia Colish suggests that "the failure of reality to correspond with the ideal cosmopolis is not used by any Stoic as a justification for civil disobedience or revolution" (1985: 39). Even in its modern formulation the insistence on the self, even when it is understood within the structure of self-care, has two essential determinations. The first is linked to a conception of care where the primacy of the individual not only precludes the possibility of insisting on the care of the world, the world becomes the mere, thus unthought, setting of human activity. Cosmology would exclude the incorporation of human being as worldly being. The world could not be the locus of primary concern. Were it to be understood in this way then the relation to the world, and the world as the place of relation, thus enjoining its own sense of relationality, would have had to prevail. Here, in contradistinction to that possibility, the nonrelational self maintains its priority. Secondly, even with the primacy of the individual, the latter is not defined by an intrinsic quality that would then yield the criteria in relation to which self-care is in fact possible and, as a result of that possibility, also able to yield criteria of judgment. There may be intrinsic properties (or the semblance thereof) that identify a given individual as who he or she is. However, those qualities only identify a given proper name. They cannot be generalized to provide an overall philosophical anthropology defined by abstract intrinsic properties and in which the world as a locus of definitionally worldly concerns would be that in relation to which human being was thought.

Pico and Seneca have an elective affinity. Both exemplify a philosophical project in which the concerns of the philosophical (and the theological)—ones which are as much metaphysical as they are ethical—are those in which what predominates is firstly a singular subject whose self-definition is simply self-referential rather than defined by a shared worldliness with others. An individual that remains delimited by the affirmed possibility of a staged withdrawal from the world. And then, secondly, for Seneca, there is a cosmology in which the world is there as that which can occasion both connection and withdrawal. The very possibility of such an oscillation is premised on the refusal of any form of original relationality. In a sense this position is captured succinctly in Seneca's description of the "happy man" (*beatus*) that can be found in *De Vita Beata*. In that context Seneca's claim is clear, namely:

> The happy man, therefore, is the one who has right judgment; the happy man is content with his present lot, no matter what it is, and is reconciled to his circumstances; the happy man is he who allows reason to fix the value of every condition of existence.
>
> *Beatus ergo est iudicii rectus; beatus est praesentibus, qualiacumque sunt, contentus amicusque rebus suis; beatus est is, cui omnem habitum rerum suarum ratio commendat.* (7.1)

The world as the place of human circumstance remains unthought. Reason thinks, but not the world. While "reason" is shared between Gods and humans, humans attain only its "shadowed" presence. The relation between Gods and human is given in terms of "semblance" (*similitudo*). The distance is maintained because "reason," according to the formulation given in *Epistulae Morales*, "is already perfected" in God, while "in us it is capable of being perfected." Perfecting its use is, of course, the project of self-making. Self-making for Seneca, as should be clear, has a particular *telos*, namely the *summum bonum*, which is described by Setaioli as the "restoration of harmony with Nature and the logos, which is identical with happiness, wisdom and virtue" (2014: 255). The essential point here is a link between the "highest good" and a sense of harmony. Self-making becomes therefore a form of recovery. And yet, the essential point endures, what allows for that project is a capacity. Human being can self-mold, self-create, and thus fashion itself. The condition allowing for the actualization of that capacity is the necessary absence of intrinsic qualities. In Pico, what is admired is a capacity. The presence of the finite individuated subject is set over against the extrinsic which occasions self-definition. Human beings do not contain dignity. They may simply become dignified. It might be argued therefore that there is an important correlation between individualism and the enforced and necessary absence of intrinsic qualities. If there is a countermeasure to the continual possibility of the individual's twofold priority, then it lies in the affirmation of intrinsic qualities which then becomes the affirmation of the primacy or priority of relationality as that which allows for individuation. Relations precede particulars.

4. Arendt

For Arendt what occasioned survival within the realm of the totalitarian was what she describes in *The Origins of Totalitarianism* as a "persistent stoicism." It allowed for the preservation of a form of individuality; the "individual" in question is of course one defined by "isolation" and thus "a personality without rights or conscience." This reiterates the point made in *The Human Condition* where she argues that Stoicism "rests on the illusion of freedom when one is enslaved" (Arendt 1958: 235). This illusion cannot be separated from the work of the imagination. For her the imagination is a power; quite simply, it is the power to produce images. The imagination is therefore productive and yet while such a claim is true, it establishes, equally, the limit of the imagination. She goes on to note in relation to the imagination's power that it

> can exert itself only as long as the reality of the world and the living, where one is and appears to be either happy or unhappy, either free or slave, are eliminated to such an extent that that they are not even admitted as spectators to the spectacle of self-delusion. (Arendt 1958: 235)[31]

Here the work of the imagination is tied to both a disavowal of the world and a refusal of relationality. In addition, the imagination would be held apart from the process of judgment. In *What is Freedom?*, an essay in which certain formulations overlap with elements of the argumentation of *The Human Condition*, a connection is established between freedom and acting: "Men *are* free—as distinguished from their possessing the gift for freedom—as long as they act, neither before nor after; for to *be* free and to act are the same" (Arendt 1961: 151). While it is clear that there is an identification of freedom with acting, it is equally true that acting involves the enacting of a capacity. Indeed, later in the same paper she can be taken as conceding that point. In a demanding expression of her position she argues:

> What usually remains intact in the epochs of petrification and foreordained doom is the faculty of freedom itself, the *sheer capacity to begin*, which animates and inspires all human activities and is the hidden source of production of all great and beautiful things. But so long as this source remains hidden, freedom is not a worldly, tangible reality; that is, it is not political. (Arendt 1961: 167, emphasis added)

This is a crucial formulation. There are two decisive elements. There is the identification of what is henceforth the "faculty of freedom" with a "capacity." Then, there is the related point that this capacity can, in her terms, remain "hidden." This she describes as the withdrawal from a "tangible reality," which amounts to the refusal to allow that capacity to become political (i.e., to become worldly). There needs to be an additional point made here concerning the sense of agency involved. While it looks as though what is at stake are the acts of a single individual, the claim is far more complex. In *On Revolution*, political freedom is defined in terms of participation, that is, participation within those specific acts that comprise governance.[32] In the end, this becomes a reapplication of aspects of Rosa Luxembourg's understanding of workers' councils to Thomas Jefferson's conception of the "ward." In relation to the latter Arendt wrote that the

> basic assumption of the ward system, whether Jefferson knew it or not, was that no one could be called happy without his share in public happiness, that no one could be called free without his experience in public freedom, and that no one could be called either happy or free without participating, and having a share, in public power. (Arendt 1961: 218)

Sharing or participating in the practice of public power overcomes two senses of individuality. In the first instance, what would be overcome is the identification of the individual qua individual as the locus of either the political or the ethical. Secondly, what is displaced is the identification of a collective will with either an individual will or an individual as representing the individualization of a collective will. The force of this position is that in displacing the priority of the individual what occurs in its place is the affirmed centrality of relationality. The latter is present in the passage cited earlier in terms of "participation" and thus held in place by the "share." The question to be addressed however concerns the extent to which all that is available to further a description of human being—and thus to develop a philosophical anthropology—are modes of relationality identified by terms such as participation and the "share." Even if a return is made to "the space of appearance," which is a key formulation, as already noted, in the context of *The Human Condition*, it might still be suggested that all that is being adduced is a description of the space of freedom, and that the "space of appearance" is a formulation that is essential in the move from freedom understood as a predicate of an abstract individual to freedom as a space of activity; an activity demanding appearing. However, the argument to be sketched here is that terms such as "participate," "share," and the interconnection of "acting" and "beginning" all invoke threshold conditions. As such the appearance of freedom—and it is essential to recall the invocation by Arendt of a space of freedom in which "virtuosity can appear"—has to be understood as a coming to appear. Virtuosity involves relationality and placedness. This is not virtue as the predicate of an isolated and isolatable individual. Hence the overall insistence on the link between freedom and action, and thus on *enacted freedom*. Appearance occurs at a threshold. There needs to be more therefore than the simple invocation of participation as opposed to individuation.

If there is going to be a genuine departure from the language of self-molding and self-making, let alone a return to it, and the concomitant commitment to the refusal of relationality—and this amounts to a departure from the philosophical anthropology that underpins what she takes Stoicism to be—then it can only be found in Arendt's description of freedom as a "faculty." The description not only complicates the presence and nature of relationality, it also complicates her overall argument. Accepting this description means that freedom is then defined in terms of its capacity for actualization. In other words, what occurs is the introduction of the language of potentiality. In sum, and while it is a position that has to be developed, the fundamental point of difference that has emerged with Seneca and Pico in the end resides in the role of potentiality once the world as a place of enactment has to be thought philosophically. The refusal of its actualization is the refusal of what might be described as *worlding*. Worlding is linked to *enacted freedom*. There is the important further claim that *enacted freedom* is the enacting, and thus the living out of relationality. If it can be argued that not only is freedom the actualization of a capacity, unfreedom would then figure as the structural or enforced refusal of the actualization. This conception of the relationship between freedom and unfreedom comprises the locus of judgment to the extent that there is a concomitant identification of an intrinsic quality which is proper to human being. Actualization is the enactment of that precise sense of propriety. In this context, unfreedom is the enforced or policed non-actualization of that which is proper to human being. The example that has already been identified is "dignity."[33]

In a sense Arendt must be committed to this latter description of unfreedom since she argues, as has been already noted, that were the source of all beginnings to remain "hidden," then the consequence would be that this "source" had become (or remained) unworldly. It then becomes no more than the freedom to imagine. It reverts to Stoicism. In other words, freedom, as a result of its "hidden" quality, would not be *enacted freedom*. The contrast is with imagined freedom. The latter is the province of the individual, while *enacted freedom* is necessarily both worldly and relational. In regard to the individual, freedom occurs within the space of the imagination, such that it would only be present as a potentiality; there, awaiting enactment, though only for that individual. Again, while it will be essential to return to this point, the claim itself is only viable if that which is "hidden" is equated with the suppression (at times the policed suppression) of that "source." In other words, though the claim is consistent with her own analysis of the totalitarian, it is not enough to use the term "hidden." The "source" about which she writes would have been hidden, that hiding would have to have been maintained. Hence, it is policed suppression. (And this will be the case whether it is the suppressive qualities resulting from the naturalization of normativity or the presence of the actual police.) The term "hidden" obfuscates. The implicit sense of value, the sense linked to the presence of that which is proper to the being of being human and which is already there in the "source" and the presence of a "faculty of freedom," would itself have been overlooked.

Once Arendt writes of the "sheer capacity to begin" and joins the presence of that capacity to the coterminous presence of the faculty of freedom, what then has to be acknowledged is that any beginning is already a form of transformation. Beginnings within the world open up the possibility of the world's containing acts which are actual beginnings rather than repetitions of the Same masquerading as beginnings. The world therefore rather than enduring as a locus of indifference is able to be reconfigured by such acts. Beginnings take on a different quality. They become acts of pure creativity. They are pure in the precise sense that they are withdrawn from any immediate inscription into forms of calculation. Such acts need to be understood as *countermeasures* insofar as they are also creative. In this instance, what is countered is the conflation of acting and instrumentality. A beginning, with its attendant link to world-creating through processes or narrativization, is not the simple furtherance of the world as given. (Nor implicitly does it accept the identification of the world with the world that is given. Undoing the given means that another cosmology attends.) The world becomes the place of actualizations that further the world by breaking the identification of continuity with a repetition delimited by the continuity of sameness. Hence the term *worlding* with its implicit actative dimension. There is a fundamental reciprocity here: the givenness of the world is enclosed within acts of beginning, and acts of beginning, the transformations of the given, are inherently worldly. The elements at work in this setting—a setting that joins "acts" and "world"—need to be developed. It is not as though individual acts by individual agents comprise the realm of pure beginnings. Arendt has already argued that what she calls political freedom has to be understood as "the right to be a participator in government." A position that has to be thought in term of the world's inhabitation not just by an insistent plurality but by an already-present plurality whose affirmation has to work against the now-current essentializing forces of both populism and nationalism.

In order to develop further the setting noted earlier, a start can be made with the understanding of political freedom in terms of participation. However, her claim is not limited to participation. Indeed, political freedom is defined in terms of participation as a "right." What then does participation as a form of "right" mean? What here is a "right"? A number of preliminary elements have to be identified before these questions can be addressed adequately. Another encounter with Arendt's engagement with Stoicism opens the way. Arendt comments on Epictetus in *What is Freedom?* as follows:

> Epictetus transposed . . . worldly relationships into relationships within man's own self, whereby he discovered that no power is so absolute as that which man yields over himself, and that inward space where man struggles and subdues himself is more entirely his own, namely, more securely shielded from interference, than any world home could ever be. (Arendt 1961: 148)

There is an obvious affinity here between Epictetus and Seneca in terms of self-creation. Self-molding and self-creating remain internal to a self over which that form of the self then exerts or attempts to exert control.[34] The self as the site of its own sovereignty. While this is a clear instance of a turn to the self that becomes self-care, what endures is a conception of self that is predicated on the suppression of the self as always already present within relationality. The sense of self that Arendt identifies in Epictetus involves a form of disjunction in which a concern with what is simply a putative sense of sovereignty, that is, sovereignty of the self which is there in name alone, leads to what she describes as "the exchange of the real world for an imaginary one" (Arendt 1958: 234). This is a form of autonomy that would be undone by an insistence on the ineliminability of plurality as definitional of the human condition. At work here is a reiteration of the position in which the assertion of the individual involves a closure to the world and thus the refusal of worlding. The refusal of worlding is the refusal of relationality. The subject within the process of *enacted freedom* is the relational subject. Thus not the subject that aspires to command itself, where such a position necessitates forms of disassociation; rather, it is one in which there is only ever an autonomous sense of self within relationality. (There is still responsibility. However, it is now responsibility within relationality.) Though, it needs to be noted that the move from the individual to the relation is not the pluralization of the one. Present here is a configuration that is more complex of a network of relations. If it can be argued that the anoriginality of relationality entails that the assertion of individuality, thought as having priority, is the refusal of the grounding setting, then what counts as an individual within relationality is the individual as an aftereffect of a network of relations. This is not the pluralization of the individual.

From the position noted earlier, it follows that the "right" to participate is not one that can be predicated of a singular subject. The subject does not exist in itself. Rather, as emerged in the analysis of both Seneca and Pico, that subject is the aftereffect of the refusal of relationality. The singular is always produced. The presence of that right therefore needs to be set in the context in which freedom as a "faculty" is inextricably bound up with what Arendt describes as the "sheer capacity to begin." Beginning and participating occur within a setting defined by a series of thresholds. To begin necessitates an act that crosses the threshold between the capacity to begin and the act which is the beginning. Neither acts nor beginnings are arbitrary. This position is formulated with great care in *On Revolution*:

> What saves the act of beginning from its own arbitrariness is that it carries its own principle within itself, or, to be more precise, that beginning and principle, *principium* and principle, are not only related to each other, but are coeval. The absolute from which the beginning is to derive its own validity, and which must save it, as it were, from its inherent arbitrariness is the principle which, together with it, makes its appearance in the world. The way the beginner starts whatever he intends to do lays down the law of action: for those who have joined him in order to partake in the enterprise and to bring about its accomplishment. As such, the principle inspires the deeds that are to follow and remains apparent as long as the action lasts. (Arendt 1973: 212)

Arendt's use of the term "coeval" is fundamental here. What is it that is "coeval?" While the answer is clear insofar as it refers to the copresence of act and "principle," a fundamental part of that question remains unanswered. What is the "principle?"

Answering this question has to begin with the recognition that the principle is not the act. Otherwise, the term "coeval" would be simply redundant. The answer to the questions hinges on the copresence of a "principle." If the path that has been created here is followed, it becomes possible to discern what is intended by "principle." The "act of beginning" is the enactment of the "faculty of freedom." That faculty is present as the "sheer capacity to begin." The place of enactment is the world. Worlding is the continuity of acting. The principle therefore is bound up with freedom as a faculty or a capacity. Moreover, along with the identification of this "capacity" there is the already-noted definition of political freedom in terms of the "right" to participate. This "right," if understood in a way similar to "the right to have rights," is already there as a precondition. These "rights" attend acting. Precisely because what is at stake is a precondition, all such preconditions must have a quality that repositions human being in terms of the continuity of a *potentiality-to-be* insofar as acting has a nonnecessary relation to any principle. That *potentiality-to-be* locates a threshold. However, once the idea of the threshold is taken seriously, then acts have to be linked continually, not just to the question of their actualization. This is a position that moves from generalized forms of appearing, to simple acts such as promising and forgiving, to acts that are the enactment of freedom, such as participation in governance, but equally to how actualization is to be conceived. All these acts have to be understood as the actualization of a potentiality. The presence of the threshold condition is necessary once freedom has to be accounted for in terms of its enactment. As significantly, the presence of the threshold also enables an account of unfreedom to be given. Unfreedom which is an enforced denial of appearance—and which here is the enforced denial of the actualization of being as appearing—is not a passive state, even though unfreedom can result in enforced passivity. Unfreedom is the policing of borders. That policing can take radically different forms; it may deploy legal strategies, it may be maintained by the institutionalization of racism or sexism, and it could involve sporadic though effective outbreaks of hate speech. In regard to institutions, what occurs is the sustained elimination of the possibility of participation and therefore freedom. This occurs through a shift in democratic concerns (though they will be democratic in name alone) away from that which might be linked to management and governance and toward the celebration and championing of individual or personal freedom.

What is emerging from this attempt to elucidate what is implicated in Arendt's use of the term "principle," a question rising out of Arendt's critical engagement with Stoicism, has, nonetheless, an inbuilt complexity. Even though it is not part of her argument, what was discovered in the engagement with both Seneca and Pico was the absence of intrinsic qualities within their accounts of human being. As a result, both the regulatory and the criteria ground judgment were external. At work here now is the move from the extrinsic to the intrinsic. The principle identified by Arendt that overcomes the arbitrariness of acts is coeval with all acts and yet is always in excess of any one act. (The excess that emerged in Hyginus's fable, as both figure and quality, namely *Cura/cura*, and then its incorporation into the logic of breath in *Genesis* returns.) As a principle it must have unconditional force. Moreover, as a principle it must be an intrinsic quality. Indeed, her claim that the "right to have rights" is explicable in terms of the "right to belong" has to hold unconditionally. That unconditionality is already there in the separation of the plurality of rights from the singular right that is the principle that would then shatter any incipient relativity that might begin to emerge within the plurality of rights claims. However, despite the unconditionality of principles, they are not located in a neutral field. The policing and restriction of thresholds entails that "freedom," "participation," "appearing," and "acting," as Arendt uses these terms or, "worlding" and "enacted freedom," as these terms have been developed here, are held in place by an insistent quality that defines human being in terms of a *potentiality-to-be*. There is a fundamental reciprocity here, since that quality delimits a threshold while being delimited by one. If there is an intrinsic limit to the way that Arendt understands her own project, then it emerges because of a failure to recognize that appearing involves crossing a threshold, one inevitable positioned by a naturalized disequilibrium of power, and is thus the actualization of a potentiality. Principles—understood here as rights—attend conditioned acts because of their unconditioned nature. They attend them, in the sense that they are coeval, allowing for judgment. Arendt is forced to this position even if there is in her work a sustained reluctance to think it.

The *potentiality-to-be* is located at a threshold, one that can be policed, restricted, one at which there may be a constant diminution of the possibility of appearance. The ineliminability of a threshold means that the question that has to be posed concerning any potentiality is its actualization. The *potentiality-to-be* comprises a repositioning of what might be described as that which underscores the dynamic quality of intrinsic principles. The "right to have rights," where the latter is understood as the "right to belong," once coupled to the principles that are coeval with actions, then identifies different forms of propriety that define and delimit human being. They are potentials whose actualization is an integral part of worlding. Their enactment is *enacted freedom*. If a general term can be used to describe unconditioned intrinsic qualities, then it is not difficult to argue that they comprise human dignity.

Notes

1 This chapter forms part of larger project funded by Australian Research Council (ARC DP160103644) entitled Place, Commonality and the Human: Towards a New Philosophical Anthropology. It was first presented to the Department of Philosophy at Uppsala University on September 27, 2018. I want to thank Sharon Rider for the invitation and her and her colleagues for the generosity with which they heard and discussed it. I would also like to thank Emmanuel Alloa, Kurt Lampe, Richard Lee, Francesco Borghesi, and Lucy Benjamin for their comments on an earlier draft.
2 The project here continues as one that was first begun in A. Benjamin (2018a).
3 It is defined in Arendt thus: "The space of appearance comes into being wherever men are together in the manner of speech and action, and therefore predates and precedes all formal constitution of the public realm and the various forms of government, that is, the various forms in which the public realm can be organized" (1958: 199).
4 The necessity for concentrating on enactment is underscored by Miriam Leonard when she writes in an investigation of Arendt's relation to Antiquity that "for Arendt there is no politics without freedom and no freedom without the emancipation from the economic necessitates that characterise the social" (2018: 55). The question, of course, is how "emancipation"—emancipation would be a mode of enactment—is understood. Arendt also identifies the limit of Stoicism in relation to the question of freedom in Arendt (2018: 27).
5 While Seneca will argue in the *Ep.*75.12 that one should be open to changes in government and other forms of transformation—indeed in writing of the world he notes that "it will not always preserve its present order (non semper tenebit hunc ordinem)"—it remains the case that the causal agent is "God." Human agency is not linked to the world's possible transformation.
6 Note also the following which clarifies what she means by virtuosity. Its link to *fortuna* is in the long-term decisive: "Freedom as inherent in action is perhaps best

illustrated by Machiavelli's concept of virtu, the excellence with which man answers the opportunities the world opens up before him in the guise of fortuna" (Arendt 1961: 151).

7 I have tried to argue this position in a number of contexts. See in particular A. Benjamin (2018a).

8 The position itself is presented in Arendt (1951: 296–7). On the complexities involved in the formulation "the right to have rights" in Arendt, see Hamacher (2014), Bell (2018). And then in regard to the way the question of rights is posed in Giorgio Agamben's work, a position that has direct relevance for an understanding of Arendt, see Birmingham (2011).

9 On the way thresholds are reconfigured as borders as a result of policing, see Longo (2018).

10 In terms of the relationship with seventeenth-century French thought, a clear example can be found in Boileau's life of Epictetus, in which he describes "ses sentiments" as "conformes au Christianisme" in part because of his commitment to the immortality of the soul and in part because of his attack on atheism (Boileau 1655: 70).

11 The complex set of questions concerning the relationship between *dignitas* and *otium* demands a sustained treatment in its own right. See Anastasiadis (2004), Bondanella (2008), Vickers (1990). Arendt also notes the connection between *otium* and slavery (Arendt 2005: 117).

12 All references to the *Oratio* are to Mirandola (2012).

13 An important discussion of the connection between the "happy life" and the presence of the individual can also be found in Asmis (1990).

14 This is the passage about which Descartes was so harsh in his letter to Elizabeth, August 18, 1645. He described the position as one in which wisdom is "to acquiesce to the order of things" (*d'acquiscer à l'order des choses*) (Descartes 1901: 273).

15 Though it should be noted that Seneca's conception of nature is far from fixed or consistent. For a discussion of the issues, see Rosenmeyer (2000).

16 For a discussion of this passage and its link to military command, see Star (2012: 26).

17 It is also true that a connection can be drawn with Stoic physics. However, the affinities with *Genesis*, despite the problem of actual historical influence, are the most telling and also the most exact.

18 Also, it is important to note that the major philosophical study of this fable, apart from Heidegger's fundamental engagement (2001), namely Blumenberg's (1987), misunderstands what is at stake in it. There is for Blumenberg a form of arbitrariness involved in the decision that leads to the figure's production. The centrality of reflection, the image that Cura sees in the river, that prompts her and allows Blumenberg to interpret that fable in Gnostic terms, is left out by Hyginus.

For Blumenberg, the guideline of "judgment" has been removed. It is however significant here to note that Blumenberg has systematically ignored what might be described as the implicit temporality of the Fable. Care does not "cross a river." Note, firstly, that the Fable begins, "Cura cum quendam fluvium transiret" (when Cura was crossing a certain river), and, secondly, that the question of her own deliberative (and thus reflective) act is introduced thus: "While she was pondering on what she had done (*dum deliberat secum quidnam fecisset*)." At work in both formulations are two temporal markers that point in a different direction, namely acting within the already continuous. What happens occurs as Cura was crossing the river. Cura does not cross the river in order to create. What the Fable recounts is what happens while an activity is occurring. Note the repetition of *dum*. Blumenberg's interpretation seems hasty. See in addition Larivée (2014), Adler (2014, 2015).

19 The most significant study of the actuality of this text is to be found in Hamilton (2013).
20 I do not pursue this point here. I have however taken up the problems posed by the image of God in A. Benjamin (2017b, 2019b).
21 I have described this opening in much great detail in terms of "law's constancy." See A. Benjamin (2019a).
22 See A. Benjamin (2017a).
23 A position also held by Garin (1993: 123–4).
24 According to the register of Pico's library complied by Kibre (1966: 186), the library contained a copy of Ambrosius Traversarius's Latin translation of Diogenes Laertius (1472).
25 There are, of course, other slightly better possibilities for dogs. Note Friedrich Schlegel in the Critical Fragments [54] "There are writers who drink the absolute [*die Unbedingtes*] like water; and books where even the dogs refer to the infinite" [*die Hunde sich aufs Unendliche beziehen*]" (1991: 7).
26 This is identified by Kant in the following terms: "This holiness of will is nevertheless a practical idea, which must necessarily serve as a model to which all finite rational beings can only approximate without end" (1999: 166).
27 For a further discussion of verticality in Seneca, see Williams (2016: 176). This is the ethical position—one that demands both the singular and the nonrelational subject, as well as "uprightedness"—against which Cavarero (2014) writes. Though for a defense of Seneca which highlights ambivalences and openings within his work that such a critique might have ignored, see Rimell (2017).
28 See in this regard Roller (2018: 275–89).
29 As Malcolm Schofield notes (1999: 3), for "Seneca the true city is a cosmic city."
30 There is of course a form of the *imago dei* in Seneca which is linked to forms of moral action. Being like God enables action in the world. However, that action leaves the world unaltered. See Russell (2004), in particular page 253.

31 See also Sari (2017).
32 See also Arendt: "political freedom . . . means the right to be a participator in government or it means nothing at all" (1973: 218).
33 As a separate concern, it should be noted that an intrinsic property would then be linked to the presence of a noncoercive "ought." That intrinsic qualities ought to be actualized cannot lead to their axiomatic actualization. What a noncoercive ought provides is a ground both of judgment and then of subsequent actions based on such judgments.
34 Despite the details of his engagement with Stoicism and his recovery from Seneca of the identification of life with a training to live, what endures in Foucault's detailed development of the "care-for-self" is the primacy of the nonrelational. The latter is retained without critical engagement. See Michel Foucault (2001), in particular the discussion of Seneca throughout pages 435–57. Some of the limitations of Foucault's interpretation are also noted by Shadi Bartsch (2012: 191).

Works Cited

Adler, Anthony (2014), "Fractured Life and the Ambiguity of Historical Time: Biopolitics in Agamben and Arendt," *Cultural Critique*, 86: 1–30.

Adler, Anthony (2015), "Deconfabulation: Agamben's Italian Categories and the Impossibility of Experience," *Diacritics*, 43 (3): 68–94.

Anastasiadis, V. I. (2004), "Idealized ΣΧΟΛΗ and Disdain for Work: Aspects of Philosophy and Politics in Ancient Democracy," *The Classical Quarterly*, 54 (1): 58–79.

Arendt, Hannah (1951), *The Origins of Totalitarianism*, New York: Schocken Books.

Arendt, Hannah (1958), *The Human Condition*, Chicago: University of Chicago Press.

Arendt, Hannah (1961), "What Is Freedom?" in *Between Past and Future*, New York: The Viking Press.

Arendt, Hannah (1973), *On Revolution*, Hammondsworth: Pelican Book.

Arendt, Hannah (2005), *The Promise of Politics*, New York: Schocken Books.

Arendt, Hannah (2018), *Thinking Without a Bannister: Essays in Understanding, 1953–1975*, New York: Schocken Books.

Asmis, Elizabeth (1990), "Seneca's *On the Happy Life* and Stoic Individualism," *Apeiron*, 23 (4): 219–56.

Bartsch, Shadi (2012), "Senecan Selves," in Shadi Bartsch and Alessandro Schiesaro (eds.), *The Cambridge Companion to Seneca*, 187–98, Cambridge. Cambridge University Press.

Bell, Nathan (2018), "In the Face, a Right Is There: Arendt, Levinas and the Phenomenology of the Rights of Man," *Journal of the British Society for Phenomenology*, 49 (4): 291–307.

Benjamin, Andrew (2017a), *Virtue in Being*, Albany: SUNY Press.
Benjamin, Andrew (2017b), "Oikonomia, Incarnation and Immediacy: The Figure of the Jew in St John of Damascus," *International Journal of Philosophical Studies*, 25 (3): 407–22.
Benjamin, Andrew (2018a), "Being and Appearing: Notes on Arendt and Relationality," *Arendt Studies*, 2: 215–32.
Benjamin, Andrew (2018b), "Metaphysics of Nudity: Notes on Seneca, Arendt, and Dignity," *Classical Philology*, 113 (1): 39–52.
Benjamin, Andrew (2019a), "God and the Truth of Human Being," *Journal for Continental Philosophy of Religion*, 2: 141–69.
Benjamin, Andrew (2019b), "Listening to God and the Founding of the Law: Notes on *Exodus* 32:19-20," *Journal of the British Society for Phenomenology*, DOI: 10.1080/00071773.2019.1687976
Benjamin, Walter (1980), *Gesammelte Schriften*, eds. Rolf Tiedemann and Herman Schweppengäuser, Frankfurt: Suhrkamp Verlag.
Benjamin, Walter (1996), *Selected Writings*, eds. Marcus Bullock and Michael Jennings, Cambridge, MA: Harvard University Press..
Birmingham, Peg (2011), "The Subject of Rights: On the Declaration of the Human," *Epoché: A Journal for the History of Philosophy*, 16 (1): 139–56.
Boileau, G. (1655), *La Vie d'Epictete et sa philosophie*, Paris: Guilliaume de Luyne.
Blumenberg, Hans (1987), *Die Sorge geht über den Fluß*, Frankfurt: Suhrkamp Verlag.
Bondanella, Julia Conaway (2008), "Petrarch's Rereading of *Otium* in *De vita solitaria*," *Comparative Literature*, 60 (1): 14–28.
Cavarero, Adrianna (2014), *Inclinazioni*, Milan: Raffaello Cortina Editore.
Colish, Marcia (1985), *The Stoic Tradition from Antiquity to the Early Middle Ages*, vol. 1, Leiden: Brill.
Descartes, René (1901), *Oeuvres de Descartes. Correspondance*, eds. Charles Adam and Paul Tannery, Paris: Léopold Cerf.
Diogenes Laertius (1472), *Laertii Diogenis Vitae et sententiae eorum qui in philosophia probati fuerunt*, ed. B. Brognolus, trans.. A. Traversarius, Rome: Giorgio Lauer.
Foucault, Michel (2001), *L'Herméneutique du sujet. Cours au Collège de France (1981-1982)*, Paris: Éditions du seuil.
Garin, Eugenio (1993), *L'umanesimo italiano*, Bari: Laterza.
Hamacher, Werner (2014), "On the Right to Have Rights: Marx and Arendt," *CR: The New Centennial Review*, 14 (2): 169–221.
Hamilton, John T. (2013), *Security, Politics, Humanity, and the Philology of Care*, Princeton: Princeton University Press.
Heidegger, Martin (2001), *Sein und Zeit*, Tübingen: Max Niemeyer.
Kant, I. (1999), *Practical Philosophy*, trans. Mary J.. McGregor, Cambridge: Cambridge University Press.
Kibre, Pearl (1966), *The Library of Pico della Mirandola*, New York: AMS Press.

Kristeller, Paul Oskar (1947), "The Philosophy on Man in the Italian Renaissance," *Italica*, 24 (2): 93–112.
Larivée, Annie (2014), "*Being and Time* and the Ancient Philosophical Tradition of Care for the Self: A Tense or Harmonious Relationship?" *Philosophical Papers*, 43 (1): 123–44.
Leonard, Miriam (2018), "Arendt's Revolutionary Antiquity," *Classical Philology*, 113: 53–66.
Longo, Matthew (2018), *The Politics of Borders. Sovereignty, Security and the Citizen after 9/11*, Cambridge: Cambridge University Press.
Mirandola, Giovanni Pico della (2012), *Pico della Mirandola: Oration on the Dignity of Man; A New Translation and Commentary*, eds. Francesco Borghesi, Michael Papio, Massimo Riva, Cambridge: Cambridge University Press.
Mirandola, Giovanni Pico della (2013), *Conclusiones nongentae*, Florence: Leo S. Olschki.
Rimell V. (2017), "Philosophy's Folds: Seneca, Cavarero, and the History of Rectitude," *Hypatia: A Journal of Feminist Philosophy*, 32 (4): 768–83.
Roller, Matthew B. (2018), *Models from the Past in Roman Culture*, Cambridge: Cambridge University Press.
Rosenmeyer, Thomas G. (2000), "Seneca and Nature," *Arethusa*, 33 (1): 99–119.
Russell, Daniel C. (2004), "Virtue as Likeness to God in Plato and Seneca," *Journal of the History of Philosophy*, 2 (3): 241–60.
Sari, Yasemin (2017), "An Arendtian Recognitive Politics: The Right to Have Rights as a Performance of Visibility," *Philosophy Today*, 61 (3): 709–35.
Schlegel, Friedrich (1991), *Philosophical Fragments*, trans. Peter Firchow, Minneapolis: University of Minnesota Press.
Schofield, Malcolm (1999), *The Stoic Idea of the City*, Chicago: University of Chicago Press.
Seneca (1928), *Moral Essays*, trans. John W. Basore, Cambridge, MA: Harvard University Press.
Seneca (1979), *Epistulae Morales*, trans. R. M. Gummere, Cambridge, MA: Harvard University Press.
Setaioli, Aldo (2014), "Philosopy as Therapy, Self-Transformation and 'Lebensform,'" in Gregor Damschen and Andreas Heil (eds.), *Brill's Companion to Seneca*, 239–56, Leiden: Brill.
Star, Christopher (2012), *The Empire of the Self. Self-Command and Political Speech in Seneca and Petronius*, Baltimore: Johns Hopkins University Press.
Vickers, Brian (1990), "Leisure and Idleness in the Renaissance: the Ambivalence of *otium* (Part I)," *Renaissance Studies*, 4: 107–54.
Williams, Gareth D. (2016), "Minding the Gap: Seneca, the Self and the Sublime," in Gareth D. Williams and Katharina Volk (eds.), *Roman Reflections. Studies in Latin Philosophy*, Oxford: Oxford University Press.

9

Hans Blumenberg and the Anthropology of Stoicism

Kurt Lampe

1. Introduction

Few historians of ancient philosophy outside of German-speaking countries are aware of the work of Hans Blumenberg (1920–96). Likewise, few of the Germanists and contemporary philosophers working on Blumenberg have first-hand command of the immense array of Greek and Roman texts he cites in their original language. The number and length of his publications, many of them posthumous, make it challenging to appreciate his philologically rigorous and philosophically creative reception of specific topics in the study of classical antiquity. While a recent collection has illuminated his handling of Plato and Lucretius (Möller 2015), his readings of Stoicism appear never to have received any sustained attention.

My aim in this chapter is to gather, explain, and critically evaluate some of Blumenberg's most noteworthy engagements with Stoicism. By far the most important text is *Paradigms for a Metaphorology*, throughout which Blumenberg uses Stoic positions in order to illustrate his claims (2010 [orig. 1960]: *passim*). His arguments there are developed further in *The Legitimacy of the Modern Age* (1983 [orig. 1966]: 243–62) and *The Genesis of the Copernican World* (1987a [orig. 1975]: 8–21). Also significant is *Höhlenausgänge* (Leaving the Cave[1]), in which he offers an extended commentary on a long passage in Cicero's *On the Nature of the Gods* (1989: 193–206). Though I shall concentrate on these four sources, it is worth mentioning that Blumenberg also discusses ancient Stoic doctrines or texts in *Die Lesbarkeit der Welt* (The Legibility of the World) (1989: 40–1), *Shipwreck with Spectator* (1997 [orig. 1979]: 12, 64–5), *Care Crosses the River* (2010 [orig. 1987]: 31–2, 42, 148), and "Imitation of Nature" (2000: 33–5).[2] He also discusses the role of neo-Stoicism in early modern intellectual history, as Angus Nicholls discusses elsewhere in this volume.

The difficulty of explaining and assessing these scattered passages illuminates both Blumenberg's erudition and his interpretive method. With regard to the former, it should be noted that Blumenberg's approach to Stoicism, like that of today's specialists in ancient philosophy, combines doxography and surviving complete sources. In *Paradigms*, *Legitimacy*, and *Genesis*, he relies primarily on Hans von Arnim's four-volume *Stoicorum Veterum Fragmenta* (SVF) (1903–24). This goes some way toward demonstrating his mastery of both ancient languages and the Stoics's overall system, since the testimonia in SVF are fragmentary and untranslated. But Blumenberg also cites passages from surviving Stoic sources, especially Seneca's *Letters* and the exposition of Stoic theology put in the mouth of Balbus in Cicero's *On the Nature of the Gods*. If his interpretive claims and arguments about these passages are often hard to evaluate, there are at least three reasons for that. The first is that his concern is generally with the evolution of narrative and imaginal patterns across the grand sweep of Western intellectual history, not with the integrity of theoretical and practical systems. The second is that this intellectual history takes its orientation from Blumenberg's own philosophical preoccupations, even though that agenda often fades into the background. The third is that he takes it for granted that his readers' erudition rivals his own, so that he takes little trouble to explain the doctrines and arguments he discusses.[3]

In the following sections, I will therefore undertake several tasks. One is to sketch how Blumenberg's lifelong philosophical concerns structure his approach to Stoicism. Another is to clarify the meaning and evaluate the cogency of his compressed readings of ancient Stoic sources. In order to do this I will both adduce additional Greek and Latin texts and draw on up-to-date scholarship. My final goal is to reflect on the philosophical significance of Blumenberg's approach. I will suggest that he gives us a way of thinking about pre-theoretical dimensions that are crucial to Stoicism as what Pierre Hadot calls "a choice of life and an existential option" (2002: 3), or Anthony Long calls "an experiment in philosophical power" (2006: 19). In this respect, Blumenberg's reading complements mainstream scholarly approaches to Stoicism as a "way of life" (e.g., Brennan 2005) as well as cognitive-behavioral modern Stoic reception (e.g., Robertson 2013).

2. The Metaphorics of Stoic Epistemology

Blumenberg's *Paradigms for a Metaphorology*, which was published in 1960, arose from a lecture he delivered to the inaugural conference of the German "Senatorial Commission for the History of Concepts" in 1958 (Nicholls 2015: 14).

Thus, as Blumenberg later puts it in "Prospect for a Theory of Nonconceptuality," at this stage his theory of "metaphorics" was "directed mainly toward the constitution of conceptuality" (1997 [orig. 1979]: 81). He argues that the history of concepts must be understood against the backdrop of what cannot be fully conceptualized, namely "absolute metaphors." Stoicism is one of the conceptual systems to which he returns throughout this work in order to illustrate the ineliminable and generative presence of metaphors.

"Conceptual" and "metaphorical" thinking must be defined in relation to one another. Even in *Paradigms*, which is Blumenberg's most accessible work, definitions are in short supply. Following his allusions there to Descartes, we can stipulate that "conceptual" thinking connotes its objects "clearly and distinctly," such that they can be "logicized" without ambiguity (2010b: 1–3). Turning instead to Blumenberg's emphasis on Husserl in "Nonconceptuality," we can add that conceptual suppositions are characterized by being fulfillable through intuitions (1997: 82–6).[4] We might synthesize these two perspectives as follows: conceptual thinking consists of propositions whose sense is unambiguous, on the basis of which apodictic conclusions can be deduced, whose correspondence to reality can be assessed via one or more self-evident experiences.

"Absolute metaphor" can now be defined by contrast with conceptuality as a mode of thinking whose connotations are *not* "clear and distinct," so that its expressions can neither be logicized apodictically nor assessed via self-evident experiences.[5] To this initial polarity we must add that metaphorical thinking is epistemologically prior to conceptual thinking:

> By providing a point of orientation, the content of absolute metaphors determines a particular attitude or conduct; they give structure to a world, representing the non-experienceable, non-apprehensible totality of the real. To the historically trained eye, they therefore indicate the fundamental certainties, conjectures, and judgments in relation to which the attitudes and expectations, actions and inactions, longings and disappointments, interests and indifferences of an epoch are regulated. (2010b: 14)

In other words, absolute metaphors suggest answers to questions too big to be addressed conceptually—for example, theoretical questions about the totality of existence, or practical questions about basic emotional and active orientation (Wetz 2004: 20). Conceptual thinking takes its starting points from these metaphors; they are a "a catalytic sphere from which the universe of concepts continually renews itself, without thereby converting and exhausting this founding reserve" (Blumenberg 2010b: 4). The task of "metaphorology" is to illuminate how they coordinate thought and action and explore how they change over time.

It is best to understand "full conceptualization" and "absolute metaphor" as two limits of a continuum, neither of which thought ever occupies (Blumenberg 1997: 85). That said, I suggest that Blumenberg's metaphorological approach to Stoicism complements scholars' usual conceptual approach. Let us begin with his investigation of the metaphorics of truth, which reveals the Stoics's implicit answers to the following questions:

> To what extent does mankind partake of the whole truth? What situation do those who seek the truth find themselves in? Can they feel confident that what exists will freely reveal itself to them, or is knowledge to be acquired only by an act of violence, by outwitting the object, extorting information from it under duress, interrogating it on the rack? Is our share in truth meaningfully regulated by the economy of our needs, for example, or by our aptitude for superabundant happiness in accordance with the idea of a *visio beatifica*? (Blumenberg 2010b: 7)

While "To what extent does mankind partake of the whole truth?" is a clearly conceptualized question, about which Stoics and Academic skeptics carried on refined debates for centuries, Blumenberg's questions about truth's "free self-revelation" or the truth-seeker's "outwitting," "extorting," and "interrogating" the object of inquiry are metaphorical. They represent emotional and practical attitudes to be adopted by the philosopher. Likewise, the phrase "economy of our needs" suggests a situation of scarcity, prioritizing, organizing, and disposing.[6] Blumenberg's claim is that metaphors such as these are prior to the epistemological systems rooted in them.

We can illustrate this claim with the Stoic theory of the "cataleptic impression" (*phantasia kataléptikē*). Sensory and linguistic "impressions" (also translated "representations") occur to our minds constantly (LS 39A-G), but they only have epistemological or ethical consequences if we "assent" to them: the wise person gives assent only to "cataleptic" impressions. These are the primary criterion of truth, and therefore the most fundamental building block for understanding nature and harmonizing yourself with it. Their definition evolves over the history of the school, but they generally have the following attributes: (1) they arise from something that is the case and (2) are stamped and impressed with all the peculiarities of their source (3) in such a way that they could not arise from anything else (LS 40E). Some Stoics add the proviso that (4) they must not be impeded (LS 40K). To take a simple example, the impression "I am typing," if it is cataleptic, arises from an actual state of affairs and is stamped with the peculiar attributes of that state of affairs. In other words, if I am not typing, or this activity does not present itself clearly and distinctly to my awareness, in such a manner that it could not come from another activity, then the impression is not cataleptic. Finally, I must not have a compelling reason to doubt this impression, such as remembering that moments ago the dental surgeon administered a general anesthetic (in which case I am probably dreaming).

Blumenberg has little to say about how cataleptic impressions relate to the rest of the Stoics's conceptual system, which in any event scholars understand much better today than in the 1950s. Rather, he draws our attention to the pre-understandings suggested by the Stoics's words and phrases. The word "cataleptic" is simply a transliteration, which many English scholars retain; others translate it as "cognitive," "apprehensive," or "graspable." *Katalambanō* means "grasp firmly" or "seize," which gives rise to the question, who is seizing what? "The original Zenonian idea," Blumenberg writes, "seems to have been that a 'cataleptic' impression is one that seizes and masters the object as it 'exists' itself, bringing it to presence in the fullness of its concrete characteristics" (2010b: 9, translation modified).[7] Here Blumenberg undoubtedly has in mind Zeno's performative elucidation of his position: he likened his open hand to an impression, his semi-closed hand to mental assent, his clenched fist to "firmly grasping" (*katalēpsis*),[8] and "when he'd put his left hand over his right hand and tightly and forcefully gripped it, he said, 'Knowledge is like this'" (LS 41A).[9] The implicit metaphor of "cataleptic impressions" can also be reversed, as Blumenberg points out: "The second meaning of the cataleptic impression seems to have dawned at a later date: the mind seized and overwhelmed by the evidence of the impression is now the object of *katalēpsis*" (LS 41A). Here Blumenberg explicitly cites Sextus Empiricus's report: "The cataleptic impression . . . being self-evident and striking, all but seizes [*lambanei*] us by the hair, they say, and pulls us to assent" (LS 40K3). It is undoubtedly because Sextus attributes this position to "newer Stoics" that Blumenberg claims it "dawned at a later date."

The upshot of this is that the Stoics's most fundamental epistemological concept establishes opposing theoretical and practical pre-understandings. On the one hand, Zeno's performance suggests that truth-seeking is a matter of grasping and securing your grip on the right kind of impressions. We might speculate that this metaphorical orientation underlies the Stoics's conceptualization of knowledge as "secure" (*asphalēs*) and "stable" (*bebaia*) due to the systematicity of its true propositions (LS 41C3, 41G3, 41H, Vogt 2012: 158–71). Ultimately we could connect this with the metaphorics of security highlighted by Pierre

Hadot's influential study of Marcus Aurelius, *The Inner Citadel* (1998). (It is not coincidental that Hadot counted Blumenberg among his friends, as he records in his deeply Blumenbergian final work, *The Veil of Isis* [2006: xi–xii].)

On the other hand, the image of the criterial impression "all but seizing us by the hair" points in a different direction. According to Blumenberg, we are dealing here with an attitude that became prevalent in Hellenistic philosophy, "that felt itself obliged to place enormous demands on a truth before being prepared to accept it" (2010b: 9). Scholars usually explain this in terms of the rise of skepticism, of which the figureheads were Pyrrho and Timon of Elis and the Academics Arcesilaus and Carneades. We can reconstruct in considerable detail how the latter influenced the evolution of Stoic epistemological concepts and arguments (Hankinson 2003). The metaphorical inversion highlighted by Blumenberg complements this conceptual evolution. He connects this with the metaphorics of "uncarelessness" in Stoic dialectic:

> In their logic, the Stoics had elaborated the doctrine of judgmental qualities from the standpoint of a "position" taken by reason in relation to the pure contents of utterances: the sovereignty of reason is manifested in its freedom to suspend judgment in the ἐποχή, in its refusal to give its assent until the object has been fully ratified. Yet here the probable reveals its power to seduce the judging subject to precipitancy (προπτωσία). . . . Stoic dialectics wants to immunize reason against the probable; it inculcates an attitude of wariness as the stronghold from which reason can best hold out against the allurements of probability: "By wariness they mean a strong presumption against what at the moment seems probable, so as not to be taken in by it." (2010b: 89, citing DL 7.46 and 7.89)

Here Blumenberg mentions two of the four dialectical virtues recognized by Stoicism, namely "non-precipitancy" (*aprosoptōsia*) and "wariness" or "uncarelessness" (*aneikaiotēs*). The other two are "irrefutability" (*anelenxia*) and "non-randomness" (*amataiotēs*) (LS 31B). As one contemporary scholar of Stoic dialectic remarks, "It's remarkable . . . that the four virtues are designated by privative neologisms . . . . The ensemble gives the rather curious impression of *defensive* virtues" (Gourinat 2000: 77, my italics). For Blumenberg, this "curious impression" suggests a fundamental posture of suspicion and vigilance, in which non-cataleptic impressions attempt to "take in" and "allure" the mind. Thus, the truth-seeker's attitude is no longer one of firmly grasping materials and constructing a secure foundation, but rather of caution. In Blumenberg's words, the mind is "sovereign" and safe in its "stronghold" precisely by *not* giving assent to impressions.

This metaphorological approach can enrich our understanding of many Stoic passages, of which I will mention just two. The first comes from Herculaneum Papryus 1020, most of which has only recently been published. Its editors, Michele Alessandrelli and Graziano Ranocchia, argue that Chrysippus is its most probable author (2017: 8–10). It is entirely preoccupied with expounding the Stoic sage's avoidance of cognitive errors. The sage will never mishear (*parakouein*), mis-see (*parorān*), miscalculate (*pararithmein*), or misthink (*paranoein*) (columns 105–7). In other words, although many of his sensory and mental impressions will of course be non-cataleptic, he will vigilantly withhold assent from them. The final legible words of the recently published columns focus entirely on "non-precipitancy":

> For the non-precipitate man must be incapable of being dragged [*anelkuston*] by a non-cataleptic impression; he must be strong [*iskhuein*] in impressions, so that he isn't dragged [*helkesthai*] by non-cataleptic impressions; he must rule over [*kratein*] his assents, so that he isn't dragged [*helkesthai*]. (col. 112.16–26)

This passage's metaphorics is remarkably emphatic[10]: in quick succession, the author repeats three times that the sage cannot be "dragged," inserting between these repetitions two assertions of the sage's strength and sovereignty. This oscillation between images of coercive impressions and images of stable discernment attests to the same attitude Blumenberg has identified. Blumenberg would claim that this attitude not only complements but in fact underpins the conceptualized arguments made elsewhere in the papyrus about the sage's freedom from error (col. 108–10).

At the opposite chronological end of the ancient tradition, we might connect this with Epictetus's surprising instruction to beginning Stoic practitioners: "For the time being remove your desire entirely" (*Ench.* 2.2, *Disc.* 1.4.1-2; cf. *Disc.* 3.12.8). Desire arises when we assent to impressions that something would be good for us, so Epictetus is advising his listener not only to vigilantly guard against non-cataleptic impressions about what is good but "for the time being" *to withhold assent from all such impressions*. Of course we can supply a conceptualized explanation for this austere guidance: beginners are liable to assent to non-cataleptic impressions that this or that event would be good for them. They should therefore suspend assent to evaluative impressions until they thoroughly digest the Stoic theory of value (Long 2002: 113).

But this reasonable explanation leaves niggling doubts. Could not Epictetus say instead that beginners should assent only to the impression that philosophical progress would be good for them? Is not this impression the key to their motivation? In order to think this through, we would need to articulate an entire series of arguments and counterarguments, adducing Stoic doctrines about progress and passion, selection and "disselection," and preferred and "dispreferred" indifferents. Rather than hazarding such terrain, I will conclude by remarking that metaphorology suggests a different angle of illumination. Inasmuch as Epictetus has internalized Stoic metaphorics, we will say that he is *predisposed* to frame impressions as temptations and the philosopher as evasive and vigilant. This suggestion by no means obviates the need for reconstructing and criticizing Epictetus's conceptual thinking, but it helps to explain how it arose and why it appears sound to him.

3. The Anthropology of Stoic Physics

Hitherto I have focused on epistemology. But for both Blumenberg and the Stoics, epistemology is inseparable from questions about humans' position in the universe and frameworks of meaning. While meaning and positionality are merely hinted at in *Paradigms*, they become increasingly prominent in *Legitimacy* and *Genesis*, and receive their clearest exposition in *Work on Myth* (1985 [orig. 1977]). There Blumenberg borrows and adapts ideas from the German tradition known as "philosophical anthropology" in order to articulate a framework for tranhistorical analysis.[11] This framework is minimalist in its premises, and might better be approached as a heuristic device rather than a dogmatic foundation (Wetz 2004: 98; compare Nicholls 2015: 116; contrast Hudson 1993). It revolves around two propositions: first, humans require "relief from the absolute," and second, they achieve this relief through "self-assertion." Let me concisely explain each of these.

First, Blumenberg defines "the absolutism of reality," like absolute metaphor, as a "limit concept" (1985: 3). It designates a situation of complete disorientation, in which, on the one hand, someone is entirely unable to anticipate defensively what might happen, or from which direction danger might come; and, on the other hand, they are equally unable to anticipate any possibilities with an attitude of hope and desire (1985: 4–7). They are therefore in a state of "indefinite anticipation," or "intentionality of consciousness without an object"—in short, a state of anxiety (1985: 4).

The solution to this anxiety is to create horizons of caution and desire, which is the task of "self-assertion." Varieties of self-assertion include absolute metaphors, which give shape to the totality of being and value; myths, which give names, qualities, or personalities to cosmic powers; and conceptual thought, which renders phenomena logically and practically manageable. All of these make possibilities matter in determinate ways, and thus enable people to take positions toward them. In order to designate the horizon of possibilities that emerges from self-assertion, Blumenberg sometimes borrows the term "lifeworld" from Husserl. "The life-world [sic]," writes Husserl, "for us who wakingly live in it, is always already there, existing in advance for us, the 'ground' of all praxis whether theoretical or extratheoretical" (1970: 142 §37; cf. Nicholls 2015: 102–8).

With this minimalist anthropology in mind, let us now return to our investigation of Stoic metaphorics. Elsewhere in *Paradigms* Blumenberg expands his commentary on Stoic epistemology. In Hellenistic philosophy in general, he writes,

> The fulfillment of existence is to be secured by *shielding* an inner space of subjectivity that now breaks away from the world, rather than by *enriching* one's stock of truth in interaction with the world. On the other hand, a specific stock of statements is now pooled into a fund of truths deemed necessary for salvation, first and foremost the legacy of moral insights inherited from the Stoics. (2010b: 19)

The first half of this statement correlates with the metaphorics we have already outlined. We have seen that Stoic wisdom lies partly in "vigilance" and "wariness," here expressed as "*shielding* an inner space of subjectivity that now breaks away from the world." What this passage adds is a distinction between two sets of impressions, which invite two kinds of attitudes—precisely the two attitudes between which the metaphorics of Stoic inquiry oscillates. The first set is "a specific stock of statements . . . deemed necessary for salvation, first and foremost the legacy of moral insights inherited from the Stoa." In other words, Blumenberg suggests that Stoics focus on achieving confidence with regard to moral impressions. This is the domain of "seizing" and "holding firmly." On the other hand, he suggests that they contradistinguish all other sorts of impressions—such as logical, physical, and metaphysical impressions—as the domain of wariness.

This is only the beginning. If we pursue the correlation between the bipolar metaphorics of knowing and the binary sorting of impressions, we will find it is connected to the fundamental doctrines and metaphors by which Stoics position themselves in their world. For instance, Blumenberg relates this distinction to "a teleological economy for the fulfillment of human needs" (2010b: 83). That quotation requires some unpacking. By "economy" he means *oikonomia* or "administration." (Compare Giorgio Agamben's *The Kingdom and the Glory: for a Theological Genealogy of Economy and Government* [2011], for which Stoicism is a recurring point of reference.) The administration in question is that of Zeus's divine providence, which is coextensive with Right Reason, Nature, Fate, and the Law (LS 63C3–4, Sen. *NQ* 2.45.1–2). In fact, Stoics sometimes explicitly refer to this power as an *oikonomia* (SVF II.937, III Chrysippus 178, cited by Agamben 2011: 19), although they prefer the etymologically related word *dioikēsis* (e.g., SVF I.87, I.98, II.416, LS 63C3). This power is "teleological" in the sense of being purposeful: it is the cause and reason why everything in the universe is what it is and happens the way it happens. So Blumenberg is saying that the division of impressions into a limited "salvific" set and a larger "alluring" or even "deceiving" set is not arbitrary; it is part of Zeus's providence "for the fulfillment of human needs."

It is therefore the twin task of Stoic philosophy both to demarcate the limits beyond which inquiry becomes hazardous and to direct attention to the salvific knowledge divine providence has placed within our reach (Blumenberg 1983: 258). This tension manifests differently in different areas of theory. For example, Blumenberg sees it not only in the dividing line between catalepsis and suspension of judgment in Stoic epistemology but also in the Stoics's emphasis on the logic of conditional and conjunctive propositions (1983: 258–9).[12] He connects it with Seneca's repudiation of most of the so-called liberal arts (1983: 261–2, citing *Ep.* 88). With regard to ethics, it is surprising that he does not mention the doctrine of "reservation," which would certainly support his argument. According to this doctrine, Stoics should bear in mind their cognitive limitations when making decisions, which they should therefore formulate with the proviso, "If I can, if I should, if this is the way things turn out" (Sen. *Ben.* 3.39).[13]

But it is Stoic physics that most interests Blumenberg. Let us begin with the Stoics's general attitude to the study of nature. On the one hand, since Nature is purposeful and benevolent, and since it has implanted in human beings a desire to understand, this desire must lead toward happiness. In this connection, Blumenberg quotes Seneca's *On Leisure* 5.3–4 in both *Legitimacy* and *Genesis*:

> Nature has given us an inquisitive spirit (*curiosum ingenium*), and being aware of her own skill and beauty, she has brought us forth as spectators of the great spectacle of things, since she would lose the fruit of her labor[14] if she had displayed her works, so vast, so wonderful, so artfully constructed, so luxuriant, and so various, to empty solitude. That you may understand that she wants to be

investigated and not only contemplated, notice the position that she has assigned to us: she has set us in her center and given us a panoramic view in all directions. (1983: 260–1; cf. 1987a: 18, where Blumenberg also quotes Sen. *Helv.* 8.3–10)

As Wetz recognizes (2004: 21–2), Blumenberg sees here an absolute metaphor that is central to the Stoic lifeworld. What is the totality of reality? It is a beautifully crafted artifact. How should we orientate ourselves to reality? We should become its inquisitive and appreciative contemplators. This metaphor performs an anthropological function: our impulse to contemplate and the universe's need to be contemplated give us meaning and positionality, setting the absolutism of reality at a distance. It recurs in many other Stoic texts, such as Epictetus's claim that Zeus "introduced humankind as spectator of himself and his works, and only spectator, but also interpreter" (*Disc.* 1.6.19-20), or Balbus's claim in Cicero's *On the Nature of the Gods* that "humankind was born to contemplate and imitate the world" (2.37; cf. 2.140).

But Wetz elides a crucial point about this metaphor, namely that the Stoics do not presume a perfect fit between mind and cosmos. In keeping with his emphasis on the metaphorics of wariness, Blumenberg insists that the Stoics retreat from Aristotle's theoretical optimism, for which "Man's life is . . . in principle capable of fulfillment in its essential pretension to knowledge, and the objectivity to which he has access exceeds neither his powers nor his finitude" (1983: 256). As a leading scholar puts it, for Aristotle "There is . . . a single activity—contemplating the world—which at once manifests the world's intelligibility and also reveals what man most truly is" (Lear 1988: 117). In other words, the human desire to understand meshes with the cosmos' impulse to be understood. This is only partly true for the Stoics, some of whom not only warn against "precipitancy" and other forms of cognitive vice but also proclaim the sterility of many fields of inquiry. Seneca is particularly fond of this topic, as *Epistle* 48.12 succinctly exemplifies: "Even if we had many years left to live, we'd need to be parsimonious in order to meet our needs. As it is, when time is so short, what madness to learn useless things!" (Cf. 59.5–12, 82.23–24, 87.37–40, 108.12, 117).[15] Physics is not among the subjects Seneca decries as "useless"; to the contrary, he explicitly defends it against this accusation (*Ep.* 65.15–24)—not to mention the effort he devotes to *Natural Questions*. Blumenberg's claim that Seneca rejects "The great integration of human culture into the meaningful context of nature, which had been carried out by Posidonius," is therefore simply wrong (1983: 262).[16] While Posidonius's attention to empirical natural research and mathematics was unusual among Stoics, his valorization of physics was completely orthodox. In fact, it would be truer to say that much of physics, like all of ethics, belongs to the "salvific truth" a Stoic must grasp cataleptically. Yet there remains a subtle tension in the Stoic metaphorics of contemplation, as I will now explore with two of Blumenberg's own examples.

The first comes from *Genesis of the Copernican World*, where Blumenberg discusses an obscure report that Cleanthes, the second scholarch of the Stoa, accused the astronomer Aristarchus of impiety "on the grounds that he was disturbing the hearth of the universe because he sought to save the phenomena by assuming that the heaven is at rest while the earth is revolving along the ecliptic and at the same time is rotating around its own axis" (Blumenberg 1987a: 16, citing SVF I.500). In other words, Aristarchus developed a heliocentric mathematical model of the cosmos. Cleanthes, we know, wrote an entire work *Against Aristarchus* (SVF I.481), from which only this testimony survives.

Blumenberg's reading of this polemic can only be understood against the backdrop of his sweeping argument in *Genesis*, which concerns the connection between geocentrism and the meaningfulness of the way the world appears to us. Citing Cleanthes's poetic claim that the cosmos is an "initiation rite" (*mustērion*) and the sun its "torch-bearer" (*dāidoukhos*, SVF I.538), Blumenberg infers that for Cleanthes, Aristarchus's crime is to attempt to "see through" the cosmic spectacle instead of embracing "the aesthetic immediacy of appearance" (1987a: 16–17). In other words, Cleanthes believes we should behold astronomical appearances like initiates at Eleusis behold the torchbearer, whose sacred meaningfulness cannot be fully articulated. Thus, the reason Cleanthes attacks heliocentrism is that his astronomical doctrine is governed by a metaphorics not only of contemplation but more specifically of sacred beholding (*theōria*).[17] Stoic geocentrism rests on this metaphorics of beholding; as we read earlier, Seneca writes that Nature "has set us in her center and given us a panoramic view in all directions" because otherwise she would "lose the fruit of her labor" (*perditura fructum sui*).

Blumenberg's interpretation promises a deep significance in this obscure evidence, but it requires both criticism and clarification. For instance, it is not clear how beholding is supposed to relate to firm grasping and wary vigilance. Does Cleanthes intend us to firmly grasp the cataleptic impression that the motions of the heavenly bodies are beautiful, which we can behold as a matter of "aesthetic immediacy," but to warily suspend judgment about the specifics of those motions? That would conflict with Seneca's statement that Nature "wants to be investigated and not only contemplated," and Epictetus's claim that Zeus "introduced humankind as spectator of himself and his works, and only spectator, but also interpreter." It would also make Cleanthes a poor philosopher, since his metaphors would severely curtail his conceptual thinking.

It would therefore be better to apply Blumenberg's method with greater nuance, suggesting that geocentrism, while not an object of aesthetic immediacy, should nevertheless be grasped cataleptically. On this interpretation, Cleanthes does not forbid empirical observation or speculative reasoning about astronomy; he simply thinks Aristarchus's reasoning is bad. Thomas Bénatouïl has cogently argued that Cleanthes's doctrines regarding the sun were developed in dialogue with an array of interlocutors. Most importantly, they were directed at both the Stoic Aristo's wholesale repudiation of physics and Aristarchus's Peripatetic assumption that mathematical astronomy can be separated from theological and biological cosmology. Against Aristo, Cleanthes develops theories that go far beyond what is immediately evident. His doctrine that the sun follows a spiraling path around the earth not only accounts for its observed motion along the ecliptic but also coheres with his belief that the sun is a divine being, nourished by terrestrial waters, whose rays orchestrate the harmony of nature. Against Aristarchus, he argues that cosmobiology is more cogent than mathematical modeling, just as he prefers the Heraclitean harmonics of opposing elemental processes to the Pythagorean harmonics of numerical proportions (SVF I.501–4, 541–2; Bénatouïl 2005: esp. 215–1). It is on this basis that he recommends wariness toward Aristarchus's geometrical reasoning in particular, not toward nonevident propositions about the heavenly bodies in general.

The upshot is that the anthropological imperative operates more subtly than Blumenberg's thumbnail discussion leads us to believe: it coordinates an entire network of metaphors (not only grasp, vigilance, and beholding but now also the cosmos as organism and harmony), which collectively establish a framework of meaning. This framework neither replaces theoretical reasoning nor rigidly limits it. However, it does imply that solar motions are beyond our powers of precise mathematical analysis. For this reason, we must adopt an attitude of wary vigilance toward geometrical astronomy.[18]

My second example comes from Blumenberg's untranslated *Höhlenausgänge*, an entire chapter of which is devoted to a long passage in Cicero's dialogue *On the Nature of the Gods* (*De Natura Deorum*, abbreviated *ND*). In this passage, the Stoic Balbus is defending the reality of divine providence against the Epicurean Velleius (*ND* 2.72–96, Blumenberg 1989: 193–206). Blumenberg asserts that what drives this argument is Cicero's need, as a Roman politician, to demonstrate the gods' responsiveness to public cult (1989: 179). That Roman state activity was inseparable from religious observance is not in any doubt; indeed, Mary Beard has argued that the real accomplishment of Cicero's trilogy *On the Nature of the Gods*, *On Divination*, and *On Fate* was to establish the parameters of "religion" as a discrete topic for Roman intellectuals (1986). Blumenberg is probably right that Cicero's authorial position on this question aligns with that of his speaker Balbus, whose Stoic point of view is what really interests us. At the beginning of his long discourse, Balbus boasts that Rome excels all other nations in the scrupulousness with which it consults the gods, and laments how some of these traditions have become degraded in his day (2.8–10). Thus, Blumenberg is correct to claim that Balbus aims not only to defend Stoic doctrine in general but also to prove the gods are "sufficiently reliable" to sustain a relationship that is "one of reciprocity, nearly of contractual rights" between themselves and the Roman state in particular (1989: 179).

Balbus's elaborate sequence of metaphors—only part of which I will address here—obviously fascinates Blumenberg, since he addresses other parts of it in *Paradigms* (2010b: 65–6) and *Die Lesbarkeit der Welt* (1986: 40–1). It is a treasure trove for historians of ancient literature, because it contains lengthy quotations from two lost works: the Roman tragedian Accius's *Medea* (*ND* 2.89) and Aristotle's *On Philosophy* (2.94–5).[19] Blumenberg focuses on the latter in *Höhlenausgänge*, since it features the metaphor after which the book is named: departure from the cave. For our purposes, it will be more productive to concentrate on the former. Both metaphors belong to what Blumenberg aptly calls "a kind of thought experiment" intended to reveal the divine activity Balbus's contemporaries have become too jaded to discern (1989: 198). In other words, they are designed to help us look afresh at the universe, in such a way that providence will become apparent. Balbus relates that the Stoics divide arguments for providence into three categories, of which the last is "from our sense of wonder at celestial and terrestrial phenomena" (*ex admiratione rerum caelestium et terrestrium*, 2.75). These metaphors accordingly attempt to restore a sense of wonder at the sight of the world, which grounds arguments for the reality of divine power.

Balbus's quotation from Accius opens this argument from wonder. He recalls how the tragedian depicts a shepherd, who has never seen a ship, "astonished and completely terrified" (*admirans et perterritus*) as he witnesses the Argonauts's vessel from a coastal mountain:

> Such an immense mass flowing,
> Raging out of the vast deep with roaring winds,
> It revolves the wavy vortexes violently before it,
> Rushes falling, blowing and spattering back the ocean!

> Just so, while you think an odd-shaped rainstorm is revolving,
> a high crag snatched and thrown by winds and gales,
> or globular waterspouts struck by the concourse of waves—
> unless the sea prepares a massacre for the land,
> or maybe Triton, rooting up in the wavy straits
> some underground cave right from the bottom
> heaves out this stony mass toward heaven! (2.89)

Obviously the shepherd finds the spectacle both awe-inspiring and confusing: notice not only the violent elemental and divine forces he invokes but also the extravagant alliteration and broken syntax through which he attempts to express his experience. Even when he sees the sailors, at first he likens them to sea animals or gods: "Like swift excited dolphins they roar out [*perfremunt*],"[20] he says; "it brings to my ears a sound and song like [the god] Silvanus' melody" (2.89). But Balbus makes it clear that the shepherd eventually recognizes that these are human beings and the Argo a product of divine and human craft. His argument depends on an analogy between the shepherd and his opponents, philosophers who doubt that the gods care for the world:

> In the same manner, though the first sight of the world may have dismayed the philosophers, after they had seen its precise and balanced motions and all its parts managed with decisive orderliness and unchanging stability, they should have recognized the presence in this world of not only an inhabitant, but a governor, administrator, and as it were architect of this immense work and immense spectacle. (2.90)

Just as the shepherd witnesses the semi-divine Argo with no prior experience of seafaring, so too we must imagine these philosophers' "first sight of the universe" (*primus aspectus mundi*). It is obviously impossible for them to have spied the universe "for the first time," as if from some extra-mundane mountain. But Balbus wants to help his listeners suspend "the mode of givenness of the everyday" (*die Gegebenheitsweise der Alltäglichkeit*, Blumenberg 1989: 198). If they can manage this suspension, they should experience a kind of wonder (*admiratio*), which would stimulate further investigation and reasoning, the culmination of which would be to recognize "a governor, administrator, and as it were architect of this immense work and immense spectacle."

That is how the argument works at the conceptual level. At the metaphorical level, we should begin by adducing Blumenberg's argument in *Shipwreck with Spectator* that "Humans... seek to grasp the movement of their existence above all through a metaphorics of the perilous sea voyage" (1997 [orig. 1979]: 7). Within this metaphorics, the sea generally represents "the sphere of the unreckonable and lawless, in which it is difficult to find one's bearings" (1997 [orig. 1979]: 7). Thus, the metaphorics of seafaring lends itself to expressing humankind's primal anxiety regarding the absolute. Blumenberg explicitly alludes to this metaphorology when he remarks:

> The shepherd from Accius' tragedy inevitably perceives the Argonauts' ship in the metaphorics of the violent appearance of nature, and in the dialogue this translation makes it possible to move in the opposite direction as well: to perceive nature as a masterpiece of artistry. (1989: 199)

When Blumenberg says this perception is "inevitable," I suggest that he is adopting the author's point of view: Accius "inevitably" represents the shepherd's encounter with the Argo, the mythical paradigm for the hybris of seafaring, in terms of "the unreckonable and lawless, in which it is difficult to find one's bearings."

Let us examine more closely the "translation" (*Übertragung*) Blumenberg highlights between perceiving the world as a well-designed artifact and perceiving it as a violent chaos. Balbus has borrowed a surprisingly complex passage to begin his arguments for providence "from the sense of wonder" (*ex admiratione*). Although he believes the cosmos is beautiful, intelligent, "perfect and complete in all its numbers and parts" (2.37), he admits that the philosophers in his thought experiment may have been "dismayed" by their primordial experience of it (*eos . . . conturbaverat*), just as the shepherd was "astonished and completely terrified" (*admirans et perterritus*) by the Argo. These are not the responses one might have expected to beauty and perfection. Only in a second moment are the philosophers supposed to "recognize . . . the architect of this immense work and immense spectacle," just as the shepherd's disturbed imaginings, informed by the sounds of the sailors, resolve into the contours of a human activity and vessel. Even here Balbus hints that human cognition remains overstretched, since the object of contemplation is simply too enormous: "this immense mass" (*tanta moles*) is now perceived as "this immense work and immense spectacle" (*tanti operis tantique muneris*).

The whole passage can be used to deepen our understanding of the metaphorics of beholding. In Cleanthes's case, I argued that this metaphorics does not replace arguments about solar motion, which take account of both empirical observation and cosmological principles. Rather, in cooperation with other metaphors, it gives those arguments their parameters. This is even more obviously true for Balbus, who laments the fact that "because of daily repetition and visual habit people's minds get used to [the sight of the universe], so they don't wonder at it or seek explanations for the things they always see" (*neque admirantur neque requirunt rationes earum rerum quas semper vident*, 2.96). At the level of conceptual reasoning, it is the very purpose of wonder "to impel us to search for causes" (2.96).

Yet the metaphorical significance of wonder is not used up in that motivating function. Wonder defines the beholder's complex affective relationship to the object of beholding: awe-struck, frightened, fascinated, or worshipful. On the one hand, this relationship establishes a position of emulation. Balbus concludes his argument by claiming that "by observing these things [i.e. the motions of the heavenly bodies], the human mind comes to know the gods, and from this arises piety, to which justice and the other virtues are conjoined, from which emerges a blessed life similar and equal to the gods" (*ND* 2.153). This recapitulates his opening claim that human prudence and intellect come from the gods (2.79). In both cases, as Blumenberg notes (1989: 197–8), the metaphorics of beholding takes on a political dimension. "For the world is a sort of shared home for gods and human beings," Balbus perorates, "or a city belonging to both. For they alone, since they have the use of reason, live by law and justice" (2.154; cf. 2.78–9). In other words, the feeling of astonishment at the heavens' regularity and beauty leads us to infer not only that they are intelligently and purposefully administered but also that this is the very same reason and purpose we ourselves possess. Thus, we are not only spectators and interpreters but also collaborators. The role of wonder is to trigger this emulation of divine reason and law, which binds us together as a polity of rational beings. This means that Roman state rituals, which presume communication and reciprocity with the gods, continue to make sense.

But we should note that wonder also frames an affective relationship of inferiority and being overwhelmed. "Who would call that man a human being," Balbus asks,

> who, although he sees such precise motions in the heavens, such stable order in the stars, and all things so connected and conjoined with one another, denies that there is any reason in all of this, and declares it happens by chance? By no thought of our own can we follow by how great a thought these things are administered. (2.97)

Here the emphasis falls on that dimension of reality that escapes our cognitive organization: "by no thought of our own can we follow by how great a thought these things are administered" (*quae quanto consilio gerantur nullo consilio adsequi possumus*). Inscrutable divine power, which is one of the major concerns of *The Legitimacy of the Modern Age*, is the precursor in Blumenberg's thought to "the absolutism of reality." A number of passages in Seneca's *Natural Questions* hint at this facet of providence:

> How many things besides these [comets] follow secret paths, and never emerge into human sight? For God didn't make everything for humankind! What fraction of this immense work has been committed to us? (7.30.3)

> The observations of the Chaldaeans have recognized the powers of the five planets. What? Do you think so many thousands of stars shine in vain? . . . They don't lack rights or dominion over us . . . but it's as hard to know their powers as to doubt they have them. (2.32.7–8)

> [Some] lightning bolts signify nothing, or something we cannot recognize, like those that are scattered over the vast ocean or empty deserts: either they signify nothing, or their signification perishes. (2.51)

Neque enim omnia deus homini fecit: god did not make everything for humankind. This is surprising for anyone accustomed to the truism that Stoic cosmology is anthropocentric. The doctrine that "it was for the sake of gods and men that the world and everything in it was created" (LS 54N = Cic. *ND* 2.133) is often abbreviated as "god made everything for the sake of human beings" (*omnia deus hominum causa fecit*, LS 54R; cf. Cic. *ND* 2.153). Compare the Stoics's notorious claim that the qualities of all plants and animals have been designed for the benefit of human beings (SVF II.1152–67). But this neglects the possibility that Zeus organizes many things for the community of gods, which includes "so many thousands of stars" (*tot illa milia siderum*), and not for human beings. We are excluded from understanding what is happening, even though we know it matters to us: these multitudes of stars "don't lack dominion or rights over us" (*non extra ius dominiumque nostri sunt*).[21] It is much harder here to describe the position and attitude defined by the metaphor of beholding. Perhaps we can even appreciate why, in another context, Blumenberg suggests that the Stoic posture of "letting go of what is indifferent" could be compared to "a sacrifice to the sea god" (2010a: 32).[22]

It is time to gather together some conclusions from this investigation of the Anthropology of Stoic physics. First, I have attempted to show that all these texts are structured not only by their concepts and arguments but also by their metaphors. I have focused on the metaphor of beholding and some of its relations to metaphors of grasping and vigilance. By looking carefully at some ancient Stoic texts and scholarship, we have seen that this metaphorics is more complex than it first appears, and relates more subtly to conceptual reasoning than Blumenberg's own readings suggest. Second, such metaphors help to define basic theoretical and practical orientations, without which Blumenberg claims that human beings are exposed to intolerable anxiety. I have indeed argued that an awareness of that which precedes or overflows conceptualization remains at the margins of Stoic physics. Even admiration and emulation, which are unquestionably the dominant modes of wonder in Stoic texts, preserve a remainder of unfathomability. Moreover, their interplay with fear and awe points toward nuances of Stoic practice that are usually neglected. Is "anxiety" an adequate description of the experience at which these texts hint? It is on this that I would like to focus in my final section.

4. The Complexity of the Stoic Life

As I noted in my introduction, it is now common in both the history of philosophy and the modern Stoic movement to approach Stoicism as a way of life. I would like to use the foregoing reading of Blumenberg in order to suggest that some possibilities within this way of life are too often ignored. Descriptions of it concentrate almost exclusively on the pursuit of conceptual lucidity, practical resolution, ethical concentration, emotional satisfaction, and—when Stoic physics receives attention from anyone other than specialists—the benevolence of divine order. Let us by all means admit that these are central characteristics of all Stoic lives. Nevertheless, this description flattens and homogenizes those lives.

Let me begin with the claim that it flattens them, meaning it occludes many of their dimensions. What is valuable about Blumenberg's approach is that it gives us critical and reflective distance from the Stoics's own self-understanding. His anthropological thesis allows us to question how any Stoic valorizes a horizon of possibilities, and so not only makes her universe theoretically intelligible and practically manageable but also reduces anxiety to a tolerable level. This fundamental question about anxiety, which for Blumenberg subsumes existentialist and psychoanalytic insights (Blumenberg 1985: 4–11, 89–95, 109–10, 269–70), simply does not arise in ancient philosophy. Analysis of the Stoics's concepts and arguments obviously provide one way of answering it. Blumenberg's metaphorology complements rather than replaces analysis of concepts and arguments, as I have attempted to show in this chapter. It allows us to recognize a recurring image like "beholding the universe," to analyze its vicissitudes and its relations to theory, and to consider the possibility that it is not "merely a metaphor": rather, its recurrence might signal a posture and an attitude in which its authors have invested care and significance. In this respect Blumenberg's reception of Stoicism should be placed alongside others that, without downplaying the centrality of conceptual reasoning, attempt to understand the Stoic life also in terms of unconscious, imaginal, embodied, and extended cognition (Lampe 2013, 2016).

We can go a little further here, and in the process pose a question for Blumenberg as well. We have shown that Stoics cultivate a sense of wonder, and that this wonder implicitly acknowledges "the absolutism of reality." Blumenberg would explain that Stoicism, like every apparatus for human self-assertion, inevitably fails to domesticate the absolute in its entirety; Stoic metaphors, myths, and concepts simply do their best to contain it. But we could instead propose that measured exposure to (and identification with) an overwhelming power is part of what makes the Stoic life worth living. Blumenberg is well aware of Rudolf Otto's neo-Kantian theory of "the holy" as a sui generis category of experience (Otto 1959; Blumenberg 1985: 14, 20–1, 28, 62–4), but *Work on Myth* neglects the ideas of Otto's most well-known German-language successors: it casually dismisses Carl Jung's work, and disregards that of Mircea Eliade.[23] Today we might add Jeffrey Kripal to this tradition, which defends the theoretical and practical value of the numinous. With regard to Blumenberg's philosophical anthropology, incorporating these thinkers could mean balancing reduction of anxiety with cultivation of spirituality. With regard to Stoicism, it could make better sense of their theoretical and practical commitment to divination, which in Posidonius's case—the most radical attested—extends not only to astrology, oneiric and ecstatic visions, and augury by birds and lightning bolts but also the reading of muscular spasms.[24]

Having ventured this suggestion, it is important to stipulate that it is descriptive rather than normative. In other words, there have always been many ways of living a Stoic life. Some Stoics will have been more invested in the epistemic posture of seizing and securing, others in the posture of guarding and vigilance; the attitude of wondrous beholding will have enchanted some more than others. Jordi Pià Comella has recently traced the oscillation in the history of the ancient Stoa between rationalist critique and conservative defense of rituals such as divination (2014). Modern Stoics are even more widely divided between atheists and those with spiritual orientations (Vernon and LeBon 2014). Thus, I by no means argue that we have, through Blumenbergian anthropology and metaphorology, come to a fixed and abiding truth about "authentic Stoicism." My suggestion is rather that a critical reading of Blumenberg gives us one way to appreciate that for some practitioners, some of the time, the Stoic life supplements lucidity and cheerfulness with a dose of mystery and awe.

Notes

1 *Höhlenausgänge* is plural, but *Exits from the Cave* misses the metaphorical resonances that are key to the title.
2 These are merely the discussions of which I am aware; there are undoubtedly others.
3 Wetz's suggestion is apt: "Sicherlich hätte Blumenberg als Schriftgelehrter auf den alten Ausspruch zuruckziehen können: '. . . Für mich selbst habe ich geschrieben'" (2004: 10).
4 Regarding Blumenberg's lifelong engagement with Husserl, see Wetz (2004: 132–51) and Nicholls (2015: esp. 73–6, 103–8). The relation of Husserl's "scientific" aspirations to Descartes is concisely presented by Moran (2005: 43–6).
5 As Angus Nicholls reminds me (via personal communication), Blumenberg cites the brief discussion of "symbols" in section 59 of Kant's *Critique of the Power of Judgment* as the impetus for what he calls "metaphorology." Cf. Wetters (2012: 107–12) on the difficulty of defining "absolute metaphor."
6 See further in the following text.
7 Blumenberg's translator uses "presentation" for this Stoic technical term. In keeping with the convention among specialists, I have in every case replaced this with "impression."
8 "Firmly grasping" or *katalēpsis* is assent to a cataleptic impression (LS 41C).
9 For all passages from LS, I have adapted the author's translations; all translations of Greek, Latin, French, or German passages for which no translation appears in the bibliography are my own.
10 Indeed, the repetition is so striking that we must acknowledge the possibility of scribal diplography.
11 Nicholls (2015: 79–121) is particularly good at setting Blumenberg in his German philosophical context. Wetz (2004: 28–114) illuminates how *Myth* emerges from Blumenberg's earlier preoccupations. See also Hudson (1993).
12 Blumenberg actually speaks of "special cultivation . . . of the topic of hypothetical inference," which I interpret to mean conditional and conjunctive logic. See LS 35–6 with Bobzien (2003). I omit Blumenberg's mention of "the doctrine of modalities with its 'weak' intensities of judgment" (1983: 258), since it is not clear what relation he intends to imply between modality (LS 38) and "intensity of judgment."
13 Cf. *Ben.* 34.4–5; Epict. *Ench.* 2.2; MA 4.1, 5.20, 11.37.

14 Here Blumenberg (1983: 260) has "sacrificed the enjoyment of herself," which is neither clear nor representative of the Latin (*perditura fructum sui*). I have accordingly replaced it with the translation from Blumenberg (1987: 18).
15 One should not overlook how much knowledge of these supposedly pernicious topics Seneca demonstrates, nor fail to admit that he may intend for his readers to appreciate this self-deprecating irony.
16 Blumenberg quotes Sen. *Ep*. 88.13–17, which in isolation appears to repudiate astronomy and astrology. But in context, its primary target is geometry.
17 Blumenberg later devotes an entire book to the metaphorics of *theōria*, focusing on the anecdote about Thales falling into the well. This study scarcely mentions Stoicism (1987b). It would be worthwhile comparing Blumenberg's diachronic study with Nightingale's focused reconstruction of how Plato appropriated the religious metaphor of *theōria* for philosophy (2004).
18 Compare Seneca's criticism of geometrical astronomy, *Ep*. 88.24–28.
19 Balbus also quotes two lines from a lost Roman tragedy by Pacuvius here (2.91). Aristotle's *On Philosophy* is cited as well at 1.33, 2.44, and 2.46.
20 While *perfremunt* sounds odd for dolphins, Accius had probably never heard one.
21 The context makes it clear that *nostri* is an objective rather than subjective genitive.
22 However, Blumenberg's claim that *pereant ne peream* is a "Stoic byword" must not be taken to mean that any classical Stoic ever penned this phrase: it appears nowhere in the database of classical Latin.
23 Blumenberg (1985) discusses Jung only in passing, and primarily in connection to his break with Freud. Eliade is not cited.
24 Key sources on Stoic theoretical attitudes to divination include SVF II.157.605, II.270.939, II.281.967, III.304.1018; Sen. NQ 2.32–51; Cicero *On Divination passim*, esp. 1.6, 39. 64, 117–32; 2.33–5; Posidonius F104, 111–13 Edelstein and Kidd. The only sources which address the actual use of divination by Stoics are Epictetus, *Ench*. 18, 32; *Disc*. 2.5.

Works Cited

Agamben, Giorgio (2011), *The Kingdom and the Glory: For a Theological Genealogy of Economy and Government*, trans. Lorenzo Chiesa with Matteo Mandarini, Stanford: Stanford University Press.

Alessandrelli, Michele and Graziano Ranocchia, eds. (2017), *Scrittore Stoico Anonimo, Opera Incerta (PHerc. 1020), Coll*. 104–12, Rome: ILIESI digitale. Accessed at http://www.pherc.eu/publications.html.

Beard, Mary (1986), "Cicero and Divination: The Formation of a Latin Discourse," *The Journal of Roman Studies*, 76: 33–46.

Bénatouïl, Thomas (2005), "Cléanthe contra Aristarque: Stoïcisme et astronomie à l'époque hellénistique," *Archives de philosophie*, 68: 207–22.
Blumenberg, Hans (1983), *The Legitimacy of the Modern Age*, trans. Robert M. Wallace, Cambride, MA: MIT Press.
Blumenberg, Hans (1985), *Work on Myth*, trans. Robert M. Wallace, Cambridge, MA: MIT Press.
Blumenberg, Hans (1986), *Die Lesbarkeit der Welt*, Frankfurt am Main: Suhrkamp.
Blumenberg, Hans (1987a), *The Genesis of the Copernican World*, trans. Robert M. Wallace, Cambridge, MA: MIT Press.
Blumenberg, Hans (1987b), *The Laughter of the Thracian Woman: A Protohistory of Theory*, trans. Spencer Hawkins, London: Bloomsbury.
Blumenberg, Hans (1989), *Höhlenausgänge*, Frankfurt am Main: Suhrkamp.
Blumenberg, Hans (1997), *Shipwreck with Spectator: Paradigm of a Metaphor for Existence*, trans. Steven Rendall, Cambridge, MA: MIT Press.
Blumenberg, Hans (2010a), *Care Crosses the River*, trans. Paul Fleming, Stanford: Stanford University Press.
Blumenberg, Hans (2010b), *Paradigms for a Metaphorology*, trans. Robert Savage, Ithaca: Cornell University Press.
Bobzien, Suzanne (2003), "Stoic Logic," in B. Inwood (ed.), *The Cambridge Companion to Stoicism*, 85–123. Cambridge: Cambridge University Press.
Brennan, Tad (2005), *The Stoic Life: Emotions, Duties, and Fate,* New York: Oxford University Press.
Comella, Jordia Pià (2014), *Une Piété de la raison: Philosophie et religion dans le stoïcisme impérial*, Turnhout: Brepols.
Gourinat, Jean-Baptiste (2000), *La Dialectique des stoïciens*, Paris: J. Vrin.
Hadot, Pierre (1998), *The Inner Citadel*, trans. Michael Chase, Cambridge, MA: Harvard.
Hadot, Pierre (2002), *What Is Ancient Philosophy?* trans. Michael Chase, Cambridge, MA: Belknap Press.
Hadot, Pierre (2006), *The Veil of Isis*, trans. Michael Chase, Cambridge, MA: Belknap.
Hankinson, R. J. (2003), "Stoic Epistemology," in B. Inwood (ed.), *The Cambridge Companion to Stoicism*, 59–84, Cambridge: Cambridge University Press.
Hudson, Wayne (1993), "After Historicism: Blumenberg and Philosophical Anthropology," *History of the Human Sciences*, 6 (4): 109–16.
Lampe, Kurt (2013), "Obeying Your Father: Stoic Theology Between Myth and Masochism," in V. Zajko and E. O'Gorman (eds.), *Classical Myth and Psychoanalysis: Ancient and Modern Stories of the Self*, 183–97, Oxford: Oxford University Press.
Lampe, Kurt (2016), "Kristeva, Stoicism, and the 'True Life of Interpretations,'" *SubStance*, 45: 22–43.
Lear, Jonathan (1988), *Aristotle: The Desire to Understand*, Cambridge: Cambridge University Press.

Long, A. A. (2002), *Epictetus: A Stoic and Socratic Guide to Life*, Oxford: Oxford University Press.

Long, A. A. (2006), "Hellenistic Ethics and Philosophical Power," in *From Epicurus to Epictetus: Studies in Hellenistic and Roman Philosophy*, 3–22, Oxford: Oxford University Press.

Nightingale, Andrea (2004), *Spectacles of Truth in Classical Greek Philosophy: Theoria in Its Cultural Context*, Cambridge: Cambridge University Press.

Möller, Melanie (2015), *Prometheus gibt nich auf: Antike Welt und modernes Leben in Hans Blumenbergs Philosophie*, Paderborn: Wilhelm Fink.

Moran, Dermot (2005), *Edmund Husserl: Founder of Phenomenology*, Malden: Polity Press.

Nicholls, Angus (2015), *Myth and the Human Sciences: Hans Blumenberg's Theory of Myth*, London: Routledge.

Otto, Rudolf (1959), *The Idea of the Holy*, trans. John W. Harvey, Harmondsworth: Penguin.

Robertson, Donald (2013), *Stoicism and the Art of Happiness*, London: Hodder & Stoughton.

Vernon, Tim and Mark LeBon (2014), "Do You Need God to Be a Stoic?" *Modern Stoicism*. https://modernstoicism.com/the-debate-do-you-need-god-to-be-a-stoic/. Accessed February 12, 2019.

Vogt, Katja Maria (2012), *Belief and Truth: A Skeptic Reading of Plato*, Oxford: Oxford University Press.

von Arnim, Hans (1903–24), *Stoicorum Veterum Fragmenta*, Leipzig: Teubner.

Wetters, Kirk (2012), "Working over Philosophy: Hans Blumenberg's Reformulations of the Absolute," *Telos*, 158: 100–18.

Wetz, Franz Josef (2004), *Hans Blumenberg: zur Einführung*, Hamburg: Junius.

10

Planetary *Askēsis*

Peter Sloterdijk's Stoic Journey into Existential Spatiality

Sam Mickey

1. Introduction

Peter Sloterdijk has a dream:

> The dream that I pursue is to see the dying tree of philosophy bloom once again, in a blossoming without disillusionment, abundant with bizarre thought-flowers, red, blue, and white, shimmering in the colors of the beginning, as in the Greek dawn, when *theoria* was beginning and when, inconceivably and suddenly, like everything clear, understanding found its language. Are we really culturally too old to repeat such experiences? (Sloterdijk 1987: xxxviii)

In this dream, the blossoming tree of philosophy is a rejuvenation of the tree that bloomed among the ancient Greeks. In some respects, this rebirth of philosophy modeled after early Greek thinking seems like a very traditional dream, not one that would set Sloterdijk apart from his philosophical peers. Nonetheless, by pursuing that dream throughout his career, Sloterdijk (b. 1947) has earned a reputation as one of the most provocative of contemporary philosophers. He is a prolific writer, exhibiting a hyperbolic style and broadly interdisciplinary erudition with sophisticated displays of scholarly rigor, sardonic wit, and contemplative reserve. He eludes simple categorization, as is evident from his attempt to describe himself. "If I had to examine myself from a distance, then I would say that this Sloterdijk is a strange bastard, comprising a lyrical extremist and a damned school master. Or a mystic and compère" (Sloterdijk 2011b: 297). Poetic and pedantic, he is a lover of wisdom and an ostentatious showman. Sloterdijk is a compère in a figurative and literal sense. He writes like a master of ceremonies enthusiastically introducing various people, ideas, and events; more literally, Sloterdijk was a cohost for a late-night talk show from 2002 to 2012, *Im Glashaus: Das Philosophische Quartett* (In the Glass House: The Philosophical Quartet), which aired on the German national channel ZDF (Sloterdijk 2016: 120).

From the success of his books to his national television fame, Sloterdijk has become something like a "celebrity philosopher" (Meaney 2018). That celebrity status did not come without controversy. For instance, criticism arose in response to a 1999 essay in which Sloterdijk reflects on Heidegger's "Letter on Humanism" and considers how the tradition of humanistic education relies upon the practice of "reading" (*Lesen*) as a method of "selection" (*Auslesen*) for avoiding barbarism and maintaining the openness in which humans exist (Heidegger 1998; Sloterdijk 2017). Some people misheard tones of eugenics in his emphasis on "selection," his image of civilization as a "human park" (*Menschenpark*), and his sympathetic references to Heidegger, whose philosophy is troubled by affiliations with Nazism and antisemitism. Rather than tarnishing his reputation, the academic criticism that Sloterdijk receives only seems to heighten his celebrity status.

Sloterdijk's popularity lies partly in the way he appears to be outside the fray of academic debate. He seems detached from the concerns of intellectual elites. His style of thinking expresses a self-confident ease, what one commentator describes as serenity:

> A distinctive mark of Peter Sloterdijk's philosophy, especially within the context of the German tradition, seems to be its striking serenity. Sloterdijk is obviously amused by what he observes (for example, postmodern cynicism), and he comments about it with a polite smile reflecting something between a certain kind of love and a slight contempt for a more or less silly object. This detached attitude appears to save psychic energy and to subsequently allow for a pleasurable release in beautiful and witty poetic verbalizations. So even where Sloterdijk is sharply critical, he is never passionate. This has apparently made him popular and readable even for people who may otherwise stay away from philosophy. It is the reason why some of his "disinvolved" findings have generated more debate and social concern than any "alarmist" criticism would have been able to. And it may also explain why traditional critical academia in Germany finds it difficult to deal with his work. (Pfaller 2011: 67)

The traditional critical academia in Germany is exemplified in the critical theory of the so-called *Frankfurter Schule*, which is among the main targets of Sloterdijk's polemics, especially its second generation, of whom Jürgen Habermas is the most prominent representative.[1] In terms of German philosophy, Sloterdijk's lineage is not critical theory. It is more of an existential lineage, with references and allusions to Nietzsche and Heidegger making regular appearances throughout Sloterdijk's writings, including two monographs on Nietzsche (Sloterdijk 1989, 2013b). Post-existentialist French thought also figures prominently in Sloterdijk's work, such as the orientation toward the life of practice in Pierre Hadot and Michel Foucault, and the processual and systems-theoretical language of assemblages from Gilles Deleuze. Sloterdijk also devotes a short book to Jacques Derrida, interpreting his deconstruction as a project to construct "an undeconstructible survival machine" (2009: 9).

Sloterdijk's work reflects his own spiritual practice. He says that the time "between 1974 and 1980 was the experimental phase of my life," which he calls "the wild years of groups," including "communes, psychotherapy, meditation groups, the New Left, the New Man" (Sloterdijk 2016b: xiv). Part of this experimental phase included a trip to India, which was not an uncommon element in the spiritual aspirations of Sloterdijk's generation, embodying therapeutic, spiritual, and countercultural developments. He spent time with the famous and controversial Indian mystic Bhagwan Shree Rajneesh (also called Osho). While his experimental years changed him, Sloterdijk was not thereby converted to Indian modes of philosophy and spiritual practice. "On the contrary," as he puts it, "it was only since then that I consciously became a European" (Sloterdijk 2016b: xv).

Sloterdijk's conscious effort to become European was an effort to draw on his own background and develop a "private meteorology," that is, to cultivate an inner revolution that does not need to wait for a social revolution in order to attain emancipation (2016b: xv). In the European philosophical tradition, such self-cultivation has ambivalent status. It is a particularly prominent practice across the schools of ancient European philosophy, but it is quite lost among contemporary theoreticians, who have witnessed the "liquidation of the ancient European subject of theory" (Sloterdijk 2012: 86). Questions about the self are converted into questions about the complex systems and underlying processes that constitute or situate the self, such as social hierarchies, economic relations, political power, ideologies, paradigm shifts, language games, and biophysical constraints.

Privately and professionally, Sloterdijk has sought a reconstitution of the ancient sense of subjectivity. His unique use of late classical and Hellenistic thought for his private meteorology entered the public arena in 1983 with his first book, *Critique of Cynical Reason*. That book recovers the ancient philosophical school of Cynicism—what he calls Kynicism (*Kynismus*)—as means for overcoming the incredulity and inhumanity that characterizes the "cynical" (small "c") attitude of malaise, criticism, resentment, and disbelief pervading modern, postindustrial societies.[2] However, Cynicism is not the only Hellenistic school of thought informing Sloterdijk in that book and in other writings. A closer look shows many connections between Sloterdijk and a direct descendant of Cynicism: Stoicism. Sloterdijk's reception of Stoicism can be found directly in his references to Stoicism and Stoic thinkers, especially the philosophers of the Late Stoa (e.g., Seneca, Epictetus, and Marcus Aurelius), and in his use of Stoic concepts, especially the idea of philosophy as a practice that involves *askēsis* ("exercise," "training") and the idea of cosmopolitanism. The Stoic side of Sloterdijk also can be detected indirectly, in his engagements with other schools of thought, from Cynicism and Skepticism to phenomenology and media theory, and in his theory of intimate, inhabited spaces or "spheres."

Sloterdijk adapts Stoic practices of self-cultivation for the milieus of contemporary life, rethinking Stoicism in light of the unprecedented conditions of a globalized social system, which is so massively scaled in its technologically mediated impacts that it has occasioned a transformation of planetary proportions. When humans in industrial societies began impacting the strata of Earth's crust—distributing plutonium, plastic, Styrofoam, high amounts of carbon, and numerous artificial chemicals across the face of the planet—the geological epoch of the last 12,000 years (the Holocene) gave way to a new one, which bears the indelible stamp of *Homo sapiens*—the Anthropocene. "The concept of the Anthropocene includes the spontaneous *minima moralia* of the current age. It implies concern regarding the cohabitation of the citizens of Earth in human and nonhuman forms. It prompts us to cooperate in the network of simple and higher-level life cycles" (Sloterdijk 2015: 338–9). Sloterdijk brings the practice of philosophy to bear upon the challenges of understanding and responding to the conditions of the Anthropocene, in which the natural and the artificial have imploded under the weight of the Earth-shaping impacts of humans. He considers how a recuperation of ancient European theory can facilitate the design of viable spaces of cooperative cohabitation across local and global scales.

While integrating Stoic practice into the planetary design project underlying contemporary coexistence, Sloterdijk seeks to avoid what he takes to be reactionary or resentful tones in Stoicism, what he (2012: 46) calls "loser romanticism." Sloterdijk also holds in suspense metaphysical postulates of Stoicism, although not without remaining engaged in some aspects of metaphysical thinking. Sloterdijk's Stoicism could be described as post-metaphysical, but unlike the ethical and non-metaphysical proposals for "new Stoicism" (Becker 2017) and "Stoic pragmatism" (Lachs 2012), it is not constrained within secular rationality. To elaborate on Sloterdijk's reconstruction of Stoicism, this chapter (1) situates Sloterdijk's approach to Stoicism within his rejuvenation of Hellenistic philosophy, (2) elucidates the function of Stoic *askēsis* in his method of theoretical inquiry, and (3) describes his study of spheres as Stoic journey through the history of human cohabitation, arriving at the emergence of planetary forms of *askēsis*.

2. Cosmopolitanism

For Sloterdijk, Diogenes the Cynic is a figure of singular importance (1987: 102). "The appearance of Diogenes marks the most dramatic moment in the process of truth of early European philosophy." It was the "cheekiness" of Diogenes that Sloterdijk finds so significant. That which is "cheeky" (*frech*) is not just irreverent, naughty, or amusingly insolent, but more fundamentally, it is "a productive aggressivity, letting fly at the enemy: 'brave, bold, lively, plucky, untamed, ardent'" (1987: 103). A good example of this effrontery is the story about a lecture in which Plato received applause for defining the human (*anthrōpos*) as a featherless biped, and Diogenes plucked a chicken and brought it to the lecture, declaring, "Here is Plato's *anthrōpos*" (DL 6.40).

Some of the actions attributed to Diogenes are more transgressive than others, but they all involve an existential boldness that flies in the face of accepted norms. He is known for parodying his culture's customs, including relatively extreme actions like defacing money, publicly masturbating, having only a barrel as a home, and ordering Alexander the Great to stop standing in the way of the sunlight. Diogenes demonstrated that Cynicism is a way of life that takes "practical embodiment to an extreme," while holding in abeyance "idealistic abstractions" that render thinking stale and stuck in the head (Sloterdijk 1987: 102). This way of speaking and living the truth is full of irony and laughter, but it is not flippant or haphazard. It is not as if personal integrity is unimportant or unbelievable; in that sense, Cynicism is not cynical. Rather, "kynics [*sic*] support their 'cheekiness' with a life of ascetic integrity," exercising personal restraint by withdrawing from society, refusing praise, and bearing harsh material conditions (1987: 103). It is the integrity of someone committed to embodied practices of social subversion, practices that are productive and not simply negative. Not unlike the drilling and blasting practices of miners, whereby the controlled use of explosives opens passages for excavation, Cynics use their cheeky asceticism in order to produce political transformation, specifically a transformation that opens the local to the cosmic.

The Cynical focus on personal integrity and social subversion is relevant for contemporary life because the political situation has not changed in any fundamental way, notwithstanding the immense differences of scale between Greek city-states and today's planetary civilization.

> For politics—of yesteryear, and more than ever, of today—is just as the kynics of the degenerating Greek city-states experienced it: a threatening coercive relation between human beings, a sphere of dubious careers and questionable ambitions, a mechanism of alienation, the level of war and social injustice—in brief, a hell that imposes on us the existence of Others above us who are capable of violence. (1987: 106)

There is a gesture within Cynicism toward an alternative to the options of either actively contributing to this malfunctioning politics or wallowing in cynicism. The alternative is cosmopolitanism. It is reported that, when Diogenes "was asked where he came from, he replied, 'I am a citizen of the world [*kosmopolitēs*]'" (Laertius 1970: 6.63). It is not clear to what extent the Cynic meant those words as a repudiation of his responsibilities, whether to his homeland (Sinope) or to his current residence (Athens), or as an affirmation of a more universal homeland that includes all of Greece and extends to the whole world. Whatever the specific details might be, it is a politics grounded in philosophy as a way of life, and it is a politics that opens the local to the cosmic.

While Diogenes and the Cynics provide a "good antidote" to the "drug of false certainty," Sloterdijk suggests that such an antidote can be found anywhere one retraces "the lines and paths of ancient thinking" (2013c: 13). Sloterdijk observes that "no one believes anymore that today's learning solves tomorrow's 'problems'; it is almost certain rather that it causes them" (1987: xxix). A better today and tomorrow require a rejuvenation of an ancient yesterday. A common thread in Cynicism and most ancient thinking is the practice of philosophy as a way of life. For Sloterdijk as for the ancients, "the discipline of philosophy must present itself, first as a way of thinking, and then as a way of life" (2013c: xviii). In this regard, Sloterdijk finds himself allied with the French philosopher Pierre Hadot, whose writings are thoroughly oriented around the recovery of philosophy as practical embodiment and not simply theoretical abstraction, which is to say, a way of living and not only a way of thinking (Sloterdijk 2013c: 9; Hadot 1995). The definitive question of philosophy for Hadot and Sloterdijk is thereby reoriented, as Adam Robbert puts it (2017: 3), from "What is philosophy?" to

"Who is the philosopher?" Cynics, Stoics, Platonists, Epicureans, and all ancient schools shared the conviction that the answer to that question has to include exercise.

> Philosophy that would not have operated as a transformative exercise (*askesis*) would have remained suspect to its ancient acolytes also as a source of knowledge. When Diogenes of Sinope succeeded in having Alexander step aside so that he would not block the sun, the goal of the exercise was also achieved. In this sense the wise pantomimes of cynicism are the equal of loquacious Platonism. (Sloterdijk 2013c: 10)

Of all the schools in ancient Greece, it is arguably Stoicism that most resembles Sloterdijk's practice of philosophy.

Much of what Sloterdijk admires about Cynicism is maintained in Stoicism. As Hadot points out, "Cynicism and Stoicism were very close to each other with regard to their conceptions of life" (1998: 57). Like Cynics, Stoics emphasized practical embodiment, focusing on ethics, virtue, and a disinterest or withdrawal from worldly or social dealings. The leading figures in Stoicism frequently include Cynics among their lineage. For example, Epictetus mentions Cynics, particularly Diogenes, as extreme yet exemplary practitioners, who should only be followed with the utmost deliberate effort and caution (*Disc.* 3.22). Marcus Aurelius attributes to a Cynic named Monimos the idea that all human thoughts are a matter of judgments of good and bad that are not rooted in reality, which means that, while humans cannot change reality, they can avoid clinging in vain to their thoughts and judgments about reality (Hadot 1998: 56).

The cosmopolitanism of Diogenes reaches a more articulate expression among Stoics, beginning with the founder Zeno of Citium and attaining further elaboration among subsequent Stoics, including Seneca and Marcus Aurelius (Nussbaum 1997: 7). For Stoicism, the foundation of human belonging is the commonality of reason. "Human reason, which seeks logical and dialectical coherence with itself and posits morality, must be based upon a Reason possessed by the All, of which it is only a portion" (Hadot 2002: 129). Marcus spells out the argument clearly in his *Meditations*: "If reason is common, so too is law; and if this is common, then we are fellow citizens," and "the world [*kosmos*] is as it were a city-state [*polis*]" (MA 4.4). Participation in that cosmopolis is more important than one's specific locality. "It makes no difference whether a person lives here or there, provided that, where he lives, he lives as a citizen of the world" (MA 10.15).

It could be said that Diogenes expressed a "negative cosmopolitanism" in the sense that he was subverting and parodying political norms without positing a replacement, whereas Stoics present cosmopolitanism as a positive political program, which relocates political solidarity from local traditions to the universal capacity to reason shared by all humans (Kent and Tomsky 2017). In Sloterdijk's terms, Stoicism is a movement of "de-domestication," which demanded of its followers that they "break with traditional domesticating systems" and replace those systems with bigger and better ones: "Uprooting from former dwelling places is part of a relocation effort to higher domesticity" (2018: 29).

Like Cynicism, Stoicism seeks to take up the burdens of life through exercises that cultivate wisdom and patience, but Stoics are more constructive, more explicitly oriented toward a goal. This is conveyed in Sloterdijk's summary of Stoicism as "a general system of being-in-the-world-enduring-suffering," including two main aspects: "the theoretical conviction that the world is a place where human beings are exposed to burdens, and the practical resolution to harmonize with this belief by performing daily exercises that involve burdens" (2018: 170).

Like a ship crossing a sea, Stoic exercises are carefully constructed.

> Among Stoics in general, as a metaphor for life, seafaring remains as self-evident as it is indispensable, and philosophy was considered by them to be a preschool for foundering. We thus read in Seneca: ". . . who sails this sea that has no other shore but death." In which case, to philosophize means daring to cross the sea of life, and, indeed, not on the raft of emotions and bad habits, but on the carefully constructed boat of practice and tranquility. (2018: 171)

The Stoic sense of seafaring involves the development of a "shore subjectivity"—the subjectivity of one who has stepped out of the river of ordinary life and onto the shore of practice (Sloterdijk 2013d: 225). The shift from Cynic cheekiness to a more carefully constructed and ordered shore subjectivity can be seen in Stoic uses of dialectical and deductive argumentation and the presentation of a coherent system, in contrast to Cynicism's irony and refusal of abstract systems. Sloterdijk notes that, for the Stoics, "being and being-in-order mean the same thing" (2016a: 437). Along those lines, the Stoics were less hostile to popular norms and social conventions than the Cynics.

Stoics sought acceptance in the Roman Empire, an acceptance undermined by associations with the shamelessness of Cynics. "Stoic philosophers resolved the tension by rewriting Cynicism, ridding it of its amoral and asocial characteristics," purifying it of "its most obscene gestures," and filtering it through Stoic teachings (Shea 2010: 5). A Cynic emperor is a contradiction in terms, whereas a Stoic emperor like Marcus makes sense. In much the same way, a professor like Sloterdijk fits with Stoicism more than Cynicism, as Stoics seek harmony with their conditions and thus affirm participation in institutional roles. There is a fusion of the practice of *wisdom* and the practice of detached tranquility or *patience*: "*sapientia* and *patientia*" (Sloterdijk 2018: 170). Philosophers should transform norms, but they should do it with a sense of peaceable reserve. Sloterdijk notes that Stoics are in agreement with Platonists and Epicureans in "defining the philosopher as the expert for investigating the peace of the soul" (Sloterdijk 2013c: 4). Sloterdijk is in agreement as well, and his own "striking serenity" and "detached attitude" are consistent characteristics of his writing and his public presence (Pfaller 2011: 67).

Along with his detached attitude and his integration into his social surroundings, Sloterdijk also echoes some ontological and ethical aspects of Stoicism: "I start from a strong ontological thesis: intelligence exists. This leads to a strong ethical thesis: there is a positive correlation between intelligence and the will to self-preservation" (2016b: 230). Sloterdijk does not elaborate the details about this intelligence, like whether it is implicit in the universe like the cosmic *logos* of the Stoics; but in any case, there is intelligence, and it is correlated to practice, namely the practice of self-preservation. That is not a selfish practice in an individualistic or egotistic sense. Rather, the self exists in relation to its surrounding conditions. Like the Stoic self, it is harmonized with a cosmopolitan community that shares this intelligence, which for Sloterdijk suggests the imperative "to build a global immune system that opens up a common survival perspective," that is, "co-immunism" (2016b: 230).

Intelligence is not pure or perfect. It is always entangled in biases, habits, and passions, and even with the best of intentions it can still yield unintended consequences. The recognition of the many ways that "intelligence can go in the wrong direction and confuse self-destruction with self-preservation" is, for Sloterdijk, "the most promising idea of older Critical Theory" (2016b: 230). However, one cannot rest with critique, since that simply breeds mistrust. Modern cynicism is the result of a society of universal mistrust, a society that critiques everything, unmasking every theory and practice to show the unconscious dynamics, political power, and economic relations at work underneath. An affirmative or positive theory is needed, which does not negate critical theory but includes its core insight within a viable, peaceable way of life. "A philosophy in the spirit of Yes also includes the Yes to the No" (Sloterdijk 1987: xxxvii).

Saying "Yes" to the critical "No," Sloterdijk includes critique within a rejuvenated practice of philosophy as a way of life. His recovery of Stoicism does not return to precritical metaphysics. Sloterdijk is a post-metaphysical thinker. He develops a "post-metaphysical spherological analysis," whereby he describes the circumstances of human existence while avoiding any metaphysical thinking that purports to escape those circumstances or observe them from the outside (2013d: 234). This is not precritical metaphysics, but it is not critical theory's total prohibition of metaphysics either. Sloterdijk (2014: 450) considers the possibility that the "post-metaphysical age" that began with modernity might be more accurately described as a "differently metaphysical" age that has yet to be understood.

Sloterdijk (2013b: 34–5) follows Nietzsche's diagnosis of the resentment operating in premodern metaphysics, which he sees as "the first impulse toward maligning reality in the name of an over-world or an anti-world, which has been specifically approved for the sake of humiliating its contrary. [. . .] In metaphysical-religious discourse contemptuousness becomes an insidiously twisted self-praising force." This suggests that the problem with metaphysics is not its exaggerations and speculations but its contempt for the world. Sloterdijk's post-metaphysical thinking emancipates the hyperbolic expressions of metaphysics from the escapism and hostility whereby metaphysics becomes a means of mistrust, revenge, and reaction against the circumstances of life. Keeping hyperbole while overcoming resentment, Sloterdijk's post-metaphysical thinking is actually a form of "solidarity with metaphysics," and it thereby stands in stark contrast to the anti-metaphysical thinking of critical theory, which gets rid of hyperbole and keeps cynical reason, making a "post-hyperbolic" gesture that amounts to "boasting about the merit of having no merits of which one could boast" (2017: 172).

Post-metaphysical Stoicism need not be drained of metaphysical imagination or universal aspirations. It does not need to divorce the ethical and pragmatic side of Stoicism from its metaphysical side. A post-metaphysical Stoic can still produce speculations and systems that take on cosmic and spiritual proportions. The post-metaphysical difference is that Stoicism is drained of its resentment, what Sloterdijk calls its "loser romanticism" (2012: 42). According to Sloterdijk, the emergence of Plato's Academy, Stoicism, and other Hellenistic philosophical schools happened partly in response to the collapse of the classical model of the *polis*. Philosophy began as type of "loser romanticism" by "reinterpreting a defeat as a victory on another field," such that collective defeat was painted as a victory for individual pursuits of wisdom. The tendency of the "romantic loser" led to "a proud defeatism that presented itself as the art of winning by losing" (2012: 43). That defeatism fosters hostility toward the whole of social existence, a sense of "revenge against the disappointment of reality," even going so far as to reject human dependence on life and the material world (2012: 58).

Embroiled in the contradiction between its pure self and the external world, the romantic loser tends to seek harmony while avoiding anything that would compromise or contaminate its purity. This yields a "free-floating intellectual" who is "involved nowhere" yet embraces the cosmopolitan ideal of being at home everywhere (Sloterdijk 2012: 46). Sloterdijk observes that this tendency produced the "preconditions for Stoicism's widespread success. Concern for community has become concern for oneself" (2012: 46). It was "the popularized Stoicism that excelled" above all other schools in "the counseling of enlightened losers," particularly by enjoining them to realize the difference "between that which depends on us and that which does not" (Sloterdijk 2016a: 395). Moreover, this defeatism does not preclude philosophers from taking exalted positions as lawgivers, rulers, or experts. The soul can maintain its purity by looking at society from outside or from on high. Indeed, a visualization commonly practiced in Stoicism and other Hellenistic schools involves a view from above, where the practitioner imagines looking on all people and earthly things from some exalted place, thereby relocating seemingly immense struggles of human existence within the far more comprehensive context of the Stoic's cosmic consciousness (Hadot 1995: 245).

While critical theory would like to situate itself after the metaphysics of antiquity, it emerged with much of the same world-weariness, bringing with it a "second romantic loser atmosphere," that is, an atmosphere not of the pure soul but of the cynical subject (Sloterdijk 2016a: 48). It is the atmosphere of "complaint-addicted moderns" (Sloterdijk 2014: 29). The aim of Sloterdijk's philosophy is to free intelligence from its alliance with resentment, and thereby "create a space for future paradigms of detoxified worldly wisdom" (2010: 228). To function as an antidote to resentment, a rejuvenated Stoicism will produce metaphysical exaggerations and speculations, but they must emerge with exercises and must affirm the dynamics of practical embodiment and social involvement instead of reacting against them. To the extent that Sloterdijk's post-metaphysical spherology undertakes this rejuvenation, it has to be understood in light of his recovery of Stoic exercise.

3. *Askēsis*

"Anyone on earth who understands their situation will face the fact that no one leaves this place alive. People on this gloomy orb must practice" (Sloterdijk 2014: 770). Humankind inhabits the "planet of the practising" (2013d: 17). It is impossible not to practice, but it is quite possible to practice in ways that are ineffective or destructive. Practice includes any actions that transform the capacity of the actor to engage in the next performance of that action. Every human being is engaged in some kind of design of the self or practice of self-transformation, which is to say, some kind of *askēsis* ("training" or "exercise"). Sloterdijk proposes a generalized study of training—"general ascetology"—for which *askēsis* is indicative of the "autoplastic constitution" of human beings, the "operationally curved space" whereby practices of thinking, feeling, and acting reflect back on the practitioner, changing the practitioner and the practices in "self-referential relationships" of subjective design (2013d: 110). The openness of human existence, which Heidegger named *Dasein*, is its own ongoing design project. "*Dasein ist Design*."[3]

General ascetology is the study of the varieties of existential design, in other words, it is "a doctrine of life practice," "a comprehensive theory of practicing existence" (2013d: 6). This theory attends to the training regimens in wisdom traditions like Buddhism, Stoicism, and Christianity, as well as the exercise routines of athletes, the practices that train artists and musicians, the exercises of politicians, and more. In sum, Sloterdijk translates "religious, spiritual and ethical facts into the language and perspective of the general theory of practising" (2013d: 6). The use of practical language might sound like it brings the religious and spiritual tones of *askēsis* into a secular frame. That is not exactly the case. Sloterdijk could be described as post-secular. However, like the label "post-metaphysical," Sloterdijk's post-secularism is more of a continuation or explication of what it overcomes, not a negation.

Continuing the secularism of Enlightenment rationality, Sloterdijk is attempting to bring religious practice into more explicit articulation, available for public scrutiny and reconstruction, but two things set him apart from secular perspectives on religion. First, Sloterdijk avoids the cynicism and resentment infusing many secular critiques of religion, and second, he rejects the very category of "religion," upon which the secular-religious opposition depends. In short, "no 'religion' or 'religions' exist"; "The false dichotomy of believers and unbelievers becomes obsolete and is replaced by the distinction between the practising and the untrained, or those who train differently" (2013d: 3). The distinction between *vita activa* and *vita contemplativa* occludes their shared dynamics of training, which cuts across active and contemplative lives (Sloterdijk 2012: 6).

Contemplative prayer and meditation are not different in kind from athleticism, farming, surfing, dramatic acting, chemistry, or motorcycle maintenance. They are all practices that involve exercise regimes, very different exercises of course, but with no great religious/secular divide. Each training regime offers different possibilities for individuals and groups to design themselves, to transform themselves in light of "vertical tensions," which mark different capacities for acting and being acted upon (Sloterdijk 2013d: 13). Verticality implies that practices are always "achieved more or less well and done better or worse" (Sloterdijk 2012: 8). The category of verticality allows Sloterdijk to situate within the field of practice any metaphysical claims about whatever divine, angelic, or demonic entities might be involved in one's training regimen. General ascetology studies training as an endeavor of *human* design, marking "an anthropotechnic turn" in the study of religion, spirituality, and ethics (Sloterdijk 2013d: 1).

The term "anthropotechnics" (*Anthropotechnik*) can be misleading. It might sound "anthropocentric," as if anthropotechnics implies a hierarchy that gives more value to humans than to animal, vegetal, and elemental modes of existence. That is not the case. The point of anthropotechnics is that the human is plastic, adaptable to design and redesign. Furthermore, the emphasis on cultivating and redesigning the self might sound individualistic. However, as the notion of vertical tensions implies, the call to practice and engage in self-improvement comes from something that is higher than you. The title of Sloterdijk's book on anthropotechnics is *You Must Change Your Life*, meaning the call to change comes from outside the self. The content of that specific call comes from a poem by Rilke, "Archaic Torso of Apollo" (2013d: 21). The subject of the poem is observing a sculpture of a torso and feeling seen by the torso ("there is no place/ that does not see you"). It concludes with these words, "You must change your life" (Rilke 2010: 230). Being seen is not about a symmetrical reciprocity of seer and seen—me observing and being observed by the torso. As Sloterdijk (2013d: 23) observes, it is a reversal of the seer-seen dynamic, such that the torso "eyes me more sharply than I can look at it." It grasps me when it sees me, compelling me to change my life. Meanwhile, I am rendered incapable of seeing the torso, blinded by its provocative gaze, by the glow and glisten of the torso.

With the outside folding in, anthropotechnics happens in a curved space, internalizing the external call to change your life. "The outside is the most proximate, the innermost and the native, and everything inside is merely a molding or folding of the outside" (Sloterdijk 2014: 633). Nonetheless, it is ultimately the responsibility of the practitioner to heed the call from the outside. Sloterdijk mentions that Seneca "knew best of all that even in the demanding relationship between master and student, everything ultimately depends on the latter's willingness to mould themselves" (Sloterdijk 2013d: 372). A Stoic willingness to change one's life is a willingness to profoundly break from the lifestyles of others. On this account, Stoicism is not a shortcut or problem-solving technique for living a better life, contrary to some popular accounts of Stoicism as a mental tip or trick, a so-called mind-hack (Wallace 2014). Stoicism is not a set of strategies for hacking or cutting through life's problems in an efficient or productive manner. It is not a set of procedures that can be applied piecemeal or as pertinent situations arise. It demands that you change your whole way of life.

From an anthropotechnic perspective, philosophy is not a set of doctrines to be learned or professed. Rather, as Hadot says of Epictetus, to be a philosopher is "to profess, as a result of a conversion which caused a radical change of lifestyle, a way of life different from that of other people" (1998: 5). It is a way of life in what Sloterdijk calls "secession" (2013d: 217–30). Secession from others facilitates a lifestyle of self-control or self-mastery, which Sloterdijk describes as a sovereignty that requires a profound interruption of one's integration into conventional lifestyles:

> We live constantly in collective fields of excitation; this cannot be changed so long as we are social beings. The input of stress inevitably enters me; thoughts are not free [. . .]. They come from the newspaper and wind up returning to the newspaper. My sovereignty, if it exists, can only appear by my letting the integrated impulsion die in me or, should this fail, by my retransmitting it in a totally metamorphosed, verified, filtered, or recoded form. It serves nothing to contest it: I am free only to the extent that I interrupt escalations and that I am able to immunize myself against infections of opinion. Precisely this continues to be the philosopher's mission in society. (2011b: 84)

It was a common conviction among schools of Hellenistic thought that humans have the power to free the self from whatever it is that confines or conditions it. Nonetheless, Stoics get specific credit. The "rebuilding of the subjective space" as a space of a free identity is something that "began with the Stoics's invention of the self-sufficient individual" (Sloterdijk 2011a: 200).

For Sloterdijk (2013d: 225), "the Stoic principle of *cura sui* [concern for oneself]" facilitated the development of a "shore subjectivity"—the subjectivity of one who has stepped out of the river of ordinary life and onto the shore of practice. Like a poet being grasped by a compelling injunction issuing from a statue, "You must change your life," Stoics heard a call to change their lives, to cultivate the inner statue of the soul. The statuary soul reflects the statues of ancient Greece, where that which is best and most divine (gods) resembles, or is even identified with, that which is most attentive, vital, and capable (athletes)

(Sloterdijk 2013d: 27). In other words, the "training consciousness" of Stoicism emerged with "statuary philosophers," who equate a concern for self-sufficiency with "sculptural work on the inner statue" (287).

One of the practices Stoics take up in their existential sculpting, a practice for which the contemporary popular use of the adjective "stoic" still applies, is the cultivation of a disinterested attitude or a sense of detachment: *apatheia*, which is perhaps better translated as "equanimity" than "apathy." Not totally without concern or engagement, Stoic exercise involves the cultivation of attention (*prosokhē*). Accordingly, *apatheia* is not inattentive, but it does mean being indifferent toward circumstances that are independent of oneself or out of one's own control, circumstances that Stoics consider "indifferent" things, "such as health, fame, wealth, and even death" (Hadot 1995: 245). Stoic exercise pays the utmost attention to the world while also remaining calm, peaceable, indifferent to indifferent things. Philo of Alexandria captures this Stoic sensibility: "All who practice wisdom" have as their goal "a life of peace" and are "the closest observers of nature and all that it contains"; they are "'cosmopolitans' who have recognized the world to be a city," and they train themselves "to hold things indifferent as indeed indifferent" (*Special Laws* 2.44–46).

The bold aspirations of a virtuous life of peace, attentive participation in all of nature, and cosmopolitan unity are cultivated with disinterested reserve. "Philosophy becomes exact boasting, as well as the feat of speaking of overwhelming things with a dry soul" (Sloterdijk 2014: 31). To practice *apatheia* is like drying one's own soul, a desiccation almost unto death, the ultimate indifferent thing. The "self-generation of the disinterested person" is not unlike transforming oneself into a dead person, or more accurately, since the dead is still technically alive, it is more like entering into a state of "suspended animation" (*Scheintod*) (Sloterdijk 2012: 2).[4] The capacity for entering into states of suspended animation is foundational for the practice of philosophy. Method in this context "is not merely the scientific path to things but also the approach to a state of near-death, a cognition-enhancing condition," like "the art of dying that the Stoics of antiquity [. . .] regarded as a supreme ethical discipline" (2012: 3).

The practice of suspended animation is related to the phenomenological method of suspense (*epochē*), which enacts a "bracketing" whereby consciousness withdraws from the assumptions and positions of one's everyday situation (18). *Epokhē*, as Sloterdijk observes, originated among the Skeptics of ancient Greece, for whom it described an abstention from judgment or a free floating between possible positions (20). Nonetheless, the practice whereby thinkers "cast off their bodies and apparently become pure intellects or impersonal thinking souls" is a common thread running from antiquity through the mystical theologies of the Middle Ages (3). Furthermore, *epokhē* is not simply a cognitive endeavor. It has spatial and political manifestations. The spaces where philosophers and contemplatives would gather are themselves a kind of *epokhē*, putting into brackets the world of conventions and opinions, opening up an "Elsewhere" within the here and now, like churches, monasteries, Plato's Academy, and the painted porch (*stoa poikilē*) where Zeno of Citium began Stoicism (2012: 30, 33). *Epokhē* can also be seen at work in politics. Hellenistic cosmopolitanisms manifest a kind of "global *epochē*" that resulted from the (supposed) decay of political life at the time (45).

For Sloterdijk, the practice of calmness and stillness required for suspended animation "reached its ultimate peak in the Stoic ideal of *apatheia*" (54). Reaching cosmic proportions, a calm reception of philosophical lessons transforms into a calm acceptance of fate. Hadot describes the Stoic love of fate as a "cosmic consciousness," in which "I want that which universal Reason wants, and identify myself with it in my feeling of participation and of belonging to a Whole which transcends the limits of individuality" (1998: 145–6). The art of dying becomes the art of loving fate, which overcomes the loser romanticism of one who rejects the quotidian world. Hence the description Marcus gives of a virtuous person: one who "loves and welcomes whatever happens" and whatever "fate may bring," one who is "pure, calm, ready for release," and feeling "no resentment against anyone" (MA 3.16).

The ideal of a disinterested observer, even one free of resentment, has come under attack in modernity. "The pure observer is dead," and Sloterdijk enumerates ten guilty parties that have contributed to its assassination, which is paradoxically a matter of "killing an apparently dead person" (Sloterdijk 2012: 4). Through a "critique of neutral reason," shore subjectivity has been thrown back into the river of life (2012: 87). The ten parties contributing to this lethal critique were involved in activities like (1) changing the world (Marx), (2) affirming irreducibly many perspectives (Nietzsche), (3) defending a political party (Lukács), (4) being in a phenomenological situation (Heidegger), (5) facilitating mass destruction like the bombings of Hiroshima and Nagasaki (technoscience), (6) having resolute commitments (existentialism), (7) producing knowledge within a paradigm (Thomas Kuhn) or discourse (Michel Foucault), (8) situating theory in histories of heteronormative patriarchal domination and gender performance (Judith Butler), (9) specifying the neurological determinants of cognitive activity (António Damásio), and (10) taking away any extra-political authority from philosophers and experts and treating them and all other entities as actors in social assemblies (Bruno Latour) (2012: 87–93).

Those various assassination attempts saturate the space in which the cultivation of an inner statue happens in the contemporary world, rendering highly improbable the suspended animation required for disinterested theory. The statuary space is also saturated by mass media. Humans today inhabit "saturated infospheres" that are pervaded by advertising, which "no longer passes on what people should know in order to access advantageous innovations; it creates illusions of purchasable self-elevations that *de facto* usually lead to weakenings," that is, "downward training" (2013d: 368). Further saturating the space of practice is the global ecological crisis. Endangering the basic conditions for life on Earth, the global ecological crisis compels humans to train as if life depends on it. "Today, the phrase 'You must change your life' is no longer interpreted only in terms of Buddhism, Christianity, or Stoicism, or in Nietzsche's sense, but as a mission to develop a form of life that makes human coexistence on this endangered planet possible" (2016b: 236). Sloterdijk calls for "universal co-operative asceticisms," and he recognizes the tremendous urgency of this task; "monastic rules must be drawn up now or never," so that people can practice "the good habits of shared survival in daily exercises" (2013d: 452).

4. Spheres

The operational curvature whereby humans transform themselves is made possible by the spherical shape of human existence. Sloterdijk explicates his theory of spheres in his trilogy bearing that title, with three large volumes, *Bubbles* (2011a), *Globes* (2014), and *Foams* (2016a), originally published in 1998, 1999, and 2004, respectively. Together they account for the history of intimate dwellings that make up subjectivity (microspheric) and social systems (macrospheric), from the relatively singular spaces of premodern and modern societies ("globes") to the radical plurality of contemporary societies ("foams").

Spheres are not physical or metaphysical containers, but "multi-significant universes of existential spaciousness" (2011a: 34). They figure what Heidegger describes as the "being-in" that comprises "being-in-the-world," which is reinterpreted as "being-in-spheres" (2011a 46). Spheres form the ecstatic openness of human existence—the "there" (*da*) of *Dasein* (2011a: 541). For Heidegger (1962: 140), *Dasein* exhibits "*an essential tendency toward closeness.*" Bringing-close entails "*making room*," that is, making an existential space of concern (Heidegger 1962: 146). A sphere is a "ball of care [*Sorge*] in which existence has spread out in an original being-outside-itself" (Sloterdijk 2011a: 335). Carefully attuned to the being-outside-itself of existence, humans are open to the distance of the world, bringing the outside in.

Spherology gives comprehensive attention to all the ways that humans make room. While it bears traces of many philosophical schools, it is uniquely Stoic, particularly insofar as it focuses on practices of self-cultivation and cosmopolitanism. Furthermore, Sloterdijk exemplifies Stoic *apatheia* in his survey of the variety of the spherical designs of *Dasein*, unlike Heidegger, who clearly has preferences for some epochs over others within the history of being, with particular antagonism to modern technology. Sloterdijk (2016a: 15) himself describes his *Spheres* project as Stoic. He mentions that the first volume of *Spheres* is a "stoic journey into the first ecological niche of humans."[5] It is a journey into the first formations of the inner statue, in other words, the first formations of a cosmic citizen, beginning with the intimate space of a fetus in the womb. This cosmopolitan journey is continued in the second and third volumes, which explores not the subjectivity of the citizens but the shape of the worlds they inhabit, from classical and modern images of the globe to the foaming plurality of the Anthropocene.

The first ecological niches of humans are microspheres—the titular "bubbles" (*Blasen*) of the first volume of *Spheres*. Bubbles are the small-scale intimate spaces that constitute subjectivity, which Sloterdijk examines across numerous registers, including the intrauterine space of mother-child relations and child-placenta relations, the space of face-to-face relations, the resonant space of the welcoming voice (from the maternal voice to messianic voices), the loving space of heart-to-heart relations, the "magical" space of bonding (e.g., hypnosis, Mesmerism, and psychoanalytic transference), and the space of the care of one's own genius, angel, or true self (2011a: 540). An overarching point of these analyses is that, while it is possible to practice solitude, self-sufficiency, indifference, and sensory deprivation, it is impossible for a human to be truly alone. There is always some relation, some context, channel, or significant connection through which one finds oneself. Spherology could be described as a generalized media theory (2011a: 31). Being-in-spheres means being-in-media, never being alone.

If a sign was hanging at the entryway to Sloterdijk's *Spheres* trilogy, like the sign hanging at the entrance to Plato's Academy ("Let no one enter who is not a geometrician"), the sign would say something about prohibiting entrance to anyone who is unwilling "to refute loneliness" (Sloterdijk 2011a: 9, 13). For Sloterdijk, "ultimately the individual does not exist":

> My project is based on a philosophical hostility to the ideology of the solitary individual. [...] I reject the fallacious idea of ontological solitude that the society of the modern age is based on. In reality, Being always means being accompanied, but not necessarily by a visible companion. An invisible couple is always hiding in the apparent solitude of the individual. Being single therefore means forming a couple with a hidden Other—even if it is only my unknown "I." (2016b: 306)

By situating the self in the curved space of practice, a Stoic concern for the self can function as an antidote to individualism, opening up modern selfhood to an unknown "I" and to the world. To put it colloquially, a Stoic sage is not a solitary individual, but a well-rounded person, an individual that makes itself at home in the world through a development process of "appropriation" (*oikeiōsis*). *Oikeiōsis* can be paraphrased as a process of "recognizing what belongs to you" (Lampe 2013: 187). This resonates with Hierocles's image of each individual as the center of concentric rings, starting with one's individual body and then moving through immediate and distant relatives and then to neighbors and citizens, with the process of appropriation drawing outer rings back toward the center (LS 57G).

The well-rounded Stoic exemplifies a well-sculpted inner statue, what Hadot calls "the inner citadel" (Hadot 1998: 120, discussing MA 4.3). A sphere functions like an immune system. Similar to the process of *oikeiōsis*, spheres protect the self not in a way that closes off from the world, but in a way that facilitates robust relationships with others. Spheres are "immune-systemically effective space creations" (Sloterdijk 2011a: 28). Spherology is General Immunology, which avoids the resentment whereby premodern metaphysics theorized about the world as a way to escape the world, and likewise avoids the cynicism whereby modern critique gave up on articulating any grand narratives or integrative systems. "General Immunology is the legitimate successor of metaphysics" (2013d: 451).

As an immune system, the inner citadel is protected, but not solitary. The self makes contact with concentric circles of others while remaining intact, going toward things without being penetrated by them. Sloterdijk calls the Stoic selfhood of the citadel "enclave subjectivity" (2013d: 228), citing Marcus's injunction to maintain "the retreat into this little territory within yourself" (MA 4.3.4). Part of that retreat requires control of one's use of speech. "The Stoic philosophical life," as Hadot (1998: 50) observes, "consists essentially in mastering one's inner discourse." Enclave subjectivity thus requires that one's own speech be restrained with the utmost reserve, such that one adopts what Sloterdijk (2013d: 234) calls "endo-rhetoric," which includes speech that reinforces one's detachment from conventional ways of being, facilitates improvement of one's habits and character, and envisions one's participation in the whole.

The enclave subjectivity of a Stoic sage who is practiced in endo-rhetoric is different by a matter of degree, not a matter of kind, from the subjectivity of a fetus listening to the welcoming voice of the mother, the subjectivity of an artist following an inner genius, or the subjectivity of a lover falling in love with a beloved. All of those subjects are in immunological bubbles. A bubble can include more than two people, like a family, a therapy group, or a circle of friends sharing stories around a campfire. The worlds within which bubbles are embedded are macrospheric systems, "globes" (*Globen*), wherein "being-in on a small scale returns as a political and cosmic relationship" (Sloterdijk 2011a: 671). Care of the subject returns as care of the world.

Humans first began thinking of themselves as inhabiting some kind of globe with the emergence of metaphysical and religious representations of the world as a single, encompassing whole, in which the self participates. What had been viewed as a plurality of "surroundings" became viewed as "the orb," which "inspires the leap of the soul into the whole" (2014: 49). The orb is the cosmos of Cynic and Stoic cosmopolitanism. It marks the beginning of globalization according to Sloterdijk. Globalization did not begin with the development of electronic communication technologies in the twentieth century, or with modern colonialism 500 years before that. As sphere construction "on the grandest scale," globalization began with a cosmic phase that "preceded its terrestrial variety by over two thousand years" (2014: 46). Sloterdijk thus demarcates three phases of his grand narrative of globalization: "cosmic-uranian globalization," which begins with ancient myth and speculative thought, "terrestrial globalization," which spans approximately five centuries from the beginning of modern colonialism to the end of the Second World War, and "electronic globalization," marked by the development of new technologies and media beginning in the latter half of the twentieth century (2013a: 9).

Insofar as spherology can diagnose "sphere pathology," this history of globalization indicates that the domination and alienation issuing from modern forms of globalization have an ancient metaphysical source (Sloterdijk 2011a: 73). The idea of "the One Orb" already exposed "the limit and danger of metaphysical imagining," a danger that "begins with the ancient instructions for viewing the orb blissfully from without," in a "lordly observation of the outside that would one day lead to polytechnical dreams of control and the tyranny of knowledge over concretely interpreted life as a whole," in short, the "betrayal of humanity's existential place" (2011a: 79). Ancient and modern forms of globalization share that betrayal. The difference is the shift of focus from the heavens (ancient) to Earth (modern) as the site of the global integration project. With modern scientific discoveries in astronomy, it became increasingly untenable to believe that Earth is "enclosed by spherical forms like warming heavenly mantles," so people began believing that humans exist "only on a ball, but no longer inside a ball" (2011a: 24).

The monotheism of the ancient orb was replaced by a geological unity, "monogeism," which expresses a fidelity to the singular Earth (2013a: 161). The cosmopolitan ideal of a peaceful world persisted, but in an immanent form. As a form of cosmopolitanism, it became a support for emancipation from the river of local conventions and the extension of the concentric circles of *oikeiōsis*. However, as it hardened into abstractions and certainties, it became more of a regulative ideal and lost its grounding in *askēsis*, and universal reason became critical of metaphysical exaggerations and lost its intimate connection to the cosmos. Just as the attempt to find peace in a metaphysical orb had its problems and successes, so too did the attempt to find the good life through terrestrial means, whether cosmopolitan or colonial. A very small few benefited at the expense of the vast majority. Terrestrial globalization made cosmopolitanism look like "the provincialism of the pampered," producing "a comfort-animated artificial continent in the ocean of poverty," a continent Sloterdijk designates as the "world interior" (*Weltinnenraum*) of capital (2013a: 196).

The electronic phase of globalization continues the monogeistic turn while abjuring the imperial, colonial projects of history. It includes new technological developments (e.g., social media, information and communication technologies, and virtual reality), which operate with such speed that feedback happens relatively immediately across global systems. The result of this phase of globalization is that humans are connected yet plural, congealed in a "hyperactive vibrating jelly," not integrated into a cosmic orb or terrestrial globe (2013a: 11). Without the integrative process of appropriation, the macrosphere becomes a massively distributed plurality—"foams" (*Schäume*). "In foam worlds, the individual bubbles are not absorbed into a single, integrative hyper-orb [. . .]. What is currently being confusedly proclaimed in all the media as *the* globalization of the world is, in morphological terms, the universalized war of foams" (2011a: 71).

The foaming of multiple worlds is not only a foaming of human worlds through individualism and multiculturalism. Nonhuman worlds have also entered the fray, as scientific inquiries (notably, Jakob von Uexküll's ethology) have disclosed the world-forming capacities of all sentient beings, thereby suggesting "a pluralistic ontology that estimates as many worlds as there are eye types and other sensors to see and feel them" (Sloterdijk 2016a: 230). Furthermore, not only are nonhuman worlds intruding into human worlds, the relationship between humans and their environment has become inverted. In the Anthropocene, all of Earth's basic systems (land, biodiversity, water, and climate) are impacted by humans, specifically by humans inhabiting the pampered island of global capital. The environment as the background against which human design takes place has inverted, becoming a product of human design.

> This situation can be described with the term "environmental inversion." While the natural situation is such that the environment surrounds and humans are surrounded, the construction of the absolute island creates a situation in which humans themselves design and set up the surroundings in which they will later reside. [. . .] Environmental inversion sets about technical implementation following the hermeneutical maxim "seize that which seizes us." (2016a: 308)

While Earth functioned as a stage for worlds and globes throughout history, environmental inversion means that the stage has become an actor, and that upon which all human life depends now depends on humans. The foam worlds of the Anthropocene must now converge on the task of maintaining their survival on a shared Earth, finding commonality not in the uninhabitable globes of metaphysics or colonialism, but in the shared fate of humankind with one Earth. The "common point of reference" for humanity "would no longer be an Olympus populated by gods removed from the world. It would be an Earth that the mortals themselves share, in all its diverse regions, an Earth too real to perform the role of conventional transcendence, yet also too transcendent to ever become the possession of a single imperial power" (Sloterdijk 2015: 338).

For Sloterdijk, "monogeism" describes "the appropriate cognitive relationship of human beings" to Earth not as a background but as a vibrant, dynamic agent, called by various names (e.g., "Spaceship Earth," "Gaia or Terra or Sphaira"); at the minimum, it entails "non-ignorant relationship to Earth's pre-eminence" (2015: 336). Sloterdijk envisions the monogeism of the Anthropocene in Stoic terms of self-preservation. The construction of the inner citadel coincides with the construction of a planetary citadel. "We must decide to build a global immune system that opens up a common survival perspective. We have to work now on a protective shield for the earth, for humankind and for its technological environment. That will require global ecological management. I call this co-immunism" (Sloterdijk 2016b: 230).

Bruno Latour (2017: 123) observes that, with this kind of global ecological thinking, Sloterdijk's spherology is inaugurating "the first *anthropocenic* discipline!" Latour admires how "Sloterdijk rematerializes in a new way what it means to be *in* space, *on* this Earth, offering us the first philosophy that responds directly to the requirement of the Anthropocene that we bring ourselves back down to Earth" (2017: 124). The immune systems of globalization were tainted with resentment for Earth, from the ancient aversion to the disorder of embodied existence to the domination and exploitation of human and natural resources through colonialism and capitalism. Like all immune systems, co-immunism protects "the own" from something other, except the other is not a foreign people, nor is it the nonhuman environment. The foreign element against which co-immunism immunizes humankind is the "dominant exploitative excess" that is endangering humankind and the habitats and inhabitants of Earth (Sloterdijk 2013d: 451).

This attention to Earth assigns "existential significance to climatology," explicating the fragile dynamics of the climate constituting the habitable sphere without which the good life is strictly impossible (2016a: 673). Spherological ethics is "atmosphere ethics," which "formulates the good as the breathable" and "describes the most fragile as the starting point of responsibility" (2016a: 242). Transitioning from the world interior of capital to the atmospheric ethics of co-immunism requires a just and generous distribution of the burdens and abundance of life on Earth, and as Sloterdijk observes, justice and generosity ultimately demand that all humans be afforded sufficient uplift and pampering for them to practice their own freedom. In co-immunism, the practice of freedom is a practice of facilitating the freedom of others. "Freedom, therefore, means the ability to affirm the egotism of others" (2016a: 753). Co-immunism is an affirmation of a shared atmosphere of political life, a cooperative asceticism of mutually enhancing self-sufficiency.

From bubbles to co-immunism, spherology is Stoicism for the Anthropocene. The conditions for practice have changed. The Stoic can no longer imagine the world in a view from above. The retreat space of enclave subjectivity has to emerge within the dynamics of planetary coexistence. Scientific discoveries, critiques of reason, and ecological crises demonstrate that there is "no outside view" in "the hothouse" of a planetary civilization; rather, one "must move within immanence" to explore it (2016a: 767). The disinterested observer must hold in suspense an impossible amount of cognitive biases, social systems, and biophysical constraints. Furthermore, the environmental inversion of the Anthropocene has radically transformed life on Earth from something that does not depend on humans to something that does, thereby synthesizing self-preservation and ecological preservation. The orderly nature that provides a basis for inner freedom and cosmopolitan collectivity becomes a nature that humans design.

As an epoch "in which human-made emissions have begun to influence the course of 'planetary history,'" the Anthropocene demands emission control (2015: 330). Stoic *apatheia* can be seen as the first systematic exercise for emission control, cultivating reserve and restraint in thinking, feeling, and acting. The climate crisis does not simply demand a reduction in carbon emissions, but a reduction in the emission of resentment throughout the history of globalization. "We can't live in one-sided negativity all the time. In this respect we could use a bit of emission control for the intellectual climate" (Sloterdijk 2016b: 120). This emission control must be cheeky or it will fall into cynicism. Stoicism in the Anthropocene must boldly affirm the fate of being in spheres, overcoming the resentment that accompanies metaphysical and critical rationalizations, which includes the resentment whereby Stoics sought a second world, a spiritual world separate from the mundane opinions and conventions of the normal world. Salvation in divine Reason must now be replaced by survival, comfort, and pampering here on Earth—in short, relief. "From a spiritual viewpoint we are entering a period where what matters is no longer salvation, but relief. [...] We have been going through a gigantic spiritual transformation that has led from a spirituality infused with denial of life and the world to a form of spirituality based on affirmation" (2016b: 310).

Affirming the conditions of the Anthropocene, Sloterdijk's Stoicism recovers cheekiness after critical theory, rejuvenates the practice of suspended animation after the assassination of the indifferent theoretician, retrieves vertical tensions of practice after secularism, rethinks the spatial and immunological shape of existence after metaphysics, relocates anthropotechnics at a planetary scale in the Anthropocene, and redefines cosmopolitanism as cooperative *askēsis* in foam worlds without a globe. The inner statues of the ancients become the breathable bubbles of the Anthropocene, and cosmopolitanism becomes the design of atmospheres for shared survival. "Foam," wonders Sloterdijk (2016a: 674), "would that now mean the air from gasps of relief in unexpected places?"

Notes

1 The public controversy about Sloterdijk's "*Menschenpark*" essay involved an antagonistic and accusatory exchange of newspaper articles between Habermas and Sloterdijk (Peacock 2000).

2 Sloterdijk (1987: xxix) uses a spelling difference to distinguish between the ancient school of thought, *Kynismus,* and the modern attitude, *Cynismus.* In the present inquiry, unless directly quoting Sloterdijk, the distinction is made by capitalizing the school of thought (Cynicism) and maintaining a lowercase spelling for the modern attitude (cynicism).
3 This pun, coined by Henk Oosterling, is reiterated by Bruno Latour with much appreciation for the way Sloterdijk's conception of humans as designers of spheres avoids any human/nature bifurcation (Latour 2011: 157).
4 *Scheintod* ("suspended animation") is a prominent theme throughout Sloterdijk's (2012) book *The Art of Philosophy: Wisdom as Practice,* the German title of which is *Scheintod im Denken,* which could be literally translated as "Suspended Animation in Thought."
5 The word "stoic" is lowercase here and elsewhere throughout this text, but it is clear in other uses that Sloterdijk is referring to the Hellenistic school and not simply using the adjective to refer to a relatively detached attitude. For instance, Sloterdijk (2016a: 229) describes a process "leading from stoic beginnings to Epicurean culminations."

Works Cited

Becker, L. (2017), *A New Stoicism,* Rev. ed., Princeton: Princeton University Press.
Epictetus (1928), *Discourses,* trans. W. A. Oldfather, Cambridge: Harvard University Press.
Hadot, P. (1995), *Philosophy as a Way of Life: Spiritual Exercises from Socrates to Foucault,* ed. A. Davidson, trans. M. Chase, Malden: Blackwell Publishing.
Hadot, P. (1998), *The Inner Citadel: The Meditations of Marcus Aurelius,* trans. M. Chase, Cambridge: Harvard University Press.
Hadot, P. (2002), *What Is Ancient Philosophy?,* trans. M. Chase, Cambridge: Harvard University Press.
Heidegger, M. (1962), *Being and Time,* trans. J. Macquarrie and E. Robinson, New York: Harper and Row.
Heidegger, M. (1998), "Letter on 'Humanism,'" in W. McNeill (ed.), F. A. Capuzzi (trans.), *Pathmarks,* 239–76, Cambridge: Cambridge University Press.
Kent, E. and T. Tomsky, eds. (2017), *Negative Cosmopolitanism: Cultures and Politics of World Citizenship after Globalization,* Montreal: McGill-Queen's University.
Lachs, J. (2012), *Stoic Pragmatism,* Bloomington: Indiana University Press.
Laertius, D. (1970), *Lives of Eminent Philosophers,* vol. 2, trans. R. D. Hicks, Cambridge: Harvard University Press.
Latour, B. (2011), "A Cautious Prometheus? A Few Steps Toward a Philosophy of Design with Special Attention to Peter Sloterdijk," in W. Schinkel and L. Noordegraaf-

Eelens (eds.), *In Media Res: Peter Sloterdijk's Spherological Poetics of Being*, 151–64, Amsterdam: Amsterdam University Press.

Latour, B. (2017), *Facing Gaia: Eight Lectures on the New Climatic Regime*, trans. C. Porter, Cambridge: Polity Press.

Lampe, K. (2013), "Obeying Your Father: Stoic Theology Between Myth and Mashochism," in V. Zajko and E. O'Gorman (eds.), *Classical Myth and Psychoanalysis: Ancient and Modern Stories of the Self*, 183–98, Oxford: Oxford University Press.

Marcus, A. (1983), *The Meditations*, trans. G. M. A. Grube, Indianapolis: Hackett.

Meaney, T. (2018), "A Celebrity Philosopher Explains the Populist Insurgency," *The New Yorker*, February 26. https://www.newyorker.com/magazine/2018/02/26/a-celebrity-philosopher-explains-the-populist-insurgency

Nussbaum, M. (1997), "Kant and Stoic Cosmopolitanism," *Journal of Political Philosophy*, 5 (1): 1–25.

Peacock, M. (2000), "Philosophical Rumblings in the German Republic: Der Philosophenstreit," *Philosophy Now*, 26. https://philosophynow.org/issues/26/Philosophical_Rumblings_in_the_German_Republic_Der_Philosophenstreit

Pfaller, R. (2011), "Disinhibition, Subjectivity and Pride. Or: Guess Who Is Looking? Peter Sloterdijk's Reconstruction of 'Thymotic' Qualities, Psychoanalysis and the Question of Spectatorship," in W. Schinkel and L. Noordegraaf-Eelens (eds.), *In Media Res: Peter Sloterdijk's Spherological Poetics of Being*, 67–82, Amsterdam: Amsterdam University Press.

Philo (1937), *On the Special Laws*, trans. F. H. Colson, Cambridge: Harvard University Press.

Rilke, R. M. (2010), "Archaic Torso of Apollo," trans. E. Snow, in S. Burt and D. Mikics (eds.), *The Art of the Sonnet*, 230, Cambridge: Harvard University Press.

Robbert, A. (2017), "The Side View: Hadot and Sloterdijk on the Practice of Philosophy," *Cosmos and History: The Journal of Natural and Social Philosophy*, 13 (1): 1–14.

Shea, L. (2010), *The Cynic Enlightenment: Diogenes in the Salon*, Baltimore: Johns Hopkins University Press.

Sloterdijk, P. (1987), *Critique of Cynical Reason*, trans. M. Eldred, Minneapolis: University of Minnesota Press.

Sloterdijk, P. (1989), *Thinker on Stage: Nietzsche's Materialism*, trans. Owen Daniel, Minneapolis: University of Minnesota Press.

Sloterdijk, P. (2009), *Derrida, an Egyptian: On the Problem of the Jewish Pyramid*, trans. W. Hoban, Cambridge: Polity Press.

Sloterdijk, P. (2010), *Rage and Time: A Psychopolitical Investigation*, trans. M. Wenning, New York: Columbia University Press.

Sloterdijk, P. (2011a), *Bubbles: Spheres Volume I: Microspherology*, trans. W. Hoban, Los Angeles: Semiotext(e).

Sloterdijk, P. (2011b), *Neither Sun Nor Death*, with H.-J. Heinrichs, trans. S. Corcoran, Los Angeles: Semiotext(e).
Sloterdijk, P. (2012), *The Art of Philosophy: Wisdom as Practice*, trans. K. Margolis, New York: Columbia University Press.
Sloterdijk, P. (2013a), *In the World Interior of Capital: For a Philosophical Theory of Globalization*, trans. W. Hoban, Malden: Polity Press.
Sloterdijk, P. (2013b), *Nietzsche Apostle*, trans. S. Corcoran, Los Angeles: Semiotext(e).
Sloterdijk, P. (2013c), *Philosophical Temperaments: From Plato to Foucault*, trans. T. Dunlap, New York: Columbia University Press.
Sloterdijk, P. (2013d), *You Must Change Your Life: On Anthropotechnics*, trans. W. Hoban, Malden: Polity Press.
Sloterdijk, P. (2014), *Globes: Spheres Volume II: Macrospherology*, trans. W. Hoban, Los Angeles: Semiotext(e).
Sloterdijk, P. (2015), "The Anthropocene: A Process-State at the Edge of Geohistory?," trans. A.-S. Springer, in H. Davis and E. Turpin (eds), *Art and the Anthropocene: Encounters Among Aesthetics, Politics, Environments and Epistemologies*, 327–40, London: Open Humanities Press.
Sloterdijk, P. (2016a), *Foams: Spheres Volume III: Plural Spherology*, trans. W. Hoban, Los Angeles: Semiotext(e).
Sloterdijk, P. (2016b), *Selected Exaggerations: Conversations and Interviews, 1993–2012*, trans. K. Margolis, Cambridge: Polity Press, 2016.
Sloterdijk, P. (2017), "Rules for the Human Park: A Response to Heidegger's 'Letter on "Humanism",'" in P. Sloterdijk, *Not Saved: Essays after Heidegger*, trans. I. A. Moore and C. Turner, 193–216, Cambridge: Polity Press.
Sloterdijk, P. (2018), *What Happened in the Twentieth Century?*, trans. C. Turner, Cambridge: Polity Press.
Wallace, L. (2014), "Indifference Is a Power," *Aeon*, December 24. https://aeon.co/essays/why-stoicism-is-one-of-the-best-mind-hacks-ever-devised

Contributors

Andrew Benjamin is Distinguished Professor of Architectural Theory at the University of Technology, Sydney (and Emeritus Professor of Philosophy at Monash University Melbourne). His recent publications include *Towards a Relational Ontology. Philosophy's Other Possibility* (2015), *Art's Philosophical Work* (2015), and *Virtue in Being* (2016).

Gene Flenady is Lecturer in Philosophy at Monash University. His research concerns German Idealism, particularly Hegel, and its relation to contemporary metaphysics and critical social theory.

Josh Hayes is Associate Professor of Philosophy in the Department of Humanities at Alvernia University in Reading, Pennsylvania. He has published numerous articles and chapters on Heidegger, especially his reception of the ancient Greek philosophical tradition (Heraclitus, Plato, Aristotle). He is a founding member of the Pacific Association for the Continental Tradition (PACT) and currently serves as coeditor of the *Journal of the Pacific Association for the Continental Tradition* (JPACT).

Hedwig Gaasterland defended her thesis *Nietzsche's Rejection of Stoicism. A Reinterpretation of Amor fati* in March 2017, at Leiden University, under the supervision of H. W. Siemens and F. A. J. de Haas. She has taught courses on Stoicism and Nietzsche's Reception of Antiquity.

Kurt Lampe, Senior Lecturer in Classics and Ancient History, University of Bristol, is the author of *The Birth of Hedonism: The Cyrenaic Philosophers and Pleasure as a Way of Life* (2015) and of numerous articles on ancient philosophy and its reception, and was Principal Investigator for the UK AHRC international networking grant, *Continental Stoicisms: Beyond Reason and Wellbeing* (2016).

Sam Mickey is Adjunct Professor in the Theology and Religious Studies Department at the University of San Francisco, San Francisco, California. He is an author of several books, including *On the Verge of a Planetary Civilization*

(2014) and *Coexistentialism and the Unbearable Intimacy of Ecological Emergency* (2016).

Angus Nicholls is Professor of Comparative Literature and German at Queen Mary University of London. His books include *Goethe's Concept of the Daemonic* (2006), *Thinking the Unconscious: Nineteenth-Century German Thought* (co-edited with Martin Liebscher, 2010), and *Myth and the Human Sciences* (2015).

Paula Schwebel is Associate Professor of Philosophy at Ryerson University in Toronto. Her research focuses on Walter Benjamin, twentieth-century readings of early modern political philosophy, political theology, and modern Jewish thought.

Emidio Spinelli is Full Professor of the History of Ancient Philosophy at the University of Rome La Sapienza and President of the Società Filosofica Italiana. His primary areas of interest are ancient skepticism, the Presocratics, atomists, Socrates and the Socratics, Plato, the Stoics, the Epicureans, literary and philosophical papyri, the reception of classical antiquity, and Hans Jonas.

Index

Abel, Günter   3, 10–11, 67
absolute, the   195, 212–24, 250
actualization   6, 8, 23, 37, 176–9, 190, 192–8
affirmation   85, 99, 252
Agamben, Giorgio   139, 214
agency   25–32, 39–40, 65–6, 115, 119, 170–1, 191
alienation   145–6, 153, 234, 248
anthropology
   Hegel's Anthropology   24–5, 32, 36–7, 39, 42–3, 46
   Stoicism and   6–8, 10–11, 169, 175, 177, 189, 192, 212–23
anthropotechnics   241, 252
apatheia, *see* impassivity
appropriation (*oikeiōsis*)
   and denaturing   13
   and *Ereignis*   9–10, 137–54
   and self-cultivation   17
   and spherology   246–49
Arendt, Hannah   8–9, 175–8, 190–8
Aristotle   45, 71, 121, 162, 215, 218
ascetics
   asceticism   99–103
   ascetology   240–1
   planetary *askēsis*   232–52
assent (*sunkatathesis*)   15, 168, 208–11
astronomy   224–5
authenticity   139–53

Benjamin, Walter   11, 109–25, 180
Blumenberg, Hans
   anthropology of Stoicism   212–25
   metaphorics of Stoicism   206–12
   on neo-Stoicism   65–7
Bodin, Jean   11, 110, 119

care
   for dialectic   210
   Hyginus' fable of   146–8, 180–2
   of the self (*see* self-cultivation)

Sorge   138–48, 246
   for the world   5, 10, 171, 188–9, 219, 246–8
cataleptic impressions, *see* impressions
Chrysippus   141–9, 211
Cicero
   On Fate   149
   On The Nature of the Gods   215–21
   theory of concept acquisition   71–2
Cleanthes   15, 216–27, 220
common sense (*sensus communis*)   68–78
constancy, *see under* passion; virtue
contemplation (*theōria*)   139, 167, 215–32, 240
cosmopolitanism, *see under* politics
Cynicism   230–40, 247–8, 252

danger
   of ecological crisis   245, 251
   knowledge and   9, 97–8, 100, 102–3
   of metaphysics   248
   of technology   170–1
Dasein   36, 137–54, 240, 245–6
death
   being-toward-death   144, 148, 152
   fate and   119
   fortune and   185
   freedom and   16–17
   indifference of   243
   pain and   96–9
   truth and   97
   virtue and   117
Deleuze, Gilles   3, 231
desire
   inconstancy and   111, 121–2
   indifference to   8, 25–7, 35, 39, 42–6
   satisfaction of   26, 31–2
   suspension of   211–12
   for truth   89–91, 99, 102–3
   to understand   215–16
determinism, *see under* fate

dignity   8, 171, 175–98
Dilthey, Wilhelm   10–12, 57–78
ecology   171, 245–52
emotion, *see* passion
Epictetus
   Bonhöffer on   2
   on contemplation   215–16
   and Cynicism   235
   ethics of self-cultivation   5, 10, 232
   retreat from the world   194, 242
   suspension of desire   211–12
   therapy of emotions   85, 90, 92, 100
Epicureanism
   attack in Stoic theology   218
   Kant on   7, 26
   Nietzsche on   87–8, 91–2, 101, 103
   Sloterdijk on   235, 237
epochē
   suspended animation   243–5, 252
   suspension of judgment   210–11, 214, 216
Ereignis, *see under* appropriation
eudaimonia   26, 87, 107–8

fate
   determinism and   163–5, 172
   and historicity   13–14
   love of fate   9, 85–8, 99–103
   and providence   112–16
   and resoluteness   10, 148–50
   and suffering   116–19
Foucault, Michel   5–6, 10, 177, 231, 244
freedom
   actual or enacted   36, 175–7, 190–8
   and chance   185
   and death   16–17
   from error   211
   and immunization   242, 251–2
   inner   14, 23–4, 27–8, 41, 168–9
   and necessity   168–72, 177–84
   from sensation and desire   44
   as sovereignty   110–11, 116
   as theme in this volume   5–10
   as thrown projection   148–50

Gadamer, Hans-Georg   75–8
globalization   242, 248–52
god(s), *see also* fate; physics; providence; sovereignty; theodicy
   assimilation to   167–8, 180–9, 221
   awe and wonder toward   217–24

immutability of   110–24
and self-assertion   65–6

Habermas, Jürgen   12–17
Hadot, Ilsetraut   5–6
Hadot, Pierre
   and metaphorics, 209–10
   philosophy as a way of life   6, 206, 231, 234–5
   spiritual exercises   16, 239, 242–4, 247
happiness
   amor fati and   85–7
   appropriation and   166–7
   inner   185–6
   morality and   6–8, 26–8
   participation and   191–2
   passions and   98–9
   physics and   214
Hegel, G. W. F.
   idealism   58, 61
   influence on reception of Stoicism   7–9, 12–17
   interpretation of Stoicism   23–47
Helmholtz, Hermann von   58–61, 68, 74–6
history
   historical consciousness   12–16, 74
   historicality   148
   historicism   4
human sciences, *see under Wissenschaft*

impassivity
   and emission control   243–4, 246, 252
   and mourning   120–1, 125
impressions (*phantasiai*)   168, 208–16
impulse
   natural or spontaneous   93–4, 100, 111, 120
   Stoic technical term (*hormē*)   123, 143–4, 147–8, 152
indifference (*adiaphoria*, *Gleichgültigkeit*)
   and constancy   120
   and detachment   90
   to fortune   185–6
   Hegel on   8, 23–47
   and impassivity   243
   preferred and dispreferred   212
   and relationality   246
   and sacrifice   222
   to the world   193

Jonas, Hans, 8–9, 161–72

Kant, Immanuel   6–7, 25–30, 60–1,
    67–78, 170–1
knowledge, *see also* Wissenschaft
    empirical   29, 34
    exercise and   235
    Hegel's story about   30–1
    metaphorics of   208–9
    modern philosophy of   164
    passion for (*see under* passion)
    pretension to   215
    salvific   214
    tyranny of   248
    of the whole   167
    wisdom as   179
    worldly   183–4

Lipsius, Justus   63–5, 109–25
Löwith, Karl   12–17, 65

Marcus Aurelius
    cosmopolitanism   235–6, 244
    and ethics of self-cultivation   10, 210,
        232
    reducing pain   95
    retreat from the world   36, 90–1,
        247
martyrdom   117, 122–4, 130
metaphor
    metaphorology of Stoicism   205–25
    in Stoic theory   166, 168
metaphysics
    and divine will   110, 119
    of essence   142
    historical   73
    of *humanitas*   152
    Kantian   29–30, 39
    of language   3
    overcoming   247–52
    Platonic   140–1
    post-metaphysical   232–3, 237–40
    pre-Socratic   145
    of substance   139
Mirandola, Pico della   178–84
Montaigne, Michel de   16

nature
    accord with   142, 189, 208
    Anthropocene and   251–2
    destructive   119, 220

human   6, 12–16, 27, 30, 39, 121, 125,
    138, 141, 154
    immutability of   111, 115–16, 123
    independence from   32
    in itself   60–1
    laws of   64, 110, 188
    power of   178–9
    and self-assertion   65
    and self-consciousness   36
    of souls   182
    state of   31
    technology and   169–70
    teleology and   67
    temperament as   90
    theology of   165
negation
    Hegel on   29, 33, 44–5
    Nietzsche on   87, 101–2
Nietzsche, Friedrich
    and *Altertumswissenschaft*   2, 4
    reception of Stoicism   9, 85–103
    and Sloterdijk   231, 238, 244, 245

oikeiōsis, *see* appropriation
oikos   9, 137–40, 142, 152

passion
    eupatheiai   90, 92
    for knowledge (*Leidenschaft der
        Erkenntnis*)   86–103
    and self-consciousness   42
    suffering and constancy   112–25
    therapy of   85–92, 102–3
    tranquility   177, 188, 236–7
physics   10–11, 16, 35, 164, 214–23
Plato   12, 137, 141, 161–2, 213, 233
Platonism   153, 235, 237–8, 244, 246
Pohlenz, Max   2–5
politics
    co-immunism as   251
    common sense and   71–2
    constitutive of freedom   8, 10, 17,
        24–7, 36–8, 176–7, 191–6
    of contemplation   221
    as context for theory   162–3, 217–18
    cosmopolitanism   234–7, 244, 248
    early modern   67
    of German *Wissenschaften*   58–9
    Heidegger and   13
    Löwith and   14
    and psychology   119–25

and responsibility   169
of Stoicism   31
and theology   109–16
and tyranny   116–19
Posidonius   2, 4, 215, 224
potentiality   145, 151, 176, 177, 192–3, 197–8
providence
arguments for   217–20
and common sense   76–7
and freedom   165–8, 175
and history   15, 112–16
and thrownness   147
psychoanalysis   223, 246

Rabbow, Paul   5–6
reason
acting according to   8, 23–47, 169
autonomy of   64
and constancy   111
cosmic   16, 149
criterion of being-human   138–9
divine   116, 221
early-modern   65, 72
hēgemonikon and   167
historical   68, 73, 78
and impassivity   92–4, 99, 103
as motivation   87, 100
natural   13, 64, 67, 112
right   115
secular   233
sovereignty of   119–25
of the state   67
universal   76
value of   89
Reinhardt, Karl   4
relationality   139, 141, 150–1, 185–95, 246
responsibility   7–10, 41, 149, 169–72, 195, 241, 251

Schmitt, Carl   110–13, 119–20, 123–5
self-cultivation
and appropriation   17
Nietzsche and   85, 88, 92
scholarship on   5–6
Sloterdijk on   10, 231–2, 243–6
and spirituality   224
and unity of thought   8, 32

Seneca
Dialogues   25, 72, 214–16
and Hume   17
Moral Epistles   15, 72, 141–4, 146–8, 214–16
Natural Questions   16, 215, 222
and neo-Stoicism   63–5, 112, 121
on seafaring   246
on self-making   178–90
on sickness   15–16
slavery
bare life and   181
condition of elite leisure   177–8
master-slave dialectic   31–4, 37–8, 40–1
political   8, 198
virtue and   187
Sloterdijk, Peter   6, 10, 229–52
Sorge, see under care
sovereignty   11, 109–25
space
of appearance (activity)   75–6, 192
detoxified   239
of *epoche*, 244–5
of free choice   167, 172
of imagination   193–4
inhabited   232
operationally curved   240–1
of reasons   25, 40–2
of self-actualization   14
of self-cultivation   8
spherology and   246–7, 250–1
of subjectivity   213, 242
spheres   10, 232–3, 245–7, 252
spiritual exercises, *see under* Hadot, Pierre
Stein, Ludwig   2–3
subjectivity
enclave   247–51
inner space of   213
intersubjectivity   27
intimate dwellings and   245
self-identical   25, 34
shore   236, 242, 244
suicide   16–17
suspended animation, *see under* epoche

theodicy   116–19, 165–6
Trauerspiel   11, 109–25

truth
    of being (*alētheia*)   137–8, 147, 153
    desire for (*see under* desire)
    metaphorics of   208–12, 213, 216
    and method   75–8
    natural   64
    pain and   90–4
    process of   233
    pursuit of   9, 89
    scientific   72
    temperament and   90
    untruth   145
tyranny   113, 121–5, 248

verticality   11, 241, 252
Vico, Giambattista   75–7
virtue
    Arendt on   8
    of constancy   111–25
    dialectical   210
    and the gods   221
    Hegel on   8, 37, 41, 45
    Kant on   7, 26–8
    Nietzsche on   89, 100–1
    and relationality   185–92
    W. Benjamin on   125–6

Wilamowitz-Moellendorf,
    Ulrich von   4
wisdom
    cultivation of   236–7, 240, 243
    following nature as   178, 189
    of god   118
    loser romanticism as   238–9
    Löwith's lack of   16–17
    melancholic   123
    in pain   96
    patience and   237
    relationality and   186
    rhetoric of   37
    vigilance and   213
Wissenschaft
    Altertumswissenschaft   3–5
    Geisteswissenschaft   57–78

www.ingramcontent.com/pod-product-compliance
Lightning Source LLC
Chambersburg PA
CBHW072135290426
44111CB00012B/1878